Surviving Violent Crime

and the
Criminal Injuries Compensation Authority

A Guide for Progress and Living Well

T.S. Duckett

Introductory

ISBN 0-954.3444-0-5

Typeset by Inner Circle Services Limited,
137–149 Goswell Road, London, EC1V 7ET
Tel: 020 7253 5252 EMail: info@inner-circle.co.uk

Printed and bound by Witherbys Limited,
2nd Floor, 32-36 Aylesbury Street, London EC1R 0ET

This handbook is dedicated to:

The memory of the dead
and all those affected
and neglected in the
New City Cinema Fire.

All those who have suffered
through violence and those
who have suffered injustice
through neglect and in silence.

All the people working to
provide excellent services
with sensitivity, against
huge obstacles.

Disclaimer

This handbook is written with the intention of guiding people affected by, and those working with, victims of violent crime. At the date of publication, all information is accurate and every effort has been taken to select the best service providers within a chosen field to provide the most helpful and accurate advice. Inevitably, some individuals move on to other jobs but the service will remain.

However, I cannot take any responsibility, nor provide any guarantee, for any specific service provided or for acting upon the guidance or information volunteered by any of the agencies listed.

Advice on how to go about selecting competent organisations, and how to complain about a sub-standard service, is detailed throughout my handbook. Any seriously sub-standard service that is experienced regarding any agency included within my handbook should be addressed to me via my e-mail address available on my website - see back cover for my web address. If I am satisfied that the grounds for complaint are legitimate, the agency will be removed from the list of best-practice entries.

Everything in my handbook and website is copyrighted and not to be used without my prior written permission.

Contents

Acknowledgments

The Department of Health, the Criminal Injuries Compensation Authority (CICA) and the Justice and Victims Unit were consistently disinclined to assist me effectively. It made securing simple, basic research data almost impossible. Thank you for reminding me why justice is not given. However …

There are brilliant civil servants and other professionals who were encouraging and generous in sharing their knowledge and time. I am truly indebted to all for making this handbook possible. They are diamonds in a bleak terrain of service exhaustion, dwindling morale and resources and entrenched cynicism. They stand apart and shine as beacons of service excellence, humour and remarkable compassion. They give us cause for real hope.

I thank profoundly the emergency services, the police, the Florence Nightingale Hospital and Dr Colin Wilson for saving my life. Within my unfolding terror, I wish to acknowledge the exceptional, abundant personal talent, patience and professional brilliance of Detective Constable Tony Poole. I thank my remarkable family and friends for staying by me throughout my years of pain, turmoil and transformation.

The expertise in editing and proofreading of Arthur Boulton and Karen Howatson saved this work. The expertise and guidance of many have contributed towards this handbook. I wish to thank: Will Anderson, Alex Thorn, Rabbi James Raphael Baaden, Alberto Capaccioli, Merle Baars, Mike Bell, Berni Spivak, Dr Cesar Lengua and the remarkable men and women of Tyne and Wear who remind me why we must never be silent, Dr Shaun Russell, Doreen Lawrence OBE, Professor David Alexander, Dr Richard Shepherd, the librarians at the National Police Library at Centrex Bramshill, David Freeman, Neville Udall and colleagues at the Northern General NHS Trust, Sheffield, the Justice Department of Alberta, Canada, the Procurator Fiscal's Department, Scotland, the Justice Department of the Netherlands, the London Transport Museum, Dr Andy Watts, Mr James Laughland, barrister-at-law, Professor Mardi Jon Horowitz, Carol Jackson, Carol Brooks-Johnston and Richard Scorer from Pannone and Partners for abundant talent and assistance, Detective Superintendent Trevor Fordy of Northumbria Police and the other police officers who gave invaluable talent and time to comment on my section about police work.

Also: Carol Peace, Millivres Press, Adrian Johnston, TalkBack Productions, the BBC, DocuText Limited, the gifted craft and diligence of Inner Circle Limited for their artwork and typesetting in putting together my work against great odds and with style, the musical artists who kindly gave permission to reproduce their lyrics, and Malcolm Wright of ampheon.co.uk for bringing professionalism to the world of website design. Thank you.

Victims of crime need to have clear guidance of their rights and what to do. Our lives are becoming more and more fraught with danger as we move around our environment. The ordinary man and woman on the street are more likely to suffer attack of one description or another.

In these circumstances where and to whom do you go for help? Who will hold your hand when you need it most? What are the structures that would kick- start and take control when you become a victim?

As human beings we are at our most vulnerable state when we are hurting. We lose our confidence and no longer do we feel that we are in control. We all know that it is finding the help you need and is it readily available? In times like this it is practical advice we need.

Doreen Lawrence OBE

A violent crime can have a devastating effect on the survivor and the survivor's family. The experience is likely to challenge their previous assumptions about how much they are in charge of their own destiny, and about how fair and just is the world. What did I do to deserve this? Why do people not really understand the way I feel? Will I ever get my life back to normal? What will I do now?

These, and other fundamental questions commonly trouble those who become the victims of violent crimes. Such an event can also leave the individual feeling vulnerable and uncertain as to what they can do to get help. The help they may require may come from different quarters: medical, social and legal. Unfortunately, the routes to such help are not mapped out very clearly and, when one is upset and traumatised that is when one needs very clear guidance. In particular, advice and information are particularly necessary with regard to the legal domain as it can be an intimidating and bewildering one for the ill prepared and inexperienced.

Simon Duckett has sympathetically identified the impact of violent crime on individuals and the problems and pitfalls for them as they seek to adjust to their misfortune. He has compiled some very valuable information about how to engage the medical, social and legal services. His contribution through his text is not just, however, at the important practical level but he has also raised a number of challenging medico-political and social issues relating to the provision of the care for those whose lives have been thrown into disarray because of the effects of violent crime.

Professor David A. Alexander, Centre for Trauma Research, Aberdeen

What constitutes heroism? Is it the courage to endure physical injury and acute pain, or to bear the torture of mental violence against oneself and one's friends and relatives? Is it rising above systematic personal and institutional discrimination during the course of one's life, or is it strength of conviction in pursuing a principle regardless of personal loss and the obstacles thrown in one's way? Is it perhaps the power to speak out against injustice and be an inspirational voice for the dispossessed? Or is it the ability to bring succour and empowerment to those who are victimised and least able to defend themselves? It can be all of these things and more of course. But how rarely during the course of our lifetimes do we come across someone who exhibits these characteristics?

The author of *Surviving Violent Crime and the Criminal Injuries Compensation Authority* is an exceptional individual who displays the above qualities. Simon Duckett has brought a unique combination of background, experience and painstaking research to the task of providing victims of violent crime with a unique guidebook to surviving the aftermath of their trauma and loss. His remarkable work offers not only reassurance and comfort, but also detailed practical information for those in need of assistance following criminal injury or bereavement. Equally importantly, the handbook highlights what is missing in the system of support for victims of crime, and the obstacles and difficulties that are faced by those seeking aid from state and non-governmental agencies in their time of need.

Simon Duckett has worked in the social services sector for much of his career and has an inside perspective on the institutional response to casualties of social and criminal abuse. He has been involved at strategy-setting and grass roots levels in many community and charity projects with disadvantaged groups. An even more compelling reason for him to be heard is that he is also the victim of a horrific crime, an arson attack in which 11 people died and during which he was seriously injured. The author has used the criminal injuries compensation that he received following this attack, to pay for the research and preparation of this publication.

These qualifications lend a rare credibility to the work, which is at once courageous, independent and outspoken. The author casts off the epithet of 'victim' and inspires other sufferers to do likewise. By so doing, it not only informs people of their just rights and entitlements, but also empowers them to rise above feelings of vulnerability and exclusion so as to face their futures with confidence and new hope.

Surviving Violent Crime and the Criminal Injuries Compensation Authority is inevitably political, and consciously attempts to move forward both debate and action on support and compensation for those affected by violent crime. It is also a work of compassion and integrity that offers valuable insights for the victims of crime, but should also be required reading for personnel of state and non-governmental agencies who work with people affected by violent crime.

Dr Shaun Russell, Tan-yr-Allt, Wales

Just over 170 years ago, the foundations for British policing were laid down and these became known as the primary objects of the police. They were the protection of life and property and the prevention of crime. The sentiment was sound and for almost the next 150 years police officers based their role on these objectives, but, it was obvious by the 1980s the police had been trying to stem the tide of ever increasing crime and public disorder – and to put it bluntly they could not cope.

Numerous agencies were set up to take over some of the roles of the police and calls from senior police officers and some politicians made calls for more police. Sir Kenneth Newman, in his last annual report to the Home Office, called for a dramatic increase in police numbers of over 7,000 in London alone.

Nothing like that number has ever been recruited even though nearly twenty years have elapsed, and crime has continued to rise. Unsurprisingly, violent crime has risen and become almost accepted as a way of life.

From the inside looking out, the police still thought they were the only people who could and should have the last word when it comes to crime and, almost as an excuse, blamed everything and anything, but were reluctant to look at themselves. At this time, in the early 1980s, changes were on the cards but I have to admit the police did not look kindly to change. Confidence in the police was on the wane and almost a siege situation started to take a hold within the police. Internal reforms came and went and the Home Office set about their reforms, but in my opinion successive government reforms have never been to the benefit of the communities that make up the people of England and Wales. To my mind, it seemed, reforms benefited the Treasury.

The present government seems to have taken note of the public call for more police and we are told we have more police officers than ever before. But is this good news? This brings with it problems that the police have encountered before. When you embark on a massive recruitment drive and you recruit from society at large, a risk exists of recruiting some wrong people and the dreadful examples mentioned in the handbook by Simon Duckett could increase.

Leadership, supervision and first-class training should be at the top of the agenda. The public deserves, indeed should demand, the very best, but the economics of everyday life tells me in some areas the police may have to settle for second best – I hope I am wrong.

Simon Duckett appears to have recognised many of the failures within our criminal justice system and instead of simply becoming a critic he has set out to help those people who, like him, are, or have been, a victim of violent crime. Not all police officers have the qualities needed to be a Family Liaison Officer, indeed not all FLOs have the same qualities. In my opinion the secret of being a good police officer is never make the same mistake twice.

Police officers do make mistakes and hopefully any mistake will be acknowledged and apologies given. I found the police, like our politicians, saw an apology as a sign of weakness that I think is a sign of strength.

I served for 37 years in the Metropolitan Police Service and the changes from when I joined in 1961 to when I retired in 1998, both within the police and within society, have been immense. I comfort myself with the fact that for every nasty individual or criminal there are tens of thousands of decent, honourable people. I have no doubt that if you are a victim of violent crime you will come across some of these people – Simon Duckett deserves our thanks.

Mike Bennett MBE FRSA
Former Chairman, Metropolitan Police Federation, 1986–1998

Surviving Violent Crime and the CICA has been written to address a disturbing lack of information that helps people make connections and decisions when affected by violent crime. The handbook is, in part, common sense, part reference and part directory – so it is a signpost to what you may need to know. When I was affected by violent crime it was beyond my comprehension how poorly and condescendingly I was treated and the appalling manner in which the Criminal Injuries Compensation Authority made my life difficult and almost impossible to endure. I was made to feel like a criminal and a pest for asking questions about my compensation and had to pay £8,000 from that compensation for a mediocre legal service while the murderer received free, expert legal representation. I was amazed how little existed in terms of effective guidance and help, so I decided to research and find out if this was just my bad luck or if it was a common experience. It was depressingly common and most suffered more than myself – the isolation, poor advice, exhausted and cynical services, dubious 'victims' groups and running the gauntlet of a one-way street called compensation was the norm.

It is important that people understand and make connections about crime, their health, public services, compensation, our communities, our voting (or not voting) and the state we are in. When horror enters our lives its touches every facet of our being – and we can never be the same again. If our country is to become really democratic and a place of safety and pride then we all have areas of responsibility to enable this to come about and be universally accessible. It is also up to each of us to aspire to the best that we can and not be numbed in anger or silence. It will be up to emerging lobby groups, the media and victims to use their electoral power to have the needs of victims taken seriously and dignified provisions made available by politicians. It will be victims who will lead the way.

Surviving Violent Crime and the CICA outlines what to do when a crisis affects your life and tries to offer how to constructively seek the right help from the right services in a common sense manner. The layout roughly traces the services you are likely to encounter once violent crime has taken place. Short lists of solicitors and post-traumatic stress disorder experts are included. There is a section about us all being more responsible and active in making vulnerable people affected by violent crime visible and politically and socially assertive – if not, nothing will change for the better. The final section has a small directory of some of the more dynamic advocacy organisations and groups assisting people affected by violent crime.

Introduction

I experienced a lot of obstruction from government departments and the Criminal Injuries Compensation Authority and so some detail, that I would have preferred to include is lacking, but with the skilled help of others I believe the handbook has sufficient details to help you progress.

Surviving Violent Crime and the CICA will hopefully be offered freely by both the police and Primary Care Trusts to people in need, at an early stage of contact – I hope this handbook and my website are of practical use to you at a point of disbelief and unravelling pain in your life. It is also intended to prompt professionals about what they need to be mindful of. I hope this little contribution helps you face your nightmare with useful information and that good-quality help is willingly offered that will create safety and dignity in your life. This handbook is my way of making constructive progress and giving something back to society, while encouraging others not to stay stuck as permanent 'victims'. It is written mainly for people who are coping with the significant and devastating effects of violent crime.

This handbook is written to assist innocent victims of violent crime who may wish to make a legitimate and honest criminal injury compensation application. There are some amazing people 'out there' – find some time to break your silence and meet them!

Simon Duckett, London

Personal

When we speak we are afraid our words will not be heard, nor welcomed.
But, when we are silent we are still afraid.
So it is better to speak,
Remembering, we were never meant to survive.

Audré Lorde: *Litany for Survival*

When horror crashes into our lives, we instantly lose all sense of what was an ordinary and average life. Nothing can ever be the same again. Suddenly, our lives are full of people we are more used to seeing dramatised on television, but this time they are real and they are talking about us or a loved one. These may be the police, doctors, the media or officials, all asking the same questions, while, inside, we are possibly reeling from what has just happened to us, or what we have recently been told.

We know, from visits to general practitioners, police stations and hospitals, that walls are littered with posters advertising services. Yet, despite this, we somehow manage to remain unreceptive to this information – in part because of information overload.

A state of sickening dread starts to envelop us, as we answer questions, cooperate and plead, in our hearts, for this horror to disappear – for life and the loved one to return to what they were. At this early stage, a concise handbook has a role to play, which explains what is happening and why this army has descended upon you. It is important because, to the best of my knowledge, no other handbook tries to make connections between what the violent crime has done – the consequential effects on your mind and body – and how to access the right services, community action and how to make progress with life. If we choose not to assert our needs and legal rights, we will be left to sink or swim – and many do sink – especially after a trial, when police services withdraw.

If we are to get beyond being forever trapped as a victim, to aspire, over time, to achieve the dignified status of surviving and progress, then we will all need help. This help has to be of the highest quality. It is about making our suffering visible and breaking the silence of trauma. We do this by asserting our rights and expectations to be treated well and cared for until all areas of our life return to something like normality. This is why a handbook for innocent victims of violence is needed.

If Violence Has Just Happened

If you need urgent help because of violent crime, the following suggestions are worth considering.

If you feel terrified, shocked or overwhelmed, ask a police officer to arrange for you to see a consultant psychiatrist – preferably one who understands the early symptoms of post-traumatic stress disorder (PTSD). Psychiatrists are trained doctors who specialise in mental health and they really should be the preferred experts who see you in the first instance rather than some other, less experienced professional. If you are at home, in the immediate hours after a violent crime, it may be necessary to have a general practitioner (GP) help you calm down enough to cope with the intensifying distress. The GP should be encouraged by the police and social services to refer those in need for early trauma assessment. (See sections on the role of GPs and trauma as well as the listings of trauma experts, in the Directory section.)

Ask your appointed police officer to make contact with the local social services and for one of their professionals to come to see you at home as a priority, or the hospital social worker if you are an in-patient. Most hospitals have social work departments and the police can liaise with hospital staff to make sure you are seen quickly.

It is important to consider asking social services to see you, especially if you have an urgent crisis. You should expect to have all appropriate services at your disposal, for example, to arrange a special meeting to discuss and make arrangements to protect you, to make you feel secure and in control. At this meeting, having someone competent, as a supporter, to speak or just be there for company, can be useful as you may feel that what is happening is just a blur – as in a film. This could be the police or someone that they suggest. These meetings help identify what services you need. Sadly, you will find many agencies ask the same questions in the midst of your emerging horror – social services and a supporter can reduce this institutional reaction by preparing a standard written response. Sometimes, this is necessary to make sure you can receive the best service available. Sometimes, it is about services failing to communicate well with each other or cooperate with each other. Please read the section on how to ensure your real needs are not overwhelmed by seemingly irritating questions. (See section on social services and preparing a standard list of matters, pp. 160–172.)

Social and health services have a duty in law to reduce suffering and hardship. It is important the serious issues arising from the violent crime can be confronted quickly and that a good service is secured. It is therefore very important to ask the police to arrange for social services to intervene as early as possible.

It may be you find yourself being approached by victim groups, which may have little value to you in your initial state of abject terror and horror. The standards and role of victim groups are discussed elsewhere (see section on the *victim club*, pp. 242–251). It is important to secure statutory expertise, not only for mental and physical care but, in some cases, also for relocation to a secret place away from the scene of violent crime. Last, but not least, it may be important that you ask the police to protect you from unwanted media attention and from invasion of your well-being.

New Labour's approach, in the first Queen's Speech, was more evolutionary than revolutionary. However, Mr Blair made plain that the drive to modernise the welfare state and to tackle the £90 billion Social Security Bill were two of the main priorities. All the new measures sought to represent an alliance between progress and justice. The mandate was clear: to modernise what was outdated; to make fair what was unjust; and to do both by the best means available ... The era of neat phrasing, political catchphrases and buzzwords had truly arrived. The most telling of all was: The Third Way.

Audrey Leathard: *Healthcare Provision – Past, Present and into the 21st Century*

If you or a loved one are in hospital, there are some important matters that you must ensure are sorted out both while there and when ready to be discharged.

Public service workers try to provide the best services possible, in the face of extremely low morale and inadequate resources. They do life-saving work that is tough, with little recognition by governments by way of resources, pay or respect. This is the culmination of various governments over several years making changes to save money without letting workers adjust to the latest changes before further changes are put in place. Victims of violent crime have to face this reality with all its flawed compromise and still ensure they get the very best of care.

In April 2002, the government massively overhauled the structure and power base of the National Health Service (NHS) in a drive for efficiency. We will have to wait to see whether this does lead to improvement in how services are delivered.

In relation to serious criminal injuries, it is worth bearing the following in mind. If you ensure this stage of your ordeal is organised as it should be, you will save an enormous amount of stress, avoid mislaid medical records, capitalise on medical treatment and reduce legal fees in securing medical reports. This will be especially true if it becomes necessary to apply to the Criminal Injuries Compensation Authority (CICA) for assessment for compensation. The correct documentation will be in place, which has a crucial role to play in surviving violent crime in, for example, planning future health care and life priorities.

Priorities
The priority is to receive the best care available and to regain steadily the best level of health and rehabilitation you can. In the early days of

hospitalisation there are bewildering and competing pressures within and all around you: for example, a desire to know the extent of your injuries; to start comforting distressed friends or family; an intense sense of vulnerability, fear and shock. All these experiences will require expression and assistance. Remember to be polite, take as much control of your health and environment as is possible and accept as much expert help, from as many sources, as you can. This is your life, or that of someone dear, so it is right to expect the best.

Taking care

When you are able to eat, ensure you have a good balanced diet (see section on basic nutrition and exercise, pp. 114–141). Because your body has been subjected to great stress, it is important to put as much nourishment back into it as possible. It is sensible to try to eat as much fruit as you can; have friends bring healthy microwaveable food to supplement food provided by the hospital. Nervous energy and medical operations may lead to weight loss, despite the fact you are lying in bed; this may call for extra care in your effort to survive and progress. If you are taking strong painkillers, such as morphine, you may find a sudden craving for sweet things like chocolate; this will disappear when you come off such medication.

Resting

In the wake of your ordeal, recovery may well seem impossible, but it will help if you try to find time each day to practise breathing and relaxation. The breathing exercise (see section on basic nutrition and exercise, pp. 114–141) will also help to control panic attacks and the sense of anxiety, which are perfectly natural in the circumstances. Try to spend ten minutes, twice a day, practising the breathing exercise from your bed or hospital chair. Better still, if your hospital has grounds, and you are well enough to move, practise in the grounds of the hospital. Remember to allow a little time to be alone and rest; rest is crucial to getting better. Plenty of rest, plenty of good food, plenty of good visitors and plenty of good services; all are part of the recovery process.

Visitors

Visitors, as I said, are a very necessary part of feeling wanted and helping to get your confidence back. Unfortunately, though, not everyone will have family or friends who are in a position to visit. If you find yourself in these circumstances, ask the hospital to arrange for a police-checked volunteer to come to spend some time with you. Whoever your visitors may be, there are several things that should be taken into consideration with regard to them. They should not all come at once as, particularly at first, this can be overwhelming; try to get people to visit at different times so no period of the day is too empty. Often it is when alone at night that people feel most frightened, remembering traumatic events and other forms of distress. Therefore, it is worth asking whether a friend (or a police-checked volunteer) can 'bed-sit' with you for company at night-time. On the whole, people mean well, but sometimes they need to understand you need their support when it suits *you*. Visitors must be realistic and encouraging, allowing the victim space to express emotion, to cry, to talk of his or her experience. Visitors must not be surprised if this retelling needs to be repeated often. Touch is important, too, as is honesty. Use the care sheet (see opposite page) to plan hospital tests, appointments and visits.

	Morning	Afternoon	Evening
Monday			
Tuesday			
Wednesday			
Thursday			
Friday			
Saturday			
Sunday			

Say what you need

Although surrounded by many professionals, friends or family, it is sometimes hard to feel able to say what you want. Friends and family may themselves be overstressed and, while it may be important they get support, it is important to be clear that *you* are number one.

Your physical and mental health are paramount and often your mental health needs are not considered by doctors so you need to make them aware of the importance of having a qualified expert in trauma assess you at an early point.

Be sure your doctor understands whether or not you are sleeping, or experiencing PTSD (see section on post-traumatic stress disorder, pp. 104–113), and proper help is made available. This is part of the doctor's duty in caring for you, so try not to be intimidated – some doctors try to be, and some do not realise they are, intimidating. In both cases, they scare victims because they have power over their bodies.

While still an in-patient, you, and those close to you, should arrange a care plan to include health matters and, if it has not already been brought to hospital attention, now is the time to request proper services to be made aware of any non-hospital concerns.

It is your body and your life: do not feel inhibited about requesting frank answers to questions that concern you, or someone very close to you. Ask for and expect openness from professionals.

Hospital social services

These professionals have an important role to play and can assist in various matters. They can assist in simple, reassuring gestures, from ensuring that your home is secure to arranging pet care – assuming you have no one else who can do this for you. They can ensure a care plan is in place for your discharge. Remember, if you are badly injured you will need time to recover or if you have become disabled as a result of your injury, you may need structural alterations to your home – you may even need to move house. These professionals can help with social security applications and liaise, on your behalf, with other agencies including consultants and GPs, ensuring special needs and home visits are all organised. Use the hospital social work service well; ensure a meeting takes place prior to your discharge from hospital, with agencies and friends to discuss your needs. All must be in place and everything necessary must be done to help you, allowing you to return home with minimal anxiety. Hospital social workers can also assist in ensuring injuries are fully documented and that necessary copies of reports and related evidence will be available. These professionals are well placed to see people affected by violent crimes are supported within legislation and not left to the lottery of dubious voluntary groups. Expert help is a right that you must expect and assert.

Before you leave hospital

Do not leave hospital without going through your hospital records with your consultant, as each and every injury is important. What currently may seem minor may develop over months or years into a serious condition, e.g. degenerative back injury, and, if not listed at the point of hospitalisation, having the CICA accept such injury can be problematic. So, ensure you check that a clearly and properly documented signed list of all your injuries, with the consultant's full name and position, is in your hospital records. A good consultant will understand the importance of this request, and it will be invaluable for future health, when dealing with the CICA and in keeping costs for independent medical reports to a minimum.

It is important medical records state what treatments, if any, were given for all injuries, including specialist PTSD treatments, and any prognoses. It is also a good idea to have copies of X-rays and dated hospital colour photographs of all injuries. Preferably these should be taken by a medical photographer, who will produce better results than will a friend. Although the hospital may think this odd – it is your body, your life; and, if you consider making an application for compensation, you are going to be greatly assisted if all of these medical records are readily to hand. A hospital may, of course, charge a reasonable fee for any costs incurred in providing these services.

If you succeed in securing sets of all these documents, it is important to make copies and to keep them safe. These records will also greatly assist various people and agencies involved in your future care or in any compensation claim you may make, e.g. GPs, physiotherapists, solicitors and other agencies.

Ideally, you should politely request that a copy of all of these documents be handed to you prior to discharge, which should not constitute a problem as the records should be kept up to date. If, for any reason, this is not possible, arrange for them to be forwarded to you as soon as possible. These issues can be coordinated with your hospital social worker before any discharge date is considered – *don't* think of leaving hospital without these matters being definitely resolved!

When care is unsafe

It is important all of your energy is focused on getting better. When you are well enough, the police will need your help to try to gather information about your experience and to prepare a statement while the horror is still clear in your mind. In extremely serious cases, the police will try both to allocate a family liaison officer (see section on the police, pp. 22–53) and to provide support with other issues in your life. This is an area in which the police have made huge improvements in developing their skills and knowledge. Unfortunately, things can go wrong while in hospital and it is important to tell the police what is seriously interfering with your ability to get well and be safe.

Early on, possibly, you were too ill to be part of any meeting, but a written decision should have been reached with your next of kin, the hospital and police about what information the media might have. A decision about what method is used to convey information is also important and must be respected. For example, it may be decided that only police or hospital staff will read written statements. The media in situations of 'news' are known to go to outrageous lengths to get a story to please their editors (and make money). In doing so, it is almost as though they derive some satisfaction from dwelling on the plight of victims of serious crime. If, as has happened in the past, the media dress as doctors or nurses and burst into your room to take photographs and try to get you to speak, ring the emergency button immediately. In a situation such as this, you should take action against them through either the Press Complaints Commission, the courts or both. The Human Rights Act 1998 makes clear a person has a right for privacy to be respected. It is best to say nothing at all to them; rather, let the police or solicitors deal with them until you are well enough.

If it transpires hospital staff have released information to the media, contrary to agreements, or without your consent, it is best to pursue an action against the hospital, as this constitutes a breach of the legal duty – a breach of trust. (For tips on how to deal with the media, see section on court, pp. 208–241.)

You do not need to put up with, and hospital staff should protect you from, unwanted volunteers, whether they are from a charity, religious group or some undesirable legal firm trying to 'hustle' business from you. (See section on choosing a competent solicitor, pp. 260–270.)

If a patient starts to abuse you in any manner, report this immediately to the hospital and police. Similarly, if a hospital worker or anyone else working within a hospital, of any description, starts to abuse you in any manner, report this immediately to the police or a friend.

When people are ill and vulnerable, it can bring out both the best and worst in basic human nature. To survive, you must be prepared to break the silence of any form of abuse. Therefore, never be silent if you are abused or violated while in hospital – it is your unconditional right to be kept safe from harm as you recover and regain your health.

Saying 'thank you'

When a service goes well, it is natural and good to want to find a way to say 'thank you'. Take your time and do not spend all your money on making a gesture of appreciation. Remember, you have been and remain in, the early stages of an intense roller-coaster which may have been or seemed life-threatening; it is going to take time to feel safe with the world again.

Generally, a letter recounting your recovery will be reward in itself for those professionals who have helped you. So, in the short term, if appropriate, maybe you could write to the hospital trust or to the Department of Health to commend their services. In time, perhaps you, friends or family might donate something to the ward, or put a little money towards the staff Christmas party. Maybe one day, if your health allows, you can take part in a charity event to raise funds for the hospital for machinery or special treatments such as cosmetic surgery. The need to express gratitude is strong and important and you will find the right way and the right time.

The majority of people working within the NHS are talented, committed and remarkable people and we owe them a great deal. Amidst the horror that has happened, and with the unknown challenge that lies ahead of you, take time to consider both the skill and humanity of the hospital workers. This can be seen as part of remarkable goodness in people – and counters the vileness of others.

A complaint against the NHS

Sometimes services get things wrong, but often these problems can be easily remedied without fuss. Try to make sure what you need is clearly stated as, sometimes, although perfectly clear to you, it can be misinterpreted. Sometimes, things go wrong and workers do not seem to want to do their job in an efficient way. If you have been clear and, having allowed enough time for an issue to be rectified, it has not been, then making a complaint may be your only option.

This is the procedure to follow.

If you have unsuccessfully tried to resolve your complaint within the hospital with a doctor, administrator or other person employed by the NHS trust, you must request the trust's complaints procedure. Then, write in detail about your complaint to the convenor. Provide as many details of dates and the specifics of your complaint as you can, including dates for replies (see example of lay-out of a complaint in section on complaining, pp. 173–187).

It is vital to consider having a competent agency or individual represent you (see section on advocacy organisations and groups, pp. 200–201). If you choose to have a representative to act on your behalf, it is essential you write a letter of consent, confirming the person's status, name, address and, if relevant, his or her professional position. You must also give consent for information to be released to and exchanged with your representative. This letter also needs to be sent to any other agency involved in the complaint. Without these steps being taken, an investigation into your complaint cannot get off the ground.

The body with the statutory responsibility of investigating the validity of your complaint is the NHS trust or health authority convenor. By law, the convenor is supposedly impartial. But, in reality, how likely this is when the same NHS trust appoints the post-holder and sits on the board is open to speculation. Herein lies the difficulty for the system to work at its best.

Under existing rules, the convenor decides whether or not there is a complaint to be answered. There are only certain decision outcomes available to the convenor:

1. Upheld: your complaint may be upheld; the matters raised need to be addressed.
2. No grounds for complaint, or no further action shall be taken.
3. Referral: the complaint is referred back to the service about which the complaint was made so that further discussions can take place.

Outcome 3 reflects the most common outcome of complaints: they are referred back to allow 'further avenues to be explored' in an effort to find resolution. Sadly, this can be used as a delaying tactic, which often deters complainants from continuing, thereby allowing the complaint to become 'cornered' or dormant and eventually being recorded as having been successfully dealt with by the convenor. Assuming you discuss, either personally or in writing, your complaint with the service concerned, you will either reach, or fail to reach, a satisfactory conclusion, from your point of view. In the latter case, or in the case of the convenor having found no grounds to uphold the case (see outcome 2), you must write again to the convenor, saying you remain dissatisfied and requesting a review of the decision and relevant progress of your complaint. This means that you must support your initial complaint with any new facts you have and, where possible, reinforce the elements of your complaint that have not been satisfactorily addressed.

The convenor *reviews* their decision and will either agree or refuse to proceed to an independent review. The convenor may propose certain actions take place as an alternative or prior to the date of an independent review.

An *independent review* includes an independent chairperson (who is usually from another NHS trust), the convenor and a professional layperson. The independent review considers all the arguments and reaches a decision that is final. There is no further local action after this decision by the NHS trust.

If you remain dissatisfied, it is possible to complain to the Health Ombudsman, forwarding all the documentation and providing reasons as to why you request they take up your complaint. (For address details of the Ombudsman, see section on Criminal Injuries Compensation Authority, page 280.)

This process can take years to conclude, and the Ombudsman's powers are limited to stating whether parties acted correctly and making suggestions for improvement. The last Conservative Government significantly reduced the powers of the Ombudsman.

If you are represented by an advocate, signed originals of your letter of consent will have to be included for every public service agency involved in the complaint. This prevents delays about 'consent' and 'confidentiality'.

Problems with the NHS complaints procedures

Prior to forming the government in 1997, Labour stated that, when they came to power, they would radically review the functioning of the NHS complaints process – we must wait to see what value this statement has in reality.

Patients Advice and Liaison Services (PALS) exist within each NHS trust to provide a conciliation service for complainants. In the future, the government is to establish Independent Advocacy Services to assist complainants in progressing a complaint in a more committed manner, and with greater hope of experienced representation and a just outcome. The litmus test will be to see what level of power this service will have; what levels of autonomy and genuine independence. We must hope it is not a reworking of the redundant former Community Health Councils.

The complaints process is draining, costly and a very time - and energy - consuming experience for a protracted and generally inadequate outcome. It is flawed in structure and administrative weight and puts pressure upon complainants to produce enormous quantities of documentation. Competent representation should be considered to alleviate pressure and complex manoeuvrings, allowing you to remain one step removed and therefore more able to focus on your well-being.

The process is not a good use of public funds, as it fails to produce an efficient service and rarely produces decisions challenging standards of NHS performance.

As with other 'independent complaints procedures', it is far from genuinely independent; in effect, it's a one-way power street. We await change to see if the public are to be provided with a fairer, more efficient system.

It is a tough decision to make whether to progress and fight or whether to walk away – which may be the most sensible act. It depends on the gravity of the complaint and its future implications for the quality of your life.

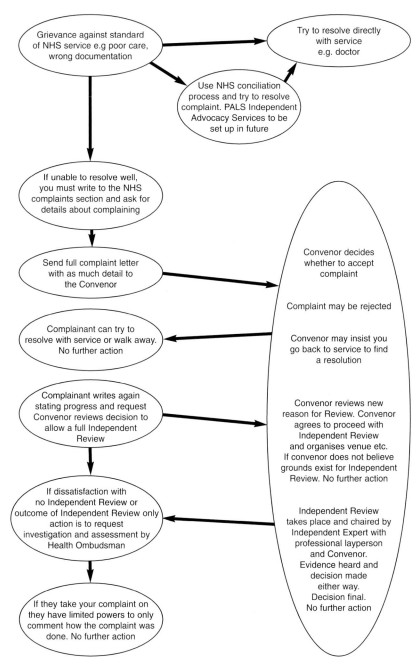

Grievance against standard of NHS service e.g poor care, wrong documentation

Try to resolve directly with service e.g. doctor

Use NHS conciliation process and try to resolve complaint. PALS Independent Advocacy Services to be set up in future

If unable to resolve well, you must write to the NHS complaints section and ask for details about complaining

Send full complaint letter with as much detail to the Convenor

Convenor decides whether to accept complaint

Complaint may be rejected

Complainant can try to resolve with service or walk away. No further action

Convenor may insist you go back to service to find a resolution

Complainant writes again stating progress and request Convenor reviews decision to allow a full Independent Review

Convenor reviews new reason for Review. Convenor agrees to proceed with Independent Review and organises venue etc. If convenor does not believe grounds exist for Independent Review. No further action

If dissatisfaction with no Independent Review or outcome of Independent Review only action is to request investigation and assessment by Health Ombudsman

Independent Review takes place and chaired by Independent Expert with professional layperson and Convenor. Evidence heard and decision made either way. Decision final. No further action

If they take your complaint on they have limited powers to only comment how the complaint was done. No further action

Standard NHS Complaints Procedure

The new NHS

There has been a lot of media coverage about how improved the new NHS is going to be and we must hope the government gets this right for the people it serves. It will be a greater success if it is appropriately resourced; it has to be staffed with good resources, less bulky management structures. Staff within the NHS have endured change after change imposed by successive governments and it is a miracle any staff know what it is they are supposed to be doing. As with the complaints procedures and the Patient and Public Involvement Services that are to be established, the government must start to address the basics and allow services to settle down before they totally disintegrate through lack of consistency and lack of staff. The government will need to make the NHS and all public services professions attractive, worthwhile professions. All of this will take a great deal of time, commitment and skills. Society will have to wait a long time before the damage to morale, skills and resources created by destructive government policies over the years can be rebuilt.

See the diagram opposite of where the power and influence now lies within the new NHS.

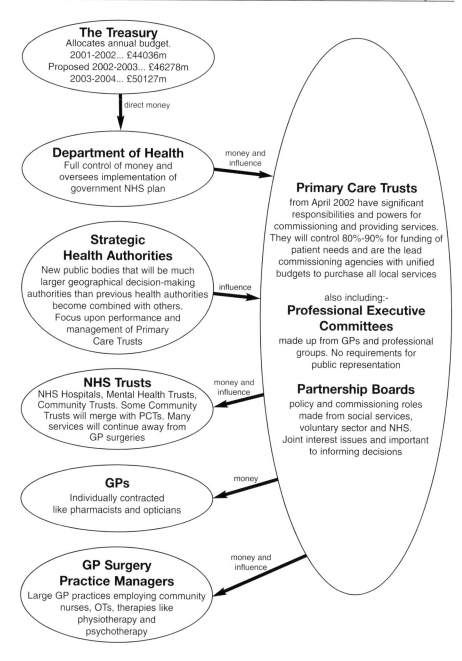

The Treasury
Allocates annual budget.
2001-2002... £44036m
Proposed 2002-2003... £46278m
2003-2004... £50127m

direct money

Department of Health
Full control of money and
oversees implementation of
government NHS plan

money and influence

Primary Care Trusts
from April 2002 have significant
responsibilities and powers for
commissioning and providing services.
They will control 80%-90% for funding of
patient needs and are the lead
commissioning agencies with unified
budgets to purchase all local services

Strategic Health Authorities
New public bodies that will be much
larger geographical decision-making
authorities than previous health authorities
become combined with others.
Focus upon performance and
management of Primary
Care Trusts

influence

also including:-

Professional Executive Committees
made up from GPs and professional
groups. No requirements for
public representation

NHS Trusts
NHS Hospitals, Mental Health Trusts,
Community Trusts. Some Community
Trusts will merge with PCTs. Many
services will continue away from
GP surgeries

money and influence

Partnership Boards
policy and commissioning roles
made from social services,
voluntary sector and NHS.
Joint interest issues and important
to informing decisions

GPs
Individually contracted
like pharmacists and opticians

money

GP Surgery Practice Managers
Large GP practices employing community
nurses, OTs, therapies like
physiotherapy and
psychotherapy

money and influence

The New National Health Service

© T.S. Duckett 2003

17

Primary Care Trusts

Primary Care Trusts (PCTs) are now responsible for assessing local health needs and for planning future health provision. Accordingly, they are *the* lead organisation for partnership with local authorities and other community resources. They have huge powers and cover a wide range of national health responsibilities. The PCTs will have duties to involve 'partnerships' that reflect the social and economic issues within regions. It is hoped the needs of people affected by violent crime will figure strongly and dynamically within this new order and, interestingly, will have a more defined link with social services. Community involvement will play a large role in the shaping and delivery of future services. Clinicians and local people will lead the PCTs. The government is keen to stress that, in the new order, devolving power and responsibility to PCTs provides real opportunities to involve local and regional groups. We must hope the groups genuinely reflect community issues and needs, as opposed to individual, dysfunctional egos. PCTs will take a clear lead in developing local services and apparently 'tailor' services according to the area and take responsibility for all family health practitioners. At best, if properly developed, this could offer an enormous positive step forward for all health care – especially for those affected by violent crime. A lot of emphasis is placed upon integrating local authorities with health and social care and implementing both the Local Government Act 2000 and the Health and Social Care Act 2001. This, along with developing work within the police service, could finally see the emergence of placing victims of violent crime positively within institutional responsibilities that, so far, have largely lacked enthusiasm from some services. PCTs will be *the* agency for modernising social and health care.

Partnership

The following is an extract of what the government means by the Patient and Public Involvement that it is promoting. The public remains objective by judging the government on the length of waiting lists – and why waiting lists exist at all – the quality of in-patient and out-patient care and, in relation to victims of serious violence and injury, the redevelopment of old-fashioned convalescent homes. People affected by violent crime will look to see the establishment of specialist trauma treatment centres for children, adolescents and adults, which offer more than a redundant 'debriefing'. People will want to see access to free, expert trauma services, which are not budget-dominated but sufficiently flexible to meet needs effectively. People affected by violent crime will judge the government's value of what it says by how it has modified the one-way, pressurised complaints procedure and, of course, how it deals with criminal medical workers. People will judge success by the resources hospital workers are given to treat people. People affected by violent crime will judge the government's value of Partnerships by the quality and diversity of groups for victims represented on Partnership Boards.

The new Patient and Public Involvement system provides people affected by violent crime with a rare opportunity to become directly involved in highlighting their needs. It must be hoped that the government and PCTs invite more than just the usual groups to be involved and nurture involvement from as wide a spectrum as possible. This presents a new opportunity for emerging and organised groups that genuinely reflect the needs of people affected by violence to place victims of violence positively within the institutional arena in these forums. But where are our diverse groups for people affected by violent crime to choose from?

What Patient and Public Involvement System will offer

In every Primary Care Trust and NHS trust there will be a Patients' Forum that will:
• Monitor and review the services arranged and/or provided by the trust from the perspective of the patient – not just the operation of services, but the range of services provided too;
• Seek the views of patients/carers receiving services provided or arranged by the trust;
• Inspect premises where NHS services are delivered, including private premises;
• Make reports and recommendations to the management of the trusts;
• Refer matters of concern to OSCs, StHAs, CHI and NPSA, etc. – and any other person or body the forums deem appropriate including the media;
• Be represented on the Board at Non-Executive Director level.

In addition the PCT Patients Forum, supported by Commission staff, will:
• Promote the involvement of the public in decisions and consultations on matters affecting their health;
• Commission and provide independent complaints advocacy (ICAS);
• Collect anonymous information about the patient experience, identify trends and make reports to decision-makers;
• Put forward the views of the public on health issues to key local decision-makers, including wider community planning mechanisms and processes;
• Help forums work together across boundaries;
• Have to take account of forums' views when setting priorities for their work;
• Provide a one-stop shop service by providing advice and information to the public about public involvement;
• Monitor how well the NHS is meeting its duty to involve and consult the public under s.11 Health and Social Care Act 2001.

And in every NHS trust and PCT there will be a **Patient Advice and Liaison Service** that will:
- Resolve problems on the spot;
- Provide information to patients, carers and their families about local health services and put people in contact with local support groups;
- Tell people about the complaints procedure and direct people to independent complaints advocacy support;
- Act as an early warning system for trusts and patients forums by monitoring trends and highlighting gaps in service and making reports for action to trust management.

In all local authorities with social services responsibilities there will be an **Overview and Scrutiny Committee**. They will:
- Take on the role of scrutiny of health services including the NHS;
- Be able to refer contested service changes to the SofS;
- Be able to call NHS managers to give information about services and decisions;
- Report their recommendations locally;
- Have to be consulted by the NHS where there are to be major changes to health services.

Nationally there will be a **Commission for Patient and Public Involvement in Health** that will:
- Set standards for patients' forums and providers of independent complaints advocacy;
- Monitor and make recommendations about the performance of patients' forums and providers of independent complaints advocacy support;
- Submit reports to the SofS on how the whole system of patient and public involvement is working and advise him about it;
- Make reports as it sees fit to other national bodies such as CHI, the NCSC and the NPSA on patient and public involvement issues and issues that in its opinion give rise to concern about the safety or welfare of patients that have not or are not being dealt with properly;
- Carry out national reviews of services from the patients' perspective – collating data from forums and making recommendations to the Secretary of State, and to other bodies and persons it considers appropriate.

© Department of Health, June 2002

Useful reading and contacts

Websites – NHS

www.doh.gov.uk/nhscomplaintsreform
www.doh.gov.uk/involvingpatients
www.doh.gov.uk/patientadviceandliaisonservice

Contact your local hospital NHS trust for information about local complaints procedures and service changes. Some details may be available from your local library.

Books and documents

Healthcare Provision – Past, Present and into the 21st Century, *by Audrey Leathard,* published by Stanley Thornes. An excellent text, detailing the practices and policies that have shaped our health service from 1900 to the present.

A Remedy for Medical Complaints – A Guide to Complaints Procedures, *by Rosamund Rhodes,* published by Sweet & Maxwell, 1998. An excellent, legally framed text about the processes of negligence and complaints and still very relevant. Very expensive: use a reference library.

Shifting the Balance of Power within the NHS – Securing Delivery, published by the Department of Health, July 2001. A very useful outline of the changes taking place within the NHS with the government's 'everything's going to be wonderful' shining through. Also, it is free from: Department of Health Publications, PO Box 777, London SE1 6XH; fax 01623 724524; E-Mail doh@prolog.uk.com or website www.doh.gov.uk/shiftingthebalance

Supporting Doctors, Protecting Patients, published by NHS, 1999. A consultation paper on preventing, recognising and dealing with poor clinical performance of doctors in the NHS in England. An unsurprising catalogue of medical negligence, fraud and policies that pre-empts the new 2002 NHS service changes and post-Dr Shipman murders. Time will tell what usefulness this government document and proposals will have.

A lot of people think this is a job that you go to.
Take a lunch hour – job's over – something like that.
But it's a twenty-four hour deal – no two ways about it!
And, what most people don't see – is
Just how hard it is to do the right thing.

People think if I make a judgement call, that
that's a judgement on them – but that is not what I do.
And that's not what should be done!
I have to take everything and play it as it lays.

Sometimes people need a little help.
And sometimes, people need to be forgiven.
And sometimes, they need to go to jail.
And that is a very tricky thing on my part – making that call.

I mean, the law is the law – and heck, if I'm going to break it
If you can forgive someone – well that's the tough part!
What can we forgive?
Tough part of the job – tough part of walking down the street.

Law enforcement officer's narrative from final scene of film Magnolia ©

The police force, our law enforcement service, has been rigorously scrutinised, in recent years, with intense external and internal change as a result. Much of the media attention has focused on our urban police forces. We know from certain high-profile cases of abuse and corruption within the forces that such elements exist within the system. Without doubt, the police force has, within its ranks, some appalling officers who should be subject to legal proceedings or dismissal. Like all public services, when criticised, the police force tends to react defensively, rallying as an 'institution' rather than confronting public criticism. It is natural to feel defensive if unfairly criticised, but the challenge for public institutions is to be proactive: to root out corrupt elements or sub-standard practices. Otherwise, these negative elements will simultaneously drain the morale of its own service workers and weaken general public confidence.

Public inquiries are on the increase and bring us ever closer to those in power. This has taken reactionary, less contemporary or competent officers by surprise and left them feeling unfairly judged. Sadly, and all too often, however, some drawn-out cases of sub-standard police practice have shown that public inquiries and their findings were justified in their criticism.

It was not so long ago that, at a police station, a police officer was subjected to a campaign of sustained prejudice and hate to try to force him to leave his job, because he was gay. This included the burning of his car while parked in the police car park, anonymous hate mail and cowardly telephone calls to 'out' him to his mother. Skilled and hardworking police officers who are offended by this kind of behaviour constitute the majority; but, it is incumbent on them for that very reason to speak out against such base bigotry. By refusing to accept such cowardly conduct, they can identify and help to eradicate the bad apples. Add to this the peculiarly and disturbingly high number of deaths among young black and Irish men in police custody or whilst on remand, and you have a picture of institutional racism: power plus prejudice. Recently, an Asian police sergeant had to lodge a complaint against his superiors, after enduring lengthy and bizarre investigations resulting from allegations that he had sent himself abusive e-mails, before he was cleared of the charge. No one else has been apprehended, or dismissed, for this – at significant cost to police morale and public money.

A crucial issue was not developed in the media reporting (*Evening Standard*, 6 November 2001) of a white man, and the murder of his wife and two of their four children in August 2001 in Kent. It was a frenzied attack with a hammer following years of domestic violence that included kicking his pregnant wife in the stomach, an alleged threat against her with a meat cleaver and disruptive extra-marital affairs with peer colleagues. The killer was a serving police officer in a county Tactical Support Team, who was authorised to carry and use guns. He had a reported history of domestic violence. These issues were never properly confronted within his management hierarchy, which, if they had, would surely have led to immediate protection from the appropriate agencies for both wife and children. Clearly, he would have been dismissed and a tragedy averted. The passive collusion of the killer's peers and management will one day require an explanation from two traumatised, orphaned children. How could this man be allowed to serve in a job of protection while simultaneously proving to be such a danger – all with such tragic yet predictable consequences? Silence can kill!

> We've waited nearly six years since my son was murdered.
> And yet again, the police seem to have failed us, and
> I want to know why?
> Why is this police officer allowed to retire?
> Why on earth should a family have to go through this?
>
> Doreen Lawrence OBE: *Evening Standard*, 14 January 1999

The passionate perseverance of Stephen Lawrence's family, in the end, forced the Metropolitan Police to accept criticism of its standards of practice and service and to spearhead a campaign of change in work practices. This is to be applauded. Therefore, when fine officers express frustration and feel attacked by strong criticism, they must remain objective about the calibre and performance of individuals within their service that they know are unsuitable. What are they doing to remove them? The unacceptable face of police abuse is carried out because rogue elements believe they will not be held responsible or accountable and, in some hierarchies, it is institutionally tolerated or ignored. Equally, we, as citizens, must remain objective and explicit in our need to support the best in law enforcement and support greater training, selection and resourcing of officers for the benefit of all in society. We must hail the remarkable men and women who protect us.

Our society needs a buoyant, well-resourced and qualified police force. One that is genuinely receptive and has the conviction to confront the abuse of power within its own ranks. Like all public agencies with extensive power over citizens, the emphasis and expectation from society for clear quality and performance are not a fashion but a social necessity. However, it is also a fact that, generally, within the police force there is a large majority of talented, committed men and women performing an extremely hard job in difficult circumstances: dwindling resources, bewildering organisational and political change; and against a backdrop of increasing violence and social fragmentation. We need a police service that is accountable, but we also need to temper our criticisms and generalisations of those 'bad apples' within its ranks with respect for the high standards of the majority. We should be prepared to ask our government how it is addressing the needs of citizens' safety beyond political condescension. Our government needs to encourage our officers and needs to make the police force a dynamic and attractive profession. After all, would you don a police uniform to go out on the streets of Britain to protect its citizens? Where good service is offered it should be commended because, when we criticise it, we must also reflect on the fact that we want and need it to protect us and our diverse communities. We are interconnected to one another as citizens and service providers; despite what some politicians say, there is such a thing as society.

As with all public services, the police force is witnessing a decline in the number of new recruits. Simultaneously, we are seeing a steady flow of workers leaving the profession due to severe demoralisation, excessive stress, inadequate coherent executive guidance and support where the work is good. All this is going on at a time when we, as a society, need a dependable, well-resourced, confident and non-prejudiced service to cope

24

with the increasing incidence of violent crime. It is an unpleasant, often unrewarding, but essential service that requires disciplined, competent, non-prejudiced and dynamic people who exercise the powers bestowed upon them with skill. Young people are disinclined to view law enforcement as a viable professional career – this is a tragic reflection on what has been happening within our society for years and what is continuing to happen. We need a government that is receptive to the needs and resourcing of the police in contemporary society. We need a government that does not undermine the workforce as we have seen in both the NHS and education; we do not need patronising politicians.

One criticism that came out of the Stephen Lawrence inquiry (officially known as the MacPherson Inquiry) was that the police force was 'institutionally racist', something that hurt officers who are fine policemen and women. The professional police officers who are positively challenging racism within their institutions, within unmanageable social and work environments, can justifiably feel stung. However, they must also acknowledge the unacceptable canteen banter that, at times, does filter into the work attitudes of some peers who generally are not confronted.

We saw excellent working practices among the police officers who apprehended the individual responsible for the bombing of minority communities in London during 1999. The first affected was the Bangladeshi community in east London, then the largely African–Caribbean community in south London and, finally, the gay community in central London. In trying to gather information for the investigation into who was responsible for the attacks, police officers retrieved 1,097 CCTV tapes from key sites in south London. This entailed over 4,000 hours' viewing and, after two weeks, produced a suspect, who was indeed the culprit. During the third attack, best practice could be seen in the rapid deployment of 36 Family Liaison Officers (FLOs) providing support to the 139 injured and the families of the three fatalities. As one person affected commented:

> The Met Family Liaison Officers supported the
> victims and their families above and beyond the
> call of duty with great compassion and humanity.
>
> Peggy Hall, mother of Brixton bomb victim, quoted in *The Job*,
> Friday, 30 June 2000

One of the recommendations of the MacPherson Inquiry was that all forces develop skilled FLOs, but more officers are also required. It is against the backdrop of an increasingly polarised and volatile society that the police force has to function. Against low morale and a lack of resources, there is emerging an increasingly vocal and positive change spreading through the ranks of the police force – especially in relation to differences in race and sexuality. The parents of Stephen Lawrence symbolised by their dignity and stealth showed a refusal to accept the abuse of power and the prejudiced attitudes of the police. The Lawrence family made a huge contribution to, and was a significant force in, accelerating the change that ensured effective markers for new, standardised best practices to be set in motion across the nation.

The police officer's job – policing society

The police's job is ensuring the protection of society from individuals and groups who break existing laws and place at risk the safety of individuals and communities. It is law enforcement. A police officer is the physical embodiment of our civilised laws and of our society's wish to know that there exist right and wrong; the police are our bridge between the two. They should offer protection, service without prejudice; they maintain the laws that reinforce our code for society's benefit and individual safety. Police work is also about preventing crime, which is a tough task to implement and accomplish.

The core elements of their job include: gathering as much accurate and consistent information about a crime and suspected criminal as possible; the pursuit of an investigation without personal prejudice; successful interrogation and charging of an individual or group; and helping to take the case to trial. Increasingly, the police force is developing experience and success in taking up the allied issues of people in need – once the preserve of social services – such as pastoral caring or a befriending role (which is discussed in the section on the failings of social services and the NHS). Police services are initiating codes of practice for those affected by violent crime – this is a positive development, which gives us cause for real hope.

Once a case has reached court, it is no longer possible for the police to have any influence beyond the communicating of accurate facts to the court. Often, the police are left in almost as much despair as a bereaved or violated person when an individual or group appears to 'get away with murder'. We are familiar with the staggeringly low sentences passed down by the courts, which woefully fail to reflect the gravity of the crime. This may be because of the nuances of interpretation of the wording of the law by senior barristers or judges, against all the evidence and common sense. The police force works within a very narrow area of public service and duty with little power to influence the legal process that ultimately impacts upon the lives of victims of violent crime.

The police force, then, generally, stands out as a beacon of hope for securing compassion and justice for people affected by violent crime, notwithstanding the reservations mentioned, and some of our police officers are nothing short of diamonds. These are highly pressurised men and women who take, head-on, the often justified criticisms of the public and their right to know what the police do and why. The police service has, at times, been forced to adapt, mould and develop expertise and, within this process, we are seeing the work of force liaison officers almost replace the statutory duties of other agencies, such as psychiatric and social services. (See section on social services, pp. 160–172.)

In contemporary law enforcement practice, where there has been a serious violent crime and especially where a murder or suspicious death has occurred, at an early stage of police involvement, a trained police officer will be assigned to the individual or family.

The role of the Family Liason Officer (FLO)

> The primary function of [an FLO] in all cases is that of an investigator. In performing this role officers must seek to achieve the primary goals of family liaison.
>
> © MPS Family Liaison Policy and Fundamental Guidelines: Second Draft

Parallel with valid criticisms of poor police practices, the media and some government ministers fail to make sufficiently clear the generally high standard of police work that is taking place daily. If a tragedy has recently entered your life, it is more likely you will find an early degree of sanity, anchor for coping, and comfort from within the ranks of the police than any other statutory or voluntary agency. This is not simply because they have a statutory duty that leads to immediate early involvement. Today, the work of the police, as FLOs, in the midst of shrinking public services, can be outstanding. They are willing, gifted and dynamic men and women working to the highest standards, delivering their service with tremendous humility despite lack of both resources and real government support.

In some ways, we can understand the mission and goals of FLOs as a natural response to public need and progress in policing. In fact, FLO work has always been assumed to be 'part of the job' – for better or worse. The difference is that what, for years, has been an implicit set of sensitive, intense, investigative and arbitrary skills is now rightly required to be explicitly stated and formally practised. Formally, as in: written codes of training, practice and supervision for the service and service users in the wake of human tragedy, which was originally pioneered by the Avon and Somerset Constabulary and made standard by the fight of the Lawrence family.

The written concept becomes a strategy – the idea – the need.

This is made into the policy – how the idea will happen: the training, the daily practice of contact with citizens in need and the need for the police to investigate violent crime.

This is what citizens receive, at the point of trauma, through the legal, investigative and compassionate agency of a skilled man or woman – policy in legal human practices and need.

This is policy in practice with a finite beginning, middle and end – because all professional relationships must have an end – and a purpose that starts with an agency's idea – a strategy. Our other relationships, like those with family, friends, lovers or voluntary groups, are not duty bound by statute or formal codes of practice. That is why this handbook explains agency duties and relationships – because they are different and because they are professional, task-focused relationships. These different relationships provide avenues of hope, emotional nourishment and the chance to rise above the status of victim, of getting beyond merely surviving – to reclaiming a life as fulfilling as one possibly can.

Changes in society are inevitable and good services learn to yield to, and grow alongside, the dynamic public they serve. In Britain, with increasing levels of violent crime and diminishing public services that harbour a national culture of low morale, this is a mighty tough role for the police to get right. We place a high, and maybe unreasonable, expectation upon the police when too many of society's ills, in fact, lie at the feet of the government. For FLOs to function properly, a sea change in both law and attitudes has to take place in order to support this increased workload, secure optimum results and avoid placing unachievable goals upon all police services. We know that violent crime occurs across the land; we know that increasingly violent crime affects masses of people – and secondary victims – within a single devastating incident. This requires comprehensive services which are able to respond effectively to the often horrendous and complex human misery that results from such crime. Our police force cannot be everything to everyone all of the time – nor should it aspire to be or to do so.

Selection of an FLO

Serious attention is given to the selection, additional training requirements and supervision of FLOs. Candidates who choose to become FLOs will have successfully completed a set of accredited courses and personality tests. In the future, we can expect to see these tests become even more sophisticated with the possibility of them starting, as an option, during the initial phase of basic training for officers. These officers would still require a mandatory minimum number of years of qualified general police experience as a prerequisite to accreditation. All these points are crucial, because, for people in the grip of horror, it is common and human for them to become intensely attached to the first person(s) – public workers – to become involved and invariably these will be police officers. For FLOs to provide the very best service, they must be psychologically adept in maintaining a very difficult balance between human compassion and a methodical investigation of information that will lead to the arrest and conviction of the proven criminal. FLOs, therefore, require expert psychological skills, objectivity and the ability to deal effectively with the fact that many violent crimes are committed by someone within, or known to, the family of the victim. FLOs must have secured a degree of objective, analytical knowledge about themselves and their own personal experiences alongside any professional requirements. This can be a tall order, as it is invariably the police who must disclose extremely horrific information to families of victims.

FLOs and accountability

To safeguard everybody involved, FLOs are accountable to senior, specialist investigating officers and must detail, in writing, every contact with the family. It is the responsibility of every investigation managing officer to develop a local or regional FLO response strategy – that is, strategic plans for responding to the needs of victims and their families so that services are not random or reactive. These, in practice, will be not dissimilar to the Community Care Plans that local social services are compelled to produce annually by law – but FLO strategies are of superior, practical service value and have less 'babble' or 'politically patronising' content, so the result is more dynamic and genuine. The working practice of FLOs has yet to be quantified and analysed to review their impact and indicate where their roles may require change. However, FLOs do portend a radical shift by the police in gaining greater influence of the experience of dealing with victims and in defining service needs.

Strategic politics

There exists a potential double bind in FLOs' work: although a lot of superb work is being undertaken daily, it is undertaken without placing it in a wider statutory domain beyond the monopoly of the Home Office, which translates everything solely in terms of a mono-service. However, from a positive point of view, and, if developed well, this could enhance services for people affected by violence if the appropriate allied services came under the jurisdiction of the Home Office and adequate resources were made available for FLOs.

For FLOs to reach their optimum goal, and for people affected by violence to reach their optimum rehabilitation, other skills are needed; for example, social and health care, housing issues and compensation matters. The current necessity for an FLO to withdraw eventually can be counter-productive for those in need, if these other skills are not provided. Given policy changes, it could work well if the FLO role was expanded to take on more long-term family work in new teams. Then, this would be a constructive reason for maintaining a monopoly on victims' needs, for which other government departments are failing to provide adequate services. We require diversity, choice and quality in practice, not government pressure resulting in more political 'condescension' and cost cutting – diversity of services creates constructive competition and greater potential for people to really survive violent crime. The police force has adopted its expertise in many areas that were once the domain of social services, which generally fail to enact their role with interest, desire or in a dynamic manner. The potential for an exclusive government department that undertakes a comprehensive service beyond the legal, including assisting in the completion of the criminal compensation process, is worth serious debate and implementation of pilot schemes. It requires common sense and skilled resources.

> But I couldn't wait any longer. I pulled myself to my feet and crossed unsteadily back to the desk. The young officer was dealing with someone else, but if this didn't take priority what possibly could? He looked up helplessly as I approached. I could tell straight away that nothing had been done.

> There was a policewoman behind him now and he turned and said something to her. I couldn't catch what it was. The look she gave me was less than sympathetic. However, they went to the side of the desk and opened the lock to let me into their side of the station. As I came through, both of them kept their distance. I suddenly realised that they thought I was a raving lunatic.

> 'I've been told what you said when you came into the station,' said the policewoman. 'A police officer would never have told you that on the phone!' Her voice was hard as nails, the words pronounced with relish.

'We're not allowed to', she added.

The world was completely mad. I had expected that things would be handled with speed and compassion but instead here I was, on top of everything, having to fight to prove that I wasn't completely insane.

She continued: 'We've been trying to get through to Wimbledon to find out what's going on. But this just doesn't sound right. This isn't the way that we do things.'

'He didn't want to tell me!' I managed to say, 'He didn't want to tell me.'

They weren't sure, either of them. They were hesitating. Eventually they showed me into what must have been an interrogation room of some kind. There was a phone on the table and the policewoman picked it up. It didn't work. She led me into another room and picked up yet another phone. Again there was a problem with it. Time was going past and this was just a shambles. Alex was on his own. I had to get to him. She led me back out into the corridor and wanted me to go back to the waiting room until they sorted something out. This was unbearable.

A door opened at the end of the corridor and an officer with grey hair appeared. I assumed from the way they looked at him that this must be a senior officer. He must know what was going on, I thought, and would undoubtedly take charge and sort this mess out. But he just stood and watched. By now there were several male officers just standing at a distance and watching. I felt like the main attraction in a freak show. I felt completely dehumanised.

Only the policewoman was doing anything. But far from offering help and understanding, she seemed to be relishing the opportunity to display her gung-ho spirit and 'hard as nails' persona. I got the impression that she only wanted to show her male colleagues how capable she was in dealing with a lunatic. And how useless they were in their inability to react.

'I've got to go', I said. 'You're not doing anything for me.' I had no other choice. These people were going out of their way not to understand. In a minute I could find myself locked up in a cell with no way on earth of getting to Alex. The officers all looked at the one with grey hair. He nodded in a way I understood to mean: 'Let him go'. The policewoman unlocked the door, saying, 'You're in no state to drive.' I knew I wasn't. But I had no choice. I tried to take stock of myself once again. I felt a little stronger. I wouldn't ride fast. I couldn't take any stupid risks – I had to keep myself alive for Alex, there was absolutely no way I could afford to take any chances. Even if I took the greatest effort of concentration I had ever made I knew that I would get there in one piece – I had to.

The officers followed me out on to the drive beside the station – all of them, including the senior officer. A couple of police cars were parked outside.

The scene was completely surreal, but again, what did I expect? Again the male officers kept their distance while the policewoman continued to try and convince me not to go. The others remained silent. 'Why don't you wait till we get a car for you?' she said. The cars were there but I didn't see anybody rushing to get the keys. 'You're not doing anything for me,' I said. She tried to physically block my bike as the others stood and watched. I pulled on my helmet.

She was still in my way. The last thing I wanted to do was push her. Instead, I silently pulled the bike upright and made to climb on. I wanted to make it clear that I was going. She seemed equally determined to prevent me. Nevertheless, she glanced round to see the reaction of the one with the grey hair. 'Let him go,' he said again.

'It's the least you can do,' I thought to myself. I pressed the starter and the motor caught. The policewoman moved out of the way just enough to let me roll past and out of the driveway ... I had hours to go before I could get to Alex ... it seemed like an eternity.

© André Hanscombe: *The Legacy of Rachel Nickell – the Last Thursday in July*

André Hanscombe had demanded, by telephone, to know what had happened to his companion – the mother of his child – and was reluctantly told by an officer. Police failed to arrive quickly to collect him as promised. After waiting a long time, he motor-biked across London. In deepening shock, he arrived at a police station, saying he had been told his companion had been murdered: the above extract recounts the initial reaction that he received.

Summary of the work of an FLO

The stated objectives of an FLO's role may vary slightly between different forces, but the core areas of concern, intervention and duties are consistent throughout the country. The goals cited here are from the second draft of the Metropolitan Police Service. A final draft is now amended and future amendments will periodically alter some aspects, but the core elements that are provided, for the foreseeable future, remain relevant. Because the Metropolitan Police Service serves a major world city with a concomitant level of violent crime, and has seen some of most deplorable police practices, it is rapidly developing an expertise founded on the core skills developed within the Avon and Somerset Constabulary (as discussed above). You may find it worthwhile asking your local police authority for a copy of its FLO guidelines.

The core elements of FLO duties will remain the pursuit of, and securing, accurate information to progress enquiries that will lead to the apprehension of a violent criminal (investigation) – as well as the psychological and practical needs identified and provision for individuals or families.
People affected by murder or other violent crime need to be aware that if an

identification (ID) parade of suspects takes place, the FLO would not be involved by law (D2.2: Police and Criminal Evidence Act 1984). This includes neither informing nor accompanying people in grief when attending an ID parade and is in keeping with not prejudicing bereaved people's knowledge or opinions or unconscious desires to show gratitude or other feelings. This is about maintaining a legal objectivity during a time of intense and unknown emotional outcome and to prevent the possible influence or prejudicing of a vulnerable potential witness where it might be argued, in a court, that bias was used.

It is up to FLOs to anticipate this situation and, with their managers, to provide appropriate alternative agency involvement to help those in need – as required by law. For example, with the process of viewing and identifying a loved one, the visual selection of a potential perpetrator is heavy with emotional fall-out for everyone involved.

It will be the responsibility of the main FLO involved in working with you to respond to, and write the police report for, the Criminal Injuries Compensation Authority (CICA). This report is one of the compensation authority's requirements for confirmation of the actual crime, subsequent legal action taken and any recorded injuries. The authority has been inclined to blame delays in processing compensation claims on the police failing to submit the required report. This is very rarely the case and your legal representative can easily verify this with the police force involved. It is important that the FLO is given the correct CICA reference number at the earliest opportunity when you, or your representative, receive it from the authority. Naturally, full cooperation with the police, in securing an arrest or prosecution, is a precondition to the CICA accepting a compensation claim for assessment.

> For my last seven years of service I was in charge of a department with a wide range of administrational/enquiry roles (the type of department designed to free up operational officers and keep them out on the street); among various responsibilities our remit included liaison with outside agencies including the CICA.
>
> The CICA would request a report from the police for every application for compensation they received, this was the first part of their procedure and they give the police a 21-day return period on these.
>
> We ignored their time-scale and worked on a 14-day turn round, which obviously meant they were back with the CICA long before their 21-day deadline.
> It was very noticeable to us that some of these applications were very old

when they arrived with us. They had been date stamped when received by the CICA and again prior to being sent to us and the discrepancies in these dates showed they had been lying around for substantial periods of time before being acted upon, often numbered in months rather than weeks.

It was not uncommon for us to receive phone calls from irate members of the public, who, on complaining to the CICA about the length of time being taken, were informed that they, (the CICA), were awaiting a police response. In all of these cases my department had either returned the form within time or, believe it or not, not even received it by the time the applicant came on the phone. They were telling people that applications were out with the police when their own department had not even processed them.

Anecdotal comment of retired police officer

As explained, throughout Britain, the mission and goals for FLOs are generally the same and these are the identified duties within the Metropolitan Police Service.

One of the most important considerations throughout any investigation is the relationship between the family and the police. The Metropolitan Police Service accepts that the primary responsibility for family liaison rests with the police. Families will be considered as partners in an investigation. Families will be treated appropriately, professionally, with respect and in accordance with their diverse needs. This concept must be reflected at all levels of the police service.

The primary goals of the FLO

These may be summarised as set out below.

- To gather evidence and information from the victim/family in a sensitive manner which contributes to the police investigation/action and preserves integrity.
- To provide a documented, two-way communication channel between victim/family and police, which is fully recorded using the family liaison log.
- To mitigate, as far as possible, the negative effects of the criminal justice system through the provision of timely information and practical support to victim/family concerning:
- The investigation, action, procedures, to date and ongoing which may include the interaction with other agencies such as council, media, Coroner's Officers etc.
- To liaise, keep victims aware of the ongoing processes/procedures of the criminal justice system, i.e. the Crown Prosecution Service, Coroner or other statutory bodies interacting in the process.
- To ensure that victims/family members are given information about support agencies and that referrals are made to Victim Support and other agencies in accordance with the victim's/families' wishes.

Racial and Violent Crime Task Force (DCC4) MPS Family Liaison Policy and Fundamental Guidelines: Second Draft © August 2000. Reproduced with kind permission

An FLO's job – in the early hours and days of contact

An FLO will be responsible for providing clear facts about the gravity and nature of injuries and adding whatever information becomes available as examinations and investigations progress. The FLO gathers information to assist in the assessment of the victim's life and the people in their lives, about the circumstances of the crime, explains the legal procedures and will assist the closest relatives or friends in the identification of a deceased loved one.

Most individuals and families affected by murder often want to know the raw details about the murder of their loved one. Exactly what is disclosed, how and when, are decided by all concerned according to the actual information known at the time. Initially, the actual injuries may not be at all clear until a post-mortem is performed. The FLOs must discuss these facts and disclosures with their coordinating manager with reference to keeping the confidentiality of information – especially in the early hours and days of an investigation. If the police suspect a close relative, some information may be withheld. They must take into consideration just what, in fact, an individual or family can really handle: shock is a highly disturbing and disorientating state and what is sometimes expressed, at the very moment they learn of their terrible loss, is not always what is meant, so to disclose further unpalatable details at this time can compound shock. At the same time, the truth cannot be avoided indefinitely and a balance of factors, centrally informed by the bereaved, can be more safely secured by asking the family how often, in what way and to what level of detail they wish to know what has happened – and what will now happen. This allows people affected by psychological trauma to begin a process of adjustment, while in the early grip of shock, with fewer complications via mistruths. It will also lay a foundation for professional directness and integrity that will forge a trusting relationship. This will be successfully achieved by FLOs by taking the steps as set out below.

- Providing immediate and appropriate information to the family concerning the death of the victim and in explaining the procedures in respect of the body (of the loved one(s)) and coroner's processes. The family should be informed of their right to have a representative present at the post-mortem.
- Establishing, from the family members, any immediate evidence, information or rumours, so that it can be passed directly to the investigation team for urgent attention.
- Providing protection/assistance should a family or individual express concern for their safety or have been subject to threats or intimidation. In all cases, the FLO must act quickly and effectively, informing the Investigating Manager without delay.

- Giving or facilitating initial practical support for members of the family, e.g., transport.
- Protecting, as far as possible, the family from unwarranted media intrusions.
- Arranging temporary housing when the family home has been designated as a crime scene or a protracted search of the victim's home is anticipated.
- Facilitating the family's wishes to visit the crime scene where it is divorced from the family home. There is a need to balance evidence gathering with the emotional needs of the family.
- Arranging access to medical services for the family, e.g., family members suffering the effects of trauma.
- Where appropriate, exploring with the family, at an early stage, the involvement of statutory or voluntary local support organisations, including local community interest groups.
- Supplying at least one member of a family with a copy of the Home Office pack called Information for Families of Homicide Victims. A pack to offer help in coping.

Racial and Violent Crime Task Force (DCC4) MPS Family Liaison Policy and Fundamental Guidelines: Second Draft © August 2000 MPS. Reproduced with kind permission

At best, an FLO provides the physical and psychological parameters for beginning to absorb the impossible and intolerable. Also, while acting directly as part of a murder investigation or serious violent crime they will be able to channel those in need to the best of what is available for counselling, rehousing and other specialist agencies. This is why the work does require particular additional skills to those gained by other officers in the police force, along with additional supervision and remuneration. Equally, those people affected by violence deserve the FLO service and will often quickly develop an intense emotional attachment with an FLO. This pivotal role is one that deserves high regard, not condescension or exploitation.

General matters about an FLO Investigating Manager – boundaries of contact

At the first stage of police involvement with a murder, the policy goal involves the FLO Investigating Manager gathering as much information about the crime, the victim and the victim's family as possible, i.e. languages spoken, need for translators, Braille or sign-language, etc. When the Investigating Manager arrives to meet the traumatised family for the first time, he/she should not need to ask any unnecessarily upsetting questions. Simultaneously, the process begins to commence at the legal level, gathering as much information to progress investigations as soon as possible without leaving people further traumatised, antagonised and offended.

Where humanly possible, this takes place within the first twenty-four hours and often involves an initial telephone conversation with another officer letting the bereaved family know to expect a call and to arrange a time to visit. It is during this period that social services need to be made aware of the crisis and be available for a case/network conference to aid the family, alleviate police pressures where possible and mobilise social care support (see 'network conferences' in the section on social services, pp. 160–172). The Manager will provide information about what has taken place and find out what the bereaved family needs in the unfolding hours and any immediate concerns they may have. These concerns may include: the current whereabouts of the body or bodies of their loved one(s), where the body or bodies were found, which violations took place (mindful of restrictions on what can be revealed at any given time during the police investigation) and when those grieving may come to view the body or bodies of their loved one(s). Investigating Managers must ask difficult questions if they are to make an early move to find the killer(s) of a loved one.

Managers and FLOs never raise false expectations or state any facts of which they cannot be sure. Nor can FLOs offer assurances of confidentiality with other statutory agencies because the collection and sharing of information is an important part of their work in successfully catching the violent criminal(s) responsible for the crime they are investigating. The Investigating Manager has an important role – acting as an initial and consistent coordinator and senior representative of the police force for an individual or family. They will keep the family up to date with regular personal contact and listen to any complaints or compliments regarding the practices that follow throughout the FLOs' contact with them.

It will be common for an Investigating Manager, if requested, to attend a funeral, a court, or deal with the media and help those affected understand the legal process, such as any charges brought, committal hearings (pre-trial), trial dates and any trial outcomes like sentences or appeals. The Investigating Manager has a direct responsibility for everything legal, investigative, practical and pastoral.

What are the police doing here?
Every effort is taken by FLOs and their managers to undertake their law enforcement duties parallel with an equally and active degree of compassion for people facing trauma immediately following the tragedy and right up until a court case and even, sometimes, beyond.

Every tragedy and its impacts on all concerned is unique. In general, an

Investigating Manager will be expected to anticipate some of the legal, psychological and human needs set out below.

- Regularly review developments in an investigation and the immediate well-being of the victim/families affected.
- To ensure a consistently sensitive approach – reflecting the diversity and individual needs of each victim/family and reflecting the multicultural, multiracial, sexually diverse and familial lifestyles in contemporary Britain as a standard part of any correlation in planning – including religious requirements, interpreters, gender sensitive matters and disability matters.
- Every contact and decision relating to the unfolding trauma and needs will be recorded.
- Providing the victim/family with as full and up-to-date information as possible about the crime and the processes of investigation.
- Gathering an in-depth family history and any other important facts and information.
- To balance the investigation progress by being mindful of when and how much information is disclosed – because it is a fact that, sometimes, the violent criminal is within the family, or connected in some way with it, and should not know of any police leads or forensic discoveries – and to prevent distress to victims or their families.
- Gathering evidence such as belongings or witness statements.
- Choosing a suitable FLO who best addresses the needs of the individual or family in need.
- Being able to confirm, in writing, and explain within law, any information that might be temporarily withheld and to record any individual or family displeasure at this action.
- Any complaints to be recorded and all information willingly provided if a complaint is to be pursued, after reasons for withholding have been explained.
- All agencies involved, like Victim Support, solicitors or other agencies, will have reasons for involvement recorded.
- Any decisions or representations on the behalf of families and individuals by their chosen advocate will be recorded.
- A clear withdrawal plan involving a humane and planned procedure for ending contact with a family will be arranged at the earliest feasible stage and followed through to completion with the active awareness of the individual or family.

Abridged by author from Criteria of the Racial and Violent Crime Task Force (DCC4) MPS Family Liaison Policy and Fundamental Guidelines: Second Draft. ©MSP August 2000. Reproduced with kind permission

FLOs and the media: helping the police with the media

The media in Britain are extremely powerful in influencing how governments operate and how we think by the way in which they select and present the 'issues of the day'. Sadly, in relation to victims of serious violent crimes, the media generally tend to reduce them to the status of selected 'super victims' like characters in a soap opera or other entertainment. The British media generally fail to report accurately the complex horror of those affected. So they consistently fail to use their enormous influence and power to confront governments with the immediate and long-term needs of victims of violent crime and raise social awareness to any genuine value. The media could do so much good if inclined. (See section on dealing with the media, pp. 145–159.)

An Investigating Manager will be responsible for any poor practices like 'leaks' to the media. The negative fall-out of this is when information and specific details, which are still confidential, find their way into tabloid headlines. The Home Office should provide explicit codes for the dismissal and prosecution of police officers who ignore best practice by disclosing information that may jeopardise trials of alleged killers. Instead, we find trial by media hysteria – not by an unbiased jury.

The police must make every effort to ensure no confidential information or information that could be distressing to the victim (including the family) is leaked to the media – especially before all family members have been contacted. This is important whether someone is murdered or seriously injured and whether they are in hospital or at home. The 'need to know' rules should be applied.

Nevertheless, in relation to investigating a violent crime – especially a murder – we are now familiar with the police making use of the media with appeals from deeply traumatised families – often on television. Sometimes, the killer is within the family or even giving the media interview. Occasionally, the police may use the media for a form of entrapment, which makes constructively criticising the excesses of media sensationalism difficult. It remains a precarious and somewhat unwholesome necessity of modern times. We have seen sustained and constructive media coverage lead to successful information being obtained – securing arrests and trials. Such cases as the disappearance of Suzy Lamplugh; the New Cross fire; the Marchioness campaign; the murders of Jason Swift, the Menson family and Megan and Lin Russell. The tremendous zeal of one Midlands newspaper's campaign succeeded in helping to free, on appeal after twenty-seven years in prison, a man wrongly convicted of murder.

What does this have to do with you and how the FLO will assist you with your needs right now? Everything! It is important that the FLO explains what effects appearing in the media will have in the short term, e.g. losing the freedom to grieve in privacy by becoming known as 'that family'. In the longer term, media participation may affect your chances of continued anonymity, your desire to reclaim a sense of control in your community – on your terms. It may also adversely affect extended family members' lives, such as related children trying to survive their grief, e.g. returning to school, going out with friends – but fearful of being pointed at, or people surrounding or avoiding them. Being made vulnerable to long-term and often distasteful media attention or harassment, for some, feels like being victimised all over again. Victims simply need the personal freedom to be identified as the individuals they are or wish to aspire to become.

It is another tough call for you to make. The FLO must explain and measure investigational needs against further potential social and psychological trauma. In a raw period of naturally wanting to find the killer, thinking about the potential legacy of long-term media attention and loss of privacy may not be at the forefront of your mind. It may be that you decide to take this gamble in the hope the media will show responsibility and alert the public to help seek out the guilty person(s). You may choose to have a solicitor, and the FLO provide rules for how the media will have access and only allow written statements to be read out without you ever appearing physically. Take time and advice from many professionals about what you need emotionally; balancing your desire to assist police investigations in securing, say, the killers of your loved one(s) against your vulnerability and survival – and that of the people around you. This is why the media must show restraint and decency, allowing police agencies to decide the effectiveness of using the media and pursuit of best law.

Pertinent draft guidelines are set out below.

- The police and family ideally should share a goal in what is being conveyed – use of wording on certain descriptions of the crime or murdered person(s) and how they will be expressed via the media – and why.
- If an individual or family wish to take a dominant role with the media, support should be offered alongside universal guidance about the ramifications and options, such as remaining silent while, police, a solicitor, supporter or friend read out a statement.
- The above use of a spokesperson is a viable option, especially when a tragedy affects several people or several families, to ensure all opinions – of all individuals – are heard and are part of an evaluated decision about how to utilise any media coverage of a group tragedy.
- The spokesperson must be very clear about the specific, limited and *sub judice* [i.e., when a matter is before the courts] role they take on. They will also need to be very clear about any other contact with people that they represent. Issues of discussion would require prior consultation with the police because, at this time, they are

dealing with the extremely raw emotions of victims and have enormous legal and investigative responsibilities. These representatives should therefore not object, or be offended, if FLOs are present at any meetings – which may be recorded – as there should be no conflict of unity.

- Whether only written statements are offered, via a representative, to the press to protect against misrepresentation or *sub judice*.
- To make explicit that no pictures are to be taken of other family members – children or adults – to maintain privacy at a current or future time.
- In contentious issues, such as suspected hate crimes concerning gender, sexuality or race, a need for individuals or families to be seen together signifying cooperation and unity in an investigation. The positives of this unity cannot be understated, especially if hate groups commit crimes to encourage division.
- Always repeating the human anguish that is still raw and happening to the family and the pursuit of justice to signify the humility of police work and individual human tragedy.

Abridged by author from Criteria of the Racial and Violent Crime Task Force (DCC4) MPS Family Liaison Policy and Fundamental Guidelines ©MSP August 2000. Reproduced with kind permission

Viewing and identification of a murdered loved one

There is no avoiding the anguish of viewing and identifying the body of a dead loved one in an alien environment like a mortuary. It is hard to find words that describe, with any proximity to reality, what you must go through. It is a life story that defies description. There is nothing any agency

© T.S. Duckett 2003 Not to be reproduced without written permission

41

can do to take away this unavoidable legal requirement of identifying the body of a murdered loved one, or ease the trauma. It is one more experience to be encountered in an endless stream of traumatising events that a criminal has inflicted on you and those about you. It is the beginning of a remarkable and unwanted story both unique and tragic. Before any identification is made or request for viewing of a loved one is granted, those attending an identification, should, wherever humanly possible, have prescribed medication made available to alleviate the worst potential effects of post-traumatic stress disorder (PTSD). While not negating the police's need to progress with an inquiry, this cannot be at the expense of human need, vulnerability or frailty (see sections on PTSD and network conferences in section on social services, pp. 160–172).

There exists a need for FLOs, as investigating officers, to ensure that traumatised people are accurate in identifying the body. Mistakes, for a variety of reasons, do happen. The viewing and identification process cannot be completed in seconds and there will be forms to be signed at some stage with regard to the identification process. In this situation, the FLO can only assist those who have responsibility for identification by talking them through the mortuary environment. This can be extremely hard to endure. (See section on viewing a dead body, pp. 54–81.)

Touching
No matter how prepared one may be, this aspect of identification of the body always horrifies. When touching is to be allowed, it requires the FLO to have seen the body before the people who will need to identify it, as the body of their loved one may be extremely damaged. The FLO will need to provide an individually tailored description of the condition of the body – appearance, marks and smells – everything pertaining to the process. This provides people with a visual image as preparation for the upsetting task of viewing/identifying their loved one. (See sections on death; inquests and coroners, pp. 54-81; pp. 82–93.)

An FLO will explain, alongside the physical looks of the deceased loved one, other details that will be hard to take in. They will repeat the information over the subsequent days as necessary. These details will include what people want to say about the identification of the murdered body or bodies and about the requirements of an inquest. Here, the FLO's job is to be part of a preliminary talking-guide, before the viewing and identification of a loved one. It is at the discretion of the coroner as to who will be acceptable as next of kin. Where non-nuclear families exist, the FLO may be of great help in sorting matters out – especially as nuclear families are not the dominant familial pattern any more. Where families are split, not just by divorce but also by continent or sexuality, a different course in defining next of kin is necessary.

Please refer to suggestions for guiding children through the identification processes they apply equally to adults, in the useful reading lists about trauma, pp. 112–113.

Other services – in the immediate aftermath

It is important that agencies are in place to provide appropriate emotional and physical services to assist the individual or family in the immediate aftermath and beyond. Making sense of what has happened, as shock transforms into denial, disbelief and rage or numb sorrow, requires mitigating the worst long-term nightmares. The FLO cannot be all agencies and should not do everything where others have a legal duty. This is where social and health services have a statutory duty to coordinate community, health and social matters. If undertaken correctly, this will relieve the police of duties that belong with other statutory agencies and, in the fullness of time, aid the investigative process as well as allowing the police to maximise their skills for family liaison work and forensic detection. They do have a place as the lead agency, but are not the exclusive agency for those in need.

Returning a loved one's possessions

If you are in this situation, remember that it is always acceptable to postpone, indefinitely, the collection and return of items belonging to a loved one. Even if they are never returned, this will not be unreasonable or questioned.

An FLO will of course be sensitive to the emotional state of those bereaved and to the unavoidable fact that there will never be an easy time to broach the subject. However, an FLO will talk through every option in advance and will take a lot of time checking out with an individual or family exactly in what condition – cleaned, bloodstained or broken – they wish to have a loved one's property returned. He will ask if a family wishes these items brought to them, or for people to go to collect them themselves. Some people want the items returned stained with blood and some people want the items cleaned before getting them back. It is better for personal items to be returned, where possible, within the safety, comfort and privacy of the home. If this is not possible a favourite outdoors environment may be an appropriate alternative. Any delays in returning possessions will be explained – whether there will be a delay because some possessions are still being tested for evidence and currently cannot be returned. Some items will be retained until after a court case.

The FLO, in listening to and assisting a family, will also be accountable to the investigation and the exhibits officer for the court case as to when and how items will be returned. In this situation, again, an FLO will have chosen the most appropriate time to discuss with the bereaved when and how best to collect or receive the specific items.

Some people, before any inquest, want some locks of hair taken and want to return to see from what part of the head these locks are taken. An FLO will try to arrange to do everything possible to make these wishes heard and accommodated in the least distressing and most appropriate manner.

Potential suspects within families

Individuals and families – where a possible suspect may live with, or may be known to, them – are faced with a particularly lonely and conflicting crisis. Law agencies refer these people to a charity which was specifically established to help individuals or families where a suspect might be residing among them. (This agency declined to be included due to concerns about bias but, while regretfully not listed here, it remains an important statutory funded service and your FLO can tell you about this particular charity.)

It is statistically proven that a high proportion of violent crimes are committed by a family member or by a person known to the family. The depressingly large number of crimes resulting from domestic violence and child abuse makes 'the family' a questionable object to be cited by politicians as a bastion of normality and begs the question: what, specifically, is so good about 'normal'? Because of these statistics, an FLO, as part of his/her policing duties, must, until proven otherwise, treat as potential suspects all family members where a suspicious death, disappearance or actual murder has taken place, while simultaneously providing all pastoral and allied agency support. Sometimes, especially if a family is large and has a complicated structure or includes poor or broken relationships or conflicts, two or more FLOs may be assigned to support a family in need, ·while undertaking other core components of their investigative work – sometimes, if necessary, changing FLOs to maintain a degree of objectivity, purpose and freshness.

Victims' statements

A new idea, to allow a victim's statement to be used in court and to be accepted as legitimate evidence has finally been introduced and will become standard practice throughout Britain. This is a very long overdue improvement, which will, during court proceedings, make tangible the actual impact of the crime upon victims' lives for the benefit of judge and jury. An FLO will assist with the preparation of this statement (see section on victims' statements in section on courts, pp. 208–241). This will have other important uses – the same statement can save time, energy and stress as it can be offered to psychiatrists, social services and other agencies who will want to know what your needs are and can use the statement to help assess exactly what these are.

FLOs – help during court proceedings
FLOs have a large and positive role to play in helping to plan and explain about the experience of court and can do a lot to alleviate media intrusion and help you understand how the trial will play out and what you will be asked. They will do what they can to make this important event as safe and dignified for you as possible, but, clearly, they cannot predict the outcome of a trial. (See section on courts, pp. 208–241.)

Saying goodbye to the main FLO
All professional relationships have an ending because they came about for a specific and professional reason. The relationship that has developed with an FLO – maybe over years – will have to come to an end because it had only a professional reason for existing: to investigate a crime successfully and secondarily to see you through unforeseen horror. It is hoped that this will have included witnessing violent criminal(s) successfully being brought to justice. The FLO, who has been through extremely intense experiences with you, will also be assisting other families in the early stages of a new and equally violent trauma, needing the intense levels of intervention you previously had. By the time saying goodbye to the FLO takes place, you should have other specialist agencies actively helping you try to find some means of surviving the trauma of violent crime.

The FLO, like you, will not find parting easy because the nature of this professional contact has been one of the most intense experiences a human could imagine. FLOs are human and have their own set of images and memories from working with you, which will stay with them a long time. They will receive supervision for their needs from their superiors. It is going to be a difficult parting. But try to keep things in perspective. It's an important parting from someone who has acted as your guide towards securing some degree of justice – and a way out of hell.

It is healthy to plan with the FLO what you should do and talk about leading up to the last meeting. Maybe discuss with the FLO if it would be acceptable for you to make a modest gesture of thanks by the giving of a small gift. If the FLO says, politely, 'No thank you', this should be respected. It must be remembered he/she will have been dealing with many people going through what you went through, months or years beforehand. This does not mean the FLO does not care – you will know this is not so – he/she feels too. As professionals they have to find ways of closing off, but this does not mean their work with you was just another job. Their service, if beneficial for you and those in your family and life, is the legacy they take with them as a gift; possibly, a memory to be cherished. It is a gruelling experience both you and the FLO have come through together and you should try to find some degree of nourishment from it for you both. It is important to speak freely with your FLO about this because, when you first had contact, you had no control over anything. Now, hopefully you have more control: to be actively part of saying goodbye allows active participation for you. For many FLOs, this small gesture is acceptable.

At the point when the FLO must move on, you too must somehow move on. Perhaps you are ready to move on and want to talk about what the relationship has been like and what it all means for you – and vice versa. It may be a series of conversations about the staggering, perhaps for ever bewildering, periods of learning in your recent life and adjustments you are still making in coping with a series of memories and goodbyes. This will become another goodbye and one that offers some nourishment and hope for a life that will never be the same. Maybe you, and those around you, will see the FLO as having been a strong, human and professional signpost that offered clear and upfront facts. This will not be an easy goodbye and no one should try to make it seem easy. A part of you will be placing the murdered loved one into a level of memory that will naturally hurt. You and the FLO, together, may choose to say goodbye at a special place, away from the media gaze, or crowd. Possibly where the remains of the loved one are laid to rest, and whose death was the reason for bringing you together, is the right place … or maybe somewhere quite new and different.

Unlike the brutality that first brought you together, make this a ritual, a sort of celebration for what is now in control and what you have succeeded in achieving. This professional relationship will hopefully be an example of decency and dignity – emotionally nourishing and a marker for what is to be cherished as the best of humankind and a future, unsteady perhaps, but a future, nonetheless. Ideally, the FLO will have been a beacon of these values to you and any others affected by the violent crime.

Shortfalls and negative aspects of the FLOs' role

The dynamic progress the police are making has to be respected and applauded – albeit, as we saw, against a backdrop of low morale, inadequate resources, inconsistent support within their hierarchies and conflicting messages from central government. The failure robustly to eject sub-standard or criminal elements from within its ranks all add to the burden of skilled police officers.

The status quo presents a huge burden, physically, intellectually and emotionally, for serving FLOs because guidelines are simply not tenable in the mid- or long term for police officers in isolation. As FLOs take on more cases, their ability to function has to diminish reciprocally at some point. Total exhaustion and excessive exposure to horror must take its toll on the health of police officers.

There is a negative outcome for the police wanting to assume total supremacy over victims' needs without cooperation and intervention from other specialist services. To isolate psychiatric and social needs will be disastrous. If the people in need have not had other essential services long established, a cruel irony would exist once the FLO departs. It will create the potential for a further traumatic separation for people in need – the opposite of the objectives of FLO policy.

Current policies suggest moves toward expansionism by the Home Office to secure the domain, for better or worse, over other government departments, such as the Department of Health and the Departments of Pensions and Education. This cannot work for FLOs, or the people they serve, if the resources simply do not meet their needs. The police, generally, are facing so many reviews by government along with staff shortages that a superb service could be set up only to fail before being allowed to shine.

It is important that FLOs, and the Home Office generally, do not collude with the monolithic mono-options available to people in need by only channelling people towards Victim Support. They have an important role to play, but this cannot include, any longer, the assumption that they are the sole 'voice' of those affected by violent crime. One charity for one nation is a cause for alarm as well their monopoly in funding and media awareness for a predominant and inadequately assessed service. As part of a new era in law enforcement, the police should be encouraging the creation of diverse support groups for people affected by violent crime and groups that are not necessarily statutorily funded (see sections on advocacy groups, pp.200-201, the *victim club*, pp. 242-251, and setting up groups, pp. 338–363).

Without doubt, the energy, skills and political drive are placed within practising police officers – but should they have the sole preserve over those affected by violent crime? While sensitive to human frailty, this agency will sometimes abruptly remove itself from a situation where traumatised people have made intense human connections. This, at worst, creates a secondary and institutional level of new trauma! It can be avoided by early network conferencing without negating the fluidity of any investigation. A comprehensive network conference allows distribution of agency responsibilities that reflects any citizen's complex life needs – especially in trauma.

Future

These concerns aside, this should not exclude a reforming government and Home Office that really wishes to make effective changes for the status of victims of violence. The government 'rhetoric' could, if put into common-sense terms, make dynamic and coherent practice. Currently, it is half-done but not taken to a logical conclusion. In other words, if the police are to become the service provider for victims of violence then give them the staff, resources and laws to make this happen!

Bringing together all the laws and best practices of social and health services where a comprehensive assessment of need can be put into action would radically change, for the better, the potential for recovering from trauma and might even save government money. If this means Parliament needs to debate and amend laws to allow the police to legitimise the work it already does, and a lot of work that funded services are failing to do, why not? If people are effectively helped and placed into the right services at the right time, long-term needs and less dependence on the state can also follow. By harmonising key agencies, providing needed services promptly – potentially reducing costs in compensation. Most of all, it could place victims visibly within existing statutory law and their hardship within tangible, established laws. This will break the silence, invisibility and stigma and will both make police work more fulfilling and help those affected by violence secure for themselves a more meaningful life.

The recommendations and knowledge produced within the Allen Report have yet to be fully explored and expanded into standard practice by either the Department of Health or the Home Office. This Report was the result of a series of human tragedies involving mass loss of life and suffering, whether by natural accidents or random mass killing. The blueprints for taking expert knowledge into practice are gathering dust in government departments. Naturally, the Allen Report's recommendations will require commitment from central government to make realistic funding and resourcing a reality. It remains an important, largely forgotten source of excellent policy direction.

The work, knowledge, commitment and skills of FLOs are an example of public service at its best and this is one of the few public services providing immediate knowledge with power and compassion. It is to be respected as an example of exceptional human and professional endeavour. The police officers who take on extra training and assessment to become FLOs are, as we have seen, remarkable and highly talented individuals. The work requires a constant juggling and balancing of being humanly responsive to the unfolding trauma while simultaneously initiating a thorough, collaborative investigation to bring about the successful apprehension and charging of the criminal(s).

An alternative – new multi-agency care teams – Joint Action Combined Teams

This idea follows on from the acceptance that the police are increasingly the leading agency responding institutionally to victims of violent crime. It is worth considering the economic, social necessity and feasibility of bringing together the best of existing services in one building which would be accountable to one government department and agency – the Home Office and police: i.e. the establishment of Joint Action Combined Teams. These could be like probation services and staffed by police, FLOs, health and social workers. Combined and coordinated teams would be able to undertake existing good practice and develop new areas, relieving newly affected victims of violent crime from administrative burdens. They could allow the full vision of the work of the FLOs to become a reality, with early network conferencing setting the tone for service provision and provide full long-term care management dealing with all non-investigative matters like social care, housing, health and aspects of criminal injuries compensation work. (For further discussion, see section on the Home Office, pp. 316–322.)

When the police get it wrong – need to complain

We know corrupt, abusive police officers exist and it has taken the Home Office a long time to set out effective policies for weeding out these abusers of power. It is also taking executive police officers a long time to use disciplinary measures to reset standards of performance and accountability.

If you are having contact with the police and you are dissatisfied, it is important to try to be clear in discussing your concerns immediately with the police involved. Often, especially under extreme pressure, what we think we have explained clearly, in reality, may not have been as plainly stated as we thought. We know this from non-professional relationships. If you have taken the time to meet and be explicitly clear about what your concerns are, and no satisfactory resolution is available, then, if the issue is about an FLO, a leaflet will be offered explaining how your complaint will be investigated and what you must do. This complaint will require you to place grievances in writing with specific examples and the time taken will often be influenced by the reasons for FLO involvement, staffing levels and motivation of senior officers.

Remember to try genuinely to resolve the matter satisfactorily before embarking upon what can become an experience of stress and even trauma.

Complaining to the Police Complaints Authority (PCA)

If you cannot find satisfaction within the FLO complaints procedures, it is your right to lodge a complaint with the Police Complaints Authority. If it becomes necessary to lodge such a complaint, and the Police Complaints Authority acknowledges a need for investigation, this will be carried out by another, non-involved, police force.

This process can take years, so please see the different stages of how they will deal with your complaint. Like other public services, the police complaints process is unacceptably administrative and pressurises members of the public. At worst, in the face of genuine injustice, this implicitly creates a passive way of not encouraging legitimate complaints. Sadly, like other public service complaint processes, the Police Complaints Authority, even when it does find an officer guilty and proven to be reprehensible, shows a consistent lack of appropriate punishment or dismissal. The Home Office is reviewing these punishment issues, considering, among other measures, sanctions such as withdrawal of pension rights. To take a formal complaint to this level will inevitably require employing a solicitor or an advocate from a charity.

Confrontation with institutions can be an exceptionally draining process and if things go seriously wrong, the option of complaining should not be entered into solely on an emotional basis. It will be a lengthy experience with a low chance of success. It is recommended that you find an alternative means to find a fair and just result, which will not leave you feeling degraded, poorer and emotionally depleted. However, if the gravity of your complaint is such that you must complain, an example of how to set out a formal written complaint is provided (see section on complaining, pp. 173–187).

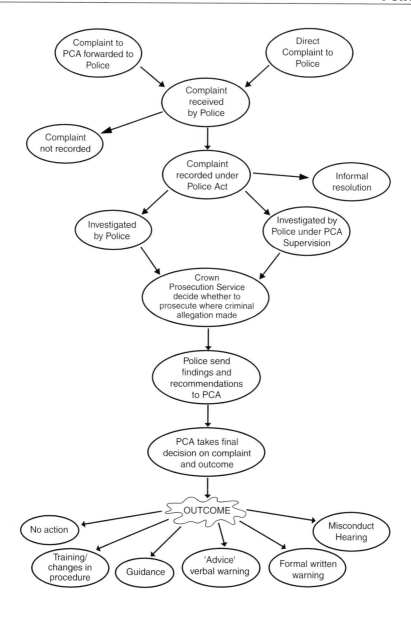

Police Complaints Authority Process

Police

Useful reading and addresses

Disasters: Planning for a Care Response – Parts 1 and 2, by the Disasters Working Party, published by The Stationery Office. Excellent response and easy to read report referred to as the Allen Report. No government has bothered to take up the many basic proposals. Excellent appendices with addresses.

The Human Elements of Disaster Management – Learning from Experience, *by the Central Advisory Facility on Organisational Health and Welfare,* published by Crown Publications. Good in parts; another document not fully developed by any government. Written for police officers.

Policing Our Communities – A Practical Guide, *by Avon and Somerset Constabulary.* An excellent short resource for understanding the diverse religious, customs and manners of our communities.

Policing and the Power of Persuasion – The Changing Role of the Association of Chief Police Officers, *by Stephen P. Savage, Sarah Charman and Stephen Cope,* published by Blackstone Press. The role of ACPO within policing and police policy-making in England, Wales and Northern Ireland, based on interviews with ACPO members, presidents and people from other relevant bodies such as Home Office, Audit Commission and the Police Federation.

Policing: An Introduction to Concepts and Practice, *by Alan Wright,* published by Willan. Aimed at police officers, but provides general information. It looks at the contemporary debate on the police and addresses what policing is. The book identifies various modes of policing practice, and discusses keeping the peace, crime investigation, management of risk and the promotion of community justice. It looks at the politics of policing in terms of the influences that are moulding it, including new public management and changes to the economic, social and technological contexts of policing.

Politics of the Police, *by Robert Reiner,* published by Oxford University Press, 3rd edn. A review of the history, functioning, sociology and governance of the British police. A very useful overview.

Family Liaison Officers, *by Richard Mason,* published by the Home Office, Police Research Group, 1998. A detective providing excellent recommendations for the selection, training and support of the Family Liaison Officers on murder enquiries.

'Family ties – the role of FLOs in relation to murder cases and areas of best practice which should be deployed', *by Peter Whent,* published in *Police Review,* 15 May 1998: 18–19. Excellent piece about the FLO: for officer and layperson.

'Softly, softly – an officer in Northumbria has developed guidelines for liaison officers working with murder victims' families', *by Margaret Nicholls,* published in *Police Review,* 16 January 1998: 28–29. A good standard for FLO work.

Alcohol, Stress, and the Police Officer – An Analysis of Drinking Behaviour and Perceived Stress across Three Divisions of the Metropolitan Police*, by William Heasman, M.A.* thesis for University of Exeter, 1995. Police work is arguably one of the most stressful occupations in modern society. A research project measured, by means of questionnaire, perceived stress levels of uniformed constables and sergeants in three Metropolitan Police areas. A warning ultimately not to confuse acute stress of work with machismo cops; pity this is not more readily available in book form.

'Psychological trauma in the police service', *by Barbara Plant*, published in *International Journal of Police Science and Management*, 2001, 3(4): 327–49. Excellent piece. Recent literature on psychological or critical-incident stress debriefing indicates it may not be as effective as originally supposed and the process in some instances might even be harmful. In light of the lack of evidence of efficacy of psychological debriefing, and the possibility that it may delay recovery and cause harm, an alternative two-stage model for post-trauma management is described to optimise protective strategies within the workplace and to ensure provision of appropriate care.

Force under Pressure – How Cops Live and Why They Die, *by Lawrence N. Blum*, published by Lantern Books. An excellent US title about police reactions to stressful duty situations, mainly those involving shootings, and the control necessary to maintain concentration and focus of attention under all circumstances, particularly emergency conditions. Discusses the need for a positive mental attitude and coping strategies.

Racism, Crime and Justice, *by Benjamin Bowling and Coretta Phillips*, published by Longman. A thorough critical analysis of racism and the criminal justice process from crime and victimisation to policing, punishment and probation. Examines criminological research and official statistics produced by the Home Office, police, courts and prisons and balances them with accounts and experiences published by minority community organisations and practitioners in the criminal justice system. Criticises New Labour's crime control policies and argues 'zero tolerance', the 'culture of control' and 'institutional racism' will intensify injustice and the criminalisation of ethnic minority communities in Britain.

Police Complaints Authority (PCA)
10 Great George Street
Westminster
London
SW1P 3AE
Telephone: 020 7273 6450
Fax: 020 7273 6401
E-Mail: info@pca.gov.uk
Website: www.pca.gov.uk

Association of Chief Police Officers (ACPO)
25 Victoria Street
Westminster
London
SW1H 0EX
Telephone: 020 7227 3434
Fax: 020 7227 3400
E-Mail: info@acpo.co.uk
Website: www.acpo.co.uk

A year ago, a number of people in my life died unexpectedly,
from unpredictable causes. They were young.
Their deaths gave me 'pause'.
These confrontations with death and dying were bold reminders,
compelling me to look at the direction of my life,
and honestly acknowledge spaces of unfulfilment ...

Many times in the past months
I have wished that just the sheer strength of knowing
that 'life is not promised'
- that death, is always happening – would make it clear.
How, I or we, must act and what, I or we – must do.

Indeed, such knowledge may
simply motivate and intensify our search for understanding,
for right livelihood,
yet, we must still struggle for answers, face the unknown,
grope towards the new future without any clear guidance or plan.
This is difficult ...

Last night I told mama ... I was afraid.
'Life is not promised'.
When I need that special push to move forward
I nurture myself with these words.

Bell Hooks: From *A Woman's Mourning Song*

Death, in all its guises, is the ultimate reminder of our fragile hold on mortality. It can be a deeply painful process, even if the person died in the 'best of circumstances'; quietly, comfortably and without pain or fear. Experts say such a bereavement can take an average two to three years' for adjustment.

To lose a loved one through violence is another matter; a wholly different type of intense loss. Life can never be the same for some people; life can never feel as safe or as unquestioned again. There is no forewarning, no last months of caring and exchanging tender memories, of resolving unfinished arguments. There is no control.

There are no easy remedies to address adequately the anguish and numbness felt by young or old alike who are left behind. In the event of violent death through crime, it is better to say what should not be avoided and many of these things are common sense – yet difficult to get right because we are vulnerable and human.

Loss and anguish

Loss and anguish can devastate lives. Parents of children who have been murdered, raped (or abducted: and having to cope with the agonising reality that their child may never be found) as well as primary victims of violent crimes may never fully recover. In death's wake, anguish leaves a profound mark on all it touches. Children and young people may be worst affected, not having the means to cope with their loss. Victims' anguish and grief will be physical as much as mental, which is another aspect of violent crime.

Such victims' grief is nothing like the grief experienced from a non-violent, foreseen loss (e.g. of an elderly relative after long illness). Following a violent crime, victims should be aware of how the symptoms of post-traumatic stress disorder (PTSD) manifest themselves; it may be a relief to learn this is common – you are not going crazy. Everything in the order of your life has been violently turned inside out. Parents of children who have been murdered tell us the loss defies the natural order of the universe. In other words, such anguish and grief could never have been imagined because it 'should' always be that your children, as adults who, will, bury you. Take time, take a lot of time, to grieve deep and long as it is going to take a long time to feel able to deal with even mundane matters of living. It is, and will continue to be, a living hell that defies description. Take care, eat a little and often and after some time practise going through the motions of some small routines you once could do – but slowly.

The experiences of remarkable people who have confronted violent horror and survived physical and mental tragedy against huge odds, to rebuild their lives are sources of inspiration for us all. Some have written of their experiences, providing us with painful, humbling and powerful records from which to learn. In time, it may prove helpful to read how other people found their own way out of the rawness of trauma and loss. There is no easy formula, and we are all different, but these tips may be a source of comfort.

The trauma of surviving violent crime requires energy and strength. Grief peels off the layers of our emotions, like an onion's many fine layers and textures, to test our core. The initial numbness gives way to sickening shock, which gives way to many emotions (see trauma symptoms, pp. 104-113). And your tears will burn. Tears for yourself and tears for who and what has been violently lost.

Early things to do
• Use professional services with police-checked individuals to get the help you need. You will need and deserve a great deal over the days that follow.

- Create a compassionate wall of friends, professionals and family to face the barrage of bureaucratic intrusions and resist the flood of door-knocking and calls.
- Avoid rushing to the media – your loss is primarily your loss and that of those about you.
- Every individual's experience of how violent death has affected him or her will be unique; don't try to fit in or follow precedents.
- Avoid destructive and voyeuristic onlookers. Tragedy can attract a retinue of strangers and 'friends' you never knew or wanted.
- Take great and exquisite care of yourself. Be tender to yourself.
- Allow time for your shock to turn into profound grief; do not feel shame about intense expressions of grief. Try to see these raw and deep emotions as natural reflections of anger, love, bewilderment and longing for your loss.
- Try not to attack one another; find ways to say when you can hear others' grief and when you cannot.
- Sudden and violent death robs victims of control, so make the funeral (or other service, if there's no burial) a ritual that you plan and control. Make the ceremony have purpose.
- Try not to turn your dead loved one into someone he or she was not; grieve for all aspects of his or her nature.
- If schoolfriends, neighbours or work colleagues cross the road to avoid you or talk about everything except your loss, this is their ignorance and fear. Do not feel this to be your problem. Do not carry others' ignorance when you carry too much already.
- If your loved one's body cannot be found, please see the advice given in the section on funerals and services (pp. 63-65). In some cases, the injuries are seen by authorities as too horrific to view. The decision of whether or not to view is a tough one which authorities will discuss with you, but what you need to think about is this: how you wish to remember your loved one and what worse effect viewing may have on you. Maybe, enraging and heartbreaking as it is, it is better not to view the remains of the person. Photographs will be taken and this situation can be discussed with an FLO; maybe, in the months to come, you will feel able to view these. Certainly, it is something to feel clear about before any trial, when images of the person may be used in court. Whether to look at such images then is another tough decision to make. Take time, take quality guidance and take heed of what you know you can cope with.
- The person who has now been violently taken was part you, so bring that person to you by not closing off your feelings for him or her. Bring out photographs and, when you can, go to the person's home – or bedroom if they lived with you.

- Bring children and young people into discussions about what has happened, but be sensitive and compassionate; temper the details as appropriate. Help the young make sense of what has happened – as you need to do.
- Never fall into the trap of self-recrimination (*'if only …' or 'maybe …'*).

Things to avoid
- Never bottle up your emotions. If necessary, take time away from work or out of your routine.
- If the entire family is affected, there may be conflict: some will be crying, while others are angry or numb – all of which may conflict with your own particular state or need. Get good help now!
- Do not pretend you can get through this life experience in a rush or without expert help.
- Try not to rush people about you into burying this loss, and let individuals make sense in their own way and time.
- Avoid the temptation of revenge – violent or otherwise. No good can come from it; stay on the right side of the law, and away from the criminal and crime.
- Avoid seeking to bury your grief in alcohol or unlawful drugs.
- Avoid dealing with the media at the height of your loss, or during the criminal investigation. The loss and injury are yours, not public property. (See section on the media, pp. 145-159.)
- Do not rush to throw away the dead loved one's possessions. There will come a time, and it may take years after the incident, to think about opening cupboards and selecting special possessions to keep.
- Avoid tactless or stupid people – always!
- Never lie to children or deny their needs.

The body of your loved one
If it is possible, agencies will find the means to let you see the body of your loved one. There are times when this is not possible: clearly, this is the case when there is no body, but also where the victim has been so terribly violated, viewing may be deemed to be too much – too distressing – to witness. This may prove an extremely difficult decision to make. If the latter is the case, it is important that you are involved in the decision, because it affects how you will make sense of the death. It may be that some form of viewing can be arranged, with careful preplanning with agencies. Remember to specify in what clothes you would prefer your loved one's body to be dressed. (See section on viewing a body pp. 58-62)

©Jacob Epstein: *Night*. Reproduced with the generous permission of the London Transport Museum. Not for recopying without prior written consent of the owners

Seeing a dead body – for any age

These suggestions are for workers, adults and young people. Whether to see a dead body will always be a highly difficult decision to make. It requires discussions with experts, friends and family because it is a profound experience that will not be forgotten. It may be necessary to show photographs and have a waiting period leading up to visiting the body. It may simply be that some people do not wish to view the body. Everyone must talk about these matters before proceeding.

Viewing the body

Evoke a picture in the mind of the person to whom you are talking of where the body is laid, what it looks like, by using familiar phrases: 'He looks like he does when he's sleeping in front of the TV'. Describe the building, the smells and colours, the walk to where the body is going to be seen and what the person's body is clothed in. You must be prepared to become an intimate guide of the streets, the building, the walk and the atmosphere. If you are too consumed to do this, then be honest, as the person can learn to deal with grief but not confusing messages. Try to think of what you need as the guide in this situation. What are the young people saying, or not saying? What will they need?

Will a chair be needed to make sure the young person can view the body? Will you need a chair? Will the young person want to touch the body? What part of the body is it best to touch? Arrange for a favourite piece of music to be played and take a tape-recorder – play a favourite of the deceased and/or a piece chosen by the young person. Make the atmosphere as unique and special as possible for everyone affected. At each stage, ask people how they are – they will tell you. This process is hugely significant for everyone. The viewing will be witnessed by professionals, but if it is clear everyone is coping and feeling secure enough, the professionals will leave you alone until you are ready to leave. The professionals are just that: skilled and sensitive. Rarely is it necessary to request that they withdraw from the viewing of a body. You will be the guide. Before each phase, building or room is entered, talk through what is about to be seen. Pause if and when other people pause. Your tools are talk, repetition and reality. You will be the guide.

Preparation through repetition
Repetition. Verbally repeat many, many times the whole process: the journey to the place of rest; everything that the young people need to know to prepare themselves. It will still have elements of risk, but preparation and repetition can reduce any disturbing fantasies the people may be carrying, especially young imaginations. Make time to explain in advance everything they will see; that the viewing is only taking place if they wish it to; that they can stop the process at any point without any pressure. When a person begins to tell you what the process will entail, and, more importantly, what they wish to happen, it is an indication that a sufficient degree of understanding is in place to proceed.

Think about what people may like to wear, as this is a special occasion; if they are old enough, they will grasp some of the significance of the visit. The burden on the responsible adults can be huge: it may require repeating the visits – in addition to the funeral itself. But the young must be allowed to become involved, which, in turn, can inspire and support the adults.

It is essential to explain to people that, should they wish to touch the body, it will be very cold. This is always shocking. This shocking fact can, with time, assist people in accepting that the 'sleeping loved-one' is more than asleep. Professionals are excellent in taking steps to reduce the impact of shock. It is also essential young people are comfortably raised to the level where the body is placed and can interact emotionally – so they are not viewing the trolley wheels.

Before leaving home, discuss with the person what it is they think they may want to say or leave behind with the dead person. To repeat: will they wish to take something of their own, e.g. a toy, a seashell from a holiday, a record, a drawing, a book or something that belonged to the deceased?

Many people fret that the body is lonely in the place of rest; so, anything the people can do to make them feel they are reducing the 'loneliness' must be liberated and praised. Young people will become, in the months and years ahead, fine, dignified adults who survived impossible loss with bravery and innocence. It is beholden on those responsible adults to make this possible.

You will be the guide. What will you need to deal with this? And, if you are family, are you clear what you will need to make the journey possible? What is it going to be like, making the journey to view the body? If you have already visited the deceased, explain openly to the young person what you saw and what you felt and feel now. To repeat: it will prepare and empower young people to cope with and express vulnerable, raw emotion without added self-consciousness.

Preparing to see or touch

Try not to be static or rigid, unless wanting to be really still, and this must be when the person is ready to focus his or her gaze and touch. We can tend to rush others because 'we' cannot cope with our own feelings.

It is important to walk around the body and if you are with a young person talking through what you see, think and hope is happening to the deceased. Prompt the person to say what they think in return and do not be frightened of silence, nor put off by outbursts or screaming. It may be that the adult/child is making sense of something with which adults can barely grapple; not the time to whisk the person away, whether screaming or not. Take confidence in people, including the young, to express whatever the emotion might be, including silence or numbness. Lest it be forgotten, you, as an adult, may also be breaking down; it may be that the young person tries to comfort you – don't reject this gesture. Comfort one another! If the screaming becomes too much, which is unlikely if all the careful preparation has been done, then steadily withdraw whether with an adult or younger person.

Touching the body – helping the young

These are reminders for both adults and younger people. Repetition of words and movements assist people in 'holding' reality, memory, dignity and control. Before a person does anything around the dead body, you must try to do the gesture yourself. As a guide, it signifies it is safe, especially when the moment comes to touch the dead body.

By physically holding someone, if you are with a young person, or by assisting the physical leaning, you hold the bridge for empowering an adult or child's sense of integrity and channel for love and loss for the one who is dead. Always, always, keep a warm physical contact and connection with young people.

It is important for an adult to explain what they are feeling and seeing – to act as guide and reassurer. It helps people feel a little better able to cope. For example, an adult should touch a body before the young person to prove it is safe, and say what they feel. For example, an adult may say, 'Gosh! Daddy feels so cold – this means he's dead doesn't it?!' ' Jack is colder than when he went shopping in the snow – so this is what a body is like when it is dead.' 'It is scarier than I thought it might be' – or maybe say 'it's not as scary as I thought it might be.'

If you suggest taking a lock of hair, this will be done by a member of staff and it will help the child (if small) to be carried and to help ask for a lock, carry the scissors, and point to where to take the hair from and how much.

Saying goodbye

If kissing goodbye, it may be best done by repetition of the person copying you as the adult–guide; you go first, allowing the child to follow suit if he or she wishes to do so. In this situation, it may be more appropriate to 'blow a kiss', or hold your hand to your lips and press them on the cheek, shoulder or hand of the deceased. It will avoid some of the shock's impact of the cold flesh on the adult or child's lips. If with a small child, ask if he or she is also going to 'blow a magic and special goodbye kiss?' And: 'Where do you think this special kiss is going?' The older the person, the more they can say what they need to do. Guide!

Take some time to repeat walking around the body. These are images of permanent significance and memories. Ask 'Shall we go now?'. If the child says 'no', then point out 'you can stay a little while longer, but, though it will hurt, you will have to leave'. Prompt the child: 'We must think about the things to do for when we have to have the funeral to say goodbye'; 'We have to go home and tell grandma how mummy looks – how will you describe her?'

Returning home

When the parting is over – resist flying out, resist flying to McDonald's, resist flying back home and resist being busy. Resist your fear, and listen. Listen to what the person's body language or words are saying to you – what do they need right now? Listen to what is going on within you.

Listen to what is going on inside you. Go to a room away from, but near to, from the deceased's temporary resting place, as someone may wish to return to the deceased briefly. This is an inconceivable experience – allow for the unpredictable.

When returning home, make time to stop and walk. It does not matter if there is a blizzard! Wrap up warm, and walk in a park or open place and verbally repeat the experience. Remember the breathing exercises and remember the importance of our animal instinct to burn up adrenalin. The person will also benefit; the detour will provide fresh air and a 'pause' about what has now happened. Words and touch are your tools for helping make sense.

Do not pretend the parting was not real, did not happen or is unimportant 'to spare the little one's feelings'. Take some time to walk and be quiet, talking when needed. This will give an indication of how you and the person are coping.

Upon returning home, encourage the person to dominate the discussion: tell everyone where you have been; what happened; what it meant. Try to resist interrupting with minor interpretations unless the person is deeply faltering. In this case, with a young person, gently repeat what happened and say 'And then what did you do – what happened then?'. It signifies the child is naturally struggling to hold on to the intensity and reality of the situation. In itself this does not denote the visit was a mistake; it signifies it is hard to cope with at present. This is the way it is.

Keep the evening as empty of agency intrusion as possible beyond key service providers and family and friends. If staying in the family home, it is better to sleep near a young person and stay in his or her room. Make his or her sanctuary as safe and comfortable as possible.

Preparing for the funeral

After the facts of your loved one's death have been established and it is possible to have the body released by the authorities, there is a crucial ritual to plan. This is the funeral and requires strength, when you have none, and treading the path of your deepest emotions to face the inconceivable.

For some, attending the funeral will be the first time they have been outside in days, so, first, once the funeral details have been arranged, it is important to get outside prior to the day of the funeral. It does not have to be for long; try, if you have a garden or access to a park or the countryside, to walk a little in these natural places. To feel the earth beneath you, at these times, is good. Practise your breathing – deeply and slowly. It may be that you find you are actually physically sick – this is natural, but will pass. Also, difficult as it may be, do try to eat – little and often (e.g. light soup and bread) – and drink a lot of liquid. These will help your body to deal with the upheaval of the trauma. Choose what you will wear: garments that reflect your dignity in grief and give you physical comfort when your body may be feverish, cold or perspiring wildly.

What type of service?

This will depend on, among other things, what you can afford and your cultural and religious leanings. Whatever your leanings and heritage, take guidance from those you trust, whether they are family, friends or religious leaders and retain control of the specific detail of what will take place. If you are from a large family or circle of friends, there may be arguments about the details of the ritual of saying goodbye because the ceremony is so important. Somehow, all must be listened to and especially those most intimately connected with the dead person. The life and loss of your loved one must be reflected in the ritual of goodbye and so, within any standard service rituals, it is important to balance, on the one hand, specific music, words on the deceased's life, achievements and its violent end; and, on the other, words that express harmony and peace for the deceased and those left behind. Make the service a mirror for all aspects of your loved one, whose imperfection will diminish neither your great loss nor your longing and love.

Funerals are very expensive and many will find the financial burden another source of stress. In these circumstances, the police and social services should be asked to assist you in resolving this matter; it's part of their role. It is worth allocating a person, not too intensely involved in the loss, to take a 'shopping list' of funeral directors and discuss arrangements with authorities while you remain focused on your unravelling grief. It is your responsibility to deal with personal practicalities and your health. Gradually, you must fumble towards finding strength, which will not always be there, to get through the following days. In the months that follow, people will often find that thoughtful content of the service, words and music and not lavish spectacle bring meaning and some comfort. Some find filming the service can be helpful.

The funeral

Many people say it is only during the funeral that they can start to grieve and that the intensity of their grief is frightening. British society generally frowns upon displays of emotions, but the funeral experience is exceptional; it can be cathartic or therapeutic. Now is the time to unburden yourself of 'what is proper' without self-consciousness and let what is within and around you flow – outwards.

Many people experience intense bodily reactions, such as intense cold or heat or nausea. This is natural and nothing of which to be ashamed, but do be aware of it.

Make this ritual yours; by which to remember your loved one and to find ways to make sure others are listening to what you want to see happen. Where there is the added anguish of no physical body, the ritual of a funeral remains as important. It may be the cremation of some possessions (not ones you wish to keep), where the ashes are scattered, to provide meaning, a sense of control and an opportunity to place these remains somewhere special – to be cherished.

Make the deep anguish a ritual for celebrating a life violently taken. Find the words you wish spoken aloud at the service and choose, with care, the person you would like to speak them. The music should also be selected with care. Some people ask for a person, not directly affected by events, to film the service because people want to keep as much as they can and they find, over the months, it is something they can watch alone or with others to help them come to terms with their loss.

Try to have a service with power, special words, music and contemplative silence. Give the ritual real meaning.

Who will attend?

The ritual of saying goodbye, then, should reflect the loved one's life and the lives of those who attend the service. If someone known to or within the family committed the violent death, this involves the added loss of trust, safety and unity in the family needs expression in a positive, non-destructive manner. Make a list of those who may attend and be clear whether you expect them to keep the details private and how you wish them to dress – some people do not want formal attire. This list can be handed to those not directly involved in the loss and they can formulate confirmations and plan the type of post-service gathering you want – if you want one at all. The police should be asked to negotiate with the media, if your loss has attracted media attention, about keeping a long distance away from the home and service. (See section on Code of Practice in media section, p. 145-159.)

Soon after the funeral

People often say they recall the funeral as a blur or a film they were involved in and, after the ritual of goodbye and returning to a reception, they feel a state of complete exhaustion. This is natural.

If a reception does take place, it can help to play the music used in the service, among other music. Although alcohol, in moderation, when used to toast and celebrate the lost life, can be good, in excessive amounts it might be counter-productive.

Do not feel you have to 'entertain' mourners; they have come to make sense and show respect. If you feel exhausted, go to a room and grieve or sleep. If you need someone to hold you, break the silence and say so.

If possible, for about one month, try to stay about your home and, after a couple of weeks, try to reclaim a little of the routine you had before your trauma. Do not take on too much too soon. After about one month, try to have arranged for you a break away from your home and go somewhere safe and pleasant as this allows for a 'pause' in events. When you return, the pause will have created a marker between unfolding events.

If your home has been the scene of a violent crime, sometime within the first month try to return with an expert worker and someone close to help you face the need to say goodbye and make plans for moving. Many people find they have no wish to return to what was once their home, and equally, many feel the need to return to the place of horror in order to move on, as it were. Nevertheless, there is work to be done in collecting mementos, old photographs and taking photographs of the home as it is now. In these situations, workers should have already made plans, with your active involvement, to find another place to be a safe home for you and your family.

During the weeks and months after a funeral, many people find that their friends have had to return to their homes and lives – maybe the police have completed their work too. Whereas, in the early unravelling trauma, you were inundated with people – family, friends, professionals and strangers – you may now find, as the shock gives way to a deep depression, there is no one or not enough people about you. It is at this point that services should have already arranged various types of assistance for you in accordance with your needs. If it is not in place, break the silence and say what you need.

There will be days of intimidating silent emptiness, exhaustion, weeping, sleeplessness, nightmares, bewilderment and rage. This is due to the effects of violence in your life and in order to survive violent crime you must walk the tough road of grief before any sense of acceptance can evolve. This becomes the foundation of a future – and 'future', in the early months, is a meaningless word. It takes a lot of time and courage.

Getting through grief

It is good to return to a place to remember the dead loved one, not mythologising him or her, but to talk and eat and hold and involve the children in sharing and eating food and to toast the memory of the dead loved one. Repetition, respect, routine and reality. Help the children by staying in reality and praising their strength and avoid making them feel 'now it's all over'; remind them how it hurts, it's not comfortable for anyone, articulate the implicit and empower the children.

About one year after a death, if the trial has convicted a killer, it can be useful to have a memorial service with the planting of a tree in a secret place or when scattering of ashes can take place. Children will be more able to say what they want and this will provide a strong marker about the young people's well-being and adjustment. A secret burial place is very important if privacy has been lost due to media attention or violation of a dead person's resting place.

Beyond violent death's damage

The love, confusion and longing will remain for ever yours and alive. In the early months these will show themselves in profound numbness, sobbing and rage and this is as it should be. In time, and with effective help, the anguish may turn towards a bearable mourning, which, in further time becomes a condition of loss that one learns to live with – and around. Our ways for surviving are unique.

In these violent circumstances, it may take years before a sense of coping really emerges. So much depends on the manner of violent death, the quality and timing of help provided, the type of person you are and the social and economic life you have. In time, there will be days when you no longer feel consumed with grief, anger or shame. Trauma of violent death has to run its own course. This is as it should be. The person, whom you loved and who now has gone, would wish you to know joy and ordinariness in living again.

It may have taken years to reach a stage where you do not perpetually think and talk about your dead loved one, or mourn deeply. It may be now that clearing out possessions becomes bearable and desirable – without guilt and with a different type of crying. Your home may start to change from being a shrine, with hundreds of your loved one's images, to a home again by selecting just a few items, e.g., maybe two in each room of your home. This a good time to think about finding a secret and sacred place, known only to you and a select group of special people, to make a memorial to your loved one. Take time to find a place that can be visited for generations, like a moorland setting, or by the sea, or by planting a tree in a park. These rituals are the rituals of having made sense of the impossible and holding on to a sense of control. These are common types of ritual where many people have suffered collective loss, such as the Lockerbie bombing or the Zeebrugge disaster, and, over the years, they offer a real sense of control and dignity.

Difficulties can arise for people if they plant the ashes of a loved one in the grounds of their home then later wish to move house: the thought of leaving the remains of the person behind might be upsetting. It is worth choosing a place that is safe, secret, can be travelled to and where you and others can meet to mark anniversaries.

In your own time, in the distant future, you may find a time and way to live with the intense loss and find new opportunities for a life with safety and joy, embracing them without fear or guilt. The anguish, with time and help, has become bearable and manageable and you have defeated the violator in not claiming you. You deserve this and those you have lost would wish you to progress as best you can!

Useful reading

Healing, Grief and Reclaiming Life after any Loss, by *James van Praagh,* published by Piatkus. Some very helpful and effective guidance about how best to cope.

For young people

> The bird flew away and perched on the roof of a goldsmith's house and
> began to sing,
> It was my mother who murdered me;
> It was my father who ate me;
> It was my sister Marjory
> Who all my bones in pieces found;
> Them in a handkerchief she bound,
> And laid them under the juniper tree.
> Oh what a beautiful bird am I!

The Brothers Grimm: *The Juniper Tree*

In relation to children and young people, ensure that they are involved in every part of the process, choosing flowers, songs, recorded songs, whether people stand close in a circle or sit in pews or other formal religious seating arrangements. Ensure children are at eye level and named and have any drawings, words or choices named when used. As a final gesture, with an elder brother or sister or adult, the child might place a small item (drawing, toy or something that belonged to the deceased) on the coffin.

A consistently depressing aspect of preparing this handbook was the reluctance that certain specialist child agencies showed towards becoming associated with it. One bereavement charity for children feared inclusion might spoil its image! Another child bereavement group stated it was 'too busy' (it had over six months) to provide information about its work. It is as though they are somewhat precious about selecting which grieving child is 'worth' helping or which project is 'worth' being associated. What a sad set of reasons and how these mirror the real value they place upon children and young people's needs. What a struggle it is for children to be allowed to know where they can say they wish to get help and be heard. What a stark reminder of how services choose to make young people feel.

The greatest insult to any young person (or adult) is to be spoken at, or about, as if he or she were not there; that such a young person is irrelevant, with no feelings. One of the early issues in dealing with children affected by violent death and injury is to make sure that they are included as much as possible from the outset.

Loss – for a young person

Within a family, and with the proper help, young people should not be censored or silenced and make to feel 'bad' or 'naughty' for upsetting mummy, daddy or granda. If, in responding honestly, you openly grieve, you are sharing the grief of your child and will bring intimacy into the rawness of your home. This can be harder for adults than it is for young people to handle. By staying true to your child you help your child share the reality and horror and make the tiny and solid steps towards a path away from hell.

If our children and young adults are to make sense of horror in their lives, heal and progress, then they require access to unbiased and good-quality services. Children are often overlooked and their needs require equal resources to adjust if they are to grow into emotionally healthy adults with a sense of their place in the world. Unlike adults, they have less power to make decisions about events and have greater dependence upon adults. So, if a significant adult has been killed violently or affected by violence, a young person's burden is huge. Equally, if his or her brother or sister has been killed, a young person has a special set of needs as they grieve too. It is hard for them to feel they can be themselves when grieving parents are naturally mourning injury or loss of another child; those left behind can find it hard to know how to still feel wanted by their grieving parents. Sometimes, especially if good help is not quickly put in place, the young start to feel left behind. Agencies must be vigilant, remaining sensitive to all family members' needs. Young people grieve in many ways; grief can manifest itself in intense sobbing, through to becoming withdrawn. Yet with good help, they can learn to express and deal with their grief, rebuilding their young lives.

Young people deserve and require constant reassurance, especially during the early months, that, yes, a terrible event has occurred, but everything possible is being done to make them physically safe and emotionally comfortable. Counter each of their fears by demonstrating how their environment is safe from harm, whether that be physical or emotional. This can sometimes be achieved by simple and practical means: a child drawing comfort from a magic drawing or toy; a young adult, from changed security locks.

Some issues young people need to know
Young people need to be spoken to in a way that helps them understand how intense fear, grieving and changes in how others treat them and, changes in their sleep patterns are all part of natural shock and trying to make sense of violent loss.

This can manifest itself in all manner of intense reactions: giggling uncontrollably; silence; staring into space for extended long periods; extreme and extended sobbing; screaming; and breaking items through to denial. (See the symptoms identified by Professor Horowitz in the chapter on PSTD, pp. 104–113; these apply equally to children and young people.)

For small children especially, using toys and use of play is a hugely useful means of helping them make sense where words fail.

Young people where possible need to be involved in drawing up plans from leaving a home of profound violence to preparation of funeral services to re-entering a family home; especially if it has been a scene of violence. Young people may feel they do not wish to live in the same home or area and this may be at odds with those feelings of parents who feel moving away is too painful for them.

Appropriate adults should explain gently and frankly to children about the intense effects of distress that may be wreaking havoc within their systems. This will assist children to maintain a sense of reality and reduce fears. For small and young people, distress may show itself in: bedwetting or incontinence; extreme night terrors; dramatic mood swings; extreme dietary attitudes; complete disorientation of time–location in their environment; through to denial or refusal to accept the tragedy.

It is also important for adults to remember that in cases where a victim is to return home (visibly physically or mentally damaged – through amputation, for example) this can present young people with similar needs and fears, exacerbated by confusion at the new image.

Like adults, a symptom which young people commonly present – which can be painful for adults and youths alike – is the need to repeat in detail everything about the tragedy. It is part of trying to make sense of it all, but must be handled properly. If not, adults can feel oppressed, while the young, being silenced, may internalise this outlet and provoke further complex, aggravated feelings of guilt and shame and complex behaviour.

Children, given the opportunity, can be a source of support to the adults around them. Offered the respect of which they are worthy, they can almost certainly help to share the grief and healing. Adults must refrain from blocking children's expressiveness. On this, expert agencies' guidance early on is crucial; accept nothing less than the best. It is incumbent on the statutory agencies to see that both child and adult are accommodated in the best possible way, and always at the right time, too. The support must be catered to the particular needs of the family members – overlooking the young or vulnerable can have dire consequences.

Young people and the media

What the public is interested in isn't the same as public interest, as Lord Denning famously quipped. We have witnessed the offensive spectacle of the media circus orbiting around children at the centre of a tragedy; this is unacceptable – the welfare and interests of the child transcends public interest. Your child's horror and family-related pain are primarily yours and must not be allowed to be annexed by the media. Adults and agencies must protect the young from such harmful influences.

Some elements of the media will regard a child's plight as 'good copy', usurping other news. The glare of such publicity can be profoundly destructive for everyone and may even give rise to permanent problems for young people – or, indeed, for their parents. It will undermine any therapeutic progress that might have been established in the safe haven of anonymity.

Resist the pressure or temptation to subject your children to abuse through the media; equally, be vigilant against allowing this to happen inadvertently. Always consult with the police and solicitors prior to any form of contact with the media.

Events convinced me that we had no choice but to go somewhere where people didn't know us. Children are very good at seeing how adults operate and then working out a way to manipulate them. Constant sympathy directed at a child growing up seemed like the recipe for all sorts of problems later on. He had to grow up where people would like or dislike him on his own merits, not because of what happened to him once when he was small. He shouldn't learn to live on sympathy. And neither should I.

André Hanscombe: *The Legacy of Rachel Nickell – The Last Thursday in July*

Similarly, never allow your children to be photographed, as this can be another avenue through which the media can victimise young people. (See section on dealing with the media and the Codes of Practice, p. 145-159.)

Summary
- Expression of grief is essential.
- Young people must be involved as far as possible with plans about dead loved ones.
- Never lie to young people.
- Protect them from ignorance around them at school or elsewhere.
- Be prepared for intense and sometimes extreme reactions (from violence, hysteria and denial, to an ability to offer support to adults – children can be resourceful and resilient).

Whether to see the body of your loved one – or not

Many adults will say that seeing the body will upset you. This is an important thing to think about, because viewing the dead body of a person that you love is important; the memory will remain for a long time. If the body is terribly damaged, it may be better not to go to see it as it may be too distressing. Talk to those around you to get a sense of what they feel will be best for you. Adults may have reservations: will you be able to cope? Will it be too much? But most young people say that, if they can choose when, where and how long to visit the dead loved one, they find it helps them. For some, this helps; but, for others this will not be so – you must never agree to view the deceased either to please others or if you are unsure. It's all right to say 'no, thank you'. And, remember, the person who is now dead would not want you to be hurting any more than you already are.

Adults will worry and start talking about you – and maybe recently you've heard them talking about whether you can see the body or not. They mean well; they are worried, though, that it may be too upsetting – for you and for them. Maybe you have recently said something like: 'I want to see mummy's body' (or daddy's; your brother's, etc.) and an adult replied 'But, it will upset you!' Children are very strong and braver than some adults realise: so, if you *really* want to see the body, ask questions about the body (Where is it? What does it look like?) Also, ask specifically why adults think it will be too scary or painful for you to see. Take time to work out what you need or want – it will not be easy. When you are young, you may have trouble finding your way, working through things or even being listened to by adults.

Take time, seek information and feel good about your decision.

What happens to a dead body

The important thing to remember if choosing to see the dead body of the person you knew and loved is that the body is *dead*. This means it is very cold because the heart and brain that keeps us alive have stopped. A dead person cannot hear you or anyone, or feel anything – anything at all – because he or she is dead.

Within a few hours of death, the body cools down and gets cold. The body gets even colder if kept in a cool place (e.g. at a mortuary) while tests are done on the body to look for answers to questions about how the person died (e.g. clues as to how a murdered person was killed and by whom). Although you will go on loving the person, that person is no longer there; the body is like any empty house, a shell – your loved one has moved on, away.

Preparing to visit someone's body

If you decide to see the body, then bear the following in mind:
Before you leave your home to visit the body, you must ask lots and lots of questions about what the body looks like. Where is it? Why is it where it is? Ask questions about who else will be there. Where and what is the building? How to get there?

When you arrive

Sometimes a dead body is a placed behind a glass window called a viewing area; that's how the chapel of rest and mortuary are designed. If you are very sure you want to see the body then, before you arrive, someone should arrange a special room – this is up to the adults to sort out and not something for you to worry you.

Remember, at any time if you cannot handle the situation, it is simply too much, too painful, too awful then say so – and leave. This is fine: it is what you want and need; it's good to say what you want and need. You thought you wanted to see the dead body, but have changed your mind – that's your choice, after all.

Remember, you can practise going in and out of the room as many times as you want – but if you find you keep trying and it's too difficult, then probably, deep down, it's not for you. In this situation, try another day, or leave a special drawing or toy or flower and ask an adult to place it where you ask (by the hand or heart – again, this will be up to you). You can walk away, knowing this is really big and hard and you have done your very best.

Seeing the body

When people first see the body lying so still, they will react in different ways: they may be moved to tears, or sob deeply, scream, a few faint and some feel that they are sick, that they will wet themselves. These reactions are common to all of us. After all, this is the last visit – a final goodbye.

Make sure someone is by your side to give massive cuddles all the time. All the time, try to hold or be held by someone warm and kind.

Walk about the sides of the body and let any tears or noises come out and if you feel sick or want to use the toilet, say so and come back if you want to do so. Remember to ask any questions about the things you are seeing as you walk around the table where the body of the person is lying. Dead bodies are, as we said, very still, feel nothing and the skin will look shiny.

It's fine to talk to the dead body of your loved one. Yes, he or she is dead, but talking will help you to make sense of the loss; you'll feel better, safer. Maybe you might want to say sorry for being naughty when you last saw him or her alive (for not washing - up your breakfast things before school). On the other hand, you might want to say thank you for being a good mum or brother. Or you might feel angry and want to ask why he or she has gone away: what will happen now? You might want to say 'I love you'. You'll be able to think of your own messages, too.

Touching a dead body

Many adults find this scary; bodies should be warm, but they know that dead bodies are cold and stiff. But, remember, if you choose to touch the body, it will be very cold to touch – like touching an ice-cube. And, of course, no one will make you do what you don't want to do – it's up to you.

When it is time to say goodbye

It is going to be really painful when it's time to go away. Goodbyes are never easy, and will be painful if you care about someone. Remember the film *ET* when the little boy and ET say goodbye? What does ET say when touching and saying goodbye? Do you remember how sad the little boy is? ET touches the little boy and says *'Ouch!'*, because it really is painful inside your belly.

You might find you want to rush out or you might find it too hard to let out the *'ouch'* inside you. This is normal. Stay a little longer to say all the things you need to say. Make sure you have put all the things (e.g. toys, music or letters) where you want them placed by the person's body. At the same time, you might want a momento of your own: ask whether a lock of hair can be cut for you to keep somewhere special. Maybe a photo of you left with the dead person, or one taken of the dead person for you would be something you'd like. Such ideas can help you cope with the painful time ahead.

Afterwards...

After visiting the dead person, you and the others should visit a nearby park, the woods or the sea to walk and take fresh air, clear your head. Don't feel under pressure to talk or pretend that you want to do so (unless, of course, you want to talk). After a big goodbye visit like this, everyone will be upset and exhausted, so not pretending is very, very important. You may want to take some sandwiches, flasks of hot soup or tea, etc., for afterwards. The exhaustion, like the stress, hurting and anger, are all natural.

Take care of what is going on deep inside you; it's natural to find your sleep routine goes from not sleeping to not wanting to wake up, and dreaming of the person. It takes a lot of time for everything to begin to make sense. But, it will and promising yourself not to keep important feelings bottled up inside is an important part of the tricks for learning to win and not get stuck. It is the same for adults - it is really tough.

Ideas for coping

Regardless of age, it's a good thing to ask people to read fairytales to you, especially at bedtime. Through fairytales, we are all reminded of how scary, difficult and cruel life can be; we are reminded of the good and the bad things in life.

It is also good to practise staying in your own bed and having stories read to you in the afternoon. This is practising feeling safe in your own bed in the knowledge that your home is all right and safe and will get safer.

When reading in bed, keep the light dim, the door ajar, the hallway light on. Talk about bad dreams or memories.

Asleep or awake, it's healthy to want to have things around you that belonged to the deceased. Remembering is normal, and 'things' can help us all.

Gradually, these things help the wounded, raw, unexpressed feelings become less painful, more easy to talk about. Eventually, you will find real words to express real feelings about real memories and real right-now desires and need. It is good to find this place inside you – with your tricks, and time, and special way of trying to understand what these really big feelings are doing to you and making changes inside, and outside of you. This is good and you are trying and this is brilliant.

In the first weeks, months and sometimes years, it can feel like everything inside your belly is hard, sore and raw. Everything on the outside is, at the same time, rushing and happening in slow motion. This is normal. Try not to be frightened, because when you practise you special tricks in your time, how you feel on the inside will be as easy to mange as the things happening on the outside of your world.

If the very special person has been murdered, you might find adults start whispering when you are about. Ask them to tell you what's going on in a way you can understand because you too have lost someone. Whispering cannot bring the loved one back, nor, if your loved one's been maimed, undoing the awful damage to the person. Say what you can cope with.

Practise eating a little and regularly – even when it feels hard. Eat a little at these times – try your favourite soups and puddings because it is important you remain healthy and live a good life despite how you might be feeling right now.

Again, if your loved one has been murdered, sometimes there is a long, long time before a funeral is allowed to take place, whether a burial or cremation. This is because when something this horrific has happened the police have to do tests on the body of your loved one to find clues as to how and by whom he or she was murdered.

A service? There's nothing to stop you from having a service of your own in the meantime. You might want to have a special in-between service where you choose some special music, or flowers that you like (and which that person might have liked), or go to a private place in the countryside or seaside with a handful of special people to read, sing or eat favourite food. It is good to take things that feel right or smell sweet to help remember things that were sweet.

If the body cannot be found, then it is important to find a place for him or her – a resting place, in effect. (In this case the above idea may be worth considering.)

Your raw pain and anger, feelings of helplessness, are normal. It's also normal to feel things within and about you are not happening (like being in a film, or leaving a cinema when it's now dark, having gone in when still daylight). Adults call this shock (or use some similar term); but, whatever you call it, it's unpleasant, and comes and goes in varying degrees and amounts of time.

Your feelings can be really big and feel unbearable. It is really important to let feelings out in the open and not hide away for long periods outside or in your room. If playing music or drawing help, then play or draw. Coping is never easy – it is time-consuming, but through breathing, feeling, expression and doing, you'll get there! It will be harder for some young people than others to find a means of coping. To get to the point of feeling able to cope with friends, school and everything else will vary depending on, among other things, personality, age and the particular circumstances of the death.

Don't even go there!

Below are some ideas about do's and don'ts, which, it is hoped, will make sense and slowly give you some feelings of confidence with your world. Maybe you will find some special tricks of your own that work well for you.

- It is very important to try very, very hard, and often, not to blame yourself if an adult (e.g. parent, big sister/brother or cousin) has been violently killed.
- It is crucial if you are trying to survive any form of abuse that you do not feel guilty; endeavour to feel alive as you once used to feel.
- If someone in your family has been abused, and you have, or are still being abused, it is extremely important that you tell a *trusted* adult as soon as you can. Make sure you ask the adult to keep you very safe. Don't be silent!
- Don't hurt yourself in any way – ever!
- Don't hurt yourself by not crying when you need to.
- Don't hurt yourself by not telling people you are hurting when you are hurting!
- Don't hurt yourself by pretending to be what you are not – even if others, like adults, might be doing so all around you – and you want to please them because they are always crying or angry and you want to make them feel better. This is very hard, but don't be like them. It is not healthy, nor the right way to go through a very hard time! It is not the right way for you to feel, get through this strange, deep and painful reality. Real is what is deep inside and big outside – neither of which is easy. With the best of help, what seems impossible becomes possible.
- Don't resort to: total escapism in TV; smashing things; taking drugs; hurting others.
- Don't pretend not be angry when you are – find ways to let the angry, raw feelings be understood without troubling you – and others.
- Don't pretend *not* to be angry when you know you are. What has happened is wrong and makes everyone feel lost and angry.
- Until your feelings and everything else change, all will be strange and scary; don't pretend you feel what you don't feel.
- Don't harm yourself by not eating at least one good meal with fruit and meat or vegetables every day.
- Don't harm yourself by eating so much you are sick and not keeping a good amount of food in your body. If you are doing things like this, it means you are harming yourself with self-hurting in shame, guilt or self-anger. Don't do these things: they are not good and not safe or fair to you.
- Try very, very, hard and often, not to pretend the horrible and painful things haven't happened – because they have happened And they are

terrible, and it is normal to feel they haven't happened. Don't believe they haven't happened – they have!

• Young people and adults, too, can be very strange about facing you when someone has died, especially if he or she died violently. You might find people can do cruel things like cross the street when they see you coming or say cruel and spiteful things that hurt you. Sometimes, young people and adults are simply stupid – and this still hurts, but is no excuse! Don't blame yourself.

• These types of people are cruel and ignorant and actually they are frightened both of what to say to you and of their own feelings. This is because what has happened in your life is rare and so powerful and violent, it brings out the worst in (some) people like the media following you and promising things if you talk with them about your loss.

• Don't try to please for the wrong reasons (e.g. pretending you want to smile when you know there is no smile inside).

• Don't try to be silent when you know you need someone to listen to you. Silence is important when you're grieving, and tired and can't sleep all at the same time. Not being silent is also important.

• Don't spend all your time being alone. It is important to be alone but not all the time. It is a way of telling yourself that it's really your fault this horrid and painful thing has happened. It is not your fault and talking helps make sense of these feelings.

• Don't feel, when losing your temper, that this is bad. It is when you never let those weird, sometimes scary, big feelings locked away like a bad secret that your temper is going to confuse you and everyone else. In such cases, you'll find yourself flaring up over a TV programme; you might start breaking personal things (like your favourite toys or music). Maybe, if what you feel is hard, try to say it very simply: 'This hurts me – I want my daddy [or mummy, sister, brother] to come home – right now!'.

• Don't destroy things that belonged to the dead person because they now upset you. A day may come, and that day may come sooner than you think, when those same things no longer provoke anger and tears. Instead, they may bring tears that are warm, loving and slow or even a slow, small smile.

The do's – real time – any time
• Look at the food and exercise section and take really great care of your mind and body.
• Be very kind to yourself.
• Learn to be cautious about people who are good and those who are not.
• Learn to express your feelings sensibly and confidently.
• Take pride in the memories of the dead loved one, remembering him or

her as he or she really was: the good and the bad; warts and all.

- It is to good to talk about the person who was violently hurt or murdered whenever you want to and when you need to.
- Try to find the special trick of knowing what your uncomfortable feelings are (e.g. really big pain; anger, or deep, deep sobbing), which you are keeping inside. Name them, and find the time to say what they are and what you want to do with these feelings. Try to find the special trick, maybe with special friends or special adults, to practise ways of letting those really big feelings come out from deep inside, out into the outside world. It is not as scary as trying to pretend that they are not there. Moreover, very often when you have found your own special trick for knowing how to let these types of feelings out, and after much practice, you may begin to feel better.
- Talk about the person who caused the violence (whether attack, murder), whenever you want to and when you need to. It is good to ask about what this person looks like; why they did what they did.
- It is good to know and believe that your dead loved one would have wanted you to recover, to get on with life. This is especially so when you are too frightened to close your eyes. Bear in mind what he or she would have wanted for you: to try hard to get on, eat well, sleep well, make new friends, do well at school and live a good life – and remember them.
- It is good to ask the people around you to listen to what you want and sometimes need to say about how you feel about everything.
- Talk to someone if either schoolwork or playground taunts are becoming too much. Tell someone what you would like to see happen to make your life better. Maybe you might want someone spiteful to apologise in front of the class, or have to write an essay about what they would feel if their mum (or brother, etc.) was murdered (or attacked, etc). (In extreme cases, it may be worth considering a move to another school, but this would be a last resort.)
- Keep your work (or schoolwork) to a high standard – perform as best you can.
- Try to regain former patterns of doing things (going to bed, rising at regular hours; playing alone, play with or going out with friends). If, after a few weeks you still can't find a trick for doing these things that are patterns and routines for living, then tell someone and ask for new tricks.
- There will be people, often adults, who, after a while, will say your mourning is over; they feel you should no longer be crying, hanging on to the dead person's belongings. In this case, you must point out that, while that is how they may feel, it's not you; that, as you try to listen to them, they should listen to you.

Uncomfortable feelings – what to do

Start to find the special tricks inside you that will be used for your inside and outside world, as a coping strategy for your pain. Start now! Try! Try, and if it is not easy or doesn't fit, try different ideas till you succeed. Try, and try, and try – try hard for your own sake.

Learn how to ask for what you need if you are not used to doing so. This is a very important trick: 'I need you to please listen to what I need to say'; 'I need to say I want to be told what is going happen if…?'.

If you live in a house where expressing your feelings is difficult, again, you'll need to find a way round this. This may mean that you will be helping the others to practise finding their own special tricks for learning to cope with loss. You can ask for people outside your family to help you, and some of these are listed at the end of this section.

Massive, safe, long, massive cuddles from safe adults and friends. Often!

Special paints – tons of paintings, tons of paintings – however old you are, it can help draw your pain out into the open.

Get a tape-recorder and talk to your dead loved one. They cannot hear you, but you want to say things and talking makes you feel better; maybe one day you will write them in a book.

Special dancing to make sense – dancing is so fantastic and you don't have to talk! There are many types of dance styles and classes around. Special dancing is like dance and drama therapy, which is brilliant fun and makes your body feel safe and good. It is a style of dancing for people who want to dance a feeling out of the system – so it is like someone teaching you not to worry about words but showing you how to use your body to make words and stories. Regular physical exercise is important – take care of yourself and enjoy regular swimming, badminton, judo or running. If very young, play with water – it's fantastic!

Maybe you feel like a holiday away from the other people around you. Maybe you and a sister (brother or cousin) feel it would be good for some special adults to arrange a holiday where you don't have to answer any questions, do any drawings, do anything you don't want to do, don't even have to think or have people whispering or pointing at you. There are not enough special places that are safe for young people to go to where they can rest, play and get help – away from all the sadness and violence.

To stay in a place where only young people who have known suffering like you and where the other thing you have in common is a plan to have a brilliant holiday.

Tricks to win …

The tricks to win back a good life are many things: eating, feelings, people, silence, talking and playing, learning about how you will help yourself stay all right and get slowly even better and live better and better. Working out how you will achieve your dreams of doing your best. Express yourself well with music, dance, art, good friends and to make a special place to remember your loved - one. Maybe find a special place a long way from where you live and plant a tree to go and visit on special occasions. Understand in time that life is uncertain and dreadful events do happen as they have in your life. Somehow, against tough odds, you will win and live well.

A feeling is like a diamond. It has many sides and colours and these are like the many types of mood within any single one feeling we have. These feelings are all confusing and all very real and all normal. These feelings settle down in time and can become part of you, like clothes, toys, music, quiet times and play and fun times. They are yours and unique and to be shared with special and good people. Watch how adults are trying to make sense just like you – maybe you are doing better than they are!

Try to practise the trick of making your feelings come out as simply as you can – this is really hard, as you can see from the adults around you who sometimes are unable to express what they feel.

Always try to find the simplest and best way of saying what you need to say well and letting others say what they feel. Sometimes it is good to bend and give way; sometimes it is good to stand by your feelings. The trick to winning life, progressing from hell to a good life, is balance and good expression.

Try to let your friends understand when and why you need to talk about the person who committed the violent crime and what it makes you feel like. As adults know, some friends are no longer worth having around if they 'block you speaking'.

It is good to keep things and memories – even the memories of when maybe you argued or were 'over the top' with the person who is dead. It is good because those things happened and they are all part of real life – as it was and as it is. These are colours in a diamond that is yours.

Sunday is gloomy
My hours are slumberless
Dearest the shadows I live with are numberless
Little white flowers will never awaken you
Not where the dark coach of sorrow has taken you

Angels have no thoughts
of ever returning you.
Would they be angry if I thought of joining you?

Gloomy Sunday

Gloomy is Sunday with shadows I spend it all
My heart and I have decided to end it all.

Soon there'll be candles and prayers that I said I know
Let them not weep
Let them know that I am glad to go

For death is no dream,
And death I am caressing you
With all this breath of my soul I'll be blessing you

Gloomy Sunday

Dreaming, I was only dreaming
I wake and I find you asleep
In the deep of my heart here – deep

Darling, I hope that my dream never haunted you
My heart is telling you how much I wanted you

Gloomy Sunday is absolutely gloomy Sunday
Gloomy Sunday … Sunday.

This section explains the reasons why people in grief cannot always have immediate control of a loved one's body. One such reason is that the legal process requires that every attempt be made to find as much medical or forensic evidence as possible to help to secure an arrest and conviction. This section also tries to demystify the medical examination that causes inevitable distress for those who wish to take their loved one's body home. In the case of a 'suspicious death', consent is not required to proceed with a post-mortem examination.

Post-mortems

It is only in rare situations that a post-mortem does not take place. For example, post-mortems were not carried out on those murdered in the Dunblane massacre. The cause of death was understood without any legal doubt, as were the identities of those murdered and where the incident took place. This was a massacre committed in open view. The killer was known locally; medical examination would have served no legal purpose. In this way, the authorities applied both law and compassion for the grieving families. Post-mortems are, by their very nature, grim. They are highly distressing experiences for grieving friends and family, because they confirm something horrendous and permanent has taken place. It means they may not see the body of their loved one for some time. It should also be borne in mind the possibility of more than one post-mortem being carried out is very real. Any person charged in connection with a death has the right to have an independent examination performed. In extreme cases, because of the most gruesome of criminal acts, bereaved people may never see the body. Post-mortems are best seen as crucial medical operations that are a necessary part of the medical–legal process. There is no way around this legal process in the pursuit of medical accuracy. It will provide facts and possible forensic evidence that will compel a trial jury to convict the right criminal.

Reasons for delay in releasing the body

The sense of bewilderment and unresolved grief is made worse if a second independent forensic post-mortem is needed. After some period of time, and this might be many months, if the police cannot make an arrest, charge and successfully bring someone to trial, a second post-mortem may be necessary. This may cause some people to feel their loved one is no longer a named human being, but something subjected to invasive acts and, moreover, now in the authorities' possession. This is yet another painful aspect of violent loss, but it is important to remember why such procedures are necessary. Every action taken by professionals in the handling of the body of your loved one is done with purpose and sensitivity.

What happens in a forensic post-mortem

A post-mortem is a meticulous and detailed medical examination, both externally and internally, of the body of a person who has been killed in suspicious circumstances. Post-mortems are carried out at the earliest opportunity. Upon the findings of the post-mortem, and simultaneous police enquiries, the legal term 'suspicious death' will cease to be used and changed to 'murder', e.g., from death due to asphyxiation or repeated blows to the head. It is at this stage that the police can intensify a murder enquiry and allocate more resources to the investigation. The professional responsible for carrying out a forensic post-mortem is a highly trained and experienced doctor, accredited by the Royal College of Pathologists (RCP). All post-mortems take place within specialist facilities such as public mortuaries, mortuaries attached to major (often university) teaching hospitals in cities or regional centres equipped for such examinations and where scientific tests may be carried out on samples and parts of the body. Any and every post-mortem examination must follow strict procedures – and standards of medical examination – laid down by the RCP. These demand sensitivity should be shown for the dead person's remains while the highest medical standards are adhered to in recording details of injuries and taking photographs, some of which may, at a future date, be used as evidence in a murder trial.

In a standard forensic post-mortem examination, the following procedures, and any other examinations regarding the dead person's specific injuries, will take place.

- The body is photographed – clothed – from many angles.
- The body is photographed – unclothed – from many angles.
- Initially, the body is lying flat on the back.
- Pathologist first makes an external examination of the body – looking for injuries as well as the body's general condition.
- Photographs, X-rays and samples of various kinds may be taken for forensic examination. Other tests may include, for example, looking to see if there is any skin under the fingernails – which may indicate that the murderer was scratched in a struggle.
- After a meticulous external examination the pathologist begins the process of the internal examination.
- The body will be returned to a position lying on the back and an incision is made above the breastbone down to the navel area.
- Each internal organ is removed. Checks for standard weight and any abnormalities or injuries to all the internal organs and vessels including the heart, kidneys, lungs, arteries, and veins are noted. When the internal organs have been examined, they are replaced – contained within a bag; the incision in the body is stitched up.
- Only if brain injuries have occurred will the brain be removed for examination.
- The pathologist examines the brain by making an incision at the base of the head and, often, small samples of brain tissue are taken for immediate examination and may be retained for further examinations.
- Removed brains need to be kept in formalin and, when examinations are completed, replaced into the body. Families are always asked if they wish the dead person's brain to be replaced once forensic post-mortem examinations are completed and the body is ready to be returned.

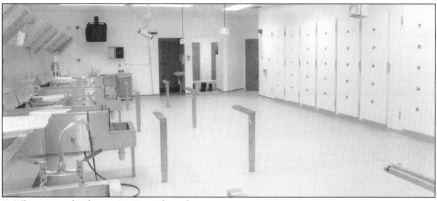

1. Where a medical examination takes place

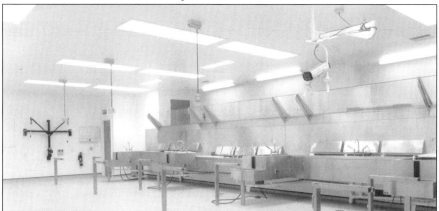

2. An examination and viewing area where officials view the procedure

3. The holding place for bodies

A mortuary technician is a member of the pathologist's team who assists in the post-mortem examination. The scientific analysis of body parts or microscopic work is undertaken by the pathologists and qualified scientists. Once a forensic post-mortem examination is completed, a mortuary technician, with sensitivity and skill, will make a body as presentable as possible for viewing by family. These skills are especially important where a person has been profoundly disfigured. In a multiracial and multicultural society, every effort is made to respect the diversity of cultural and religious obligations regarding funeral and death rituals. However, if it has been scientifically determined that a person has been murdered, it is inevitable and important in the pursuit of justice for a body to remain within the jurisdiction of the law.

What is a coroner?

The majority of coroners are practising solicitors working part-time, except in the larger cities of England and Wales, where they may work full-time and be practising doctors and barristers. In Scotland, a full-time law officer, the procurator fiscal, employed by the Lord Advocate through the Crown Office, takes responsibility for the investigation of 'suspicious death' enquiries and all other duties as performed by English/Welsh coroners. Coroners are employed by a local authority for life, or until voluntary retirement, and are ultimately accountable to the Lord Chancellor – who himself has the powers of a coroner, as have all High Court judges. Coroners work within various areas of legal statutes and, over the last decades, they have witnessed erosion of their powers, examples of which are set out below.

- Abolition of coroners' power to commit someone for trial on a charge of criminally causing death and dispensing with the need for a jury in many cases (Criminal Law Act 1977).
- Referral of criminal deaths to the Director of Public Prosecutions (DPP).
- Abolition of the need for coroners to view the body in person, prior to any inquest (Coroners Act 1980).

Nevertheless, the coroner's role is crucial to good liaison with the police, pathologist and next of kin and good practice. Compassion requires placing the needs of a family for the viewing of the deceased alongside legal matters, e.g. identification and explaining facts.

This affects families whose loved one may have died in 'suspicious circumstances', such as in prison or police custody. It is this lack of access to justice that concerns the charity INQUEST, which campaigns, lobbies government and supports families.

When a suspicious death happens – the role of the coroner

While possible criminal charges are pending, the coroner will delay issuing a disposal order for burial or cremation until the defence legal counsel has had the opportunity to perform their own expert medical examination. Where no person has been charged with a criminal death, the coroner may be reluctant to allow cremation, as this will naturally remove the possibility of an exhumation and second examination if an arrest is made at a later date.

Bernard Knight: *Legal Aspects of Medical Practice*

It is the responsibility of the coroner to ascertain the medical causes of an unexpected death and determine whether medical facts exist that require a post-mortem.

When a 'suspicious death' occurs, the police normally bring it to the attention of a coroner. The coroner, under limited powers, will be obliged to have an inquest opened and automatically adjourned – pending criminal proceedings taking place (s.20 Coroners Act 1980). This formality is to identify and permit registration of the death of the murdered or 'suspiciously' killed person. Following the adjournment, the police continue investigations. A death is referred to as 'suspicious' until such time as it can medically and legally be confirmed that death was due to a violent criminal act.

A full death certificate is rarely issued for a person whose death was 'suspicious' until a criminal is formally charged. A temporary certificate is provided to allow the funeral arrangements to be made and for matters concerning the deceased's will and estate to be executed. If charges are brought, it falls to the clerk of the Crown Court to notify the coroner of any court proceedings and verdict and, at this point, there will be no further obligations upon the coroner. It is within a coroner's powers, after notification of the outcome of any court proceedings, to arrange a brief inquest specifically to confirm and repeat the court outcome.

It is when no person is apprehended and charged that a coroner is obliged to organise a full inquest within the very reduced scope and powers of the office. Within these reduced powers, a coroner or jury no longer has any power to provide a framework for a verdict that says a 'suspicious death' was due to any criminal act on the part of a named person. Also, a coroner no longer has the historic right to commit any person for trial on a charge of criminally causing death. In the event that an inquest reveals a possible criminal element in a 'suspicious death', the coroner is obliged to report this directly to the Director for Public Prosecutions (DPP) (Criminal Law Act 1977).

In Scotland – a very different way
Sheriff's role

In Scotland, a wholly different process exists for investigation from that in England and Wales, in the person of the sheriff. Sheriffs are judges in summary courts and are legally qualified. The sheriff can also be the presiding judge in solemn criminal proceedings (more serious crime) where he will sit with a jury. In such cases, sheriffs can sentence for up to three years.

The sheriff's role with regard to violent and other 'suspicious' deaths will only ever be judicial. For example, at first instance when an accused appears from custody the sheriff is the judge who will preside over the initial hearing and take a decision about bail.

If the circumstances of a suspicious death are such that warrants are required to search for evidence, to get blood samples, etc., then such applications come before the sheriff. The procurator fiscal will submit applications for all such tests.

If an accused has been identified and there is a *prima facie* case against him, but he cannot be found, then, again on the procurator fiscal's application, a petition warrant (the document that goes before the court when the accused appears on the holding charge) will be sought for him. If granted, then this will allow him or her to be arrested and brought before the court. Again, the procurator fiscal will seek the sheriff's decision. At the time of trial, the case will go before the High Court and it will be a High Court judge who presides over the proceedings. (See section describing Scottish courts, pp. 208–241.)

Generally, this is the extent of the sheriff's involvement in the investigative process and so is very different compared to continental Europe where judges also have an inquisitorial role.

The procurator fiscal

The procurator fiscal is responsible for the investigation of all sudden, unexpected and accidental deaths in Scotland and, in this capacity, as in all criminal matters in Scotland, the police act as the procurator fiscal's agent. These deaths will be everything from a natural death where a doctor feels unable to grant a death certificate, up to, and including, homicides. In practice, the police will carry out the enquiry on the procurator fiscal's behalf but, as in all enquiries, the procurator fiscal is in overall charge of the investigation. In the case of a serious crime, the procurator fiscal (or a procurator fiscal depute) will attend the scene of crime and the subsequent post-mortem. Liaison with bereaved relatives will be carried out via the family liaison officer (see section on role of the police, pp. 22–53) and the procurator fiscal's office.

Court proceedings

If an accused is identified and there is a *prima facie* case against him or her, then there will be an appearance in the sheriff court on what is, in effect, a 'holding charge'. At this stage the procurator fiscal may seek to have the accused remanded in custody for up to eight days and the accused will be committed for further enquiry. A report will then be sent to Crown Office (head office for the procurator fiscal). If the procurator fiscal receives Crown Counsel's instructions, then the accused will be fully committed for trial at his/her next court appearance. The accused will either be remanded in custody and must be brought to trial within 110 days, or released on bail. If released, he must be brought to trial within 365 days of his first appearance in court. Previously, there was a presumption for a remand in custody on a murder charge, but, since the incorporation of the Human Rights Convention into Scottish law in 1998, that is no longer so. Although many of those appearing on such a charge are remanded, there is a possibility that an accused may be granted bail. If an accused is remanded, he can appeal to the High Court of Justiciary for bail. Similarly, if the Crown opposes bail, and it is granted, the procurator fiscal can appeal to the High Court for a remand. Bail appeals must be heard within 72 hours of the refusal/grant of bail. In practice, if an accused is given bail, and the Crown appeals the decision, the accused will be remanded in custody until the outcome of the bail appeals. Special conditions may be attached to a bail order, e.g. to stay away from particular witnesses or locations.

Defence post-mortems

If an accused appears on a murder charge, then he will be given an opportunity to instruct what is known as a defence post-mortem. The procurator fiscal retains lawful control over the victim's body and the sheriff drops out of the picture.

Fatal accident inquiries

There is no such thing as an inquest in Scotland. It is important to emphasise that, although there are a wide variety of 'types' of death where a fatal accident inquiry might be appropriate, they are the exception rather than the rule in Scotland – unlike inquests in England. Fatal accident inquiries are fact-finding missions, not finger-pointing exercises. They are neither medical courts nor trial runs for civil or criminal proceedings.

The nearest equivalent is a fatal accident inquiry, which, nonetheless differs from the English counterpart in key ways. The governing statute is the Fatal Accidents and Sudden Deaths Inquiry (Scotland) Act 1976. Inquiries will only be held if something would or might be achieved by doing so.

Fatal accident inquiries fall into two categories:
1. Mandatory – where someone dies as the result of an accident at work or while in lawful custody.
2. Discretionary – where the Lord Advocate deems it appropriate to hold one, and the circumstances of a death are suspicious, unexplained or give rise to serious public concern.

In practice, many discretionary fatal accident inquiries are held after representations are made to the procurator fiscal from interested parties such as relatives, and are deemed appropriate.

The decision to hold such an inquiry lies with the Lord Advocate. Although any representations will be very carefully considered, the circumstances of a death must come within the terms and scope of the statute before one will be ordered.

The procurator fiscal is the master of the instance at such an inquiry and investigates the death, decides what witnesses to call and puts the relevant evidence together. Once an instruction to proceed to fatal accident inquiry (discretionary) is granted, or it is apparent in respect of a 'mandatory' situation that criminal proceedings do not appear to be appropriate, then an application will be made to the sheriff to hold a fatal accident inquiry. When this is granted, the procurator fiscal proposes a date for the inquiry and places an advert in two newspapers announcing the fact that an inquiry is to be held on that date. Interested parties have the right to be present, be legally represented and lead their own evidence if they deem it appropriate. Civil rules of procedure apply and the standard of proof is 'on the balance of probabilities' not the more stringent criminal standard ('beyond reasonable doubt').

The procurator fiscal leads his witnesses first, and other parties have the right to cross-examine those witnesses. At the end of all the evidence, all parties will make submissions to the sheriff who will then make a determination (judgment) on the facts .The sheriff's role is purely judicial. The sheriff must make a judgment about where and when a death took place and the cause of death. These are known as formal findings.

The sheriff makes additional findings on one or more of the following, depending on the circumstances of the death and his view of the evidence:
1. any reasonable precaution that might have prevented the death;
2. any failure in a system of work that caused or contributed to the death (usually relates to accidents in the workplace); and
3. any other relevant facts. In this category, sometimes recommendations are made that might help prevent such a death occurring in the same circumstances. The sheriff is not limited in his role, like a coroner, by one of a set number of verdicts.

In England and Wales

In England and Wales, it is a jury, not the coroner, which decides upon a verdict. Witnesses, if asked to attend and provide evidence, are obliged to do so in order for a jury to assess all the available evidence. If a witness is required to attend, a formal summons is issued to notify the witness as to why their attendance is binding. The coroner, not the inquest jury, will make the decision as to who will be called as witness. The process of being allowed to ask questions of witnesses is referred to as 'a proper interest'. Only witness questions that specifically help the jury decide within the limited options for a jury verdict are allowed. The jury will be specifically confined to assessing the cause of death of the person named. Speeches or statements of those aggrieved are not allowed. These questions may be asked directly by a family member or close companion, but, because of the intensely stressful and legal context, are often asked by an appointed solicitor. Note that legal aid (or assistance as it's now called) is not available for representation – only the 'Legal Help' (one-hour) advice to those who qualify via means test and this offers minimal advice.

A 'properly interested person' is defined in law as being:

- a parent, spouse, child and anyone acting for the deceased;
- anyone who gains from a life insurance policy on the deceased;
- any insurer having issued such a policy;
- anyone whose actions the coroner believes may have contributed to the death, accidentally or otherwise;
- chief officer of police (who may only ask witnesses questions through a lawyer);
- any person appointed by a government department to attend the inquest;
- anyone else whom the coroner may decide has a proper interest.

The Work of the Coroner – Some Questions Answered: A Home Office Guide, 1996

Jurors are not expected to view the body of the deceased. A jury sometimes views pictures if contention arises during the inquest, which has a significant bearing upon the jury reaching a verdict. The jury may have a majority verdict as long as no more than two members disagree with the majority view and the only possible verdict a coroner may provide following a verdict is either: (a) natural causes; or (b) unlawful killing. Unlawful killing replaces the previous coroner verdicts of murder, manslaughter or infanticide.

Judicial inquiries

Recent atrocities, from the murder of Stephen Lawrence to the Marchioness Disaster and the Dr Shipman murders, show individuals have to fight hard to secure clear answers to questions about the circumstances of their loved ones' deaths and clarify issues about the conduct of statutory services. This is a small list of pointers to bear in mind if you find yourself needing to consider this path to surviving violent crime.

There are many levels and types of judicial inquiries with all manner of individual inquiry extras brought in or out and it is crucial, if this option is chosen, that these are requested, discussed and agreed beforehand and always by expert legal counsel – in writing.

Justice, as many people find out, is fought for and won only when the other party has no choice but to concede. This is about power and access, the will of the media, access to money for huge legal costs and time. This boils down to trying to access persuasive power.

This is a game of short, legal written exchanges with the Home Office or DPP that will define how future proceedings will be played out. It is a slow, time-consuming process, littered with legal blind alleys and pitfalls.

There is a need to clarify who is funding any judicial inquiry, as it is possible a group may well have to meet all legal costs. These costs can run to tens of thousands of pounds, as I do not believe legal aid is available for this type of action. Either way, clarification about funding is necessary. Contact the Bar Pro Bono Unit – a group of expert barristers and QCs who, in some circumstances, provide free representation – who will offer guidance. See section choosing a competent solicitor for the Unit's address details, pp. 260–270. On the other hand, ask for advice at a Citizen's Advice Bureau.

A judicial inquiry does not guarantee a decision to advance to court proceedings and a trial.

It is crucial that expert legal counsel writes to the Home Office to define and clarify the smallest details about the scope, seriousness and terms of reference that the judicial inquiry will have and to which it will adhere throughout the inquiry.

For example, what level of seniority will the judge have? Sometimes judicial inquiries are held by a senior barrister – a QC, a retired judge or, if the Home Office regards the gravity of the inquiry to be great, an active High Court judge, as in the Shipman Inquiry.

For example, within the written terms of clarification:
• Will the head of the judicial inquiry sit alone or with other experts?
• Will the inquiry have powers to compel or subpoena witnesses to give evidence?
• Will people be offered immunity?
• Will the inquiry be heard in public (as it should be) or private?
• Where will an inquiry take place: in a court or other public building?
• When evidence indicates a criminal trial is necessary, will the inquiry stop at that point?
• What does the Home Office see as the benefit of holding a judicial inquiry?

A judicial inquiry is probably the best course of future action if justice remains denied and all other options have been exhausted. It requires lengthy written communication by expert legal counsel, which must focus solely on the scope of the inquiry and, in very specific detail, what, in law, will be permitted, who will be obliged to attend and what will happen if evidence comes to light that requires court proceedings. This is to ensure that, if the public are allowed full access to the facts, the law can be seen to be unhindered and without prejudice in securing justice. It may provide answers about your loss and reasons for your suffering. It may even pave the way for a compensation claim (which would affect the level of any compensation awarded by the CICA) and allow for some emotional order to be re-established or, for some, to begin the grieving process.

Useful information

Legal Aspects of Medical Practice, 5th edn, 1992, *by Bernard Knight,* published by Churchill Livingstone. Excellent general text providing extremely useful information on a wide area of legal duties and roles in medical practice.

Examination of the Body after Death, *by Royal College of Pathologists,* March 2000. Highly sensitive and simply worded booklet; outlines all post-mortem processes. Does not treat in detail violent-death post-mortem or the role of forensic post-mortems, but it is helpful in trying to understand.

The Work of the Coroner – Some Questions Answered – A Home Office Guide, 1996. Available via the Home Office Publications Service.

Hedda Nussbaum, a former writer and editor of children's books, had lived for twelve years with Joel Steinberg, a criminal lawyer. It was a place that would later be described by the police as a cave – dark, littered, reeking, bloodstains on the bedclothes, the walls. There was a witness present, unimplicated in whatever had occurred the night before, a baby without language, sixteen months old … lying in his playpen on a mat that stank of urine.

Lisa Steinberg had lived with Joel and Hedda since she was seven days old. Her identity and existence were dependent upon their exercise of will. They told her she had been 'chosen'. Children themselves have no such choices.

At the age of six, Lisa Steinberg weighed forty-three pounds. She was a little thinner than most first-graders. If she had grown up she would have been called an Irish beauty … the hair hadn't been shampooed for a long time; it was tangled and matted. It hid a large red bruise on the right temple … along with two other fresh bruises on her jaw and the back of her head … in the emergency room of the hospital a very ominous sign was noticed – the child's pupils were not equal … an indication of brain damage.

When the blanket was lifted off the child under the white lights of the paediatric emergency room, the cops and medics saw the other bruises. Elizabeth Steinberg's small body was a map of pain. The marks were different colours, different vintages – red, purple, yellowish-brown. It seemed she had been hit just about everywhere – on her arms and the calves of her legs, on her chest, her buttocks. One of the biggest bruises was in the centre of her lower back. There were fresh scratches on her elbows, as if someone had grabbed her there. Her parents had just let her go dirty – her feet and ankles had a crust of black grime …

Dr Miller, a New York City medical examiner believed Lisa Steinberg had died of a subdural haematoma, specifically caused by a blow to her right temple. But there had also been two other significant blows – one to her jaw and one to the back of her head, neither of them causing fractures. Miller contended all three blows had been struck with enormous force, which he dramatically compared to the impact of an automobile collision or a fall from a third-storey window. There was no question in his mind the killer had to be a large, strong person.

© Joyce Johnson: *What Lisa Knew: The Truth and Lies of the Steinberg Case*

If you have been abused

Abuse is never acceptable. It is the abuse of power and domination of those without power or means to have control. Abuse is the violation of others through mental, physical or sexual domination against genuine, equal consent and control. If you are a young person and have been abused, emotionally, sexually and physically a lot of the tricks for surviving and the long road to recovery are the same as for young people who know a special person who has been murdered; or so badly injured they will never be the same again. It is this way because your sense of well-being has been violated against your choice and control and your helplessness and loneliness are similar to those of young people who lose a special loved one. This is important to understand. A part of your body and mind may feel as though it has been taken away from you; or, some parts of your body may feel 'dead'. So, learning to find an outlet for pain and loss is an important part of surviving. Silence will have been one of the ways the abuser kept control over your mind and your body – even maybe making you think or feel the abuse was not abuse, or not happening. But, deep in your stomach, you knew it was happening, though you were too lonely, scared, too used to being ignored, to the point that you no longer knew what was and what was not real. Therefore, breaking your silence and expressing yourself well, eating and exercising well are ways to reclaim control of your life. It is also a way of preventing the abuse carrying on or stopping the abuser having any control over you and learning to enjoy your body and mind without abuse. *Break the silence*!

Services should protect you

If you have found a safe way of breaking the silence about abuse, there are services that will take what you have to say seriously – like some of the agencies listed, the police and social services – use them and ask them to protect you.

It is going to feel hard and may take some time to feel it is safe to trust any adult after what you have been through, and this is natural. It is hoped that services will act quickly and do whatever is necessary to make and keep you safe. This is what social services can do in law to protect you if the abuse is happening in your home:

Provision of accommodation for children

(1) Every local authority shall provide accommodation for any child in need within their area who appears to them to require accommodation as a result of –

(a) there being no person who has parental responsibility for him;

(b) his being lost or having been abandoned; or

(c) the person who has been caring for him being prevented (whether or not permanently, and for whatever reason) from providing him with suitable accommodation or care.

(2) ...

(3) Every local authority shall provide accommodation for any child in need within their area who has reached the age of sixteen and whose welfare the authority consider is likely to be seriously prejudiced if they do not provide him with accommodation.

(4) A local authority may provide accommodation for any child within their area (even though a person who has parental responsibility for him is able to provide him with accommodation) if they consider that to do so would safeguard or promote the child's welfare.

(5) A local authority may provide accommodation for any person who has reached the age of sixteen but is under twenty-one in any community home which takes children who have reached the age of sixteen if they consider that to do so would safeguard or promote his welfare.

(6) Before providing accommodation under this section, a local authority shall, so far as is reasonably practicable and consistent with the child's welfare –

(a) ascertain the child's wishes regarding the provision of accommodation; and

(b) give due consideration (having regard to his age and understanding) to such wishes of the child as they have been able to ascertain.

(7) A local authority may not provide accommodation under this section for any child if any person who –

(a) has parental responsibility for him; and

(b) is willing and able to –

(i) provide accommodation for him; or

(ii) arrange for accommodation to be provided for him,

objects.

(8) Any person who has parental responsibility for a child may at any time remove the child from accommodation provided by or on behalf of the local authority under this section.

(9) Subsections (7) and (8) do not apply while any person –

(a) in whose favour a residence order is in force with respect to the child; or

(b) who has care of the child by virtue of an order made in the exercise of the High Court's inherent jurisdiction with respect to children,

agrees to the child being looked after in accommodation provided by or on behalf of the local authority.

(10) Where there is more than one such person as mentioned in subsection (9), all of them must agree.

(11) Subsections (7) and (8) do not apply where a child who has reached the age of sixteen agrees to being provided with accommodation under this section.

s.20 Children Act 1989 – Provision of accommodation for children

Society is scared to face abuse

Over recent years, long overdue attention and respect have finally come to children and young people who suffer abuse, whatever type it is. For example, being snatched, abuse at school, ongoing abuse within a family environment or abuse within services care. Breaking the silence for abused children and young people is dangerous. In British society, generally, we still fail to deliver enough for those who bravely break the silence. In our society, we still cannot deal with the impact and the extent of abuse taking place in every community. We have been taught by survivors of abuse, who often cannot break their silence until long into adulthood, that prolonged silence has a devastating effect on the quality of their lives. Abusers' menacing threats can create self-abuse and cause the victim to remain silent out of shame, guilt or fear. Service providers must find the skilled services and resources to respond effectively with the law at their disposal. This includes society facing up to its denial of the extent of abuse by showing sufficient gravity to the punishment of abusers. New agencies such as One In Four and SURVIVE are showing the right way to respond to the needs of people affected by abuse.

Children and young people who have suffered violent loss of a parent or close relative are devastated. It is similar for victims of abuse who have lost the unconditional safety and integrity of their mind and body. Eventually these lives all have to be, painfully and very skilfully, put back together. Being in a place that is safe is often one of the first and most crucial matters to ensure for someone trying to survive abuse – of any kind.

Section 20(5) of the Children Act 1989, quoted above, makes it possible for young persons to remain under the protection of social services and the courts up to their twenty-first birthday. This is very important to remember, especially if it is near your sixteenth birthday before you are able to begin to break the silence. The Children Act is very clear that the wishes of the child or young person will be listened to at each stage. So, get as much help from organisations, such as ChildLine and social services; reach out, break your silence. For those children and young people who may have single-parent families, or two parents where one parent has seriously injured the other parent or murdered that parent, then the Act, in the shape of social services, sets out how the right response is made as quickly and as humanly as possible.

In Scotland, parent–child law is significantly different, e.g. the child playing a more central role from an earlier age. A young child's views on many matters has to be taken on board; from the age of twelve, in some matters, the child's view is final. Two further illustrations: (a) the children's panel system is unique; (b) the courts enjoy a wider discretion than in England, where the courts have to run through checklists before making a decision. By contrast, the Scottish courts are unfettered so long as the welfare of the child – known as the 'welfare principle' – remains paramount – number one!

The Criminal Injuries Compensation Authority (CICA) and abuse

Within the CICA application process, the Authority often waives the two-year deadline, i.e. from a crime being committed and reported to police to the victim of abuse applying for compensation. This creates a double bind. On the one hand, victims may have struggled for years with the need to break the silence in order to secure justice and thereafter a better life. On the other hand, the pursuit of justice and possible compensation will require returning to a harrowing experience in great detail – all of which may have to take place in court. Clearly, legal expertise is essential. (See solicitors listings in the Directory section, pp. 407–449.)

When tragedy comes into a young person's life

The bank gives me some height – the cottage windows are low to start with – and by straining I have a clear view of part of the bathroom mirror, opposite. This in turn lets me see who's there.

I hear Mum shouldering open the front door, the scrape as it jams open on the hall floor and the double grind as she struggles to close it (I should have done it for her). The effect of these sounds on the steamy figures in the mirror (unless I'm misinterpreting, and I don't think so) is powerful.

Jessie is in the bath, her face dripping, her short hair clinging wetly to her scalp as if she's just ducked under the water, her tits like a burn in my brain, closer than the image in the mirror, so that I can feel the pulse beating beneath them, even while my own has stopped.

Dad is kneeling, facing her. His knees (I register this in a flash, like part of a puzzle) must be between hers. In the instant I witness, as the first scrape of the front door takes effect, Jessie's hands are scooping water to pour over the part of him that bobs above the surface of the bath – a string-operated thing, his tackle, a horse's prick, uglier and more fascinating and more threatening than I've ever seen it. Maybe I'm wrong. Maybe my mind has just run off through the rain and what I'm seeing is a waking blast from a weird dream. But …

In the mirror, my sister's eyes lock with my dad's as he lurches forward, struggling to support his hands as he clambers out of the bath, suddenly too big for it. I'm frozen for a moment longer as Dad, grabbing a towel, vacates the bathroom with a guilty speed. Jessie is left alone, left with a backward glance from him that in one shot is so much the father I know and a person I don't that I want to stick my fist through the glass to let him know I'm here.

Mum is with Jack, I can hear him crying now. I can imagine Dad walking into the bedroom, having towelled himself furiously, playing it cool: 'Sorry, Jack was so quiet we left him. I needed a bath, it's so sticky. Jessie's just gone in now'.

Alexander Stuart: From The War Zone

Contact with services

In the event of a child or adult affected by violence making contact with a statutory agency, such as social services, they must be geared up to respond in an efficient manner in accordance with both statutory provisions and best-practice guidelines.

What an emergency network should achieve

In a crisis, an emergency conference should deal with the same issues as those outlined in the section in social services – see pp. 160–172. The important addition is to ensure, if no parent or next of kin is available, that a trained, and police-checked, advocate or representative for the young person is identified quickly. These representatives will become the mouthpiece for children in meetings when they cannot or do not wish to speak. The representative protects the interests of the children in need.

An efficient network conference that places children's legal and emotional well-being as central in the response to violent crime is an example of institutional best practice. It can demonstrate both excellence in service and a humane use of lawful protection and care. It is the collective role of agencies to locate the family's hell, through articulate talking and slow planning. A small step-by-step path – constructive and flexible service of compassion, walled by common sense, for the immediate days and months ahead. The people and agencies present within twenty-four hours at the initial network meeting should include:

- The children and family – if members of the family are suspects.
- The police – Family Liaison Officers (FLOs).
- Social services – chair and responsibility for coordinated care plans.
- Consultant child, adolescent and adult forensic psychiatrists in post-traumatic stress disorder (PTSD).
- Housing authorities.
- General practitioner (GP).
- School representative.
- Voluntary agency – if known to be effective and of high standard.
- An advocate/representative chosen with the young person.

The goal must always focus on the total well-being of the abused person.

1. It shall be the general duty of every local authority in addition to the other duties imposed on them by the Part –
(a) to safeguard and promote the welfare of children within their area who are need; and
(b) so far as is consistent with that duty, promote the upbringing of such children by their families, by providing a range and level of services appropriate to those children's needs.
2. Any service provided by any authority in the exercise of functions conferred on them by this section may be provided for the family of a particular child in need or for any member of his family, if it is provided with the view to safeguarding or promoting the child's welfare.

3. For the purposes of this Part a child shall be taken to be in need if –
(a) he is unlikely to achieve or maintain, or to have the opportunity of achieving or maintaining, a reasonable standard of health or development without the provision for him of services by a local authority under this Part;
(b) his health or development is likely to be significantly impaired, or further impaired, without the provision for him of such services; or
(c) he is disabled.
4. for the purposes of this Part, a child is disabled if he is blind, deaf or dumb or suffers from mental disorder of any kind or is substantially and permanently handicapped by illness, injury or congenital deformity or such other disability as may be prescribed; and in this Part – 'development' means physical, intellectual, emotional, social or behavioural development; and 'health' means physical or mental health.

Part III Children Act 1989 – *Local Authority Support for Children and Families*

If young people have to leave home immediately

If the family home has been the place of abuse, murder or other terrible violence and it is necessary to leave the family home, either temporarily, or, it is later decided, permanently, bear in mind the following pointers. The pointers about abuse are as important as those for a violent death.

The children may know from past incidents or have witnessed what the violent crime entails. They may be trying to grapple with the shock like the adults but do not have the voice of adults. In the immediate aftermath, if leaving is for a short time, take the children around the home and have them take something from each room they are familiar with to their temporary home, e.g. toys, own duvet. If someone has been murdered, take something of the murdered person – clothing, pictures, their favourite record, the children's favourite and ordinary clothes, schoolwork. Take tons of crayons and paints to use. Unfortunately, the option of taking possessions will be unlikely for some time if the home has been the scene of the crime.

If appropriate, and the family home is not too horrific, allow the child to wander about; allow him or her to absorb everything – memories and reality. Resist the temptation to overprotect as far as possible; the adult or agency is in fact more frightened about what they themselves are feeling, rather than the young person.

Subject to expert advice, it may be helpful in the future when the child is a young adult or older and wants to return to this period in his or her life for there to be a video, to have pictures taken of every room and garden, access to police records. This is not macabre, but rather an anticipation for a future time when this child may wish or need to translate memory into fact. It may take years for a young person to feel ready to start a process of systematically dealing with the total impact.

Try to maintain as much ordinariness and routine as is possible, such as maintaining friendships and activities. If media harassment is an issue, or the former family home is the site of horror, then take the children to their friends' house or places they once felt safe in. A family member, or possibly a very close friend, should be about in the background in case the social situation becomes too much for the child and the adult can take the child away – until another day. The child will find his or her own time for breaking away from the trusted adult. A child may feel relieved to get away from the intense atmosphere of tragedy, or, equally, terrified to leave brothers or sisters or adult family and may cling like glue; and many children will exhibit degrees of all at different stages from aftermath to recovery. Give young people the chance and young people will say what they need.

What can reasonably be expected from services

It is totally reasonable to be offered very regular updates about both the progress of every aspect relating to the violent crime and why accurate information cannot always be offered. At all times, it's reasonable to expect the police, social services or any other agency to provide clear explanations about everything in a respectful manner.

What matters is young people are not bullied or silenced by unhelpful agency attitudes. Adults must make decisions which can have lifetime ramifications. These can be both painful and difficult. What can be surprising is how robust the young can be, though we must ensure that they are not (over)exposed to inappropriate elements of the incident.

> A nursery nurse killed herself because she could not get over being raped. (She, aged 18 years) took an overdose after a last night out with her friends – five weeks earlier she had been raped by a man she met in a nightclub. She found someone had intercourse with her without her knowledge at the time when she was under the influence of something that took away her consciousness. At the inquest her mother said, 'I believe that when she did this it was not a cry for help. I believe that she could not live with what happened to her – from that evening she changed'.
>
> *The London Metro,* 13 December 2000

For experts in therapeutic work with children in the treatment of trauma, see Directory section and listing for PTSD experts, pp. 449–475.

Useful reading

Fairy tales provide a wealth of reading with excellent imagery about danger, justice, struggle and transformation for small and young people. Fiction is safe as it helps young (and older) to identify safely with imagined characters. They offer warnings and education to the young and adults that help to make sense of the world, e.g. fairy tales by the Brothers Grimm – found in any library or bookshop.

The Soul Bird, *by Michael Snünit,* published by Robinson. A small, inexpensive book for 2–6 years with cartoons about a bird and how it copes with many feelings. An excellent tiny book for small children, to read by themselves or have read to them, which will help them make comparisons about how they feel and what they need. Highly useful for helping to cope with any form of violent experience.

When Father Kills Mother, *by Jean Harris-Hendricks, Dora Black and Tony Kaplan,* 2nd edn, Routledge.

Overcoming Childhood Trauma, *by Helen Kennerley.* A self-help manual published by Robinson for those who suffered childhood abuse; offers practical advice on how to move on.

Sibling Abuse: Hidden Physical, Emotional and Sexual Trauma, *by Vernon R Wiehe,* 2nd edn, Sage. Aimed at academics–professionals, but with useful points for anyone.

Drama Therapy with Children and Adolescents, *ed. Sue Jennings,* published by Routledge. About how effective such therapy is for young people seeking to recover.

The Handbook of Play Therapy, *by Linnet McMahon,* published by Routledge. Good, professional guide.

A Child Called 'It', *by Dave Pelzer,* published by Orion. An adult's story of surviving repeated sexual abuse by his father.

Help Yourself, *by Dave Pelzer,* published by Thorsons. Surviving abuse and moving on with life.

Nanin, *by Tony Thornton,* published by Book Guild Ltd. Story of family abuse and long, painful road to recovery. Very tough and powerful reading

The War Zone, *by Alexander Stuart,* published by Black Swan. A novel about incest seen through the eyes of a son. A good read on turmoil; possibly of use to young adults and adults, but not for the very young as there is much swearing and explicit language to describe fictional abuse. Like much fiction, it seems like non-fiction and may help

Beyond Trauma: Mental Health Care Needs of Women Who Survived Childhood Sexual Abuse, *by Dr Sarah Nelson,* published by Edinburgh Association for Mental Health, June 2001. High-quality academic document with important, readable parts for women (and men) affected by childhood sexual abuse, and their adult mental health. The Association is listed under advocacy organisations, page 365.

Child Abuse Compensation Claims, *by Elizabeth-Anne Gumbel, QC, Richard Scorer and Malcolm Johnson,* published by The Law Society, 2002. An excellent detailed guide aimed at law practitioners, with a wealth of expertise and case experiences. An essential reference for those assisting abused young people. Richard Scorer is a partner with the outstanding firm Pannone & Partners.

Child Abuse and the Law, *by Cathy Cobley,* published by Cavendish. Academic text that contextualises the law and needs of abused children; contains a good summary of society attitudes and services' responsibilities. Useful for professionals and those directly affected, but not a self-help book.

Creating a Safe Place, *by NCH Children and Families Project,* published by Jessica Kingsley. Helping children and families recover from sexual abuse; very informative for those affected; also geared for professionals

Shattered Dreams, *by Susan Stewart,* published by Mainstream. About domestic violence. Serves to remind us of the connections of abuse in all its forms and ages, and impact on others affected.

The Child, the Family and the Outside World, *by D. W. Winnicott,* published by Penguin. Famous academic text that is also very informative for adolescents and adults about the stages of early development and how parents affect our development.

Families and How to Survive Them, *by Robin Skynner and John Cleese,* published by Vermillion. Very user-friendly text on good and bad behaviour in families and the effect this has on people growing up.

Creative Responses to Child Sexual Abuse – Challenges and Dilemmas, *eds Sue Richardson and Heather Bacon,* published by Jessica Kingsley. Some excellent sections on different types of sexual abuse; geared for professionals, but readable for others.

The Law of Parent and Child in Scotland, *by A. B. Wilkinson and K. McK. Norrie,* 2nd edn, published by W. Green, 1999. Definitive on the subject, written by leading experts for practitioners and others with involvement or interest in this area of the law.

Children's Hearings in Scotland, *K. McK. Norrie,* published by W. Green, 1997. Specific-subject text, it is the standard reference for practitioners and others with involvement in the area.

There is a loneliness that can be rocked.
Arms crossed, knees drawn-up;
Holding, holding on.
This motion, unlike a ship's,
Smoothes and contains the rocker.
It's an inside kind – wrapped tight like skin.

Then, there is a loneliness that roams.
No rocking can hold it down.
It is alive, on its own.
A dry and spreading thing,
That makes the sound of one's own feet going
Seem to come from a far-off place.

Toni Morrison: From *Beloved*

Some years ago the Princess Royal, speaking in Glasgow, stated that people made too much of 'this counselling'. Two weeks later, she returned to Scotland with her mother, Her Majesty the Queen, to show sympathy to the parents, children and community affected by the Dunblane massacre. It seems, in our society, we are disinclined to recognise emotional need and we have a tendency to expect people to crawl through even profound life-threatening experiences silently and passively, to our collective cultural detriment.

PTSD is a condition by which many people are inevitably affected following an extremely devastating experience. We must hope that, one day, the Criminal Injuries Compensation Authority (CICA) will encourage government to review the compensation allocated for PTSD.

Unfortunately quite a few within the medical profession fail to grasp the sheer debilitating impact of PTSD and its potentially destructive legacy on the lives of people trying to survive violent crime. As the eminent Professor William Yule has noted, 'there is a requirement in law to mitigate the effects of illness'. Unfortunately though, access to mental health services is a bit of a service lottery with varying levels of expertise. Sadly, some professionals tend to claim to be a centre of treatment excellence, when they may not necessarily be quite so illustrious – self-proclamations should be treated with common sense and critical objectivity. When you consider that a leading mental health research charity states it does not regard PTSD as a serious mental illness and that some GPs will simply advise that you should 'Pull yourself together', you may find yourself having to fight to get the help and treatment you not only need but are entitled to.

I am fundamentally at odds with you over PTSD, a condition which
I perceive to be a complete disaster as a psychiatric diagnosis as it has
medicalised a condition that is best dealt with by non-medical means.
It helps lawyers – and harms everyone else.

An eminent professor of psychiatry, to author

The effects upon those exposed to trauma, directly or indirectly, are indeed
underestimated. There is a surprising failure, on the part of mental health
organisations and prominent victims' agencies, to lobby government for
specialist trauma services throughout Britain. PTSD is a condition that is
both biological and involuntary and people need to be given expert
guidance on how to manage by living with, and around, the condition. As
violent crimes continue to rise in number they are also increasing in degrees
of horror and numbers of people affected, e.g. the Hungerford massacre or
Smithfield Cinema fire.

What is PTSD?

As the behaviour of some people bears testament, and as we are inclined to
forget, we are animals. Humans, like other species, have evolved over many
thousands of years, a survival mechanism commonly referred to as the
'fight-or-flight' response. It is a natural, involuntary physical and mental
reaction to extreme stress or perceived danger to life. The experience of, and
reaction to, the endangerment of one's life causes unusually intense stress
reactions and this stress can generate extreme physical and psychological
effects. We often see this fight-or-flight response on television programmes
where other species which are stalked by an aggressor or predator either
take fight-or-flight in an effort to ensure survival. People do exactly the
same any time they feel an extreme threat to their well-being or survival.
Herein lies the biological origin and potential for PTSD in humans. PTSD is
a primal, involuntary, simultaneously physical and mental fight-or-flight
situation that causes an intolerable amount of stress in reacting to actual life-
threatening danger. It is way beyond a person's capacity to cope with what
has taken place.

There are different types and degrees of trauma and if you have people
in your life who need help, it is important to seek the appropriate
professional help.

What is going on inside our body and minds?

PTSD is how an unforeseen level of danger is experienced as extreme
involuntary physical and psychological stress. It has an immediate, and
potentially lifelong, debilitating effect upon the sufferer – especially if

ignored and untreated. In the seconds and minutes following the experience of extreme danger and excessive stress, our brain shuts certain parts of itself down – this is a biological reaction to help us cope with, and survive, extreme physical danger. It is like a massive power failure where only a minimum back-up energy supply is available. Everything is experienced as if 'on the extreme edge'.

This is the biological function of fight-or-flight – surviving by involuntarily trying to reduce emotional overload in order to stop the total 'meltdown' of your mind. The biological and uncontrollable animal desire for physical survival surpasses any other factor in a situation of extreme danger.

A person's mind and body reach a potentially chronic level of unbearable stress, or arousal, as professionals refer to this specific symptom. Although the incident may have passed, the person's perception of extreme stress is rigidly fixed in the brain (like a continuous video replay) at the point of release of noradrenaline. The individual will perpetually feel the original state of danger.

Traumatic Brain Injury (TBI) with PTSD

There is an aspect of trauma that has only recently gained scientific attention; this relates to mild brain injury and how it contributes towards PTSD. If this is part of a cluster of significant injuries with which you, or someone close, are affected, the hospital needs to ensure the mildest of head injuries is recorded. While this is obviously for future personal health care to ensure appropriate medical treatment, it will also assist in any criminal injuries compensation application.

This applies to people with an apparent short-term head injury requiring brief hospitalisation and who, as time elapses, show varying degrees of marked personality change; these changes are comparable with PTSD symptoms. People affected often return to their ordinary pattern of living and work, but, soon afterwards, experience varying degrees of difficulty with coping in the way they once did. And, as with symptoms of PTSD, relationships – within families, socially or within employment – may well deteriorate. In these situations, PTSD becomes a secondary condition following a head injury. Those affected state they have difficulty in remembering things and lose the ability to concentrate and often 'doctors [were] unable to find anything wrong with them … they were thought to have psychiatric problems, or, worse, to be malingering' (Robert B Sica PhD BCETS, *The neuropsychological basis of potential co-occurrence of mild traumatic brain injury with PTSD,* 1996). Because the physical recovery is swift, and no

A useful description of PTSD

Post-traumatic stress disorder is caused when the autonomic nervous system becomes violently over-activated when facing a life-or-death situation. The limbic system of the brain causes the body to produce vast amounts of noradrenaline. An imprinting process takes place, in the amygdala of the limbic system, within four weeks which leads to permanent flashbacks which in turn perpetuate the outpouring of adrenaline.

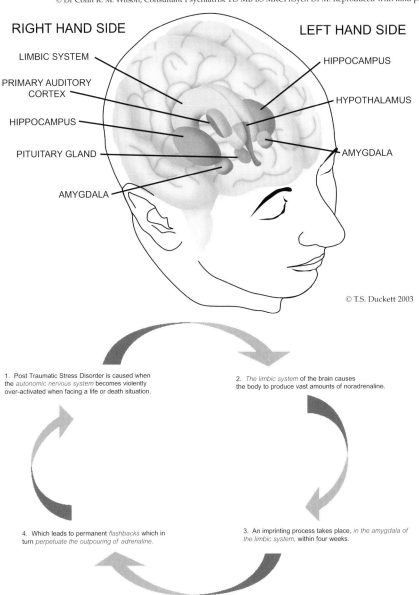

RIGHT HAND SIDE

LIMBIC SYSTEM

PRIMARY AUDITORY CORTEX

HIPPOCAMPUS

PITUITARY GLAND

AMYGDALA

LEFT HAND SIDE

HIPPOCAMPUS

HYPOTHALAMUS

AMYGDALA

© T.S. Duckett 2003

1. Post Traumatic Stress Disorder is caused when the *autonomic nervous system* becomes violently over-activated when facing a life or death situation.

2. *The limbic system* of the brain causes the body to produce vast amounts of noradrenaline.

3. An imprinting process takes place, *in the amygdala of the limbic system,* within four weeks.

4. Which leads to permanent *flashbacks* which in turn *perpetuate the outpouring of adrenaline.*

neurological basis for the behaviour could be found, the condition could easily be missed.

Symptoms of PTSD

If you, or those close to you, show clear signs of any of these symptoms, it is important to seek expert assessment at the earliest opportunity.

The best treatment is to be assessed, as early as possible, by a consultant psychiatrist, preferably with a specialism in PTSD, who, as a medically trained doctor, is in a position accurately to prescribe appropriate medication and recommend the most appropriate type of counselling. Equally, a consultant psychotherapist can immediately refer you to a consultant psychiatrist for an assessment for medication. Here are some helpful guides on symptoms of which you should be aware, developed by Professor Horowitz and his colleagues. The American Psychiatric Association criteria for PTSD is used around the world by specialists in deciding a diagnosis for this condition.

Definitions of the stress response ratings scale

Intrusion items
1. **Hypervigilance** – Excessively alert, overly scanning the surrounding environment, overly aroused in perceptual searching, tensely expectant.
2. **Startle reactions** – flinching after noises, unusual orienting reactions, blanching or otherwise reacting to stimuli that usually do not warrant such responses.
3. **Illusions or misperceptions** – a misappraisal of a person, object, or scene as something or someone else, e.g. a bush is seen for a moment as a person; a person is wrongly recognised as someone else.
4. **Intrusive thoughts or images when trying to sleep** – unwelcome and unbidden mental contents that may be difficult to dispel, include trains of thought that begin volitionally but develop an out-of-control quality.
5. **Bad dreams** – any dreams experienced as unpleasant, not just the classical nightmare with anxious awakenings.
6. **Hallucinations, pseudohallucinations** – an emotional reaction to imagined stimuli, experienced as if it were real, regardless of the person's belief in its reality. 'felt presences' of others as well as sensations of smell, taste, touch, movement, sound and vision are included, along with out-of-body experiences.
7. **Intrusive images while awake** – unbidden sensations that occur in a non-volitional manner in either visual or other sensory systems. Awareness of these images is unwanted and occurs suddenly.
8. **Intrusive thoughts or feelings while awake** – unwilled entries of simple ideas or trains of thoughts and feeling taking unwilled directions.
9. **Re-enactments** – any behaviour that repeats any aspect of the serious life event, from minor tic-like movements and gestures, to acting out in major movements and sequences, including retelling the event. Repeated enactments of personal responses

to the life event, whether or not they actually occurred at the time of the event.

10. **Rumination or preoccupation** – continuous conscious awareness about the event and associations to the event that go beyond ordinary thinking through. The key characteristic is a sense of uncontrolled repetition.

11. **Difficulty in dispelling thoughts and feelings** – once a thought or feeling has come to mind, even if it was deliberate, awareness of it cannot be stopped.

12. **Pangs of emotion** – a wave of feeling that increases and decreases rather than remaining constant.

13. **Fears or sensations of losing bodily control** – sensations of urinating, vomiting, or defecating without will, fear of suffocating, fear of being unable to control voluntary behaviour, as well as somatic responses such as sweating, diarrhoea, tachycardia.

Denial and avoidance items

14. **Inattention daze** – staring off into space, failure to determine the significance of stimuli, flatness of response to stimuli.

15. **Memory failure** – inability to recall expectable details, sequences of events, or specific events.

16. **Loss of train of thought** – temporary or micro-momentary lapses in continuation of a communication or report of inability to concentrate on a train of thought.

17. **Numbness** – sense of not having feelings, or being 'benumbed' (N.B. either patient report or your inference is acceptable here).

18. **Sense of unreality** – experiences of depersonalisation, de-realisation, or altered sense of time and place.

19. **Withdrawal** – feelings or actions indicating social isolation or experiences of being isolated or detached.

20. **Misdirection of feelings** – displacement of positive or negative feelings.

21. **Excessive use of alcohol or drugs** – avoidance of implications of the event by increased usage. Alcohol: excessive usage. Drugs: abuse of prescription agents, as well as abuse of other drugs, legal and illegal.

22. **Inhibition of thinking** – attempts to block thinking about the event. Success or awareness of the attempt is not a consideration.

23. **Unrealistic distortion of meanings** – effects of the event on day-to-day living are inaccurately appraised.

24. **Excessive sleeping** – avoidance of implications of the event by increased sleeping, as well as by simply staying in bed.

25. **Avoidance of reminders** – staying away from certain places, foods, or activities, avoiding photographs or other mementos.

26. **Seeking of distracting stimulation or activity** – avoidance of the implications of the events by seeking excessive exposure to external stimuli or activities such as television, loud music, fast driving, sexual activity, voracious reading, or other diversions.

Post-Traumatic Stress Disorder

General items

27. **Hyperactivity** – fidgeting, markedly increased pace of activity, inability to slow down or stop sequences of actions; periods of frenzied activity.

28. **Retarded pace of actions** – psychomotor retardation; clear slowing, either continuous or episodic, of thought or behaviour.

29. **Tremors or tics** – tremors or tics, including tics about the eyes or mouth. (N.B. basis of tremor or tic as neurological or characterological is irrelevant).

30. **Clumsiness or carelessness** – dropping objects, bumping into furniture, actions that are more than awkward.

31. **Autonomic hyperarousal** – sweating, palpitations, frequent urination, altered skin colour, altered pupil size, or other autonomic signs.

32. **Troubled sleep** – inability to fall or stay asleep, bad feelings about or during sleep.

33. **Restlessness or agitation** – reports of inner sensations of agitation or action and behaviour that is restless or agitated.

34. **Excited states** – thought and action is dominated by excessively high rates of arousal, information processes and expression. May include excessively high sexuality, creativity, productivity and exercise.

35. **Self-hatred** – uncontrollable suicidal preoccupation or gestures, self-loathing or hostility toward a part of the body.

36. **Rage at others** – uncontrollable hostility and anger, even if the target is unclear.

37. **Panic or disintegration** – periods of high pressure, confusion, chaos, anxiety and purposelessness.

38. **Sadness** – uncontrollable sadness or grief, floods of despair, longing, pining or hopelessness.

39. **Guilt or shame** – out-of-control experience of remorse, sense of wrongdoing, or exposure of personal evil or defectiveness.

40. **Irritability or touchiness** – relations with peers, children or strangers that are inwardly irritating, or outwardly abrupt, hostile and bristling.

Diagnostic Criteria for 309.81 PTSD from DSM IV

A. The person has been exposed to a traumatic event in which both of the following were present:

1. the person experienced, witnessed, or was confronted with an event or events that involved actual or threatened death or serious injury, or a threat to the physical integrity of self or others;

2. the person's response involved intense fear, helplessness or horror. Note: In children, this may be expressed instead by disorganised or agitated behaviour.

B. The traumatic event is persistently re-experienced in one (or more) of the following ways:

1. Recurrent and intrusive distressing recollections of the event, including images, thoughts, or perceptions. Note: In young children, repetitive play may occur in which themes or aspects of the trauma are expressed.
2. Recurrent distressing dreams of the event. Note: In children, there may be frightening dreams without recognisable content.
3. Acting or feeling as if the traumatic event were recurring (includes a sense of reliving the experience, illusions, hallucinations, and dissociative flashback episodes, including those that occur on awakening or when intoxicated). Note: In young children, trauma-specific re-enactment may occur.
4. Intense psychological distress at exposure to internal or external cues that symbolise or resemble an aspect of the traumatic event.
5. Physiological reactivity on exposure to internal or external cues that symbolise or resemble an aspect of the traumatic event.

C. Persistent avoidance or stimuli associated with the trauma and numbing of general responsiveness (not present before the trauma), as indicated by three (or more) of the following:

1. Efforts to avoid thoughts, feelings or conversations associated with the trauma.
2. Efforts to avoid activities, places or people that arouse recollections of the trauma.
3. Inability to recall an important aspect of the trauma.
4. Markedly diminished interest or participation in significant activities.
5. Feeling of detachment or estrangement from others.
6. Restricted range of effect (e.g. unable to have loving feelings).
7. Sense of a foreshortened future (e.g. does not expect to have a career, marriage, children or a normal life span).

D. Persistent symptoms of increased arousal (not present before the trauma), as indicated by two (or more) of the following:

1. Difficulty falling or staying asleep.
2. Irritability or outbursts of anger.
3. Difficulty concentrating.
4. Hypervigilance.
5. Exaggerated startle response.

E. Duration of the disturbance (symptoms in criteria B, C, and D) is more than one month.

F. The disturbance causes clinically significant distress or impairment in social, occupational, or other important areas of functioning.

Specify if:
Acute: If duration of symptoms is less than three months.
Chronic: If duration of symptoms is three months or more.
Specify if:
With delayed onset: If onset of symptoms is at least six months after the stressor.

Reproduced with permission of *Diagnostic and Statistical Manual of Disorders, 4th edn,*
© American Psychiatric Association, 1994

Experts in the treatment of PTSD

Within the Directory section are listings of some experts in the assessment and treatment of PTSD. Whoever you choose to use, or pursue with other service providers, you should always be wholly satisfied that they are competent, fully registered and police-checked with their appropriate professional body. There are a few more consultant psychiatrists in Scotland treating PTSD who declined to be included, mainly due to concerns about receiving too many referrals from outside their catchment area in an already overstretched service. So, you may wish to enquire locally through your Primary Care Trust for treatment and it is always worth travelling to get the best of any service. Unfortunately, in Wales there appears to be a markedly significant absence of experts in PTSD, with only one intensely oversubscribed psychiatrist.

While every effort has been taken, and will be taken in future editions, to ensure names and contact points are accurate, this depends partly on cooperation from the service providers included.

Useful reading

Counselling for Post-Traumatic Stress, *by Michael J. Scott and Stephen G. Stradling,* 2nd edn, published by Sage. Thorough guide to various types of PTSD conditions and techniques for treatment.

The post-traumatic stress disorder source – a guide to healing recovery and growth, *by Glenn R. Schiraldi PhD,* published by Lowell House Anodyne. Excellent value and excellent user-friendly style without missing any essential facts and issues. Very empowering and informative. Not expensive.

Going for Counselling – Discover the Benefits of Counselling and which Approach Is Best for You, *by William Stewart and Angela Martin,* published by 'How to Series'. Common-sense guide to the different types of talking therapies.

Understanding Your Reactions to Trauma *by Dr Claudia Herbert BSc (Hons) MSc DClin Psy AfBPsS.* An excellent short publication with life-saving tips and guides and part of a series of excellent quality mini series help topics. Contact Blue Stallion Publications for titles on 0845 4563 927 or www.blue-stallion.co.uk

Stress Response Syndromes: PTSD, Grief and Adjustment Disorders, *by Professor Mardi J. Horowitz,* 3rd edn, published by Aronson New York. A masterpiece; though written for professionals, it is also understandable for non-professionals. It is expensive and available by import from good bookshops, or ask your library to secure a copy (via an inter-library loan, for example).

Recovering Damages for Psychiatric Injury, *by Michael Napier and Kay Wheat,* published by Blackstone Press. Thorough guide about the legal aspects of applying for and pursuing compensation for psychiatric injury. Principally written for legal professionals. Details of specialists largely out of date, a difficulty for any directory.

NHS Psychotherapy Services In England – Review Of Strategic Policy *by Professor Glenys Parry,* published NHS Good Practice 1996 catalogue number 96PP0043. Excellent review of mental health services, standard and proposals largely ignored by governments. Excellently presented and difficult to secure a copy and worth asking your nearest Strategic Health Authority Library or a good medical library. Although written about English practices and services it equally applies to Scotland and Wales and remains a relevant document despite being written in 1996.

Websites about PTSD

Globally, there are numerous sites but the most comprehensive and valuable to date I have come across, with a fantastic wealth of information and meeting point of expert research and related aspects about PTSD, is:

> **National Center for PTSD – Research and Education on PTSD**
> **Address: refer to website**
> **Telephone : 001–802–296–5132**
> **E-Mail: ptsd@dartmouth.edu**
> **Website: www.dartmouth.edu/dms/ptsd**

International Eye Desensitation and Reprocessing Network (EDMR)
For listings and general information about this developing treatment and details about international EMDR therapists, contact:

> **Address: The International EMDR Network**
> **PO Box 51010**
> **Pacific Grove**
> **California 93950**
> **United States of America**
> **Telephone: 001 408 372 3900 ext 16**
> **E-Mail: inst@emdr.com**
> **Website: www.emdr.com/profess.htm**

Suggested reading about EMDR by its pioneer –

Eye Movement Desensitation and Reprocessing: Basic Principles, Protocols and Procedures, *by Dr Francine Shapiro,* published Guildford Press 1995 ISBN 0-89862-960-8

What is it that we see in each other that makes us avert our eyes so quickly? Do we turn away from each other in order not to see our collective anger and sadness?

It is my pain I see reflected in your eyes
Our anger ricochets between us
Like bullets we fire in battle which are not our own –
Nor with each other.
The same angry face donned for safety in the punk world is the same expression I bring to you.
I am cool and immovable – distant from what I need most.
It is easier to be furious than to be yearning.
Easier to crucify myself than you –
And perhaps easiest to ingest that anger until it threatens to consume me
Or apply a salve of substitutes to the wound.

But, real anger accepts few substitutes
And sneers at sublimations.
The anger, hurt, I feel can't be washed down with coke or a colt 45.
It cannot be danced away, mollified by a white lover nor lost in the mirror reflections of a black lover.
I cannot hope it will be gobbled-up by the alligators on my clothing!
Nor can I lose it in therapy –
I cannot offer it to Jesus, Allah, Jah
So I must mould and direct that fiery cool mass of angry energy –
Use it, before it uses me!

Anger unvented
Becomes pain.
Unspoken, becomes rage
Released becomes violence – cha cha cha!
Anger unvented
Becomes pain.
Unspoken, becomes rage
Released becomes violence – cha cha cha!
Anger unvented
Becomes pain.
Unspoken, becomes rage
Released becomes violence – cha cha cha!

In search of self I listen to the beat of my heart.
To the rhythms muffled beneath layers of delusion, pain, alienation –
Silence!
The beat was my salvation.
I let this primal pulse lead me, passed broken dreams, solitude, fragments of identity
To a new place – a home.
Not a place of harmony and sunshine – no!
But truth …
Simple, shameless, brazen truth …
Listen!

Tongues Untied, from the film by Marlon Riggs ©

As always, these handbook tips are a guide – and always consult with your own specialist. This section has been developed for people who have been through a traumatic experience including cases of hospitalisation. It reflects comprehensively healthy dietary needs as well as being practical for people living on low income or state benefits. It is good to maintain a balanced, healthy diet in any circumstances and, when under extreme pressure, it is even more important to replenish your body. In this section, the different food groups will be identified and then a number of suggestions are offered, which will help you to put it all together.

So what does 'healthy eating' mean to you? To some, it means giving up chocolate, or eating more fruit and vegetables. Some people think 'expensive', others 'cardboard' or 'boring'. 'Healthy eating' is a term used to ensure we eat the correct balance of different foods to be healthy and prevent the known complications caused by a poor diet, i.e., obesity, high blood pressure, heart disease, and so on.

Why healthy eating matters

To a certain extent, we are what we eat! Despite the confusing messages that the media portray, there is significant research pointing to the fact that what we eat can influence our health. For example, overeating, which can lead to weight gain, has been implicated in conditions such as high blood pressure, back pain and increased risk of developing diabetes. Conversely, if we do not eat a balanced diet, we run the risk of developing symptoms of deficiencies – fortunately, this is fairly rare in the UK but something to which people existing on very low incomes with high stresses are more susceptible.

If you have been hospitalised through violence, your body may require extra nutrients to support long-term repair of damaged muscle and tissues. Equally, if you are someone who is connected directly to a person affected by violence your body will also benefit from extra care and attention. Protein is a very important nutrient, as we'll see, as well as the foods that provide us with energy (fats and carbohydrates). If you have suffered fractures, you may need to take extra calcium. This is found in all dairy foods as well as white cereal products (e.g. white bread), oily fish, nuts and seeds and green leafy vegetables. If you have suffered significant tissue damage, the following nutrients may have a place in wound healing: zinc (found in meats, wholegrains, beans, peas and lentils): vitamin C (found in citrus fruits, blackcurrants, kiwi fruits and potatoes); and selenium (found in meat, fish and cereals, e.g. rice and flour products).

In addition, vitamin C is often used as a preservative, so you may find it listed on packets as 'ascorbic acid'.

Proteins

Proteins are the building blocks of food. When digested, they break down to become amino acids. These repair body tissues and are important in growth. There are two types of protein: high biological protein (HBP), where all of the essential amino acids are present; and low biological protein (LBP), where some of the essential amino acids are not present. HBP is found in animal products, e.g. meat, fish, cheese, eggs; LBP comes from vegetable sources, e.g. pulses (beans and lentils), nuts and seeds. However, by combining LBP, you will end up with all of the essential amino acids, for example, baked beans and a baked potato, lentil soup and wholemeal bread, vegetable chilli and rice. Protein foods should be eaten two to three times daily, ideally as part of a meal.

Carbohydrates

Carbohydrates are energy providers. There are two main types of carbohydrates: simple and complex. Simple carbohydrates are sugars, which give instant energy. Complex carbohydrates, like potatoes, rice, pasta and cereals, are made up of starches. Starchy foods are broken down slowly to form sugars. Starchy foods make you feel fuller for longer and give you 'sustained' energy. Meals should be based on starchy foods.

Fats

Fats are good energy providers and are both solid, e.g. butter or margarine, and liquid, e.g. vegetable oils at room temperature. Fats can be broken down into different types according to their chemical make-up and you may be familiar with the terms 'saturated' and 'unsaturated'. Saturated fats are found in animal products, palm oil and coconut oil and are identified by the body as a 'harmful' fat and should be taken in moderation, especially if there is a family history of heart disease or you have high cholesterol levels. Unsaturated fats come predominantly from vegetable sources. These can be broken down into two further groups: polyunsaturates and monounsaturates – both of which have positive and neutral effects on the body (heart). It is therefore important to take your fat mainly from vegetable sources. Even though, as a nation, we eat far too much fat, we should not cut it out completely as fat is an excellent source of fat-soluble vitamins. However, excess fat can lead to weight gain, and fats should be used sparingly, so, grill, don't fry; butter your toast lightly, not thickly.

Fibre

Fibre is the indigestible part of starchy foods, beans, lentils, fruit and vegetables. Fibre helps to keep your bowels 'regular', can prevent against certain cancers and is thought to have a cholesterol-lowering effect. Fibre-containing foods also have a 'filling-up' effect for people, so are ideal if you want to lose weight! Try going for higher-fibre alternatives, e.g. wholegrain breads, brown rice, bran flakes, Weetabix™, baked potatoes, beans, and plenty of fruit and vegetables.

If your diet is currently relatively low in fibre, start by introducing fibre foods slowly, otherwise you may become bloated and prone to excessive flatulence.

Vitamins and minerals

These are invaluable to health and allow the body to utilise the other nutrients that we take into our bodies. Many vitamins and minerals are found in fruits and vegetables. Try to ensure that these figure significantly in your diet. Five portions of fruit and vegetables per day are thought to give you the appropriate amount of vitamins and minerals from such foods. So how can we take in five? It may seem like an awful lot, but it is easily achieved. Here is an example summary of what is classed as a portion and after that is a sample meal plan of how a five-a-day diet can be achieved. NB: fresh, tinned or frozen are all acceptable.

One portion is either

> a cereal-sized bowl of salad
> a cereal-sized bowl of chopped fruit/fruit salad
> a serving spoon of vegetables
> a small glass of fruit juice
> a handful of grapes, cherries, strawberries, etc.
> an apple, orange, banana, etc.

Sample menu

> Breakfast: chopped banana/apple on cereal = 1
> Glass of unsweetened fruit juice = 1
> Lunch: piece of fruit with your sandwich = 1
> Evening meal: two servings of vegetables = 2
>
> Total = 5

What else do I need to know?

It is important to eat regularly and it is good nutritional practice to develop basic eating patterns that are as healthy as possible for your body. You should aim to eat a meal three times a day. The reason for this is that our body is a bit like a fire or stove, and needs fuel (food) to keep it going. Because of the length of time since the previous meal, and the consequent low blood sugar in the morning, it is good nutritional practice to eat breakfast before starting your day. A meal may be classed as a bowl of cereal or a big Sunday roast!

It is also important to eat a varied diet, which is not to suggest spending a lot of money. Try alternating sandwich fillings (e.g. ham and tomato, or tuna and cucumber) or have two packets of breakfast cereal on the go. Also, remember to maintain variety with balanced meals chosen from cereals, vegetables, fruit, meat or fish and limited snacks.

Healthy eating does not have to be expensive. If you have storage room in your kitchen, make use of supermarket special offers. Stock up on dried pasta, tinned beans, tinned tomatoes, tuna and breakfast cereals. Also, take advantage of reduced foodstuffs at their sell by dates. When you go shopping try to make a list rather than buying on impulse. If there is more than one supermarket in your area, compare the prices and shop at the cheapest.

Cooking facilities will influence the choice available to you. If you do not have proper access to fridges/freezers, try buying fresh foods day by day. Rely more on dry goods and tinned produce. There are many long-life, vacuum-packed goods, e.g. pasta dishes, stews and casseroles. Milk and dairy produce, e.g. yoghurts, are also available in long-life form. There are a couple of other things that should be included that are not strictly 'foods'.

Water

We all have a tendency at some point or other not to take enough fluid, or water in particular, in our diet. Water is very important to prevent dehydration. Dehydration can leave you feeling headachy, tired and weak. It is recommended we drink 1500 ml (that's six to eight cups, depending on size) per day of non-caffeinated fluids, e.g. water, juices, decaffeinated tea and coffee. Drinking a lot of water is also important when under extreme stress and helps the stomach avoid collecting too much acid: a by-product of stress.

Caffeine

This is a stimulant found in a number of beverages and some foods, e.g. coffee, tea, sodas and chocolate. It has a dehydrating effect if taken in larger quantities, and in sensitive individuals it can cause rapid heartbeat and insomnia – and an inability to sleep. If you have suffered trauma, and have been affected by violence, it might be worth your while considering low caffeine alternatives, especially if you are a poor sleeper, for example, decaffeinated tea and coffee, herbal teas, juices and carob.

Energy

Energy gives us the means to get about and can be derived from inside our bodies from the sources mentioned above, such as carbohydrates, fat and protein. Energy is released gradually inside our bodies and is controlled by enzymes which, when activated, allow us to be motivated and able to perform exertive work. They also maintain our body temperature and influence our breathing. Enzymes are special proteins and each can accelerate the rate of a specific body chemical reaction without itself being affected; they allow complex changes to take place in our bodies that would otherwise require more extreme conditions. Without enzymes, life itself could not exist.

A shortlist of cheap sources of energy and nutrients might include the following:

energy:	lard, margarine, vegetable oil, sugar, white bread, butter, brown or wholemeal bread, old potatoes, pasta, rice, biscuits, breakfast cereals
protein:	white bread, brown or wholemeal bread, pasta, liver, eggs, baked beans, cheese, milk, chicken, rice, frozen peas, old potatoes
carbohydrate:	sugar, white bread, old and new potatoes, rice, pasta, brown or wholemeal bread, breakfast cereals, biscuits, baked beans, ice cream
calcium:	milk, cheese, white bread, brown and wholemeal bread, carrots, ice cream, biscuits
iron:	liver, fortified breakfast cereals, brown or wholemeal bread, baked beans, eggs, biscuits
thiamine:	fortified breakfast cereals, old and new potatoes, brown or wholemeal bread, frozen peas, pork, liver, bacon, ham
riboflavin:	liver, fortified breakfast cereals, milk, cheese, brown or wholemeal bread, old potatoes
niacin:	liver, breakfast cereals, old and new potatoes, chicken, sausages, frozen peas
dietary fibre:	dried beans, All Bran™, baked beans, pasta, wholegrain breakfast cereals

vitamin A:	liver, carrots, margarine, butter, milk, eggs, cheese
vitamin C:	fruit juices, oranges, old and new potatoes, tomatoes, fresh green vegetables, frozen peas
vitamin D:	margarine, fatty fish, eggs, fortified breakfast cereals, liver, butter

Store-cupboard ingredients

Dry/long-life products
These are worth storing in your kitchen:
• pasta, e.g. spaghetti, shells or bows; rice, either brown or white; tins of tomatoes, baked beans, spaghetti, tuna, mackerel or sardines; plain biscuits;
• tea and coffee;
• oil, either olive or sunflower; sauces, e.g. tomato or salad cream; vinegar, Marmite™, jam, marmalade or honey.

Perishables
• Fruit and vegetables: try using fruits and vegetables in season – more salad vegetables in the summer and more root vegetables, e.g. parsnips, swede, carrots and turnip, in the winter.
• Chicken (remove the skin), or other meats. Try to buy the leanest cut you can afford and use healthier cooking methods, e.g. grill, bake or microwave.
• Cheese, butter or margarine, cold meat, e.g. ham.
• Milk, soya milks and fruit juices.

To summarise
• variety is the key to it all!;
• bear in mind that there are foodstuffs that can be harmful in excessive amounts, e.g. fats (especially animal) and caffeine;
• be aware of your limitations and try to make a plan to work around it. For example, if you are on a low income, plan your shopping trips at the times when perishables are reduced in price or, if you have limited space to store perishables, use dry and long-life goods more often;
• try to include a balance of the main food groups each day, e.g. carbohydrates, protein and fats;
• aim for five! (fruits and vegetables);
• drink plenty of water.

A final tip …
If you still have concerns about your diet and its adequacy, you are more than within your rights to ask your GP to refer you to, or seek advice privately from, a state-registered dietician.

Suggested reading

Optimal Nutrition Bible, *by Patrick Holford,* published by Piatkus.

The Hay Diet Made Easy, *by Jackie Habgood,* published by Souvenir Press.

Optimal Nutrition for Optimal Health, *by Thomas E. Levay MD JD,* published by Keats.

A Wolf in the Kitchen, *by Lindsay Bareham,* published by Penguin.

Supper Won't Take Long, *by Lindsay Bareham,* published by Penguin.

Raw Energy – Eat Your Way to Radiant Health, *by Leslie and Susannah Kenton,* published by Guild Publishing.

The Food Bible – The Ultimate Reference Book for Food and Your Health, *by Judith Wills,* published by Quadrille.

Super Foods for Children, *by Michael van Straten and Barbara Griggs,* published by Dorling Kindersley.

Food and Healing, *by Annemarie Colbin,* published by Ballantine Books.

Real Fast Food, *by Nigel Slater,* published by Penguin.

Frugal Foods, *by Delia Smith,* published by Penguin.

The Student Vegetarian Cook Book, *by Sarah Freeman,* published by Collins & Brown.

The Essential Student Cookbook, *by Cas Clarke,* published by Headline.

The Quick and Easy Student's Cookbook, *by Molly Perham,* published by Foulsham.

Exercise and stress

This section benefits greatly from the contribution of Desmond Frimpong-Manso who can be contacted via the author. All exercise photographs are the copyright property of Sam Astbury and not for use without prior permission.

Tension is a normal physiological response initiated by the body when confronted with stress. However, excessive and prolonged stress can cause health problems, because stress is a stimulus which produces strain, or even a change (deformation), in mind and body in cases of prolonged and extreme stress. Stress can be external, such as cold, heat, pain or noise; internally, it can be worry, fear, grief or excitement. Although these stressors are different in nature, they all provoke a similar response in the way our bodies address them – the fight-or-flight response that we met earlier.

When an individual experiences pressure, or even excitement, the body releases hormones (chemical messengers) into the blood, which tell the body to prepare for a response – to take action. For example, this might involve faster heartbeat, quicker breathing, more blood diverted to the muscles, or perspiration. This mechanism was a very useful response for our ancestors as it often meant that they did not end up as prey. Although a useful and normal response, it can have an adverse affect – especially if it is continually triggered when there is no fighting–fleeing, i.e. no action taken – and this is often the reality for people affected by violent crime.

What to look out for and how to counteract

It is very important that we become aware of the physiological and emotional signs of stress that affect our minds and bodies. Physiologically, reactions to stress include palpitations, drying of the mouth, sweating, shallow and rapid breathing, jaw clenching, fatigue, muscle aches and pains, headaches, indigestion, diarrhoea and constipation, insomnia and spots. Emotional reactions to stress include: an inability to relax, feeling under pressure and tense, feeling mentally tired, being easily intimidated or tearful, finding it difficult to concentrate, restlessness and fidgeting, pessimism, becoming fearful or indecisive, being unable to find pleasure and mood swings.

Physical activity, rest and relaxation in balance are key in dealing with the stressors and their effects. Being active is vital for well-being, because it helps to sustain mobility and flexibility of the joints, enhances the flow of blood and circulation. This in turn aids the supply of oxygen and nutrients to the body parts and the removal of toxins that build up as our bodies deal with the day-to-day stressors that we come across in our environment. The end result is that our body is kept well nourished, relaxed and tension free; we move and function better, improve our posture and deal much better with day-to-day stressors. It is a goal for those affected by violence to aspire towards and achieve – to the best of their ability, disability or restrictions.

Exercise and your health

More and more people are discovering the benefits of movement (being active); it produces general well-being, creates more energy for day-to-day life (stamina), better self-esteem, confidence, resistance to stress and tension physically and emotionally.

Well-being is more than just the absence of disease. Everyone can be active or do exercise – it does not matter how little you have done in the past – everybody can secure improvements and benefits. The opportunity to better our health is available and affordable to all. Our bodies provide us with signals of their current state all the time and it is imperative that we listen and take responsibility for their well-being. Through activity and relaxation, we can assist our mind and body in dealing with stress in a positive manner and it is even more important on the tough road towards surviving violent crime – to the very best of our individual abilities.

Poor posture takes up more of the body's energy and diminishes the physical abilities that we have. Every part of our body is subject to stress. Stress can induce poor posture and our backs (muscles of the back and your spine) take most of this burden. As a result, we stiffen up or stoop and sag. Are you slouching right now as you are reading this book? Alternatively, are your shoulders rounded in? Just pause … and correct this by sitting taller, opening the shoulders out and lifting the chest up and out.

Who can do these exercises?

If you are generally healthy, you can begin these exercises immediately. However, if you are under current medical treatment or have a history of cardiovascular, pulmonary (breathing) or orthopaedic (joints) problems, or you are pregnant, please consult with a physician. These are basic exercises and so you will know, from your own knowledge and with professional guidance, what is achievable and at what pace to begin, and what to aim to achieve, over the first few months.

Anyone can perform these exercises to help to relieve general stress and tension. You do not have to have any previous experience of exercise; these exercises are designed to suit a variety of individuals with different degrees of flexibility or tension in the muscles and joints. You may feel some mild discomfort during, or following, the first few sessions of exercising in areas of great tension due to prolonged periods of restricted movement. However, this should not last or persist and if the discomfort does persist, or becomes severe, stop and seek medical advice before continuing. This is about another means of taking back control of your life and this includes being sensible about what you can do in the immediate and near future – so be kind to yourself in the process of aspiring to become actively fit. The exercises can be done anywhere – all that is required is your time – but it can be difficult to isolate a certain amount of time each day, so have realistic expectations of when you can go through these exercises and how often. Where possible, try to establish a regular time in your day to exercise.

Whenever you feel in need of some stress relief or have some free time, seize the moment and take yourself through these exercises. Always go through these exercises at a slow and steady tempo to gain the maximum benefits!

A technique that has been around a long time is currently receiving a lot of overdue popularity and not only helps revitalise and relax people but also has several physical and mental benefits. The technique is called Pilates and is well documented and safe. Pilates places emphasis upon stretching and toning muscles without creating bulk or straining our bodies and has many benefits in alleviating back pain and improving joint mobility, posture, alignment and balance. It also strengthens our abdominals, which will assist posture and ability to be mobile, and it improves breathing. These benefits can extend to young and old alike, who are affected by violent crime, and help to rebuild self-confidence, which, in turn, helps us manage our stress and the sense of not being in control. If this stress-reducing and health activity interests you, there is a great deal of written material available and many day and evening classes provide lessons. It is very important to always ensure any Pilates trainer is duly qualified.

The exercises

There are times when these movements are useful, such as before or after any particularly stressful period. You may also choose to perform these in the morning, to prepare yourself for the day, or in the evening, to release the tension built up during the day. All you will need is a chair/stool, a pillow/cushion and enough floor space with a soft covering, such as a carpet/rug.

- Go through all the exercises slowly, easing into the moves and avoiding sudden movements.
- Do not bounce back and forth in an effort to stretch further.

- Breathe slowly in a gentle and rhythmic manner and never hold your breath.
- If you feel any pain, discomfort, dizziness or nausea, stop the exercise and move into a resting position.
- Count out the seconds as you hold each position or as you go through the movement.
- Do not perform the exercises under the influence of alcohol, drugs or painkillers, as your body is less sensitive and you may cause yourself an injury.

Breathing exercise

Although breathing comes naturally to us all and is automatic, this does not mean we always breathe in the best possible way. Try to avoid shallow, rapid or upper-chest breathing as they all add to the stress on our bodies, especially the muscles of the chest, shoulders and neck due to tension and overuse. These types of breathing do not use the lungs properly and thus we do not get as much oxygen into our bodies or as much carbon dioxide out – leaving our mind and body stressed, lethargic and irritable. Properly controlled breathing is a vital aspect of relaxation.

When we breathe properly, we use our diaphragm (the muscular membrane between our abdomen and chest), which means we breathe more deeply and slowly. When we breathe properly, we use the full capabilities of our lungs, take more oxygen in to feed and replenish our muscles and expel more carbon dioxide (the waste gas that is left after our bodies use up oxygen).

Breathing with your diaphragm

A very simple image to use with the breathing exercise below, until you find an image of your own, is to imagine that deep inside your stomach is a large balloon. As you breathe in, slowly through your nose, imagine you are filling this balloon with as much air as you can to make it as large as possible. As you breathe out, slowly through your mouth, imagine you are deflating this balloon by pushing the air through pursed lips (lips close together as if about to whistle – but without any sound). This requires practice but, once you get the hang of it, the rewards in calmness and relaxation are worthwhile.

© Sam Astbury 2003

Lying on your back, place your legs on a stool or chair to create a 90-degree angle at the knee joint. Place one hand gently over your stomach, breathe in slowly and deeply through your nose, and feel your stomach rise under your hand. Slowly breathe out through your mouth and push gently onto your stomach to feel the air emptying out of your lungs. As you do this, slowly tighten your stomach muscles just tight enough to feel the air being pushed out. Repeat 8 to 10 times.

Breathing is a great medium to help to ease tension and anxiety. Learning to control the speed and depth of your breathing is of great benefit when dealing with fraught situations, e.g. attending court. The use of imagery or visualisation can also be of great aid in helping to achieve confident, deep breathing, for instance, by imagining yourself in a place or at an event that fills you with calmness and well-being.

Chair exercises

Breathing while seated

Breathe in slowly and deeply through your nose and feel your body rise as you do so (pause for a count of three) and release the air slowly through your mouth (just allow the air to escape through your lips and push the air out through your mouth, towards the end of the breath, by

© Sam Astbury 2003

126

using your stomach muscles). Allow the body to deflate as you sink slightly into the back of your chair. Repeat 8 to 10 times.

Sit towards the edge of a chair, so that your back is not against the backrest. It is best to sit forward and away from what people assume is the back support of the chair because, in reality, it makes your core muscles redundant!

Make sure you are seated proud and erect with your shoulders relaxed and your hands on your lap. Ensure you keep your pelvis tucked under to help maintain a neutral spine.

Neck stretch and relaxer

This exercise is ideal for relieving the tension and tightness that can build up in the muscles around the neck.

  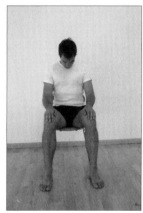

1. Sit on a chair, as erect as you can, with arms down by your sides and shoulders down and relaxed.
2. Imagine a huge clock face in front of you and, starting with your eyes in the middle of the clock face, move your neck to take your eyes to 12 o'clock – hold for a count of 5, breathing with each slow count – then return back to the centre of the clock face.
3. Repeat this, dropping your head down towards your chest, for 6 o'clock, and side to side for 9 and 3 o'clock. Repeat 2 to 3 times.

© Sam Astbury 2003

NB: Always breathe slowly in a gentle and rhythmic manner and never hold your breath.

Spine lengthener

Allow yourself to become floppy as you do this exercise, which will help stretch out your spine.

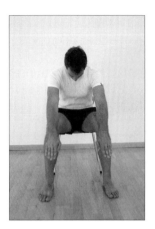

1. Sit on a chair with your feet hip-width apart (knees roughly at 90 degrees) and with your thighs parallel to the floor.
2. With your feet flat on the floor, slowly lower your upper body towards the floor with your hands outstretched in front of you.

Keep your eyes focused on a point between your hands. Aim for your hands to touch the floor, but do not strain to achieve this – drop them down as far as they will go.

3. Once you have dropped your upper body forward, and down as far as you can go, hold this position for a count of 15 and very slowly rise up again. Repeat 2 to 3 times

NB: If you begin to feel dizzy while your head is down, rise up slowly, do not continue with this exercise and try another day.

© Sam Astbury 2003

Sky reach

Ideal for relieving tension in the shoulders and provides a good stretch for the sides of the body.

© Sam Astbury 2003

1. Seated erect in a chair, with your hands relaxed by your sides, slowly take one arm up towards the sky for a count of 5 and repeat with the other arm.

2. Rest one hand in the palm of the other and gently push towards the sky until you are unable to reach any higher. Hold for a count of 10 and relax.

3. Keeping your arms raised towards the ceiling (one hand still in the palm of the other hand), gently lean towards the left side of your body until your hands are positioned at 10 o'clock. Return to the middle and then over to your right side until your hands are positioned at 2 o'clock (hold each position for a count of 5).

4. Return back to the middle and slowly lower both hands to your sides. Repeat 2 to 3 times.

© Sam Astbury 2003

Pelvic mobility

Try to stay loose and relaxed as you go through this exercise to assist with mobility in the lower spine.

1. Place a cushion or a pillow on a chair and sit your bottom right in the middle of the pillow. For the first movement, push your hips slowly from side to side, moving the air in the cushion/pillow from one side to the other (drop your shoulder down on the side where your hip is being pushed up).
2. Repeat this 3 to 4 times for each side and then push your hips forward and then to the back, repeating 3 to 4 times.
3. In pushing your hips forward, imagine that you have a tail going right through the middle of the chair and focus on moving that tail forward and upwards. In moving your hips backwards, focus on trying to stick your bottom out as far as you can without leaning forward with your body.

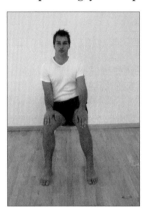

© Sam Astbury 2003

Hamstring stretch

This is an area of the body that can hold a lot of tension and, as a result, can limit the body's mobility in the lower limb region.

1. Sit on the edge of a chair, upper body upright, chest high and shoulders back. Your legs should be outstretched in front of you with a slight bend in the knees and hands on your thighs. Now, slowly lower yourself down towards the floor and allow your upper body to flop down.
2. As you lean forward, slowly slide your hands down your thigh, over your knees and towards your shins, at the same time allowing the body to flop downwards and bowing your head towards the floor as you go down.

© Sam Astbury 2003

130

3. When you have reached as far down as you are able to, hold this position for a count of 10 to 15 and then slowly return yourself to the start position. Repeat this 2 to 3 times and, as you find this exercise more manageable with time, you can increase your hold to a count of 20, 25 and then 30.

© Sam Astbury 2003

NB: Always breathe slowly in a gentle and rhythmic manner and never hold your breath on effort.

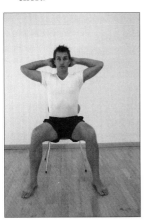

© Sam Astbury 2003

Spine rotation

Because of the constant load-bearing work our spine has to do, both in standing and seated positions, it absorbs a lot of tension. It is essential to mobilise the spine whenever possible.

1. Sit on the edge of a chair, upper body upright, chest high and shoulders back. Your legs should be outstretched in front of you with a slight bend in the knees or legs closer towards you with the knees at a 90 degrees angle.
2. Place your hands behind the back of your head, with one hand on top of the other (do not interlink fingers), and keep your elbows pointing outwards.

3. Maintaining this position, rotate your body slowly from one side to the other, always pausing for a count of 3 at either end and also pausing for a second in the middle (starting position). Repeat this 6 to 8 times.

Seated leg and arm raise

This is a three-fold exercise targeting the hip joint, shoulder joint and abdominal stability.

1. Sitting erect on a chair, slightly forward and with your back away from the backrest of the chair, gently raise one arm straight into the air.
2. Keeping the arm up, raise the leg on the same side, all the time keeping the knee bent and bringing it up towards your chest.

© Sam Astbury 2003

Concentrate on keeping a slight contraction (squeeze) on your stomach muscles just below your navel.
3. Try not to lean to one side or the other as you do this but keep yourself as central as you can. Now hold this position for a count of 3 and gently lower your arm and leg back down. Repeat this 6 to 8 times for each side.

Floor exercises

Knee hugs

This exercise offers a very good stretch for the lower back muscles, which absorb a great deal of tension through everyday living. It is essential to stretch these muscles whenever possible.

1. Lying on your back with your knees bent and your feet flat on the floor, raise your legs and move them towards your head – always maintaining bent knees.
2. Using your hands to grab hold of your knees, gently bring your knees towards your chest,

© Sam Astbury 2003

(keeping the knees together), as far as you are able to. Ensure your head is resting on the floor; use a pillow or cushion for comfort if you wish.

3. If you experience any difficulty breathing, or find breathing restricted as you hug your knees in towards your chest, try this exercise with the knees hip width apart. Hold for a count of 10 and then slowly return your legs back towards the floor. Repeat 2 to 3 times

Arm and leg raise
This is an abdominal coordination exercise, which also involves some activity for your leg muscles, hip joint and shoulder joint.

1. Lying on your back with your knees bent and feet flat on the floor (use a pillow or cushion to rest your head on), you will find that there is a small arch in the lower back. Place one hand under the arch so the tips of your fingers are directly underneath your spine. Your other arm should be resting by your side.

2. Very slowly, raise one leg towards your head. Keeping the knee bent, take it as far as it will go towards your chest and then back to the floor again. While going through this movement, ensure that you always maintain a slight amount of pressure on the

© Sam Astbury 2003

fingertips of the hand beneath the arch in your lower back.

3. To assist you in maintaining this pressure on the fingertips, imagine you are trying to suck your navel into your stomach, but just enough to keep a slight amount of pressure on your fingertips. Repeat 3 to 5 times (for each leg).

4. In progressing this exercise, go through the movement as above, but also include raising your arm together with your leg until the fingertips of your raised arm are pointing towards the sky. Once again, the movement should be performed as slowly as you are able.

5. Please note: with the progression, you will be raising the arm and leg on the same side of your body. Change over sides after your repeats.

© Sam Astbury 2003

NB: Always breathe slowly in a gentle and rhythmic manner and never hold your breath on effort.

© Sam Astbury 2003

Spine rotation

This exercise focuses on the mobility of the lumbar spine, which is essential for the well-being of your entire spine. It also involves some activity for your inner thigh muscles, the muscles at the sides of your stomach and your shoulder muscles.

1. Sit on the floor with your legs outstretched and apart to create a V-shape. Ensure you are sitting erect. Your arms should also be outstretched by your sides, but should be no higher than shoulder height.
2. Slowly rotate the whole of your upper body to one side as far as you can without straining. Turn your head as you do so.
3. Turn back to the start position and rotate to the other side. Hold at the end of each movement for a count of 5 and repeat 3 to 5 times.

Shoulder bridge

The aim of this exercise is to improve mid-section stability and involves the buttocks, stomach and lower back.

© Sam Astbury 2003

1. Lie on your back with your knees bent and your feet flat on the floor. Keep your arms by your side, but place them away from your body as this will provide you with a little more stability as you start the exercise.
2. Use a pillow or cushion to rest your head on. Slowly raise your bottom off the floor, forming a bridge supported by your shoulders and your feet.
3. Make sure that your head stays down and hold the bridge for a count of 10, then slowly return your bottom back to the floor. Repeat 3 to 5 times.

Body lengthener

Imagine that your limbs are growing away from your body as you try to stretch them out as far as you can.

1. Lie flat on your back, resting your head on a pillow. Keep your arms by your sides and your feet flat on the floor so that your knees are bent.
2. Raise one arm over your head and keep it as straight as possible for a count of 5, then repeat with the other arm.

3. Next, gently slide one leg straight out, also to a count of 5, then repeat with the other leg.

© Sam Astbury 2003

135

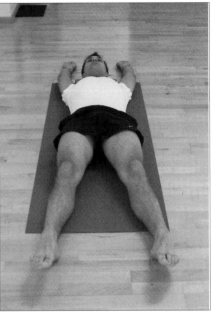

4. Now, breathing in for a count of 5, try to stretch your arms and legs as far out as you can. Breathe out for a count of 5, holding your arms and legs in their extended position. Repeat 2 to 3 times.

© Sam Astbury 2003

Dorsal raise

This exercise strengthens the spine extensors, a group of muscles which play an important role with posture and lower back strength.

© Sam Astbury 2003

1. Lie face down on the floor (place a pillow/cushion to rest your forehead on if this feels comfortable) and place your arms, palms up, by the side of your body.

2. Focus on slowly raising your upper body off the floor. Keep your head down so that you are always facing the floor and try to make sure that your legs stay down with your toes touching the floor.
3. Once you have raised the upper part of your body as high as you can, pause for a count of 2, then slowly return your body back to the floor.
4. Ensure that you breathe out as you raise your body up and breathe in as you return your body back to the floor. As with all of these exercises, keep your breathing slow, deep and controlled. Repeat 8 to 10 times.

And so we come full circle – exercising helps to relieve general stress and tension. Our bodies provide us with signals of their current state all the time and it is important we listen and take responsibility for their well-being. Through activity and relaxation, we assist our minds and bodies to deal, in a positive manner, with the extreme pressures of surviving everything that is connected with violent crime, and to progress.

Meditation

Why on earth would I be interested in something like meditation with the horror that has crashed into my life?

Why? For that very reason! Maybe not today, or this week, but sometime. Within the numbing chaos that may, right now, be going on all about you and within you, with all the strangers coming in and out of your life, amid the madness and the shocking intensity of your tragedy unfolding, it will be necessary to take some time to stop. Creating time and a space to be quiet is what can help. Obviously, everything within this handbook is easier said than done, but let us simplify what meditation is.

Meditation does not have to be the 'new age' notion or have a religious aspect – unless this interests you. Meditation is also what has been previously outlined as, simply, concentration on breathing and becoming calmer within oneself. It can help the mind to learn, under exceptional pressure, to be still – like the 'breathing from the diaphragm' exercise. This has a direct benefit as a tool for survival and control in the weeks and months ahead.

The breathing exercise, whether lying down or sitting in a chair, can be used as a type of meditation and, if you find using an image easier, make it an image that feels, even in these bleak days, an image of safety, calm and peace. Maybe it will be a holiday, a view, a favourite object or visualising a tear becoming a diamond and each diamond flowing through your veins passing all around your body. Really see this diamond – what colours and shades does it have? Really envelop yourself and, with practice, learn to control the stillness within yourself. When using this style of exercise, try to keep your eyes still, half-closed and focused on an object like a candle or a plant while counting your breathing. We can think of meditation as a form of concentration and, with practice and effort, learn to control and dispel images, especially distressing thoughts and recollections, from the mind.

If such distressing images come to mind, let them pass and return your concentration to your breathing – steady, deep breathing from your diaphragm – or visual image/meditation. Repeat this counting or imaging each time any distressing image comes to mind.

How is this going to be done with everything else that is going on all around me and when I cannot even sleep?
Meditation on its own, in the early days and months after a traumatic event, will not be a cure-all by any means. Increasingly, it can become another means of reclaiming control in your life by assisting you in everyday situations and help in dealing with the media, going to court, flashbacks or panic attacks. It is something that can be done by both young people and adults – ideally, twice a day for however long you think you can. At the beginning, it is good to practise for 10 minutes – after a bath and before going to bed. Once a week, increase the time by 5 minutes until you can comfortably manage one hour a day.

Where am I going to try this meditation?
Always use a place you feel safe in. Use your favourite room – maybe, for now, the room will be the special room of someone you loved who has been killed or seriously injured. If there is nowhere you feel safe, find somewhere! Turn all machines off – pull the plug from the telephone – maybe invite others, who live with you, to practise at the same time. Make sure the room is warm and nicely lit. Light some incense, if sweet scents please you, and sit on an upright chair with a cushion. For those who are fit, use a mat or stuffed cushion and sit crossed-leg on the floor – back upright and hands placed lightly on top of each other, resting in your middle. If you have no favourite room, maybe you only feel safe in a public place in daylight – like a swimming pool or library – find a place that is physically safe and warm.

Walking in the countryside – especially when all about you are coming in and out of your home – may be a preferred way of meditating and this also means you will be close to the earth. Try walking in the woods with someone, quietly, or along the shoreline. It is good, especially for those of us living in urban areas, to find a way to get to fresh air and space as often as is possible. It is really hard to find a solid, safe foundation within oneself with the mad circus that surrounds you in the early aftermath of violence. This is where meditation can help you ease an over revved-up mind or the sickening feeling in your belly when flying from one agency's questions to another, coping with others' grief and somehow trying to protect children, lovers and a mind bursting with images of events, dread and sorrow. Regular meditation that slowly trains your mind to find a growing measure of stillness and rhythm in your day is a fine goal to pursue in the early phases of making sense of the impossible.

Creating the time is going to be the challenge. Understanding that, once or twice a day, you should try to turn off all distractions to give something back to yourself. Be tender and patient and be realistic with yourself. Work towards inward healthy control. Stillness.

Massage
Touch! Touch is good, yet touch is something with which it is hard to feel safe when we are affected by trauma and violence. Touch – safe, friendly touch – is something we are not so good at doing with each other in our culture and yet it is something we need and deserve as living dynamic people – especially at times of extreme pressure. We do not always find it easy to ask for and receive safe touch … at the very time we need this most. Massage is a soothing and healing way of touching and being touched that can be like a meditation – something young and old should feel good about requesting in safe surroundings. Simply asking people you can trust to rub your aches does not require training.

If you cannot find a GP who will fund regular massage, ask your GP to recommend places that are accredited with people trained and registered who will charge a fee. There are books available about massage and its techniques that you may wish to explore and many courses in which you may wish to take part. It is important for young and old to know they are being touched safely and to feel uninhibited about disclosing which areas of their bodies they feel they do not wish to be touched. This is especially the case for those men, women and children who have been victims of violent crime, whose sense of well-being has been violated. Being able to say which areas can be massaged helps to take back control and also to start the process of feeling good again about being touched. It is healing and nourishing. If children and young people wish to be massaged, it is helpful for them to know a responsible adult or friend is close by – not necessarily in the room, but very close, nevertheless. If you decide to massage at home, just follow your instincts – get some baby oil or aromatherapy scents and remove all jewellery. If shy, it is fine simply to have your head and shoulders massaged while clothed. Alternatively, if you feel a bit more confident, start from the neck and shoulders, working slowly in small rubbing circles, like kneading clay or dough for bread. Slowly rub circles into all the stressed areas like the shoulders, down the back, the base of the back, the buttocks and down to the toes. It is important to have a towel cover half of the body not being massaged, to keep the body warm and to ensure this type of massage is not sexualised, and a towel to keep the feet warm. Allow roughly half an hour for the back and half an hour for the front of your body. Finish where you started at the head, neck and shoulders. If preferred, ask for only certain body parts to be massaged like your head, shoulders and feet – this is fine. It is your body and it is your time. Break the silence and say what you want and how you wish this healing touch to happen! Make the room warm, safe and pleasant for yourself to enjoy a tranquil, safe and relaxing breaking down of the intense physical and mental pressures that are pounding you.

Remember, wherever you happen to be, keep your breathing, nice, slow, smooth, deep and controlled …

Useful reading

Women's Bodies Women's Wisdom – The Complete Guide to Women's Health, *by Dr Christiane Northrup,* published by Piatkus.

Yoga, Mastering the Basics, *by Sandra Anderson and Rolf Sovik, Psy.D.,* published by Himalayan Institute Press.

Pilates – A Beginner's Guide, *by Roger Brignell,* published by D & S Books.

Pilates Body Power, *by Lesley Ackland,* published by Thorsons.

K.I.S.S. Guide to Fitness, *by Margaret Hundley,* published by Dorling Kindersley.

Fitness for Life Manual – Fitness and Nutrition, *by Matt Roberts,* published by Dorling Kindersley.

Illustrated Elements of Tai Chi, *by Angus Clarke,* published by Element.

K.I.S.S. Guide Massage, *by Clare Maxwell,* published by Dorling Kindersley.

Massage for Health, *by Susan Mumford,* published by Hamlyn.

101 Essential Tips – Massage, *by Nitya Lacroix,* published by Dorling Kindersley.

Ten Minute Stress Relief, *by Erica Brealey,* published by Cassell and Co.

How to Meditate, *by Paul Roland,* published by Hamlyn.

Teaching Meditation to Children – Simple Steps to Relaxation and Well-being, *by David Fontana and Ingrid Slack,* published by Thorson.

Meditation Exercises – Inspirations for Well-Being, *by Bill Anderson,* published by Duncan Baird.

Atlas of Skeletal Muscles, *by Robert and Judith Stone,* published by McGraw – an excellent comprehensive guide and atlas to body and muscle parts.

When these things happen it is about everything.
It is about looking at everything that has happened in your life.
It is about everything that has gone before as well as looking at what this
horror has done to you. It is about everything.

Trauma, especially related to near death, and its subsequent
effects on health are very difficult to come to terms with,
as one's sense of self has been completely shattered.
The rebuilding of a sense of security in oneself and others
is always difficult especially when it is compounded by
physical injuries that affect future health.

The brilliant, intimate and detached eloquence of a wise counsellor

Disabled people know better than others what it is like to learn to live
confidently with varying levels of impairment. Disabled people know what
it is like to be treated in a dismissive and condescending manner by others
– and what to do about it. Disabled people have a great deal to teach victims
of violent crime about how to mobilise and politicise the quality and
inequalities of basic rights and services that able-bodied people take for
granted. Because of the remarkable passion that exists within the disability
movement, many exciting changes have developed over the last ten years,
some of which place disability matters within a legal standing to prevent
prejudice and compel statutory services to listen and act. Disabled people
have actively defined what their services are and what disabled people say
is needed – rather than the way it was historically where disabled people
were told what 'they' needed. The disability movement has a great deal to
teach victims of violence about rising above the status of social, political and
secondary victimisation by institutions supposedly there to assist them. This
requires becoming totally responsible for setting the national and regional
agendas about social, political and service matters – to become visible and
assertive. This means breaking a collective silence and not being dominated
by one charity or government. Disabled people have fought hard, and
continue to do so, to retain control and central involvement of all aspects of
their lives. Consequently, over the years, they have gone beyond the stigma
others tried to place upon them to access a diverse number of services that
are exclusive and inclusive. Notwithstanding such progress, they have
much further to go.

Disabled people find themselves victims of violent crimes like every other
community in society. Mobility and sensory impairments make people more
vulnerable to attacks. Within care establishments, deplorable sex crimes and

physical abuse are now coming to light. Clearly, such crimes are pernicious in the extreme; the work of the disability movement and individual solicitors in countering such crimes is to be applauded.

When an able-bodied person is subjected to a violent crime that leaves him or her disabled to some degree, this will be a further dimension to the trauma. Someone who once took mobility and ability for granted is now confronted with the reality of needing to adjust to being and looking different. Someone who once set great store by his or her good looks, but whose looks are now scarred or impaired, will be shocked at the different attitudes from other people (the stares, the ignorance). It is tough, very tough, to hold one's head up with pride while appalling ignorance is all around. To master these situations will be part of your surviving violent crime. Ultimately, defying the violent criminal by taking total control of your destiny; by being seen when you are ready; by taking expert help and reviewing social circles is all part of powerfully moving forward – even though it is natural to want to hide away. Alongside the mental - emotional injuries, a person in this position now has a double adjustment. Such a victim has to become as comfortable as possible with disability. It almost requires restarting your life. You may, for example, have to learn to adjust to wheelchair sports, if you are a sporty type. You will have to make all the social, sexual, psychological and environmental adjustments that disability demands. For others in your life, life-changes will also be necessary: to become a carer and face the public gaze as they push you around in your chair. Some relationships cannot sustain this change, which, of course, brings yet further grief and loss affecting victims of violent crime. Although ignorance and rejection may hurt, in the long term, new and nourishing relationships which accept you with integrity can emerge. These are the relationships to develop and seek out.

When disability is added to the lot of a victim of violent crime, the potential for profound self-loathing becomes real; self-rage must be addressed. To perpetuate emotional self-abuse is no way forward. You face the simultaneous challenges of adjusting to physical pain and agility and psychological readjustment. Nothing is easy about violent crime. Finding the right services and social world to make sense of everything you have lost, and what you are going to rebuild and the transformation this requires of you and those around you, will take time. Acceptance of self, like acceptance of abrupt violent death, will not come easily. It is a slow, painful process and the more practice, the more expert help, the better.

Learning to live with physical pain and letting go of the 'way you were' is extremely hard. It may be necessary to let go of twenty, thirty or forty years – this is not moving mountains, rather shifting planets! It takes courage to work out the ways in which you can do things on your own, and the things you may be able to do – at some point – and the things you will never again be able to do on your own. Hunger for independence, being tender with yourself and not bullying yourself with setting goals that are impossible will help lay the foundations for a new mirror that in time will offer a new image of self-worth. Take time and grieve for what is lost; take a deep breath for the emergence of the new you. Set pain control activities that take you to the level of managing your pain and slowly master the periods when you can function and allow enough time to rest. The breathing exercises covered in this handbook (see pp. 125–141) can assist with the mental pain as well as physical pain. Nothing is easy within this handbook and this section deals with one of the most daunting. But it is not impossible. A qualitative life can be secured. Do not hide away in self-loathing and reclusiveness as this gives the attacker further power – take some power back and break your dilemma. Dignity will follow, and you will enter a dynamic and vocal internationally active community.

The disability organisations listed in the Directory have extensive data resources on a multitude of groups, carers and home adaptation resources as well as social groups and specialist assessment services that provide CICA reports on future and present needs. The Disability Living Foundation has one of the largest databases in Europe and all have the means to assist in varying ways about different aspects of rehabilitation from learning to adjusting to visual impairment to home adaptation for people who have become paralysed. If violent crime has resulted in some form of impairment, then it is advisable to contact an appropriate specialist service.

Three characteristics seem to mark out the behaviour of
British newspapers: an almost pathological reluctance to admit
errors and say sorry, a deep sensitivity to criticism and a marked
distaste for thinking about the consequences of what they do.

(Some) stories demonstrate how much damage and hurt can be
caused when news values take precedence over human values:
when the hunt for a story or pressure from their news editors
takes journalists, deliberately or sometimes casually, beyond
what is accurate, justifiable or even in their best interests.
There is certainly no doubt that the British press is not serving
the citizens of a mature democracy as well as it could or should.

Raymond Snoddy: *The Good, the Bad and the Unacceptable*

There have been occasions when the media have acted brilliantly and given
us reason to be proud of how they have constructively championed the
cause for justice. The media, in the way that they give us information and
make us aware, have tremendous power and when they use it with
responsibility they should be applauded. By keeping a consistent awareness
of horrific events in the public consciousness – the heinous slaughter of
Megan and Lin Russell; the unresolved murder of Stephen Lawrence; the
Marchioness disaster – the media are acting responsibly, using their huge
power constructively in the pursuit for justice. The *Matlock Mercury*, under a
former editor, took a local issue of injustice and started a sustained and
arduous campaign. Stephen Downing was convicted of a murder in 1973,
but the *Matlock Mercury* campaign, assisted by others, eventually brought
pressure to bear, which led to a review of his case. This in turn resulted in
the decision that his conviction was unsafe and that he was innocent. After
serving twenty-seven years in jail for a crime that he had not committed, his
sentence was overturned on appeal and he walked out of court a free man.

The media could do so much more good by raising the issues of violence in
society and the daily impact on, and the subsequent needs of, victims. This
would ensure that victims receive the political attention that they deserve. It
would be wonderful if the media did this more often, as well as making
pertinent observations about the lack of provisions for those affected by
violent crime. Yet, all too often, the media fail to produce sustained features
that seriously raise public debate, bringing the views of people to the
attention of government. The media could assist vulnerable groups in many
constructive ways rather than – at times – cheapening and adding a further
distressing dimension to private tragedy.

However, the media generally thrive on criminal horror and it is too often presented as if it were a TV drama. Reporting should be factual, dignified and sensitive. Their style degrades those affected and creates an unpleasant and voyeuristic perspective that sensationalises violent crime, which, in turn, desensitises us. The media have started to blend real-life violence that blurs reality and makes tragedy a form of entertainment. Too often, the media try to capture every nuance of despair with entertainment-style reporting, while the victim's own private and personal tragedy is unfolding, a situation deserving dignity and not exploitation.

It is about more than money. It is about the media taking up the broad issues that affect all regarding violent crime – access to expert legal advice, to good public services and to respect. If the media chose to champion a repeal of the punitive and cost-cutting Criminal Injuries Compensation Act 1995 and favoured a return to a common law legal basis for realistic compensation and resources for people in need, our society would be the better for it. The power that the media have does determine to a considerable extent how governments act, but do the media care enough to exert influence in the right direction?

If a recent incident has happened, the media want attention

It is not advisable to make public what is, in reality, your private agony. The media should be dealt with very carefully, for, although they can play a useful role, you must discuss with a lawyer and the police what you can and cannot say, simply because it may have a negative effect on police investigations and the potential for a successful prosecution. We have witnessed how the media have affected several publicised court cases. This author strongly urges people not to use the media as a source of attention.

It may be better to have the police or a solicitor read written statements and, for your privacy, it is best to try to make yourself invisible and refuse to be photographed. When communicating directly with the media it is worthwhile having a dictaphone and another person present to record and witness what is said. If necessary, and if the police agree, be relocated to a secret address – and remember this means not informing people beyond those agreed by the police.

When you engage with the media, you will lose all privacy and this will affect how well you are able to rebuild your life and the lives of those around who have also been affected. The British media generally do not respect the grief of people and those about you can often find themselves forever beholden to them – with or without consent.

Please refer to the Code of Practice that the press must adhere to when dealing with people affected by violent crime – see pp. 154–159.

The public's right to know

It does not seem probable that the public would wish to gloat over or feel that they are intruding into a stranger's grief, yet it would appear that the public can be manipulated into a 'mob voyeurism'. So, who are the public? It seems, too often, the 'public' is simply a byword for an editor's whim and interest to improve profit. Most members of the public would not wish to receive intense media attention if the roles were reversed and it is interesting to see, on the rare occasions when journalists are 'news' themselves, how the media seem to protect their own.

It is your life and your tragedy. Try to retain some control of what is happening in order to survive.

The issues arising from freedom of reporting versus censorship of information and the public's right to know are often debated. Naturally, these debates will not be of immediate concern if you have recently found your life turned physically and psychologically upside down. Somehow, such issues seem a million miles away from the urgency of your personal crises. However, what has recently happened in your life might, on the decision of others, become the 'news of the day'. It may transpire that your private trauma could easily become local or national news and explode into the public arena, becoming a spectacle with, for you, far-reaching and unhelpful consequences. This can mean that, on top of everything else, you have lost your privacy, which will have enormous implications for you.

If you are unprepared for, or ill-advised in, dealing with the media – or media attention imposes itself at the wrong time for you (if, that is, attention is wanted at all) – then your situation might become newspaper fodder.

For the media, new tragedy is fresh copy – but of temporary 'news value' because, in no time at all, it will be yesterday's. There are too many occasions when the industry shows us its power without adequate responsibility. The machinery of mass communication can be used for good or ill. It should not be forgotten that, in the news industry, they are constantly competing among themselves for our money – and our lives become the currency for their profit.

What has recently happened in your life may be of genuine public concern and interest but, somehow, it must be allowed to remain primarily private and dealt with in a manner that is in keeping with your needs and wishes. It would also be more justified if the media pursued governments in a sustained and committed manner to show what, in reality, the government provides for victims of violent crime. This would be a catalyst for positive change.

The Press Complaints Commission (PCC) regards its Code of Practice as a successful and self-regulatory system. Essentially, the Code provides two functions: it offers the industry a set of principles to guide it; second, it gives the PCC a 'clear and consistent framework with which it can address complaints' from the public.

However, this simply is not good enough! It remains the press industry's own drafted Code of Practice and, more obviously, fails to work in practice. It is when the press 'smell the blood' of a story that excesses take place and great private damage is done. It is a contentious issue whether it is in the best interest of society to continue to allow the media to have so much power with so little responsibility. It appears, too often, that the press cannot behave themselves, so it would be better for the public for another agency to regulate them instead.

Although the PCC has fine codes and principles, it continues to fail to implement dynamically sanctions against oppressive and blatantly excessive infringements of the PCC Code of Practice by its own profession. As suggested by the Calcutt Review, there remains a great need for an independent and robust tribunal in Britain. The absence of a robust framework in law to protect citizens and their privacy only intensifies the sense of being a victim.

The PCC Code forms part of editors' and journalists' contracts of employment, which can, if used with more commitment by the PCC and the industry at large, provide a more powerful means of disciplining wayward and substandard journalistic practices.

The phone rang one day, and I picked it up and answered in French as usual. But the caller didn't speak French. In English he asked for me formally by name. 'Can I speak to André Hanscombe please?' Only a handful of people in the UK had our number. This was no one who knew me: not one of the people I knew would ask for me so formally. And this wasn't an official, the voice didn't carry enough confidence. This was a 'journalist'.

I carried on in French and pretended I didn't understand. The speaker knew no French at all. He was soon flustered and hung up. I put down the phone in complete depression, my heart pounding. What was I going to do? Once they had the number it would only be a short time before they had the address. If they didn't have it already. When would they be on the doorstep?

Maybe we should move away as soon as possible. But I didn't want to move, we couldn't hide for ever. And if they had found us once they could do so again. I had to wait. I had to see what their next move was. I only hoped they were lightweights. Here the authorities were on our side: privacy laws were strict. They were off their patch, they wouldn't know the rules. And if they didn't even speak the language then at least I had one advantage. From that moment on I was back on my guard. Paranoia gripped me. But it wasn't paranoia – they were after us.

André Hanscombe: *The Legacy of Rachel Nickell – The Last Thursday in July*

In reality, in Britain, there is no right to privacy. Many readers will be aware that in other countries, including America and many EC member states, privacy is enshrined within their constitutional legislation. Article 8 of the European Convention on Human Rights states that:

Everyone has the right to respect for his private and family life, his home and his correspondence. There should be no interference by public authority with the exercise of this right except such as is in accordance with the law and is necessary in a democratic society in the interests of national security, public safety or the economic well-being of the country, for the prevention of disorder or crime, for the protection of health or morals, or for the protection of the rights and freedoms of others.

The Convention is now part of our law: it was incorporated into domestic law in the Human Rights Act 1998. It remains to be seen how effective the Human Rights Act will be in protecting privacy.

During the early 1990s, partly in response to the endless harassment by the press towards the British royal family and especially the late Princess Diana (who tragically lost her life fleeing the paparazzi and whose pictures were always purchased by British newspapers), an attempt was made to try to bring the British newspaper industry under control. As the press was increasingly showing belligerence and indifference to the damage it caused to individual lives, a review was established to look at how to improve the safety and privacy of citizens in Britain and the conduct of the British press. In the short term, it calmed the media down – but this was more probably due to the reaction from the public. It soon passed and the hounding of royalty continued. In January 2002, Prime Minister Blair succeeded in securing the backing of a press watchdog in his attempt to stop the press from releasing a story about one of his children going to university. He has, on more than one occasion, instructed the press to leave his family alone – very nice if you have power and are protected by state security services – but what about ordinary citizens who do not have the benefit of protection?

This review of press self-regulation was carried out in the Calcutt Review. It concluded that the PCC failed to deal with the newspaper industry effectively and that new legislation was the only remedy after years of the British press failing to regulate itself in an appropriate and democratic manner. The Calcutt Review wished to see the introduction of an 'infringement of privacy' law, as well as the establishment of a Press Complaints Tribunal, to enforce a Code of Practice and issue penalties for misdemeanours.

The PCC

Set up in 1991, the PCC is commonly described as an 'independent' organisation. Its remit was to ensure that British newspapers and magazines follow the letter and spirit of the PCC's Code of Practice. The Code of Practice, cited in full at the end of this section, considers issues such as inaccuracy, privacy, misrepresentation and harassment. The PCC receives over 3,000 complaints a year from individuals, the majority of which cite potential breaches of the Code. Many concern inaccuracy, which can be resolved directly and swiftly by editors to the satisfaction of the people complaining. The PCC adjudicates on those cases that cannot be resolved locally and all critical adjudications are published in full and given due prominence.

How to complain

If you are dissatisfied and have a complaint about an item in a newspaper or magazine which you believe breaks the Code of Practice, you should, in the first instance, write a letter detailing your complaint to the editor of the publication. As mentioned, ideally, the editor without delay will unambiguously provide a satisfactory correction or apology – it's reasonable to give the editor ten working days to reply. (Note: the PCC advises that you should not wait any longer than one month.) If the quality of the response by the editor is unsatisfactory and you are still dissatisfied, you can lodge your complaint with the PCC. NB: the PCC is not able to seek financial compensation for complainants.

Who can lodge a complaint?

Any individual or organisation directly affected by the matters about which they are complaining. Occasionally, the PCC may consider complaints from third parties but only where the complaint raises a significant issue that has not already been resolved. If you are complaining on behalf of someone else you must provide a signed statement from that person stating that he/she wishes you to complain on his/her behalf or if this is not possible the PCC must be informed why. The PCC must be informed about the nature of your relationship to the individual or organisation featured in the item about which you are complaining.

A copy of your letter is sent to the Editor of publication and suggested matter is resolved with you directly
All complaints are judged against a Code of Practice. If there is no *prima facie* breach of the Code, the PCC tells the complainant it can take no further action. PCC will normally only deal with complaints that are lodged within one month of publication of the relevant story, or if the complainant first wrote to the Editor, within one month of the Editor's reply.

The PCC writes to you if they decide not to deal with your complaint, explaining why
The PCC will not usually entertain complaints from third parties, i.e. anyone not directly involved in the published piece. However, it frequently writes to those who are concerned in the story asking if they wish to co-operate in the complaint. If not, the matter goes no further. The PCC justifies this principle on the grounds of practicality in that if the subject of the story does not wish to give his/her side of things, the evidence is bound to be one-sided.

If the matter is not resolved, the PCC decide whether there has been a breach of the Code. They may ask you and/or the Editor for more information or comment
The PCC will not deal with a complaint if litigation about the story is either in progress or about to start. At the conclusion of the PCC procedure there is, however, nothing to prevent the complainant issuing proceedings. The PCC will not normally consider the matter further if the complaint is resolved with the Editor.

The PCC reach a formal adjudication about the complaint

The PCC write to you and the Editor stating they do not intend to take the matter further

---

Complaint upheld

Complaint not upheld

Copies of the adjudication are sent to you and the Editor. The publication concerned is *required* to publish this adjudication in full whenever a complaint is upheld

© T.S. Duckett 2003

How soon must a complaint be lodged?

The PCC will expect complaints to be made within one month of the publication or of the editor's reply to a complaint made directly to the newspaper or magazine in question. In exceptional circumstances, late complaints may be considered.

Types of complaints considered

The PCC will consider your complaint if it raises a matter that falls within its responsibilities. You should tell the PCC how the publication has broken one or more of the clauses of the Code of Practice. If, for some reason, you are unable to write your complaint, the PCC will do its best to help you find a way to register it.

What to include

When you lodge a complaint with the PCC, you must enclose the following:

- The offending article or piece, or a clearly dated copy of the item(s) concerned.
- Your letter of complaint, including an indication of the relevant clauses of the Code that have been breached. The PCC's helpline can assist you in this.
- The reply from the editor and copies of all relevant correspondence or documents that you believe will help the PCC to understand and assess your complaint.
- The PCC generally forwards a copy of your correspondence to the editor, in part to confirm that that editor has failed to resolve the complaint satisfactorily.

Complaints that the PCC cannot deal with

- Legal or contractual matters, or matters that are the subject of legal proceedings.
- Advertisements, promotions, competitions and other parts of newspapers and magazines that are not considered editorial content or undermine taste and decency. These are the responsibility of individual editors and other organisations governing, e.g. advertising.
- Broadcast material, books, leaflets and pamphlets.

When the PCC receives your complaint

1. If the PCC cannot proceed with your complaint, for example because the complaint is outside its responsibility, it will inform you at the earliest opportunity.
2. If the PCC accepts your complaint, it will be carefully examined, and, if it decides that it does not breach the Code, it will tell you; a copy of your letter will be sent to the editor.

3. If the PCC decides your complaint does raise a possible breach of the Code, it will send the editor a copy of your complaint and try to reach a resolution amicably and quickly; this might be by means of the publication of an agreed correction and/or apology, a letter from you, or a follow-up article.

4. If resolution is not possible, the PCC will investigate the matter and you will be asked for further information before it can make a decision on your complaint; both you and the editor will be sent copies of the PCC's decision. If your complaint is upheld by the PCC, the publication concerned will be obliged to publish any critical adjudication in full, with due prominence, in relevant publication.

5. The adjudication will appear in one of the PCC's regularly published reports.

6. Everybody who makes a complaint is kept informed of progress throughout.

Contact details

Press Complaints Commission
1 Salisbury Square
London
EC4Y 8JB

HELPLINE: 020 7353 3732
Switchboard phone: 020 7353 1248
Fax: 020 7353 8355
Text phone: 020 7583 2264
E-Mail: pcc@pcc.org.uk
Website: www.pcc.org.uk/contact/home.htm

Scottish HELPLINE: 0131 220 6652

Please note: a copy of the Code of Practice is available in Welsh, on the website; copies of the Code and the leaflet 'How To Complain' are available in Urdu and Bengali from the PCC's office.

If readers wish to raise comments or suggestions regarding the content of the Code of Practice, they may be written and sent to:

The Secretary
Scottish Press Complaints Commission
Code of Practice Committee
Olympic House
142 Queen Street
Glasgow
G1 3BU

Dealing with the Media

Code of Practice

Ratified by the PCC on 1 December 1999

All members of the press have a duty to maintain the highest professional and ethical standards. This code sets the benchmarks for those standards. It both protects the rights of the individual and upholds the public's right to know.

The code is the cornerstone of the system of self-regulation to which the industry has made a binding commitment. Editors and publishers must ensure that the code is observed rigorously not only by their staff but also by anyone who contributes to their publications.

It is essential to the workings of an agreed code that it be honoured not only to the letter but in the full spirit. The code should not be interpreted so narrowly as to compromise its commitment to respect the rights of the individual, nor so broadly that it prevents publication in the public interest.

It is the responsibility of editors to cooperate with the PCC as swiftly as possible in the resolution of complaints. Any publication which is criticised by the PCC under one of the following clauses must print the adjudication which follows in full and with due prominence.

The PCC definition of 'the public interest' is:

There may be exceptions to the clauses marked * where they can be demonstrated to be in the public interest. [These specific areas are often the very issues of personal contention and distress for those who are victims/survivors of violent crime that the PCC effectively condones – author's comment.]

A. The 'public interest' includes

i) Detecting or exposing crime or a serious misdemeanour.

ii) Protecting public health and safety.

iii) Preventing the public from being misled by some statement or action of an individual or organisation.

B. In any case where the public interest is invoked, the PCC will require a full explanation by the editor demonstrating how the public interest was served.

C. There is a public interest in freedom of expression itself. The Commission will therefore have regard to the extent to which material has, or is about to, become available to the public.

D. In cases involving children, editors must demonstrate an exceptional public interest to override the normally paramount interest of the child.

1. Accuracy

i) Newspapers and periodicals should take care not to publish inaccurate, misleading or distorted material, including pictures.

ii) Whenever it is recognised that a significant inaccuracy, misleading statement or distorted report has been published, it should be corrected promptly and with due prominence.

iii) An apology must be published whenever appropriate.

Newspapers, while free to be partisan, must distinguish clearly between comment, conjecture and fact.

iv) A newspaper or periodical must report fairly and accurately the outcome of an action for defamation to which it has been a party.

2. Opportunity to reply

A fair opportunity for reply to inaccuracies must be given to individuals or organisations when reasonably called for.

3. Privacy

i) Everyone is entitled to respect for his or her private and family life, home, health and correspondence. A publication will be expected to justify intrusions into any individual's private life without consent.

ii) The use of long-lens photography to take pictures of people in private places without their consent is unacceptable.

Note: private places are public or private property where there is a reasonable expectation of privacy.

4. Harassment

i) Journalists and photographers must neither obtain, nor seek to obtain, information or pictures through intimidation, harassment or persistent pursuit.

ii) They must not photograph individuals and private places (as defined by the note to clause 3) without their consent; must not persist in telephoning, questioning, pursuing or photographing individuals after having been asked to desist; must not remain on their property after having been asked to leave and must not follow them.

Editors must ensure that those working for them comply with these requirements and must not publish material from other sources, which does not meet these requirements.

5. Intrusion into grief or shock

In cases involving personal grief or shock, enquiries should be carried out and approaches made with sympathy and discretion. Publication must be handled sensitively at such times but this should not be interpreted as restricting the right to report judicial proceedings.

6. Children

i) Young people should be free to complete their time at school without unnecessary intrusion.

ii) Journalists must not interview or photograph a child under the age of 16 on subjects involving the welfare of the child, or any other child, in the absence, or without the consent, of the parent or other adult who is responsible for the children.

iii) Pupils must not be approached or photographed while at school without the permission of the school authorities.

iv) There must be no payment to minors for material involving the welfare of children nor payments to parents or guardians for material about their children or wards unless it is demonstrably in the child's interest.

v) Where material about the private life of the child is published, there must be justification for publication other than the fame, notoriety or position of his or her parents or guardian.

7. Children in sex cases

1. The press must not, even where the law does not prohibit it, identify children under the age of 16 who are involved in cases concerning sexual offences, whether as victims or as witnesses.

2. In any press reports of a case involving a sexual offence against a child

i) The child must not be identified.

ii) The adult may be identified.

iii) The word 'incest' must not be used where a child victim might be identified.

iv) Care must be taken that nothing in the report implies the relationship between the accused and the child.

8. Listening devices

Journalists must not obtain or publish material obtained by using clandestine listening devices or by intercepting private telephone conversations.

9. Hospitals

i) Journalists or photographers making enquiries at hospitals or similar institutions should identify themselves to a responsible executive and obtain permission before entering non-public areas.

ii) The restrictions on intruding into privacy are particularly relevant to enquiries about individuals and hospitals or similar institutions.

10. Reporting of crime

i) The press must avoid identifying relatives or friends of persons convicted, or accused, of crime without their consent.

ii) Particular regard should be paid to the potentially vulnerable position of children who are witnesses to, or victims of, crime. This should not be interpreted as restricting the right to report judicial proceedings.

11. Misrepresentation

i) Journalists must not generally obtain, or seek to obtain, information or pictures through misrepresentation or subterfuge.

ii) Documents or photographs should be removed only with the consent of the owner.

iii) Subterfuge can be justified only in the public interest and only when material cannot be obtained by any other means.

12. Victims of sexual assault

The press must not identify victims of sexual assault or publish material likely to contribute to such identification, unless there is adequate justification and, by law, they are free to do so.

13. Discrimination

i) The press must avoid prejudicial or pejorative reference to a person's race, colour, religion, sex or sexual orientation or to any physical or mental illness or disability.

ii) It must avoid publishing details of a person's race, colour, religion, sexual orientation, physical or mental illness or disability unless these are directly relevant to the story.

14. Financial journalism

i) Even where the law does not prohibit it, journalists must not use for their own profit financial information they receive in advance of its general publication, nor should they pass such information to others.

ii) They must not write about shares or securities in whose performance they know that they, or their close families, have a significant financial interest without disclosing the interest to the editor or financial editor.

iii) They must not buy or sell, directly or through nominees or agents, shares or securities about which they have written recently or about which they intend to write in the near future.

15. Confidential sources

Journalists have a moral obligation to protect confidential sources of information.

16. Payment for articles

i) Payment or offers of payment for stories or information must not be made directly, or through agents, to witnesses or potential witnesses in current criminal proceedings except where the material concerned ought to be published in the public interest and where there is an overriding need to make, or promise to make, a payment for this to be done. Journalists must take every possible step to ensure that no financial dealings have influence on the evidence that those witnesses may give.

(An editor authorising such a payment must be prepared to demonstrate that there is a legitimate public interest at stake involving matters that the public has a right to know. The payment or, where accepted, the offer of payment to any witness who is actually cited to give evidence should be disclosed to the prosecution and the defence and the witness should be advised of this.)

ii) Payment, or offers of payment for stories, pictures or information, must not be made directly or through agents to convicted or confessed criminals or their associates – who may include family, friends and colleagues – except where the material concerned ought to be published in the public interest and payment is necessary for this to be done.

The broadcasting media

Although not perfect, with its eerie trend towards lingering shots of victims' suffering and an increasing blurring of real-life against semi-soap and semi-documentary style programmes, the broadcasting media appear to attract more professional people. They also appear to show more sensitivity and good practice.

If, in any democratic society, there are balances to be struck between the citizen's right to receive information and ideas and the responsibilities of broadcasters and journalists to behave reasonably and fairly and not cause an unwarranted infringement of citizens' basic right to privacy…

The Codes of Guidance cannot resolve that dilemma but it sets out what the Broadcasting Standards Commission considers are the principles to be observed and practices to be followed – that all broadcasters (including the providers of Teletext services) avoid unjust or unfair treatment in radio and television programmes … Broadcasters and broadcasting regulatory bodies should reflect this guidance in their own codes and guidelines.

Broadcasting Services Commission

The issues of accuracy and respect remain largely similar to those within the Code of Practice for the press and so only the main phrases are included here. Please contact the Broadcasting Standards Commission for a copy of the Code of Guidance if you wish to read them in full.

The Code of Guidance include matters such as:

1	fairness	8	door-stepping	15	crime
2	correction and apologies	9	suffering and distress	16	violence
3	opportunity to contribute	10	revisiting past events	17	current-affairs and documentary programmes
4	deception	11	children	18	explicitness
5	privacy	12	occasions of grief and bereavement	19	factual programmes
6	use of hidden microphones and cameras	13	people with disabilities or mental health problems		
7	telephone calls	14	race		

Broadcasting Standards Commission's Complaints process
Who can make a complaint?

Remember, if obliged to lodge a complaint as a last resort, you should read the section about how to prepare a complaint (see pp. 173–187).

Any individual, association or corporate body is allowed to lodge a complaint and normally complaints should be made by the individual directly affected in the programme or, in some rare circumstances, another person who has been authorised to pursue the complaint, with the explicit and written authorisation of the person affected by the programme.

If the person affected by the programme has died during the five years immediately before the broadcast, a personal representative or family member or someone closely connected to them is allowed to make a complaint. In these circumstances, the Broadcasting Standards Commission has the power to decide, when assessing the complaint, whether the connection is strong enough for a complaint to be pursued. In cases of unjust or unfair treatment, the person who is complaining must have either taken part in the programme or been subject of the alleged treatment or, whether taking part or not, has had a direct interest in the subject matter that was treated within the programme. In the case of unwarranted infringement of privacy, it must be that your privacy, or the privacy of the person whom you are representing, has been directly infringed.

The Broadcasting Standards Commission
7 The Sanctuary
London
SW1P 3JS
Telephone: 020 7233 0544
Fax: 020 7233 0397
E-Mail: fairness@bsc.org.uk
Website: www.bsc.org.uk

Suggested reading

The PCC – Code of Practice as stated.

The Broadcasting Standards Commission – Code of Guidance as stated.

The Good, the Bad and the Unacceptable, *by Raymond Snoddy,* published by Faber & Faber. An experienced journalist's observations on the British press.

Power without Responsibility, *by James Curran and Jean Seaton* (most recent edition), published by Routledge. Excellent, slightly technical but easy to access history and analysis of the British press and broadcasting up to the present.

The Media in Britain, *by Jeremy Tunstall,* published by Constable. Accessible and thorough history and analysis of British press, broadcasting and politics.

From morning to night I stayed out of sight
– didn't recognise I'd become – No more than alive
I'd barely survive – in a word … Overrun.
Won't hear a sound from my mouth –
I've spent too long on the inside out
My skin is cold to human touch.
This bleeding heart's not beating much.

He's standing on the threshold
– caught in fiery anger
Hurled into the furnace
– he'll curse the place

I'm creeping back to life – my nervous system all awry
I'm wearing the inside out.
I'm holding out for the day –
when all the clouds have blown away
I'm with you now – can speak your name,
now we can hear ourselves again

He's torn in all directions
– still the screen is flickering
Waiting for the flames
– to break

Pink Floyd: 'Wearing the Inside Out', from their album *The Division Bell*.
Lyrics: ©Anthony Moore; ©Pink Floyd Music Publishers Ltd 1994.
Reproduced with very kind permission. Not to be reproduced without prior written permission

Social work is an extremely tough profession – it is a job that mirrors the issues we prefer to turn away from as a society and in our communities. Social services are a source of derision for many in our society; yet generally, workers try to provide the highest of standards and services to improve disadvantaged and vulnerable people. Some of the derision is self-inflicted where failure to swiftly remove incompetent and ineffective social workers has undermined the safety of some service users and undermined the credibility of the profession. Committed workers perform excellent work under enormous stresses, dangers and ever-changing legislation and policies to provide an essential service for society. Like all public services, social services are facing steady demoralisation. The loss of experienced workers alongside increased social and health needs, lack of respect from the general public, lack of resources and rigid legislation within a disintegrating welfare state make social work more than a challenge to work within and, like all public service workers, social workers are exposed to violent people in their work.

In Britain, we have always been ambivalent about welfare provision. This shows itself with a sense that those in need should be 'grateful for whatever they receive and should shut up and put up'. It also shows itself in public ambivalence towards service providers. As with every sector of public service in Britain, social services are placed in an ever-critical state of collapsing against the weight of trying to respond the best they can. It is a miracle and reflection of the commitment of many workers that they remain working. Unsurprisingly, the government is recruiting social workers from abroad, e.g. from South Africa and Scandinavia. For decades, people have voted for low taxes over thorough, democratic and civilised public services, which has had a negative impact on public provision. We are mirrors of what we choose, including our governments and cultural attitudes. Now, as a victim trying to survive violent crime, or seeking compensation, is an uncomfortable time to find out what store we have set by these values.

What crisis?

Generally, social workers contacted, including a major professional magazine, stated they did not see it as their role to help victims of violent crime. The common response was 'we are stretched to the limit and can only respond to crises'. This is sad and unjust, as people affected by violent crime have a duty to be properly assisted as legislation makes clear social services have access to a wide range of laws and (albeit) dwindling resources and budgets. After all, what is a family or individual who is rendered incapacitated due to violence? What is a family abruptly and violently bereaved without a wage-earner, or a scene of crime that requires mental health services? Indeed, many of the duties once the domain of social work are now undertaken, generally, very well, by the police and some specialist voluntary organisations. It is feasible, if social services cannot show greater responsiveness and inclusiveness about how they perceive 'need' and 'duty' that they will become seriously further diminished if not redundant. The service has also inadvertently compounded the sense of secondary institutional victimisation, rendering trivial the needs of people affected by violent crime.

The way it is

Social services have a legal duty to provide provision for those in need, in accordance with the Mental Health Act 1983, the Children Act 1989, the Chronically Sick and Disabled Persons Act 1970, the National Health Service Act 1977, the National Health Service and Community Care Act 1990, the Disability Act 1995 and the Care Standards Act 2000, to name but a few. Where there has been infamous tragedy and media attention, such as the Lockerbie disaster or the Marchioness disaster, individual services responded superbly but services remain generally reactive – not unified and standard. Surely, some part, in those areas of law mentioned, allows social services to review their responses to people affected by significant violent crime – or do none of these apply to victims of violence? The service has duties to reduce illness and risk within the community that places the needs of victims of violence at the centre of any modern social work service. But, this is not generally the case. Institutions become hysterical and 'contract' and overreact instead of acting expansively and methodically to tried and tested practice guidelines and this can mean, especially if small children are not involved, that social services are never contacted. It is as though services only respond if they fear negative media or legal attention.

Social services stand at the edge of a make-or-break phase in our society. They have been an important and useful public statutory service and a dynamic opportunity exists for them to seize the needs of those affected by violent crime by providing a willing and non-cynical service for this growing minority. In doing so, they would improve their credibility among the wider public – or is it too late?

Decades of failure to provide uniform service responses to victims in need allowed the trivialisation of victims from violent crime to be offered ad hoc attention from charities for victims. This failed victims and equally diminished the role of social services and their use of legislation. It is the police service that has largely responded in the absence of goodwill and a cluster of victim's groups many of which operate in an ad hoc and dysfunctional way and without authority.

A new service without cynicism

Like all public services, social services must be prepared to rid itself of substandard workers and improve its standing within society. It will also need to rid itself of a culture of preciousness about itself and apply serious action to improving its professional image. Equally, government must constructively respond while recognising the role, needs and efforts made by social workers and allow this vital service to stabilise and produce a service with resources. For individuals, at this time, it is about chance and powers of persuasion to secure a responsive service and this does not benefit all victims. If social services respond more positively and uniformly they would immediately raise their standing in the eyes of society and be seen to be doing what they claim to do – and duty-bound to do.

It seems service exhaustion and ambivalence for 'perceived' victims of violence means that victims would be better served if a new service under the aegis of the Home Office were to be established. It would ensure victims of violence are firmly located on the statutory map instead of at the mercy of ad hoc voluntary sector groups with varying degrees of ability and authority. This is developed in the section about the Home Office.

At last!

Long overdue, and with refreshing clarity, the newly established government response in creating the General Social Care Council (GSCC) has forged the universal standards for workers' conduct and that of employers. As with all public services, the government seems more concerned with discipline and 'buzz phrases' above basic improved resourcing than letting workers get on with their job. (See Directory about their duties and note they do not provide responses to individual needs.) After decades, the government has developed the GSCC to oversee and implement training and practice standards for social care workers at all levels and their employers. We must hope this agency is not set up to fail or to overreact with punitiveness to 'prove' its existence. It is time that social services show they are worth having. The creation of the GSCC offers social work the potential to transform with professional statutory credibility. But, it has yet to resolve its failure to face the unmet needs of people affected by violent crime – among other groups. Maybe it is too late and is already being replaced by the skilled work of the police and emerging functions of NHS Primary Care Trusts?

If you need urgent help

If your need is urgent, then social services are duty-bound to respond which is why, if the police develop the practice of immediately making a referral at this early stage, much of this handbook will become a checklist. Under s.47 of the National Health Service and Community Care Act 1990, services may be activated without a lengthy assessment if it is deemed reasonable. It is on the basis of: (a) who, (b) how dire and (c) when, that social services will determine the priority of response.

(5) Nothing in this section shall prevent a local authority from temporarily providing or arranging for the provision of community care services for any person without carrying out a prior assessment of his needs in accordance with the preceding provisions of this section if, in the opinion of the authority, the condition of that person is such that he requires those services as a matter of urgency.

(6) If, by virtue of subsection (5) above, community care services have provided temporarily for any person as a matter of urgency, then, as soon as practicable thereafter, an assessment of his needs shall be made in accordance with the preceding provisions of this section.

s.47 National Health Service and Community Care Act 1990

The ripple effect

When an individual is profoundly violently injured, or bereaved, the impact is not only direct and intense for that person; it will have what Claudia

Herbert and Ann Wetmore describe as 'a ripple effect'. By this, they refer to the dozens or more of others connected with the incident. They may be people directly and indirectly affected by changes in your personality or physical disability – or aftercare. It is important for progress in life that all such persons affected are recognised and assessed by registered professionals such as family liaison officers (FLOs), social and health services. It reasonable to expect proper service.

If your needs can wait a few days but not more than a week

If, in your view, circumstances in your life or family can wait, but no longer than five working days, tell someone in a position to convey this information to social services – like the police. Ask the police to get a definite time, name of worker and place and you may wish to ask if an FLO may be present. FLOs act as a bridge and, when they have to withdraw, social services become the direct protector of need and contact point for all agencies' communication. This is also to protect the person or family from the forthcoming deluge of strangers repeating the same questions and allows those affected to concentrate upon the only real need – the horror now in their lives – and to place the communication and responsibilities where they naturally should be. Social services' involvement can protect people from the bombardment of what people in crisis find an irrelevance or worse. Social services exist for a purpose in society.

Assessment means social workers reasonably requesting to know what it is you need and them making an informed decision of your needs without prejudice to budgetary constraints. This is set out in law.

Issues needing early attention

These might include anything and everything. For example: issues about priority rehousing if your home is no longer suitable (e.g. if it was the scene of a crime), providing referrals for priority mental health services, providing some financial support for children in need of essential food or education or psychiatric referral. Assistance with completing social security forms and allied problems, investigating child abuse and protecting children from further harm, assessing unmet needs of parents traumatised or indirectly affected by violent crime, registering newly traumatised and disabled people as eligible for discounts for public transport or liaising with the police or GPs.

An assessment is finding out whether social services can offer, or are duty-bound to provide, a particular service that you or they identify as necessary. A thorough assessment requires asking information about personal matters, financial independence or dependence, your environment, such as your home or surrounding facilities if newly disabled as a result of crime and how social services can best secure your personal aspirations to reach the optimum level of good health, progress and living.

Every professional service needs to ask appropriate questions to assess which service (care package) needs to be arranged and the level of priority of need. It is about making sure public services are being used effectively. This is irritating but unavoidable and reasonable. It is a good idea to have already penned a list of issues you want to raise and have any documents you believe social services may need. A pre-planned list of facts help and can be sent before an assessment by an FLO or advocate to those who need to know to allow you to speak about what you want instead of reacting to questions that may not reflect what you want to address. (See the two examples below about the information that most agencies will want to know – pp. 165–169. The headings can be used as guidelines.)

Unfortunately, you will be asked the same information repeatedly – possibly over many years – and it may be useful to type out something along these lines for institutions to try to reduce unhelpful repetition, stress and misuse of your time. It can be adapted to your needs and specific agency. It will also save money, stress and time if whatever original documents required are supplied in half dozens to speed processes through and assist all agencies including former employers.

NB: This is an example of what a partner may be stating in the early hours of shock

IN STRICTEST CONFIDENCE

To: Assessment Team Manager: Children and Families Division
From: Mr Billy Brown
Date: 21 May 1997
Address: 269 Puzzle Tree Drive, Woolcroft, Worcester, Worcestershire
Telephone: 01567 890 123

Presenting issues and needs
1. Mother murdered en route to work
2. Mother sole wage-earner
3. No extended family nearby
4. Father house-husband – made redundant three years ago
5. No access to immediate emotional help
6. Children highly distressed, middle child has remained silent since murder
7. Father trying to keep family together – refusing to accept death of partner
8. Father in need of emotional, financial, child-care and financial help
9. Assistance needed to keep family – especially children – away from media
10. Mother's parents returning from holiday following notification

Social Services

Family composition
Alice Brown – d.o.b. 10/1/68 – Mother – Murdered 23 May 1997
Billy Brown – d.o.b. 15/2/68 – Father
Life companions since 1989 – unmarried
Clare Brown – d.o.b. 1/6/91 – daughter
Diana Brown – d.o.b. 10/2/93 – daughter
Edward Brown – d.o.b. 22/5/96 – son

Service users' wishes – father
- Conference arranged asap to help cope with everything
- To take place at my house
- I want all my family kept together
- Keep the media away
- Need people to help with shopping for food and pay mortgage next month
- My kids need help and want to know why their mum's gone away

Children's wishes and needs
1. Premature to note
2. All showing intense signs of fear, silence, insomnia, guilt

Services requested
1. We want to bury Alice as soon as her folks and brother get back but I can't afford funeral if I pay the mortgage. She deserves the best.
2. I can't tell my kids what has happened because Alice may come back.
3. Too many people taking over my home – my kids are scared.
4.
5.

Agencies involved
Police:
Detective Sergeant Liz Winger – FLO
Telephone: Mobile 002789 6765 1420
Office: 01567 121242 ext 369

Coroner's Office:
Dr Malcolm Jones

General Practitioner:
Dr Sunita Patel
Address: Wooldean Surgery, Wooldean Lane, Worcester
Telephone: 01567 868090

Family needs
1. Until this week my family was all right.
2. We have family living abroad – Alice has a brother in Australia and I have a sister in Kent but my folks are dead.

3. We have been too busy bringing up our kids to have much money or time for a social life. Can't think of any special friends to call.
4. Kids are doing brilliantly at school and have lots of friends but the youngest is everywhere – he's crying in his sleep and won't talk when awake.
5. Our unmet need is that we want Alice back home – maybe she's hurt and can't get to a phone.

Financial situation
Alice: £695 p.m. after tax
Savings – £1,500 Halifax BS
Mortgage £220 pm 20 years to completion
Billy's redundancy went mainly to reducing large mortgage 3 years ago

Family summary of situation
None of us is coping and I'm trying hard to make sure the kids are all right but I can't spend the time with the girls when I want as I got to look after Edward who's everywhere. I can't believe this is happening and Alice won't come back to us.

Requests for review of needs in four weeks

© T.S. Duckett 2003 *Sample Social Services Needs List*

IN STRICTEST CONFIDENCE

To: The name of the individual and agency
From:

Re: What Specific Issues Require Attention, e.g. i) re-housing ii) charity application for funeral expenses

Address: Your Address
** Don't offer telephone number – keep everything in writing

Principal Service User

Other Service User/s
1.
2.
3.
Presenting Immediate Needs
1.
2.
3.

Presenting Immediate Family Needs
1.
2.

Family Composition
1. Starting with adult/parents
2. Then eldest child
3. To the youngest
4. With dates of birth
5. And identifying your next of kin – and their names, addresses, telephone
   details

Criminal Injuries Reported To and When
Found unconscious by passer-by reported via emergency services to St Never
Hospital NHS Trust at 11.36pm on the 9/9/99 and Police at Hurricane Hill
Station, Ealing, West London

Injuries Sustained due to Criminal Violence
1. State one by one each injury
2. Including mental health injuries – for each member of the family if relevant
3.
4.

Ongoing Injuries due to Criminal Violence
1. What are the current injuries requiring help?
List one by one

Criminal Injuries Compensation Reference Number
State your CICA reference number – especially if social services are trying to
assist in some way

National Insurance Number
BOY – 001 – 112 – 223 – 334 – 7

Last Employment Address and Salary
The CICA, amongst many others including solicitors, will require original
information about your duties and income and status. It will be useful to have
several copies of originally signed data to offer the CICA and solicitors and
others.

Last Two Employment References
References will be required by the CICA amongst others

Financial Status
Incapacity Benefit
Disability Benefit
Any savings – every agency will want this information including the CICA

Agencies Involved
1. Social Services – name, address, telephone number
2. Solicitors –
3. Bereavement Project –
4. Advocate –
5. Any charities –

General Practitioner
Name, address, telephone number

Physical Care – Hospital number
Name of Consultant(s) treating you, telephone, address.
Treatment being offered
Physiotherapy
Plastic surgery

Mental Care – Hospital number
Name of Consultant(s) treating you, telephone, address.
Treatment being offered

Medication
List each medication taken including dosage.

All contact to be made in writing via FLO, representative, solicitor or social worker.

© T.S. Duckett 2003 *Sample Social Services Needs List*

The importance of requesting a network conference

A conference may vary slightly in name, depending on where you live, but is essential for your recovery and protection. Like the recommended form to supply to all agencies, a network conference that an FLO or social services can arrange helps to make sure all the services understand what is going on and who is doing what; and by what date. Future meetings will not require so many agencies present as one agency should be the lead agency. A network conference puts your needs on a priority list and reduces unnecessary and depressing repetition of your needs. These conferences, when organised well, allow the reduction of unnecessary form-filling, duplication of services, maintain understanding and control where possible for the people in need and hold agencies to legal and service accountability by the people in need. It places the unmet needs of victims with gravity and dignity and it removes the dangers of victims being left to the dysfunctional lottery of the *victim club*. The meeting can take place in your home or an office, and, if too weak to speak, a list of what you want discussed should be made. An FLO or appointed representative can prepare your list for you.

The purpose of a gathering all crucial agencies together is straightforward:

- to review the current circumstances requiring attention; these loosely fall into four broad areas: the physical, the mental, the practical and the environment;
- for the service user and immediate family and or friends to say what they need;
- for agencies to come together and be clear with each other about what services they will be offering;
- so that the primary person(s) know exactly where they stand and what they can expect;
- that one agency is clearly identified as the link agency that will liaise and communicate in future with the person(s) affected between future case conferences or network conferences for smooth and seamless delivery of services;
- the main objective is always to reduce stress and bureaucracy and to speed up service delivery to aid rehabilitation and to maximise recovery.

Matters that require discussion

The four broad areas reflect any person's life.

Physical

Discuss and make arrangements about needs relating to any physical matter, such as transportation for physiotherapy, occupational equipment alterations to a person's home or progress in being rehoused.

Mental

Assessment of needs of each member or carers affected by unmet need, not just the individual directly affected by violent crime. Where services are not locally available then they should be contracted in as legally directed.

Practical

A conference should discuss and make arrangements for liaising with each other or contracting arrangements for successful help and rehabilitation. These social work tasks will hugely reduce lengthy and costly telephone and electricity bills, and reduce oceans of distress, knowing competent agencies are protecting and assisting recovery within the community without prejudice. It allows those in direct need to concentrate on the raw and slow process of grieving and recovery. The sole focus must be upon the individual's safety, emotional and physical rehabilitation, transformation and progress.

The conference has a legal duty to ensure and confirm every agency has up-to-date and accurate records of injuries, immediate needs and anticipated needs for good practice as a public service, explaining what they have done with public time, service and money, bring assurance to the person(s) affected and that appropriate professionalism has been taken to record the care, injuries, needs for personal progress and any future CICA application. It is important that your voice is heard or a trustworthy agency represents your wishes and needs.

Environment

It may become necessary to move if the home has been the location of the scene of serious violence or murder. It may be necessary to move temporarily, or permanently, if media intrusion cannot be abated or privacy for the family or individual is impossible. Matters about the environment relate to everything concerning the inside and outside of the home environment such as organising occupational therapy or alterations to a home if the victim has been newly or further disabled by violent crime.

Your needs have rights – the NHS and Community Care Act 1990

With regard to the assessment process, the legislation is clear about needs being brought to attention whether in the community or as an in-patient in hospital.

(1) Subject to subsections (5) and (6) below, where it appears to a local authority that any person for whom they may provide or arrange for the provisions of community care services may be in need of any such services, the authority –

(a) shall carry out an assessment for his needs of those services and;

(b) having regard to the results of that assessment, shall then decide whether his needs call for the provision by them of any such services.

(2) If at any time during the assessment of the needs of any person, under subsection (1)(a) above, it appears to a local authority that he is a disabled person, the authority –

(a) shall proceed to make such a decision as to the services he requires as is mentioned in section 4 of the Disabled Persons (Services, Consultation, and Representation) Act 1986 without his requesting them to do so under that section, and

(b) shall inform him that they will be doing so and of his rights under that Act.

(3) If at any time during the assessment of the needs of any person under subsection (1)(a) above, it appears to a local authority –

(a) that there may be a need for the provision to that person by such District Health Authority as may be determined in accordance with regulations of any services under the National Health Services Act 1977, or

(b) that there may be a need for the provision to him of any services which fall within the functions of a local housing authority (within the meaning of the Housing Act 1985) which is not the local authority carrying out the assessment, the local authority shall notify that District Health Authority or local housing authority and invite them to assist, to such an extent as is reasonable in the circumstances, in the making of the assessment; and, in making their decision as to the provision of the services needed for the person in question, the local authority shall take into account any services which are likely to be made available for him by that District Health Authority or local housing authority.

(4) The Secretary of State may give directions as to the manner in which an assessment under this section is to be carried out or the form it is to take, but, subject to any such directions and to subsection (7) below, it shall be carried out in such manner and take such form as the local authority consider appropriate.

s47 National Health Service and Community Care Act 1990

A footnote ...

At best, social services can provide part of a wall of compassionate statutory service that will provide effective urgent and long-term access to services. The sheer breadth of their responsibilities – from the elderly, children and abuse to mental illness – provides them with an opportunity to excel for people affected by violence. The sharpening and redefining of inspection of workers' standards gives hope that they will be seen as more professional, this will require social services to act effectively and soon, as they are rapidly being eclipsed by police services who seem willing to respond.

Useful reading

Violence in Society – The Reality Behind Violent Crime, *by Elie Godsi,* published by Constable, 1999. A helpful overview of social causes and consequences of violent crime.

Good Practice In Working With Victims of Violence, *eds Hazel Kemshall and Jackie Pritchard,* published by Jessica Kingsley, 2000. A lot of excellent sections covering a range of issues including children and abuse, homophobia and bullying.

The essential ingredient is a nightmarish sense of having lost one's identity, of bewildered helplessness against a vast, sinister, impersonal bureaucracy, which is intuitively felt to be evil, yet which appears to have a crazy kind of transcendent logic on its side.

Definition of 'Kafkaesque' from *Fontana Dictionary of Modern Thought*

Increasingly, people are forced to take extreme, extraordinary and costly measures to secure an ordinary level of service from public services. Whether it is about getting a service, accurate documentation or the conduct of workers, it seems we have to force institutions either to tell the truth or to simply do their job.

Look about your town, county and country. Look and see how demoralised and angry our society is and ask how has this come about. Look into the eyes of the people about you on the streets and the muted, anxious rage that is barely concealed. We work harder than our cousins on mainland Europe but have a poorer standard of health and quality of living; we are a wealthy nation yet make basic education and health a challenge to secure. Against this backdrop is a country served by under-resourced public services of drained, overworked, sometimes poorly trained staff – the police, fire brigade, social services, the NHS – all constantly bouncing from one government policy to the next. Many experienced and competent practitioners are leaving to work in completely different jobs with less stress and money, leaving a void of talent in some of these vital services. Against this reality, mistakes and problems are inevitable.

When trauma enters the lives of people, we tend to be exposed to contact with more services and agencies than at any previous time. While this may be wanted or needed, it causes extra strain if the services are not receptive: the last thing people want is further pressure. We know remarkable people and groups such as the family of Stephen Lawrence and families affected by the Marchioness disaster go to hell and back to get answers to basic questions and to call basic services to account. Beyond the fight for justice, the personal stamina and tenacity of such people, they are also examples of where the media worked responsibly with their power. The media maintained pressure on government and other agencies and sustained appropriate public awareness to help to make changes for the better in society. Most people are not afforded this.

People succeed because of a single-minded focus for justice and a refusal to be placed in the status of perpetual victim. It requires colossal stamina of those directly affected and exacts an enormous economic and personal toll.

This section is for use when all other avenues have been exhausted and it is impossible to do anything else but lodge a formal complaint, and it shows how to prepare a standard document for complaining.

What all public agencies have in common is a strong pattern of behaviour when wrong, in failing to make early and acceptable changes, promptly and explicitly apologising, and making financial recognition for the extra legal and administrative time involved in proving your original assertions. It seems to be an impossibility for British institutions to take overdue constructive criticism or make themselves truly open to public scrutiny and accountability.

The pen-pal club from hell

The need to complain generally arises when people are confronted with inexperienced workers who work within large institutions like social services or the NHS. It is a type of menacing organisational obstruction where complex and lengthy complaints processes put people off and deter them from complaining and this in turn encourages, among some workers, an arrogant attitude towards the people they are paid to serve. It is sadly ironic that large institutions that should have the service maturity to say 'we were wrong' or 'yes, this worker is bad and will be sacked' do not welcome constructive complaint. Instead of being open, expansive and efficient they generally contract and become rigid. Generally, large institutions create complaints procedures that by their design will not elicit fairness, justice or service provider accountability. They become a huge, cumbersome, heavily one-sided, costly administrative process of 'catch-us-if-you-can' – it would be interesting to see the cost of the bills for annual legal fees for such services, costs, which are met by the taxpayer. Complaints are a recurring problem with nearly all the services a person affected by violence may encounter and they need to be dealt with swiftly and effectively by wholly independent bodies. In the arena of justice and complaining the institutions are promoting secondary victimisation.

The burden will always be upon *you* to prove the service is at fault and to show in what way it has failed, for example, substandard provision, in some provable way.

For people affected by violence, formal complaints are especially stressful and institutionally prejudiced, placing an enormous amount of control with the institutions at every stage of the power process . It starts by making someone feel ashamed for complaining – 'look what we've done for you' – and leaves the victim at the end of the process feeling punished for daring to complain.

Before lodging a complaint

Wherever humanly possible, avoid this further degrading experience of complaining and direct your energy to the development of your health, future goals and happiness.

Take time to reflect that the injustice is within the lack of standards in the way a service is delivered – and not a personality clash. The latter is unfortunate but not ultimately relevant if the standard of service is receptive and good.

Take a few days to go over the communications (these should always be in writing) to ensure that what you have said is clearly stated, bearing in mind that what we think we have made clear may not have been understood clearly – rightly or wrongly. In these situations, write a letter like a shopping list, with the points you believe have not been addressed clearly, and start afresh.

Try and try, in writing with your advocate or supporter, to find an early and constructive resolution to the issue of contention – maybe via conciliation or through a third party.

This has to be considered before embarking on a process structured to drain and deplete an individual's money and resources and where the system controls the agenda and process throughout, when you have already paid an unimaginable toll.

If you have tried everything with the service and it has produced nothing of value within a reasonable period of time, then this example for structuring your complaint may be useful.

What you will need

As with everything about the tough road to surviving and rebuilding your life, it is beholden on you to be realistic and not deceive yourself about what effect the process might have on you. Equally, in the pursuit of fairness and justice, if you have a serious grievance you must complain.

It is going to require another large ring binder and administrative control, such as is described in the section on the CICA, pp. 271–280. Maintain order and do not leave unwanted papers lying around you; all must be kept in its proper place and order.

Any large complaint will need to be typed, with copies kept for future reference. If you have access to a computer keep a copy, of all written data on a back-up disc.

It will require oceans of energy, knowledge of the law, the patience of a Buddha, money for long and expensive administrative correspondence and, in extremely serious cases, representation. This is where referring back to the section on basic nutrition and exercise has further value, especially the breathing and relaxation routines – see pp. 114–141.

Please see the Directory for experts who may be able to help you either by representing you or by undertaking some of the burden on your behalf.

When a complex complaint takes off, it is often possible for it to consume your day and life; try to avoid this. Maintain nourishing patterns of eating, seeing friends and not losing interest in other avenues of equal importance such as your rehabilitation and developing a good balance of activities.

Be prepared for those you live with, or who are close to you, to find your 'obsession' too much to handle and often relationships can falter in these times – even though the pursuit for justice is right.

Ensure that you have fixed days to deal with the complaint and do not let this spill over into days when you should be going to visit people or going to have some pleasure. Like grieving and all aspects of rising beyond trauma and surviving, feeling guilt or shame about pleasure must be faced and quashed. Your performance in any meetings will be all the better if you have just experienced a fantastic day in the countryside, spent time with friends or have been relaxing in a sauna.

Maintain the best care you can about your health, stress-management, your home and those important in your life. Do not overload yourself.

If you attend any meetings, always be willing to let your representative do the talking, with pauses to go outside to raise issues you want. The temptation to 'explode' is natural if those you are complaining about are lying in front of you. Regardless of the veneer and universal soft-voiced protestations of 'we want you to know this has been a learning experience for us' – try not to find yourself in jail by thumping anybody! Get that breathing exercise right! Retain your stress control and dignity. Sometimes, silence conveys a lot.

If the experience seems like a war, it is a war to be played with steel-like contempt and precision and not with hot, written words – save these stronger feelings and emotions for your friends, your therapist or when alone in parks or on moorlands.

At any meetings, ensure you clothe your hurt and indignation by dressing smartly. While struggling against antagonists, it is good to see yourself dressed well and comfortably. Survive with style: it will make you feel stronger.

What makes this document useful
The format suggested is straightforward. It takes a person reading the complaint through: (a) the issues; (b) the characters involved; (c) the specific dates; (d) what you think should happen; and (e) what you want to see come out of the complaint. If necessary, you can provide examples describing substandard administration or bad practice in a report like this. It should be enough to give the name of the writer and date or description of what you have when supplying examples. This requires a little advice as some things in this procedure of giving your evidence may be turned against the strength of your complaint. The numbering allows any reply to be easily identified within the headings. Keeping sentences short helps you maintain order and precision about what you are specifying and simplifies giving exact information. This format is flexible and can be used for complaining against any institution or organisation.

A scenario for a complaint
Somewhere in England, a woman's life is disintegrating and services involved are not cooperating or working well for her or her carer. A life is at risk and legislation such as the National Health Service and Community Care Act 1990, the Mental Health Act 1983 and the General Medical Council Guidelines are not being used properly or efficiently. There are issues about safety, abuse, service obstruction, poor administration and unqualified worker involvement that all place the victim at greater risk, as well as potential medical negligence. This complaint will deal with: (a) two GPs; (b) the health authority who fund the GP practice; and (c) a Mental Health Service NHS Trust.

A young woman, 22 years old, who has recently been sexually assaulted, clearly desperate and barely capable of speaking, telephoned her aunt. The niece, let's call her Tracey Anne, has an irregular contact with her mother with whom she had a nomadic early life and who consistently failed her daughter. Although Tracey Anne is not known to her extended family and has barely any contact with the aunt, Mrs Drake, she makes plans to travel 200 miles to collect her niece the same night. When Mrs Drake arrives it is clear Tracey Anne is totally disintegrating mentally. Mrs Drake drives Tracey Anne back to her home in Mellowshire where over a period of days a serious, spontaneous flood of childhood secrets pours forth. Eventually, Tracey Anne returns to Chester and Mrs Drake commutes from her home to care for her.

This complaint is about two GPs with different but equally unprofessional responses to Tracey Anne's cry for help, the failure of the GP practice to refer promptly and the equally failing psychiatric service. It involves bad administrative and bad public worker communication. It is potentially placing a vulnerable woman's life at risk and the aunt cannot continue to care or commute 200 miles to try to care for Tracey Anne. An unfair and dangerous burden is being placed on Tracey Anne and her carer during which time her medical needs seem not to be understood or grasped by professionals. As a last resort, Mrs Drake has lodged a complaint but found difficulty with this process, as apparently nobody knew who the director of mental health services was. She was patronised, and issues of confidentiality were used as excuses for non-disclosure. While Mrs Drake was actively caring for and keeping a broken woman alive, these obstructions were putting a life at real risk. Tracey Anne does not want to cause trouble; breaking a secret has caused problems and everything is her fault – Tracey Anne is scared.

All reasonable avenues open to resolve the issue of complaint have not been successful. This complaint will not be taken to the General Medical Council, but, like real-life complaints, this has rapidly involved a cast of characters with very little tangible progress.

> *Tracey Anne Drake – person in need and patient*
> *Mrs Brenda Drake – distant aunt and complainant*
> *Dr Go-Away – first GP*
> *Dr Wet-Lettuce – second GP*
> *The Care Centre – an NHS mental health service*
> *Ms Drip Dry CPN – Community Psychiatric Nurse*
> *Dr Bendie-Knee – first Consultant Psychiatrist*
> *Dr Isolated – second Consultant Psychiatrist*
> *Rodney A. Rogers – Director of Mental Health Services*
> *The Police – Duty Officer*

Letter from Mrs Drake to Health Authority

Mr Alan Bee
Complaints Manager
Feather Found Health Authority
5th Floor, Downhill House
Downhill Way
Chester
CH2 7NY

7 Colindale Drive
Waxdale
Mellowshire
WX45 1AP
11 January 2004

Dear Mr Bee

Complaint: Substandard administration and medical provision; practice obstruction

Further to our telephone conversation, I now enclose specific details of my complaint written with the greatest reluctance and regret about both the Care Centre and the Wet Lettuce Surgery. I have allowed both agencies more than enough time to act professionally and it is a misuse of my time to have to push your colleagues to do their work properly without antagonism. My time would be better used caring for my niece as she is in immediate need.

The goal of this complaint is to see that Tracey Anne Drake receives the highest standards of care and provision immediately. This includes a full and independent review of the care offered, a revised care plan, which not only needs to be agreed with Tracey Anne and her advocate but must include a new and competent mental health worker. A care plan, as required and allowed by legislation, is necessary because of the obvious unmet needs. I hope individual workers are brought to account for their actions and assessed as to whether appropriate disciplinary action is justified as the public pays them to serve the public, whom they have failed.

Please find enclosed a list of specific issues giving rise to this complaint and copies of all correspondence. The priority is to ensure no further time is wasted and that Tracey Anne is swiftly placed into the best care provision and given effective treatment. Please ensure all correspondence, from all the agencies concerned, is copied to Tracey Anne. This week you will receive written consent from Tracey Anne Drake about my decision to lodge a formal complaint and agreement with my reasons for this action.

Yours sincerely

Mrs B.C. Drake
     cc. Tracey Anne Drake
         Rodney A. Rogers: Director of Mental Health
enc.
1.   **Statement including specific issues of complaint**
2.   **Tracey Anne Drake's life story** (Tracey Anne has only given consent for yourself to have a copy of this as it is our view that agencies already in receipt of this document failed to make appropriate responses to its contents and so it is as futile to have numerous copies dispersed when nothing constructive is done. Others requiring a copy should contact Tracey Anne directly)
3.   **Minutes of meeting with Dr Cold-Flannel on 10 November 2003**
4.   **Correspondence to Wet Lettuce Surgery and Care Centre** (Tracey Anne Drake will be forwarding directly to you her correspondence to copy and return, including replies from agencies to my correspondence)

Complaint: sub-standard administration and medical provision: obstruction

Background

On 31 October 2003, three males sexually assaulted Tracey Anne while she was sleeping in a room at a party; this is currently the subject of a police investigation. Subsequently, I brought Tracey Anne back to Waxdale and cared for her while simultaneously trying unsuccessfully to motivate Chester medical services to initiate services for her return home. While staying with me, Tracey Anne disclosed in great anguish a catalogue of sustained abuse (including sexual) and mental neglect throughout her early and adolescent life, which is documented in Tracey Anne's life story. Tracey Anne willingly gives consent for you to see this because it amplifies my concerns, which are Tracey Anne's concerns and unmet needs and the failure of services to provide the appropriate level of intervention. It should be noted Tracey Anne is still awaiting the outcome of initial laser treatment for live cancerous cells of the breast. Tracey Anne was already in mental breakdown at the time of the sexual assault and if not for my direct intervention and knowledge, this complaint could easily be of an even more grave nature.

Please read Tracey Anne's life story before reading further, for an appreciation of the gravity of her needs and why I am compelled to lodge a formal complaint.

The Wet Lettuce Surgery

1. Dr Go-Away failed, in the immediate days following the sexual assault, to offer Tracey Anne a good and professional standard of response.
2. Dr Go-Away's response to Tracey Anne was written on a slip of paper, for her to look in a Directory for help, his justification for this being that he was dealing with an emergency surgery. What is a 22-year-old woman reporting a violation of her body, who has an unknown prognosis for a life-threatening physical illness, if not an emergency?
3. Dr Go-Away's telephone call to me failed to address the detail of my questions and largely focused upon his excuses, namely: the time of Tracey Anne presenting in surgery in desperate need; Dr Go-Away's need for consent; not what services were being organised for Tracey Anne's return because 'Tracey Anne would have to present herself at surgery before commencement of intervention' – this calls into question Dr Go-Away's professional skills, she was at his surgery before and he failed to assess her as an emergency before his own eyes.
4. Dr Go-Away failed to understand Tracey Anne's unsuccessful presence at emergency surgery with him was his opportunity to commence intervention.
5. Within my letter of 2 November 2003, I included details regarding the importance of early diagnosis, symptoms, treatment for trauma and standard medications. These were evidently ignored.
6. Dr Go-Away, to date, has failed to provide a detailed written explanation in addressing the issues raised by me in writing on 2 November. This is substandard administrative procedure and medically counter-productive for me – the only adult actively supporting Tracey Anne.

7. Dr Go-Away's reply of 10 November 2003 was superficial and failed to provide the detail of answers that one would expect of a doctor being asked such important and specific questions. Thus, I do not accept or believe a full reply has been made.

8. Dr Go-Away never asked to speak with Tracey Anne who was present during this call.

9. This is an unacceptable and substandard response (by General Medical Council Guidelines) and is not best practice for initiating action, or common decency. My letter requested a written explanation – not a telephone call.

10. Dr Go-Away wasted important time, while I was physically caring for Tracey Anne, by failing to approach his funding authority and not securing the services that are patently and obviously required. My letter of 2 November made this clear and the early receipt of the life story made this imperative.

11. Dr Go-Away, to date, has failed to provide a written and unambiguous apology to Tracey Anne for a substandard response within the two deadlines Tracey Anne offered.

12. In November, Dr Go-Away offered to meet with Tracey Anne and this is rightly regarded not only as a further act of trivialising Tracey Anne's unmet needs and demands but also harassment. Tracey Anne is critically ill and vulnerable.

13. There is no acceptable reason for the failure of the Wet Lettuce Surgery to act practically, proactively, compassionately and professionally early in November.

14. Consistently, the Wet Lettuce Surgery has provided neither a sound level of medical intervention nor identified the seriousness of Tracey Anne's multiple needs and mental vulnerability.

15. No services were in place when Tracey Anne returned to Chester the following week.

16. I used every energy, experience and money in 'containing' a critically disturbed woman and crisis that far outweighs a family responsibility and response. This remains unreflected in what services have subsequently offered Tracey Anne. Tracey Anne is doing, and has done, everything she can to cooperate and remains in crisis and undervalued, echoing her life story.

17. Upon Tracey Anne's return, the Wet Lettuce Surgery was already in receipt of signed, posted or faxed original letters of consent; the life story or identification of needs to a level of detail few patients could offer professionals in order to initiate a comprehensive service response. Still, Tracey Anne was made to wait an unacceptable time before any assessment.

18. Dr Cold-Flannel told Tracey Anne that she would have to identify assessment and funding for dyslexia herself. This is unacceptable: if a need is identified, the agency is duty-bound in law to ensure provision for this service is secured for the patient, regardless of exceeding educational age.

19. Dr Cold-Flannel has an unfortunate pattern of nicely avoiding her professional responsibilities; assessment is crucial to secure an informed understanding as to whether Tracey Anne has dyslexia or not.

20. If Tracey Anne does have dyslexia it should be of medical concern as to what degree this difficulty in articulating herself has compounded her problems; Tracey Anne's known difficulty in understanding what is said to her – as it is said

and meant to her; the mixing-up of words and sentences verbally and in writing (which, sometimes, under pressure, makes Tracey Anne sound disjointed and odd) and obviously the quality of her future life and employment potential, Tracey Anne's birth father is known to have dyslexia. This is further medical neglect.

21. Dr Cold-Flannel failed, as assured at the meeting on 10 November, to inform Tracey Anne or myself of further enquiries into assessment for dyslexia.

22. At each crucial junction both Dr Go-Away and Dr Cold-Flannel evidenced repeated medical neglect and placed the added burden upon Tracey Anne or myself. For example, please refer to minutes of meeting with Dr Cold-Flannel, when she asked why I had not organised mental health services for Tracey Anne in Waxdale! (Because Tracey Anne lives in Chester and that is the responsible authority!)

23. Dr Cold-Flannel told Tracey Anne she has Post-Traumatic Stress Disorder but she has failed to ensure Tracey Anne receives a full package of care for her multiple needs, including appropriate medication and levels of therapy. A referral to Dr Isolated, Consultant Psychiatrist, was made very recently, I understand.

24. In the interim, Dr Cold-Flannel prescribed a 2mg dosage of Dothiepin, which is wholly ineffective and inappropriate for the condition Tracey Anne is suffering from. Ms Drip Dry, the community psychiatric nurse responsible for Tracey Anne, shared this criticism at her assessment at the Care Centre in November.

25. I asked to meet Dr Cold-Flannel with Tracey Anne, out of respect for the Wet Lettuce Surgery and to alleviate agency concerns, administrative retentiveness and repetition about 'consent games'. This took place on 10 November at the Wet Lettuce Surgery. (For a copy of Dr Cold-Flannel's late reply, which was defensive, meaningless and devoid of any sense of duty, kindly write to Tracey Anne who holds this letter on file.)

26. At this meeting, Dr Cold-Flannel wrote on her GP notes a consent note asking Tracey Anne to sign, which she did. This was a bizarre act, to say the least! All October/November correspondence was copied or addressed to Dr Cold-Flannel, pre-empting this meaningless and repetitive gesture.

27. Tracey Anne, in her letter (dated 2 November), offered consent for details of service progress to be willingly given to me, and on at least two subsequent surgery appointments asked whether further action was required regarding consent for acceptance. Dr Cold-Flannel repeatedly verbally stated she required no more confirmation yet this was still used as an (un)acceptable excuse.

28. At no time have I received a telephone or written update from either of the Doctors Go-Away or Cold-Flannel regarding Tracey Anne's health or any written answers to the 2 November questions or those raised at the 10 November meeting. (I am ignoring Dr Cold-Flannel's strange and redundant written reply, held by Tracey Anne, as the information contained therein is vague and already historical when written.)

29. I was kept in the dark while daily holding the situation as best I could for Tracey Anne without acknowledgement and assistance, even at a basic level, from any agency. This is not only poor practice but insulting and potentially dangerous.

30. On three separate occasions Dr Cold-Flannel asked Tracey Anne, alone in

surgery, if Tracey Anne still required a written apology from Dr Go-Away. As well as being subtle pressurising of a sick patient, this behaviour is prejudiced and tantamount to harassment. On each occasion, Tracey Anne gave the same answer – yes – she did demand an apology. It reflects her wish no longer to be used by men and the failure of a male doctor to treat her body as seriously as he would his own, which is reasonable.

31. At the meeting of 10 November, Dr Cold-Flannel denied harassing Tracey Anne or placing her under undue pressure to retract a full and reasonable apology. Neither Tracey Anne nor myself accepted Dr Cold-Flannel's answer as Tracey Anne's demand is unambiguous and reasonable. (See Tracey Anne's life story for demand for an apology and minutes of the meeting of 10 November.)

32. Dr Go-Away failed to meet a second deadline for an unambiguous apology by condescendingly offering a regressive, institutionally defensive and pressurising meeting, via the practice manager. This amounted to further professional harassment and pressurising, consisting of institutional arrogance, administrative game playing and medical bullying, of a totally broken and vulnerable young woman, and requires formal and disciplinary action.

33. I conclude that the GPs at the Wet Lettuce Surgery are ill-equipped intellectually, administratively and professionally to respond effectively to trauma, abuse, sexual assault, cancer anxieties, presenting mental breakdown, mature family independent support, pursuit of natural justice, proactive medical intervention let alone the General Medical Council codes of conduct and good practice, and common decency. This practice requires an independent and generic audit, via a quality review of service delivery, within its surgery.

34. It appears that the Wet Lettuce Surgery, in practice, do not, cannot or will not respond proactively to unmet needs and is disinclined to assist medically or identify ill patients. At minimum, this requires Tracey Anne to be fully and financially compensated for extended trauma due to medical and medical/institutional substandard practice and neglect.

The Care Centre

35. In early November, I telephoned the Care Centre to try to have Tracey Anne offered an early assessment upon her return and was told that the referral would have to be made by her GP. I contacted the GP surgery (refer to letters and previous complaint issues). It transpired weeks later, from Ms Drip Dry, Tracey Anne's community psychiatric nurse, that Tracey Anne could have referred herself after all. This is frankly appalling and a waste of important time when a sick person cannot be offered clear, consistent and accurate information from staff who work at the Centre. I believe the worker was the same worker whom I now complain about following a most uncooperative telephone communication on 14 November.

36. This worker withheld basic and simple information about public services, for example, the foregoing, and on 14 November refused to provide the name of Ms Drip Dry's Line Manager – until forcefully confronted. She works with vulnerable and mentally ill people who could do without antagonism and hostility. The public funded services demand more these days in competence from those who choose to work in this sphere.

37. I want the name and rank of this worker identified and to be informed of what disciplinary action is subsequently taken. Such a worker should be sacked.

38. Later, on 14 November, I tried to identify the worker by name and was told it could be one of six persons. This is not accepted because it is very easy to establish who answered the telephone around 2 p.m. on 14 November. If needs be, I will come to the Care Centre and easily identify the voice of the individual as that type of rudeness is memorable.

39. Although this is a public service, the worker refused to reveal her identity, but supplied the name of the Director of Mental Health Services, Rodney A. Rogers, but gave the wrong workplace location for him.

40. On 14 November, it took this workplace the best part of two hours to confirm Rodney A. Rogers existed. It is a source of further complaint and concern that Human Resources at Feather Found Health Authority (Downhill House) have no listing or knowledge of him, compounding the shoddy and unprofessional standards endemic in this authority.

41. Such an important postholder's work and details should be known by both the Health Authority and the service providers that he oversees.

42. On 14 November, I realised my niece was never going to get the quality of service she deserves and has needed for months unless I actively became involved again.

43. This is why I will pursue vigorously this complaint against the named individuals, the unnamed administrative worker and agencies regardless of whether the Care Centre finally answer my letter of 20 November. I should not have to chase up professionals, if they employ basic administrative practices, standard mental health skills and common courtesy.

44. Tracey Anne's multiple needs remain unmet and cynicism and substandard provision is simply not good enough and will not be tolerated.

45. Ms Drip Dry failed to respond at all, let alone in writing as requested on 2 November, to the pressing matters relating to Tracey Anne's health.

46. Ms Drip Dry failed to notify me, again as requested in writing on 2 November, of which specific pieces of legislation she was implementing with regard to Tracey Anne.

47. Ms Drip Dry failed to notify me, as requested in writing on 2 November, of why, further to assessment, extra therapeutic sessions and counselling were not pursued via the fund holding authority. Legislation states simply, if unmet needs are known, it is a duty to ensure the service user's needs are fully met.

48. Ms Drip Dry has failed in the above and offered my niece one session every two weeks. All natural justice, common sense, academic and practice texts regarding abuse and PTSD point to the need for intensive therapeutic intervention alongside appropriate medication. (I will supply some references if the Care Centre is at a loss as to how to treat trauma.)

49. Tracey Anne has repeatedly asked the Care Centre for more therapy to cope with the sexual assault, her life experiences and the implications of breast cancer treatments. Both Ms Drip Dry and Dr Bendie-Knee failed to respond effectively in recognising obvious need and ensuring suitable service provision. I expect this to be treated as a priority and to be rectified immediately.

50. Tracey Anne has expressed concerns about the effectiveness of her current medication, Seroxat 20mg, and is unclear as to what issues/needs Ms Drip Dry

or Dr Bendie-Knee are using this medication for.

51. Ms Drip Dry failed, as requested in writing on 2 November, to provide me with a copy of a care plan of action and treatment for Tracey Anne.

52. Dr Bendie-Knee failed to respond at all, let alone in writing as requested on 2 November, to the pressing matters relating to Tracey Anne's health. This letter was addressed to her as well as Ms Drip Dry.

53. Dr Bendie-Knee failed to notify me, again as requested in writing on the 2 November, of which specific pieces of legislation she was implementing with regard to Tracey Anne.

54. Dr Bendie-Knee failed to notify me, as requested in writing on 2 November, of why, further to assessment, extra therapeutic sessions and counselling were not pursued via the fund holding authority. Legislation states simply, if unmet needs are known it is a duty to ensure the service user's needs are fully met.

55. Dr Bendie-Knee failed in the above and my niece is unsure when she will next see the psychiatrist; we had hoped it would have been at least once a month. Academic and practice texts regarding abuse and PTSD point to the need for intensive therapeutic intervention alongside appropriate medication.

56. Dr Bendie-Knee failed to respond effectively in recognising obvious need and ensuring suitable services. I expect this to be treated as a priority, and immediately.

57. Dr Bendie Knee has failed, as requested in writing on 2 November, to provide me with a copy of a care plan of action and treatment for Tracey Anne.

58. Dr Bendie-Knee failed to notify me about Tracey Anne's concerns about current medication and whether the Care Centre has initiated dialogue with the cancer treatment service providers regarding Tracey Anne's panic attacks and needs around hospitals, needles, flashbacks (to childhood experiences) and obvious fears regarding any results. This is a very important matter for Tracey Anne's well-being (see life story).

59. To date, neither Dr Bendie-Knee nor Ms Drip Dry has offered Tracey Anne or myself a diagnosis and interim prognosis about her mental health to enable the family to plan and try to help.

60. The Care Centre has shown itself to be yet another remote and unaccountable institution, which is unable to respond within reasonable times to reasonable questions and reasonable service needs. It is wholly inadequate administratively, practically and professionally.

Observations, suggestions and preferences for action

The conduct of individuals that forms the wider complaint is so consistently poor and places vulnerable people at greater risk; they would never be employed within the private sector where they would undoubtedly be dismissed immediately for such unprofessional behaviour. The public will never receive high standards of health and social services while the institutions passively collude with substandard practice. The public sector appears to promote and protect such bad practice.

This matter has come about due to the horrendous experiences of a young woman leading to her reaching out for help for the first time in her life but the response was one of institutional trivialising, arrogance and general substandard practices.

It would be interesting as part of an audit to add the combined salaries of these people, paid by the public purse, and to compare that with the cost of the essential services needed plus the sum of money I have paid to assist Tracey Anne in the community – the public, rightly, is keen to see value for money. This complaint will have to be resolved quickly, comprehensively and to my satisfaction. If the health authority fails to meet the gravity of this complaint it will be vigorously pursued as a separate complaint until I am satisfied.

What I expect as a minimum from this complaint

1. A definite date when enquiry into this complaint and the subsequent report will be completed.
2. Tracey Anne is provided, as a matter of urgency, with effective and competent experts in abuse and trauma – not a community psychiatric nurse.
3. Tracey Anne is reassessed as a priority and extra funding provided so she is given higher standards of therapeutic intervention alongside a full review of current medications.
4. It is wrong that Tracey Anne's needs should be compromised by mediocre service providers to the detriment of her rehabilitation and an alternative service must be found.
5. Tracey Anne has yet to see any benefit from any service provider.
6. Tracey Anne is compensated for the ongoing institutional medical neglect and substandard practices.
7. An assessment for dyslexia is arranged without delay.
8. A new competent and professional GP practice with experience of abuse and trauma is secured for Tracey Anne without delay.
9. The Wet Lettuce Surgery, if not formally admonished, must be sent for training on abuse, mental illness and contemporary GP responsibilities to patients as well as dynamic decision-making. At this late stage, it is more appropriate for the health authority to request the General Medical Council to assess the conduct and performance of GPs.
10. To make available to the public the failure rates in not successfully treating mental illnesses and incidences resulting in suicides while known to agencies.
11. Greater provision and education of workers regarding rape, abuse and trauma.

Mrs Brenda C. Drake
cc: Tracey Anne Drake
Rodney A. Rogers: Director of Mental Health Services

Scenario postscript

Two days before a review meeting, in June 2004, to address the complaint, which the NHS Trust insisted Tracey Anne's mother attend, Tracey Anne ended her life. Tracey Anne left a note saying sorry for causing trouble and that she only wanted to be liked and had tried very hard to be a good person. The NHS trust requested permission to attend the funeral, saying this problem had offered a challenge and learning experience for it and hoped Tracey Anne's family would reconcile their feelings about Tracey Anne. The family replied, declining the request, stating that the family had not learned anything they did not know, nor needed to reconcile anything, and asked what specifically the trust had learned. Mrs Drake is seeking legal advice about culpability and medical negligence.

Useful reading

I'm at a Loss for Words, *by Cynthia MacGregor,* published by Adams. Basic ways of writing simple letters and treating awkward situations.

Writing a Report, *by John Bowden,* published by How To Books. Excellent; easy to follow.

Organising and Participating in Meetings, *by Judith Leigh,* published by OUP. Short, excellent book full of great guidance examples on court, services and being assertive.

Writing Skills – A Problem-solving Approach, *by Norman Coe, Robin Rycroft and Pauline Ernest,* published by Cambridge Press. Short; full of useful information.

101 Secrets of Highly Effective Speakers – Controlling Fear, Commanding Attention, *by Caryl Krannich PhD,* published by Impact Publications. Excellent tips and techniques especially for preparing for intense meetings like those relating to serious complaints.

Guide to Letter Writing, *ed. Kay Cullenby,* published by Chambers. Short book; great examples.

Everything You Need to Know – Letter Writing *by Harper-Collins.* Excellent guide; great examples.

How to Deal with Difficult People, *by Ursula Markham,* published by Thorsons. Excellent tips for being confident when facing difficult and unpleasant people.

DIMBLEBY BULL SAVED FROM RAVINE...

The plight of a stranded bull belonging to Jonathan Dimbleby, royal biographer and television presenter, prompted a tricky and costly rescue operation yesterday.

The young Hereford bull, worth at least £600, became trapped at the bottom of a 30ft ravine after straying from Dimbleby's farm. Nearly 18 hours later, the 900lb animal was winched to safety by a helicopter from a nearby naval base in a rescue operation involving 20 people which cost about £20,000.

Dimbleby, author of the authorised biography of the Prince of Wales, was unaware of the cost of the operation. He said he would make donations to the RSPCA, the local fire service and the naval base, all of which helped rescue the bull.

He added: 'I feel very guilty about involving all these people. But it is a very British thing to rescue an animal and I am very grateful'.

Daily Telegraph, 8 July 2000

Social security benefits are changing so constantly to make it redundant to list current rates, and types of welfare benefits available to which you might be entitled.

It is important to note that means-tested benefits you might receive will be deducted from the gross figure of your criminal injuries compensation (CICA) award. It seems that the state gives only the bare minimum – what it can get away with – rather than providing a realistic and protected (or ring-fenced) state income to those affected by violent crime. There is an assumption that the state provides compensation in the form of social security payments, but this is neither fully accurate nor guaranteed. More importantly, the CICA will take into its calculations any benefits that you have received since being injured, or affected by violent crime, and it will also make a calculated figure and assumption that future benefits will continue as part of calculating the final offer of an award. This is unjust and built on flawed assumptions, which saves the government money at victims' expense. This is not a guaranteed reality as people receiving benefits such as incapacity benefit regularly must reapply and may lose this benefit even though the CICA calculated the availability of benefits into your gross award.

It has been increasingly difficult to guarantee basic security with state benefits over recent years and expert advice about how to claim and what benefits to apply for is a good idea. If you wish to apply for benefits with/without help, it is worthwhile asking your local library to purchase a copy of the annually updated Child Poverty Action Group books about current rules for applying for all types of benefits and the amounts provided.

If you choose to seek help in completing lengthy forms, the Citizens Advice Bureau (CAB) has developed a well-earned reputation of expertise in helping people; you can also approach your local social services.

Because you will be required to provide proof of reasons for claiming benefits, it will save time and stress if you have plenty of copies of medical reports and keep copies of sickness certificates. It is important to keep copies of any sickness certificates because it has been known for social security departments to lose applications and documents. Having spare copies of medical reports will reduce excuses from others and enable them to make early decisions.

Your local library and local CAB will provide an early pointer about what you might need to apply for. Note that the latter is often heavily booked up in advance. The suggested reading is aimed at those experiencing financial hardship and looking to organise subsequent compensation.

Useful reading

Money For Life – Everyone's Guide To Financial Freedom, *by Alvin Hall*, published by Hodder & Stoughton. Excellent guidance about coping with whatever sums of money are available.

Your Money or Your Life, *by Alvin Hall,* published by Hodder & Stoughton. Excellent guidance to coping with whatever sums of money are available.

Child Poverty Action Group Welfare Benefits Handbook, Vols 1 and 2 updated each year. An essential guide and break-down of all current benefits, and entitlement rules published by the Group. These are expensive and available from libraries or via social services.

We too, had known golden hours
When body and soul were in tune,
Had danced with our true loves
By the light of a full moon,
And sat with the wise and good
As tongues grew witty and gay
Over some noble dish
Out of Escoffier;
Had felt the intrusive glory
Which tears reserve apart.
And would in the old grand manner
Have sung from a resonant heart.

But, pawed-at and gossiped-over
By the promiscuous crowd,
Concocted by editors
Into spells to befuddle the crowd,
All the words like Peace and Love,
All sane affirmative speech,
Had been soiled, profaned, debased
To a horrid mechanical screech.

No civil style survived
That pandemonium
But the wry, sotto-voce,
Ironic and monochrome:
And where should we find shelter
For joy or mere content
When little was left standing
But the suburb of dissent?

W.H. Auden: *We Too, Had Known Golden Hours*

General practitioners (GPs) have a crucial role in helping everyone remain well in their communities and, like every other public sector service, GPs have been hindered by endless government policy changes. Consequently, it is then difficult to attract new doctors to train as GPs, which is to the detriment of all. Alongside these government changes, GPs have lost a lot of public trust and respect due to finding it difficult to get early referrals to hospitals when people need care. This was especially the case when GPs held budgetary control and the failure of the governing body for doctors, the General Medical Council (GMC) readily to address 'seriously deficient performance' or simply bad GPs. The GMC's powers are contained in the Medical (Professional Performance) Act 1995. The GMC's status and accessibility for the public have substantially diminished over the last decades. The Dr Shipman case has added to public concern about the powers of doctors and their accountability alongside deplorable practices at some English hospitals. In turn, doctors and patients are left mutually anxious about what is safe and what to expect from one another. It is becoming very hard to secure a competent GP and in some districts they often appear to dislike people who are unwell and do not get well quickly. A medical cynicism has crept into the GP service.

GPs are today struggling to deliver a good service in a society which lives longer and which has growing health needs; these doctors find their surgeries oversubscribed, especially where they enjoy a good reputation. GPs have the power to refuse to treat a patient if they choose to and this was a source of concern especially when they had budgetary powers – now the responsibility of the new Primary Care Trusts. (See flowchart and explanation in section on Primary Care Trusts in the new NHS in the Hospital section, pp. 4–21.)

Hospital reports and lists

If all reports are accurately and efficiently completed by a hospital consultant and forwarded to your GP, a great deal of anxiety about seeing a GP will be alleviated. Some people are intimidated at the prospect of having to 'prove' why they need help; some less-skilled GPs will actually add to this feeling of vulnerability. If reports have not been forwarded, your GP must follow this up. The GP has to go by the judgement of consultant hospital doctors – the importance of accuracy of hospital reports is considered in the Hospital section, pp. 4–21.

When you visit your GP, it is a good idea to make a list of the issues you need to talk about because some people can find GPs intimidating and feel they must 'please' their GP and not talk about the reasons that brought them to the surgery. When people feel overwhelmed or nervous they can be inclined to forget important issues and lists make sure they are not forgotten. If it helps, hand the list to your GP when you visit. It is a bit of a lottery as to how much any given GP might know about trauma and other mental illnesses, especially in relation to violent crime. If you believe your GP is not providing the guidance that you consider reasonable, calmly repeat what it is you are concerned about. If the problem continues then complaining may become necessary (see pp. 173–187 on this matter). It is your body and life and it is their job to make coherent diagnoses about need – which they cannot do if they do not know the condition adequately.

Being confident

If your GP is to help you effectively, then expressing yourself confidently is important. Sometimes, we think we are being clear when in fact we are not because either we may be finding the issue difficult, or we might be assuming, wrongly, that the GP knows something about our circumstances. Being confident and learning to feel good about saying what you need is in everyone's interests. If you have been seriously affected by violence it is reasonable to seek the help of social services to make sure that the GP visits you at home or has been accurately told about your circumstances in advance of any meeting.

Doctors' standards

All doctors and GPs are governed not only by rules laid out by the GMC but also by laws which we are all bound by, and some date back to the aftermath of the atrocities committed by doctors during the Second World War. Ethics are standards of what is morally acceptable and best for patients. Medical ethics in the post-war English version of the International Code state:

- A doctor must always maintain the highest standards of professional conduct.
- A doctor must practise his profession uninfluenced by motives of profit.

The following practices are deemed unethical:

1. Any self-advertisement except such as is expressly authorised by the national code of medical ethics.
2. Collaboration in any form of medical service in which the doctor does not have professional independence.
3. Receiving any money in connection with services rendered to a patient other than a proper professional fee, even with the knowledge of the patient.

Any act or advice which could weaken physical or mental resistance of a human being may be used only in his interest. A doctor is advised to use great caution in divulging discoveries or new techniques or treatment. A doctor should certify or testify only to that which he has personally verified.

The International Code refers to the duties owed by doctors to the sick:

- A doctor must always bear in mind the obligation of preserving human life.
- A doctor owes to his patient complete loyalty and all the resources of his science. Whenever an examination or treatment is beyond his capacity he should summon another doctor who has the necessary ability.
- A doctor shall preserve absolute secrecy on all he knows about his patient because of the confidence entrusted in him.

• A doctor must give emergency care as a humanitarian duty unless he is assured that others are willing and able to give such care.

Bernard Knight: From *Legal Aspects of Medical Practice*

What you can reasonably expect

It is reasonable to expect a good medical service and for the GP to be aware of all your needs and that the GP be prepared to refer you to specialist services (e.g. physiotherapy or psychotherapy). As with any public service, you should reasonably expect to be treated civilly by a GP, or be referred to a specialist service.

Below is an extract from the GMC codes of practice about standards of service.

Patients must be able to trust doctors with their lives and well-being. To justify that trust, we as a profession have a duty to maintain a good standard of practice and care and to show respect for human life. In particular as a doctor you must:

• make the care of your patient your first concern;
• treat every patient politely and considerately;
• respect patients' dignity and privacy;
• listen to patients and respect their views;
• give patients information in a way they can understand;
• respect the rights of patients to be fully involved in decisions about their care;
• keep your professional knowledge and skills up to date;
• recognise the limits of your professional competence;
• be honest and trustworthy;
• respect and protect confidential information;
• make sure that your personal beliefs do not prejudice your patients' care;
• act quickly to protect patients from risk if you have good reason to believe that you or a colleague may not be fit to practise;
• avoid abusing your position as a doctor; and
• work with colleagues in the ways that best serve patients' interests.

GMC Guidelines 2002

The GMC's duty

The GMC has a statutory duty to investigate breaches of malpractice and has a specific committee to monitor breaches of its standards. This is the same standards committee that also must adhere to international guidelines and codes of medical conduct and ethics. The new GMC guidelines following the Dr Shipman atrocities, in theory, suggest a greater willingness to take an earlier active role – after running the gauntlet of the local NHS complaints process.

The GMC accepts referrals about poor GP practice when:

- local action would not be practical;
- you have tried local action and it has failed;
- the problem is so serious that we clearly need to be involved; or
- the doctor has been convicted of a criminal offence.

A key question will be: 'Is there enough evidence of poor practice, direct from reliable sources, to show that there is a case to answer?'.

You do not have to refer performance or health issues to us immediately unless:

- patients are at risk of harm; and
- the doctor is not willing or able to put things right immediately.

GMC Guidelines 2002

If the service is bad

If you have tried to secure a good service and have repeatedly and politely asked the GP for help or reasons as to why help cannot be offered, it is reasonable to ask, in writing, for the practice surgery manager to look into your complaint. If you remain dissatisfied, a further written complaint must be addressed to your Primary Care Trust (see flowchart on new NHS and section on writing a complaint, pp. 4–21; pp. 173–187). All avenues must be explored before writing a formal complaint, because the process is, in reality, geared to put you off from complaining and to wear you out. The complaint process will not assist your recovery and normally takes over one year. Try to find a way forward that does not diminish your health without losing your right to a good health service.

GPs and people affected by violent crime

GPs have a particularly important role in assisting the successful rehabilitation of people affected by violent crime. They have a great deal of power in making sure documentation is channelled to appropriate agencies such as social security and the CICA – they are also bound by codes of confidentiality – the doctor–patient relationship is one of absolute trust. A good GP will be liaising well with other health and social cares services and providing the connections like a bridge to those agencies that are relevant to your recovery. For the needs of people affected by violent crime, it would be productive for GPs to start collecting records on specific crimes and the health needs of victims in the community. This would be a good service to make the needs of victims statutorily valid and make those affected visible as a health service category. By definition, it's a GP's role to have general medical knowledge; they are not experts in all branches of medicine. However, the GP surgery will be the first port of call for many and a good

GP will be prompt to refer you to appropriate experts. Whatever your health needs, hospital reports will play a large role in the decisions that a GP makes about further care when you are at home. Because GPs are your main connecting bridge, they hold the power to transform your status from victim to survivor. These days, a good GP is like gold dust and it is worth nurturing the relationship.

Useful information

General Medical Council
178 Great Portland Street
London
W1N 6JE
General enquiries: 020 7915 3603
Website: www.gmc-uk.org

Free copies of *Good Medical Practice* and other similar booklets are available from:

GMC Fitness to Practise Directorate
178 Great Portland Street
London
W1W 5JE
Helpline: 020 7915 3692
Enquiries about sick doctors: 020 7915 3580
Fax: 020 7915 3642

Useful reading

The British Medical Association New Guide to Medication and Drugs, *by the British Medical Association,* published by Dorling Kindersley. Excellent guide, used by medical practitioners, covers all types of medicines; common-sense descriptions of medicines and their effects. Inexpensive.

It is always true that love and will become more difficult in a transitional age, and ours is an era of radical transition. The old myths and symbols by which we oriented ourselves are gone, anxiety is rampant; we cling to each other and try to persuade ourselves that what we feel is love … the individual is forced to turn inward; he becomes obsessed with the new form of the problem of identity …

Even if-I-know-who-I-am, I-have-no-significance. I am unable to influence others. The next step is apathy. And the step following that is violence. For no human-being can stand the perpetually numbing experience of his own powerlessness …

When inward life dries up, when feeling decreases and apathy increases, when one cannot affect or even genuinely touch another person, violence flares up as a daimonic necessity for contact, a mad drive forcing touch in the most direct way possible. This is one aspect of the well-known relationship between sexual feelings and crimes of violence.
To inflict pain at least proves one can affect somebody.

Rollo May: From *Love and Will*

It takes a great deal of time and help to learn to trust the world again; even then, life can never go back to what it once was. During the time that you are seriously ill, physically or mentally, the type of people that you have around you will influence how well you can survive, and progress your life beyond that.

It may be there are existing relationships that are unhealthy and need to end – and the horrific event has speeded up the need to find a constructive way to end the relationship and move on. If the relationship is one that causes violence, then a decision must be made. Do you continue to exist in a violent and life-threatening relationship that may be placing young people at added risk? Or, do you cease to make excuses, seize control and help – and move to a better life? Working out what relationships are healthy is part of working out how well you want to survive and progress. Like everything else in this handbook, it is not easy.

When horror strikes, the most stable of relationships are thrown upside down and all people connected with the person affected are affected in their own way. For example, they may not have been the actual victim, but they feel helpless for not protecting; or they may experience fear or anger; may find adjusting to the changes in mobility or temperament as challenging as the person directly affected. Sadly, it is a fact that survivors of violence do experience a lot of relationship turmoil, such as divorces and extreme changes in behaviour, that makes sustaining old and new relationships especially hard. Relocate the goodness in you and steady yourself – relocate the standards you need in others and ensure that they are steady people.

We all need and deserve stable and nourishing relationships – some professional, some social and some sexual – all help us become satisfied and feel whole. When violence crashes into our lives, the sense of being able to trust and be intimate with others can disintegrate – it can become a daily struggle to want to deal with family or friends. This is especially the case in the immediate aftermath of horror and its effect upon you and those about you. If you are going to survive and progress your life you are going to have to face your agonised rage and helplessness, grieve deeply, protect yourself and find people who have warmth and integrity.

The people in your life must understand that if you are the direct victim of violence it takes time to cope and adjust before beginning to improve. So, one issue people around you can do to help is not to place pressure upon you to 'be your old self' and expect to you be the person you once were. It may be some people you once played rugby with or went clubbing with find it too uncomfortable to see you in any way other than 'the way you were'. You should explain quietly that something major has happened and if they cannot cope and feel too uncomfortable and do not want to visit you at home or take you for a drive, then maybe it is best that they don't contact you any more. If you start to get into the pattern of pretending or self-mocking in order to keep such people in your life, you will suffer, as you are not squaring up to what has happened, to what you are and to what you need. Equally, the intense mood swings that people can have after a violent trauma means that they may not always be the easiest company to be around at times. Professional help and genuine intimate friends and one's own heart will guide one to the right perspective.

Professionals – a wall of safety

To start making sense and getting back control, it is important to make sure you have a wall of competent professionals who communicate with each other and protect you from unnecessary pressures. They can lead the way to finding voluntary groups that may be able to provide different types of assistance. Together, these agencies create a positive wall of protection while allowing you to face the emotional and raw needs of adjusting to life after horror.

Dealing with people

(See chart of symptoms listed in section on PTSD, p. 104–113; if any of these affect you or young people about you, then how you cope, when you socialise with people, and so on, will be determined by how much pressure you can handle.) This is the way it is for people affected by violence: what was taken in one's stride (e.g. a wedding, entertaining friends or walking down a street) now may be a source of dread. Do not place yourself in situations that you know will cause you too much stress – build your confidence slowly. If you are to deal well with people, you must first learn to adjust and deal with yourself and be honest about what you can manage in social contact and be honest with them. It may be helpful to refer to the list outlined in the section on planning your week: see section on Hospital, pp. 4–21. The issues remain the same outside of hospital because it is about not taking yourself to the edge of what you can handle in any situation. It is about making sure you have sufficient good-quality social company and good-quality quiet and control over your time and the quality of activity that takes it up. This extends to young people and all those around you.

A few tips ...

- Treat young people seriously and with the respect offered to good adults. Young people especially need patience and help to say what and how they feel and they need good friends and fun.
- Learning to choose good-quality friends takes practice and time. Do not be angry if you find one or two people who have manipulated and hurt you. If all the people you are encountering are destructive and manipulative, then you are part of something that is not helping you progress and seek help.
- It takes time to feel safe again with people, so do not overload yourself with too many activities or people too soon. Take control, take care and take time to rest.
- When we start to get especially fond of someone new, it can overstimulate our minds and we can sometimes throw caution to the wind and move everything a hundred miles too far and too soon, or run away. Practise the other sections that are all part of one another. Good patience and tenderness with yourself and others, good food and exercise, good help and good professionals all play their part in learning to make sense of your return to your inner world of feelings, and the outer world of new safety – and dangers.
- Do not drown yourself in the company of miserable, long-term destructive relationships or groups. Nothing nourishing comes from the permanent status of victim; instead, only muted anxious rage and futility. If you want more from your life and for those around you, drop negative people from your life.
- Do not drown yourself in the company of alcohol and other drugs. If you need help to feel calmer, use a doctor and non-addictive drugs. When we misuse drugs, we are trying to numb our raw emotions – like putting anaesthesia on them – but it will not work. In the hell of transformation, feeling and dealing with raw emotions requires clear-headedness and suffering. Any spare money is better used towards holidays.
- Do not become isolated in any way; misuse of drugs or alcohol make people

become isolated from feelings. Join two groups – one for nothing other than fun and one that may teach you new skills or a language, exercise or how to paint. Do not become isolated or full of self-loathing for wanting to progress and live well after horror. Pleasure is very important: seek out yours.

- Do not take on the role of everyone else's problem-solver when you have not sorted your own. It is a common mistake and only attracts rather unpleasant people whom you will allow to drain you – possibly of everything.
- Avoid extremes of spending money you do not have or not eating enough, or too much. Avoid people who are like this. Seek out ordinary, stable people.
- If you have a relationship, it will be necessary to make time, e.g. to go away for weekends to discuss what each person needs for a few months to come. Try to accept the horror that has crashed into your world and that at best you are going to learn to live with, and within and around 'it' to the best of your abilities. It is not easy so going away maybe once a season with the pre-agreed 'deal' that you will spend one day of the weekend talking and listening about the three main issues you each feel are really 'bugging' you does work. It works because it is breaking the silence; going away somewhere inexpensive, being emotionally intimate allows better hope for surviving and progressing life.
- Be aware of the extreme emotions like anger within yourself and what it does to others. Is it reasonable or is it becoming a pattern of extreme overreaction that is blocking ways of your saying what is most important, or blocking closeness from others? Try to be aware of seeing matters from as many sides as possible; it allows you confidence, control and the potential for good people to enter your life.
- This applies to young people too; physical activities are especially good and police-checked activity groups that allow young people to 'let rip' and be seen as ordinary young people. This can transform their sense of being left behind, worried about upsetting parents.
- Bring into your social world people who have successfully progressed their lives beyond being a victim and people unaffected by violent crime. They provide social and emotional difference, but people affected by murder often say they do not wish to be surrounded by too many people in their position.
- In the early months after horror has taken place it may be you can never find any privacy and then one day no one telephones or visits. These are raw, volatile days and months and this is where controlling who is coming to and fro in your world needs care. Later on, it may be you decide some relationships no longer have nourishing value or have the two-way respect you require and they may be family or social relationships. In such times, clearly and constructively terminate the relationship without fuss.
- Bring people into your life who offer respect, stability, stimulation and real hope.
- People are essential to living, and progressing your life, but they need to be people who bring nourishment, pleasure and stability. People are good to have in your life and it is for you to be patient with yourself and others as you all learn to adjust to finding the best way of progressing and coping. This starts with good professionals and your ability to have control of your time and social world. People are essential in our lives for social and sexual intimacy, work, guidance, affirmation and fun and to secure these well takes courage, tough decisions and time. The prize is a world that becomes nourishing and safer for you.

> The knowledgeable man in the genuine public is able to turn his personal troubles into social issues, to see their relevance for his community, and his community's relevance for them.

E. Freidson: *Professional Dominance*

It is important to be clear and understand that nearly all voluntary charities and groups deal daily with people affected by violent crime – they may just not place the word 'victim' in their title. What sets these organisations apart is they choose to provide help, and specialise in responding to specific groups of people. Generally, they have arisen out of society's neglect through lack of protection in law and lack of equality in access to services and they often have not feared politicising what they do. At the end of this handbook, you will come across listings for organisations in various specialist issues. It is important to distinguish their history, work and fine standards from the small cluster of less effective groups we might refer to as the *victim club*. These have a wholly different calibre of stability and effectiveness, and are discussed elsewhere within this work.

Advocacy organisations and groups will always have a crucial role in directly supporting people with their given skills and within their limitations. They can be powerful and effective: they see that public awareness is kept alert, so governments are prompted towards providing better resources and making changes where necessary. Over time, such organisations develop high levels of knowledge about law and specific needs. They have replaced a lot of the actual work that was once the domain of the social services but without the training in some areas or resources to extend the areas of expertise that exist. Such advocacy groups save lives every day and we must hope they succeed in securing greater training and staffing, as well as having a role in the planning and discussions with government. A lot of expectations are placed on such organisations, by governments, to fill the gap made by decades of cutbacks in service provision. What organisations do not have are the resources and legislation to meet the growing needs of people.

The voluntary sector has always produced charismatic and powerful champions of public concern about our environment, disability, domestic violence, women's safety and dignity, gay rights and sanctuary for children, to name a few. It is thanks to these elements of the voluntary sector that hidden social issues are given a strong voice and public prominence.

Sometimes, within the voluntary sector, organisations do not have the skills or resources to make the changes people need. Increasingly, organisations are dealing with the social service gap, showing a willing awareness to train and select volunteers and have police checks on potential volunteers – especially groups working with vulnerable people. It is always better to ask for statutory services to coordinate any group of services you may need or choose, as a combination of agencies will offer you the greatest chance for healing and progress in living after tragedy. Please see listings in the Directory section.

'I believe in a real master race. I believe in a race and country first, the white as the Master race and Aryan domination of the world.' He described gay men as 'degenerate and perverted' people who served no purpose in the world and, therefore, should be killed. Although he felt 'sick' when he heard that the pregnant Mrs Dykes had been killed in the Admiral Duncan blast, he said he felt no remorse for what he had done, he felt nothing about it at all.'

The bombings were his destiny and he was aiming to do one a week ... planned to follow-up the Soho bomb with one next week in Southall, a district of west London with a large Asian population... even toyed with the idea of bombing the Notting Hill Carnival ... He would have bombed Jews, 'the devil's disciples and people from the mud' – if he had an opportunity.

Copeland's defence team maintained until the end their client was mentally unbalanced and suffering from paranoid schizophrenia, he himself made a mockery of this by writing to an undercover journalist saying he wasn't mentally ill. It was a good defence line though!

Extracts from articles on the trial of David Copeland, sentenced to six life sentences for the 1999 London bombing campaign that left three people murdered and more than a hundred injured.

© Vicky Powell: *Gay News,* July and August 2000

To be on the receiving end of someone's hate or that of a group is terrifying and can even be life-threatening. How people deal with this varies but, at some stage, a statutory agency will need to intervene. Hate is the intense and irrational dislike of an individual or a group. Irrational in that it does not add up to reasoned and mature thinking or discussion. When this feeling becomes visible and acted upon, especially during times of social and economic extreme hardship, it can lead to widespread acts of violent prejudice. The targets are invariably people who do not have access to the same level of acceptance and laws to protect them as the majority. This makes them vulnerable and politically isolated communities. These people become easy targets for violent people to blame anything and everything 'on', sometimes physically, by venting their own inadequacies upon more vulnerable groups, e.g. minority groups. Invariably, people who 'hate' are very inadequate and contribute nothing of value to the very culture and society on whose behalf they claim to 'act'.

Increasingly, reports of horrific acts of hate are coming to the attention of the public through the media and are reported to the police. For example, the terror campaign of David Copeland, the pernicious attack by Asian youths in Oldham in 2001 against a frail elderly white man because he was on a gang's 'patch', or widescale hate against women (misogyny), hate against gay people (homophobia), hate against Jews (anti-Semitism), the hate against people of differing race or ethnicity by members of a majority (racism). This is fear, plus violent rage, plus 'projected' expression – 'projected' is not for any tangible fact or reason other than a fear and hate of difference – xenophobia. Invariably, hate shows itself in ways that the violent criminals 'believe' they have some wider sense of national support or sanction. Hate, then, seems to such groups to have implicit, passive support from the wider society through power plus 'projected' prejudice, whatever the target-hated group. Felt or acted upon, it is menacing, violent and causes untold terror for those victimised by it. For innocent citizens on the receiving end, it can be life-threatening; psychological violence, too, can be very serious as it plays a large role.

Hate – power plus 'projected' prejudice – is an unrefined, ignorant, base animal instinct; it is territorial. It is a tribal reaction of fear of inadequacy and sense of being overwhelmed by the 'other'. In civilised personalities, people are able to balance the irrational dislike against the wider intellectual and emotional knowledge that there exists in any group good and bad. It is healthier to survive and feel good living well alongside with respect for difference. We see hate all around and in every era: in Zimbabwe, where attacking white Zimbabweans was sanctioned by the government; Hitler's alienation of Jews in the 1930s; Idi Amin's 1970s expulsion of Asians from Uganda; and the centuries of using African people as sub-humans – slaves – in the pursuit of early capitalism. Often, hate has some level of state complicity.

Hate has an origin. Violent acts of projected, enraged, irrational prejudice that appear 'justified' originate from ignorant fear. Invariably, sections of a society that act on projected prejudice have a real sense of being disadvantaged, socially and economically deprived and have no cultivated manner in which to articulate their fears and needs. Nor do they feel inclined to take responsibility for what they have made of their lives and environment. The means to act from animal 'projected' hate is within us all – fortunately most people are emotionally and intellectually more agile and mature and do not act so. The main difference is that most people are able to see what it is their personal responsibility to accept or change – as opposed to 'project' blame or dislike.

> It seems to me that maturity is characterised by assertion and affirmation of the personality without hostility and without competitiveness, both of which characteristics are typical of childhood. The more a man has succeeded in realising his own personality, the less compulsion will he feel to be competitive and the less hostile will he be to others.

> Men are very differently endowed; and the maturity of the man with an IQ of 80 will be very different from the man with an IQ of 140; but, provided each can make full use of his differing endowments, there is no reason why each should not be equally at peace with himself and with his neighbour.

> Common experience bears witness to the fact that it is people who have least succeeded in realising their own potentialities who are most hostile ...

Anthony Storr: From *The Integrity of the Personality*

History – identity

All nations prefer to look at what is best about themselves. It is natural and good to put your best foot forward and to take pride in what is noble and fine about your nation and its culture. But a problem arises here, which is especially appropriate for our nation. The problem is our inability to have adjusted to social history as other European nations have adjusted: we no longer have or are an empire.

Some of us do not find it easy to look at our victimising history of social and economic inequalities, past or present, and some need to cling to a past – with a few distortions along the way. We are a nation which, up until the

Second World War, set forth and dominated other nations. Since the late 1940s, however, we have had to stay put with ourselves. It seems from the behaviour of sections of society that we are not happy living with who we really are or accepting that the world is a smaller place with many people living in countries not of their birth. It seems we are not sure what of who we are any more – if we ever really were.

We are animal and sometimes need to use real power with responsibility. If irrational fear of women and the crimes that that can lead to were robustly confronted, it would quickly diminish. For example, if men who are violently scared of women or routinely violate women in the home knew that such violent acts would be judged by a predominantly female jury and judge, it is very likely that such acts of hate crime would significantly disappear – why? Similarly, this can be applied to race hate and gay hate violence. At some level, the violent attackers sense that a degree of compliance exists within the legal system. So, part of the positive way forward is to see the enactment of laws that are rigorously used when hate translates into crime. It gives social and legal power back to the marginalised groups and becomes a dynamic deterrent to the aggressors. It requires the active will of government and integrity of our citizens to help to make this happen. It can be done.

Slowly, government is turning to face what hate does and is moving towards modern legislation that will bring us into line with other European, Canadian and American hate laws.

> Offences motivated by bias, prejudice or hate. An accused who commits offences of mischief to property which are motivated by racial or religious hatred cannot be sentenced for his beliefs. Those beliefs are, however, relevant in so far as they explain his actions and an offence which is directed against a particular racial or religious group is more heinous, as it attacks the very fabric of society and invites imitation and incites retaliation. Moreover, where the offence involves desecration of a place of worship, it is even more serious, especially where it is done to cause emotional upset and injury to the members of the congregation. Such offences require a more severe penalty than mischief, which is done merely to damage property.

> An assault which is racially motivated renders the offence more heinous and the sentence to be imposed in such a case must be one which expresses the public abhorrence for such conduct and their refusal to countenance it. In this case reformatory sentences for an unprovoked racially motivated assault which caused serious injury to the victim were raised to penitentiary terms. Similarly, where sentences for assault were substantially increased to take

into account that the assaults were racially inspired by the accused who were adherents to or sympathisers with neo-Nazi organisations.

Legal Response To Hate Crimes
Martin's Criminal Code, 1998, courtesy of Alberta Justice Department, Canada

Tips for challenging hate

• Minorities must avoid acquiring the abusive mannerisms and behaviour of the hate abusers.

• Minorities must resist the temptation to resign themselves to becoming passive long-term victims where there is no real personal or social achievement.

• The above requires being articulate, self-caring and accepting diversity of attitudes and types of people; to understand difference as part of life's wonderment, and not something to be frightened about.

• People who are comfortable with themselves are not angry or fearful of people different from themselves.

• Minority groups, through long experience, know that until political will exists for change, governments offer passive collusion with hate crimes – regardless of 'political speeches', e.g. the 'race card' is always a good emotive distracter from other national issues. The government's recent misuse through the media about issues regarding immigration by playing on the animal fear of territory about asylum seekers and immigrants was disgraceful and even reminiscent of Hitler's anti-Semitic rhetoric. Minorities must take responsibility and ensure they become actively involved in local and national politics and especially vote at all elections.

• Not to vote is to act without responsibility. Governments respond to the will of the media that in turn is influenced by the nation.

• Hate crimes – like any crimes – should be reported promptly to the police.

• If you are a victim of hate, start to collect evidence on camera, dated and in writing.

• Local authorities must show themselves to act decisively when presented with victims of hate crimes.

• The Anti-Social Behaviour Orders (Powers for Local Authorities) Act 1998 has not been used well to date. It places responsibility with families and individuals.

• Known hate criminals must be seen to be unacceptable and evicted, where possible, or imprisoned. Not acting decisively is allowing institutional homophobia, misogyny or racism, as the case may be, to flourish.

Beyond hate

Europe in the 1930s saw an intense period of upheaval and tensions which, in some respects, mirrors the present day. In times of economic extremes, the animal need to blame and vent irrational, violent rage increases, which is borne out by the statistics that the police record in relation to hate crime. The world is now a smaller place and we do not have room for condoning hate crime actively or passively; it is incumbent on us all to confront hate where it shows itself.

For those agencies and individuals affected by hate it is worth referring to the excellent work pioneered by the Waltham Forest Housing Association Limited with the Housing Corporation and other agencies. (See section on witness protection, pp. 212–214.)

Lord Woolf had a stark message for the Treasury last week. In a speech for the Institute of Legal Executives, the Lord Chief Justice predicted that people would be denied justice if the Government did not provide more money to run the courts [...]

'I am very concerned that what has been achieved in regard to civil justice and what has yet to be achieved by criminal justice is going to founder on the rock of lack of resources, unless it is recognised that they are essential,' he said.

[...] Lord Woolf had been told that defendants were not being brought to court on time because the pressure on the prison system meant they were being held too far away. Witnesses such as rape complainants, who were naturally anxious, had to be turned away from court because the defendant had not arrived.

Turning to the civil courts, Lord Woolf said that when the procedural reforms that bear his name were launched three years ago, the judges decided not to wait for the necessary information technology. 'But IT needs resources' he said. 'I'm afraid that if those resources are not provided, what has been achieved will be squandered'.

'Brief encounters', *Daily Telegraph,* 23 May 2002

The build-up for going to court – either to see justice done, or to provide evidence – is a highly stressful experience. It will be another 'notch' indelibly marked in your memory. It may have taken years for the day in court to arrive, and, if you have a direct reason for being affected, the trial will have filled a lot of your waking thoughts. A few coping strategies have already been suggested – please see those sections on inquests and coroners, pp. 82–93. The first and central matter is trying to take the best care of your health and needs before and after going to court.

Take care

Take care of yourself by making sure you understand what is expected of you when you go to court. The police and other services should have long ago prepared you by taking you through the steps of what happens during court proceedings. If there is something you believe has been overlooked, then say to the statutory services what that might be – for example, ensuring that you are helped to avoid the media; that transport is provided to take you away to a specified location.

The needs of you and those about you should have been spoken about, discussed and agreed long before the trial begins and in order to progress and live well afterwards you must be actively involved. There should be no last-minute unwanted surprises for you or the police.

The sections about death and grieving and trauma are worth re-reading prior to the trial, as you may experience intense recollections; see pp. 54–81; pp. 104-113. These may not be simply because of trauma but because the trial will demand this of you whether you are sitting waiting silently for justice, or giving evidence. It is all going to come back intensely – not that it has ever left you.

It may be with the build-up to the trial it becomes a good idea to look at what medication may assist or some specific talking therapies, as many people find they cannot sleep well. Try to avoid drugs like alcohol as they are addictive and depressants and, raw as it is, now is not the time to make yourself more numb than you may already feel.

Re-read the section about basic nutrition and exercise and do the excercises: take action! (See pp. 114–141.) It will possibly be the thing you least wish to consider, but the breathing exercise is something to take into the courthouse and courtroom with you. Ideally, you may have already practised some of the breathing exercises, which you will find directly assist your ability to handle the unfolding trial and experience. Eat a little and often. A lot of people do not realise they have lost interest in food with the unfolding nightmares and with this new and awaited nightmare of a trial it is important to nourish your body. If you simply cannot take the idea of exercises, try to allow yourself a professional massage.

If you are to survive and progress beyond being 'stuck' for ever as a victim, you are going to face depths of despair and self-loathing. It will require facing cynicism from others and your own turbulent raw emotions will change you and your relationships and how you see the world. The process will make this unavoidable. Try to ensure it ultimately changes so you win in whatever way you can.

Try to eat a full evening meal the night before and watch favourite videos; keep as many people around you as possible and have them stay with you overnight. (See section on death, as preparations for funerals are similar; pp. 54–81.) Try to eat something light in the morning of the trial. If you cannot eat breakfast, take some sandwiches to court and lots of liquid and sweet things. The tension will be burning up your sugar supply.

Take a Walkman if it allows you not to listen to media or other people who distress you while waiting.

This is perhaps going to be the first time since an attack, or since the murder of a loved one, that you are going to be in close contact with the alleged violent criminal. How are you going to feel about this and what will you need to maintain your courage and dignity?

Have all your court clothes pressed and ready and shoes polished the day before court as on the morning of the trial it will be a whirl of tension. Prepare a few ironed blouses or shirts in case you find yourself in court on more than one day.

If unclear about trickily-worded questions, ask for them politely to repeat the question in plain English. It is important to take time when answering questions and this is hard to do. The jury will sympathise with the manner in which you are treated. Give the best, simple and most honest answers possible.

It is stated that you can normally take only two people to the court with you (one person in the courtroom by you if wished). Try to negotiate with the FLO and court clerk to have an army of those you care about in the waiting area or in the public gallery.

The media

The media, especially if your tragedy is 'news', sometimes behave appallingly and it is worth ensuring that you and those about you have prepared yourself for the worst with them. Seek advice from the police about privacy pre- and post-trial and do not be inclined to act on strong emotions when a trial does not turn out the way you expect. Use the police or solicitors to make pre-statements to be handed out or read to the media; if retrials or appeals take place, emotionally charged statements made before or after the trial may be used against you in proceedings. Equally, it takes many months for the days in court and verdict to filter into some type of meaning: having waited so long to see justice, do not be careless in making (understandable) but possibly lamentable outbursts. After the trial is the time to make yourself and others instantly disappear from contact, with only reliable people knowing your whereabouts. See section on dealing with the media, pp. 145–159.

The media have been known to misbehave in a very enticing manner with offers of great sums of money, or belligerently (e.g. hiding in gardens or dressing as hospital staff to take photographs of people grieving; hoping to pressurise stunned people into giving interviews). These must be resisted and advice taken from the police and solicitors. To provide the media, especially the newspapers that offer significant sums of money, with details and invent details, you may weaken the prosecution's case and break the *sub judice* rule by providing any information – especially before a trial. Friends and others around you must also understand this matter.

A few tips

• Often the media have cameras and photographers camped outside courthouses from dawn. They take film and photographs of everybody entering and as the day progresses try to match faces to different trials taking place in different courts.

• If you have to make your own way into the front entrance of the courthouse and you find yourself surrounded by media, an effective trick is: (a) to wear dark glasses and (b) to have as many family and friends as possible take photographs of the photographers. It often produces a quick reaction from photographers who realise that their photographs may be plastered about by you – or sent to the PCC or the NUJ. Try to aim for good face pictures of them and remain polite.

• Always keep moving towards the courthouse. Once in the courthouse, the media must behave. They have been known to enter areas which are specifically out of bounds to them: notify the court clerk if this occurs. The media's actions in these situations can be tantamount to intimidation or harassment – prepare yourself.

• When the trial is ending, liaise with friends and police to have taxis or cars collect you and make a rapid exit. A safe place can be found from where you can talk about the trial and this can have been agreed long before with the FLO or others. It will be important to talk each other down after the intensity of everything. One reason famous people often wear dark glasses is because although they may not be able to stop the media zooming in on many areas of their lives – dark glasses serve a powerful function. They allow you the direct control of denying 'onlookers' the voyeurism of photographing (into) your eyes. By denying the media images of your eyes – frightened, weeping or enraged – you are giving yourself dignity and control. Create a little momentary privacy in an unpleasant public circus.

• Matters may not go according to plan during the trial. It may be you are all psyched up to give evidence and then not called until the next day, or day after this. Make back-up plans for what you need and where you will stay, what to wear, and so on.

Court Witness Scheme

One of the effective services that Victim Support provides is the Court Witness Scheme; from April 2002, the service will also be offered to victims of violent crime in magistrates' courts. This service tries to alleviate distress for witnesses appearing in court by helping with pre-trial court visits to see the courtroom, providing rooms for friends and family prior to giving court evidence and protect them from intrusion like unwanted media attention. In Scotland, this scheme has only just started to be piloted (autumn 2001). At the time of writing, the scheme was piloted only in the sheriff courts and due to be extended to the Supreme Courts later in 2002.

- Check that the police have ensured that you are kept a long way from the family or friends of the alleged violent criminal. It is a disgrace that this can still be overlooked. This must be avoided and anticipated by FLOs at the appropriate time.

- Visit the courthouse as many times as possible in the weeks before the trial and sit in different courtrooms as it may be that the trial takes place in another courtroom. Take some control, break your silence and ask to see everything and sit in the different corners of the courtroom and stand in the witness box.

- Practise speaking from the witness box to feel what is like and what is panicking you. Take in the atmosphere, the smells, will you need some disability access equipment? Ask where the alleged criminal will be.

Witness Protection Scheme

People who give evidence, often against people they were once connected with, can be offered witness protection. It might also apply if the person is a complete stranger and the defendant creates an atmosphere of intimidation, directly or indirectly.

If you believe your situation falls within these areas, then it is important, long before the trial commences, that you have secured definite plans for witness protection to whatever level is decided appropriate. This will largely depend upon the crime and the threat to your well-being.

For details that will assist organisations about excellent responses and multiservice provision, the Waltham Forest Housing Association Limited should be contacted (in London). They, alongside the expertise of the Housing Corporation, have piloted and pioneered sensitive and extremely good practice. Together, they have created a beacon of superb practice, multi-agency cooperation and protection for those at risk. At the time of going to print, several extended pilot schemes are about to be started around the country. These resources and reasons for asking for help apply equally to people affected by hate crimes.

Regrettably, there is no specific law that compels a service to intervene directly when witnesses are vulnerable or actually experiencing intimidation, placing their safety at risk. It seems largely 'chance', depending upon the skills and inclination of individual authorities. The Home Office has made clear that it expects responsible authorities to apply the principles recommended in *Speaking Up for Justice*. Other developments are afoot: guidelines exist from the Home Office and the (Crime Committee) Association of Chief Police Officers (ACPO); and there is currently a White Paper drifting its way through Parliament called *Justice for All*.

If justice is to be secured so that victims can progress in life, the ACPO and Home Office recognise changes in practices and services are needed. If you believe that some of the issues that we have outlined relate to your safety, then you must alert the police immediately and local authorities to act properly. These pointers come from the (Crime Committee) ACPO, which include some for identifying witnesses likely to be subjected to intimidation.

- A witness states intimidation is likely, or is occurring. (Insufficient grounds of itself.)
- A witness, although providing information about an offence, is reluctant to provide a statement due to an implicit fear of the consequences of providing evidence.
- A witness lives in a high-density environment or extended family or close-knit community where the offender lives.
- The incident occurred in or around the witness's home (insufficient grounds of itself).
- The type of offence could suggest an increased likelihood of intimidation, e.g. domestic violence, race hate or homophobic crimes and suggest increase of intimidation will follow.
- The relationship between the defendant and witness, e.g. a personal relationship or where the defendant may be in authority over the witness, e.g. a carer in a residential home.
- The offence is one of a series of incidents and evidence of repeat victimisation is likely.
- The witness is vulnerable and intimidation is likely due to cultural or ethnic background of the witness.
- The defendant has a history of witness intimidation or police intelligence suggests that witness intimidation has occurred previously.
- The defendant and or relatives or associates have the intention or ability to interfere with the witness.
- Police and local authority officers dealing with cases should follow the guidelines to prevent the identity of the witness becoming known to the suspect.
- The witness and defendant should not be allowed to encounter each other in premises, e.g. council premises or a police station.
- Police and local authority officers should develop strategies to enable the witness to cope with the threat of possible reprisals; they should provide appropriate information and advice

- Use of the Criminal Justice and Public Order Act 1994 (s.51): offence of intimidation.
- The lead agency will keep the witnesses up to date about progress especially around court proceedings.
- The Home Office, LGA and ACPO make clear under the recommendations of *Speaking Up for Justice* that the authority should take due weight and account of a recommendation of a police witness relocation service that it is not safe for a witness to remain in a particular property.
- The police witness relocation service can be contacted via Crimes Operations within the individual police service.

© Home Office Guidance on Vulnerable and Intimidated Witnesses in Supporting Vulnerable and Intimidated Witnesses – Housing Corporation and Waltham Forest Safetynet Initiative

In court – your statement – giving evidence

In court, you are going to hear 'the issue' of the violent crime – violence against yourself or a murdered loved one, which will be dealt with in a technical–legalistic manner. It often leaves those affected very distressed. There is little to cushion the anger and disgust this generates. Try to prepare yourself to hear fabricated, inappropriate or untrue matters being stated in relation to yourself or a murdered loved one and be ready to see tragedy played out like a choreographed stage of words by experts. It is all very brutal – the human loss appears to play little part. Try to prepare yourself to hear a defence team undermine your character – so you are made to feel like a violent criminal, or hear defence teams manipulate the character of a dead loved one, adding deeper injury to the sense of being victimised and the memory of one who is unable to be there; and you are silenced by the rules of the court. It may be you have experienced cynicism or ignorance in the months preceding the trial from your community or GP, e.g. where you have encountered resistance in trying to have your mental health needs taken seriously. The trial is just another act that confirms that justice – like life – is neither given nor guaranteed. It is an inevitable and perverse aspect of defending people who are guilty by causing as much pain and pressure to be inflicted on innocent people to yield to the ritualised pressure of giving evidence.

> A boy of 15 was detained for four years for raping a schoolgirl who killed herself just weeks after he was convicted. The boy who was 14 at the time and cannot be named for legal reasons, will also spend a further three years under supervision […]

> The teenager struggled to come to terms with her ordeal and took a fatal overdose. At the time of the trial, her parents said the court experience was as much to blame for their daughter's suicide as the rape itself. She had

been 'torn to shreds' by a defence lawyer and made to hold up the G-string underwear she had been wearing at the time of the attack in the park [...] 'She was determined to give evidence and for him to be found guilty as she didn't want it to happen to anyone else. I think taking her own life was the only way she could find peace' said one of her parents [...]

Her father told how she said it was like being raped all over again ... 'We still feel very angry about the way she was treated in court'.

Daily Mail, 1 August 2002

Prepare pre-trial by reading your police statement. Also, you should have had for a considerable period expert assistance in learning to speak – about everything that matters. 'Everything' includes the raw emotions as well as the intellectual preparation for the trial. This handbook is about breaking unhealthy silence, making sense, finding connections, finding courage and control and ways of coping in the face of the intolerable, and so other sections are worth re-reading.

At long last, victims' statements are now being heard in court about the effects that the violent crime had upon the victims and those close to them. This is a small and important part of the court procedure where you may legitimately break the silence and take some time to bring to life the human cost of what this tragedy has done to you. The victim's statement is also something that should be seen as part of the documentation you should submit for any CICA application for assessment for compensation. An imagined scenario is outlined at the end of this section to offer an example of how this may be presented to the judge and shows the personal part of the statement. It does not include the written police statement. The victim's statement becomes a dynamic and powerful means for honestly detailing the impact of a violent crime; it is taken into consideration by the judge and heard by the jury. Use this opportunity well.

The shortened illustrated statement would be prepared over a period of months, possibly at night if unable to sleep, or as the trauma of shock gives way to intense turbulence. It is something to take a lot of time over and to break down into specific detail, as shown. It is not about assuming people know 'what it's like' – it is beholden on you to spell out explicitly what this terror means as it is going to be interpreted mainly within a legal context. It may well be that you add further details to the statement as the months pass before handing a final statement to your solicitor to forward with other documents to the CICA. If willing, it is something you may choose to hand to psychiatric or social services. If for no other reason than the fact that you will find you are required to repeat yourself to every agency, it is reasonable to ask them to kindly read what is stated to avoid unnecessary repetition. If you find it is too painful to read aloud yourself, or if you do not read well, do not feel unkind towards yourself. Have a friend, advocate or FLO read this for you. It will be a very potent part of your experience in court because it may be the first time you are legally allowed to not be silent and also bring to life what is lost. It may be seen, with hindsight, as the moment when you started to assert yourself and, regardless of the trial outcome, when you made the switch from 'victim' to 'warrior'.

A victim's statement

> deep to the depth of anguish
> is where
> the search must dive, aflame.
> right doun to where …
> the sound is like the echo of the belly of the ground;
> deep doun low where the anger grows, harshly.
>
> blazing the voice has to be,
> like lightening,
> lighting up the sky so moon,
> rakin up the dark place,
> showing up the foe an the way he makes his moves low,
> loud in its tone of thundah, hot.
>
> the way cannot be but blood.
> the song
> of mud caught up in the blood, dying
> holdin on to life
> but dying all the same, yet livin out the pain.
> the end cannot be but sweet, final.

Linton Kwesi Johnson: *Same Way*

Giving purpose to your words

It is good to bear in mind when preparing a victim's statement that this is your sole potential direct influence upon a court trial about how violent horror has impacted into your life. It can also assist a CICA application by placing your experience before the CICA as several other professionals will be writing about you. When putting your statement together, never lie or exaggerate the facts – the impact of violence should command appropriate legal attention in its own right. Professional services have their own duties to convey medical, social and legal facts. In going about their work, they may not fully and accurately give potency to what you are going through. It is a hard task to put pen to paper, e.g. finding the energy or skill to document the exact details and feelings. It is like knowing what has happened and what it is doing to your life but somehow not assuming it is understood by the criminal system. This is an unwise assumption. Everything must be made explicit and detailed in what might seem like a mundane way. There is no reason to feel silly or inadequate in not knowing how to prepare a style of statement because it is a specialist and professional format – not like writing a postcard or friendly letter. To have a good structure for expressing yourself gives clear expression and information to the people who need to know what this horror has done to you.

To include victims' statements in court proceedings as valid evidence is a recent and overdue concession by government. It is an important, albeit an isolated token gesture which shows victims are a significant part of the criminal justice system because victims for so long have been secondarily victimised by that system. This belated and important inclusion says victims are 'human evidence' in influencing the outcome of what has taken place and been suffered. As with so many burdens facing you since horror entered your life, it is beholden upon you to explicitly state to a judge, jury and the CICA what violent horror means in your life. If you are going to survive and progress your life it must be done well and fully. And this will take time in preparing to get right and give voice to your life.

The main parts to include
(See section on constructing a formal document in 'Complaining', pp. 173–187.)

There are some basic issues to get across in a statement and these can be narrowed down to: (a) what?; (b) when?; (c) give some example to press a point; (d) how violence has impacted upon you, e.g. physically, mentally, financially, etc.; (e) what violence has made you become; and (f) your hopes for a future and the facts of the other points that will stop these aspirations from becoming a reality. What a statement will do is take these broad areas and make very specific short statements about everything.

Unpacking pain in words – what to place in a statement
The scenario and outline for putting together a victim's statement offers a guideline for how to go about preparing a style for unpacking raw and deeply personal repercussions of living with the aftermath and impact of violent crime.

Some tips

- Do not write your statement at the last moment before forwarding to court through your solicitor or the police. Too much has taken place to make recall easy; too much will be lost.
- If you do not read or write easily, or if you have been left with a degree of disability, you may find it easier to speak into a Dictaphone. If you choose this way, remember to number and title the tapes as they will need to be typed by someone very reliable – and in order. An FLO or social services may be able to help on this matter. It will stand as a legal document and may be chosen to be used for a CICA application.
- This is a deeply private and raw document you are preparing and it is something to be used as evidence in the process of law. Therefore, the contents cannot be made freely available, nor should you wish them to be. For the contents to be lost or given away could be seen in law as breaking the *sub judice* rule and seriously affecting your court appearance and the passage of justice.
- The statement is the unpacking of everything you have suffered, what help you still need and what level of ordinary life is possible. This will be placed within a simple orderly structure.
- Try to see the statement like a diary. From an early stage, begin to make notes about all the various aspects in which the impact of violence has affected your life in simple points. Use different headings because this helps you focus on that issue and helps a judge and others read or listen to what is read aloud.
- If you can use, or have access to, a computer, all the better. Either way, remember to keep a back-up copy of everything and reduce the number of people who have access to your statement. If you have access to a computer, it allows you to add to and change the statement at your pace.
- Remember to separate feelings from facts, and facts from what you know or have been told. In these situations, it is good to place a reference like a medical or social services report.

How a victim's statement is used

A statement is used by the court separately to your police and other professional statements and will be read on its own. The other reports will have been heard or used in legal debate in court beforehand. It is a decision based on guidance and ability, whether you read your statement to the court or ask others do so. Remember, a huge pressure will be on you simply by being in court; you may not wish to read your statement. This is not something to punish and feel angry with yourself about if it is too much for you to handle.

A scenario
It is easier to convey this using an example. It is beholden on you to take guidance from what you find useful when preparing your statement, or not. Imagine …

A man has tried hard to survive since being nearly killed and has struggled for many months to sort out an accurate account of what he wants to say in court, and cope with the CICA. His life has been turned inside out; he can barely make himself understood. He has cooperated with agencies and is trying to cope with his family and himself. He is struggling to cope, he is scared and has felt helpless since being attacked, even though professionals are trying to help. He is torn between feeling enraged at human injustice and desperate for legal justice and protection. On the outside, the man still tries to be a joker to his family but inside he feels despair and humiliation and his court appearance is emotionally loaded. After speaking with his wife, he has decided to ask his FLO to read his statement to the court – naturally, this is a huge event in the man's life.

The police statement is already known to the court and will not be read, only his victim's statement. This statement can be used and updated when dealing with the CICA as the facts and experience remain true. It is a summary and if preparing a victim statement yours may be very much longer as it needs to state everything you believe is important.

Here is a story that has led to court and then a summarised victim's statement is shown. The man was one of several people attacked by a gang over a period of many months. The gang have not been charged with this man's injuries; instead they have been charged with two 'specimen' murders. In the future, this means the man will not officially be entitled to information from the Victim Liaison Service about gang members, e.g. the release or licence conditions, regardless of the fact that he was nearly murdered.

The man was attacked from behind by four adult males in a multi-storey car park while unlocking his car and placing his briefcase on the back seat. Robbery was not a motive. He was dragged across the car park and severely beaten. Then, the attackers doused him in petrol, set him on fire and threw him over a ledge from the fourth storey.

The man sustained horrific injuries, including:

a fractured skull
6 broken ribs
2 complex fractured hips
2 fractured and dislocated legs – particularly to the right leg
broken lower vertebrae
significant burns to lower half of his body
hemiplegia – paralysis of right side of his body
fractured right hand and arm
chronic post-traumatic stress
left eye retina – detached
multiple muscle and ligament damage

The man was in hospital for many months and required extensive operations, grafting for burns, physiotherapy and psychiatric assistance before returning home. He has profound long-term degenerative injuries, a neurological speech impediment, impaired vision and short-term memory loss. He will never be able to be an active parent or to work again and has a limited range of mobility. He is dependent upon others much of the time and is still receiving periodic physiotherapy and psychiatric services. His children have developed behavioural difficulties since his injuries.

He is now 37 years old with two children under 9 years of age. He had been an insurance salesman for three years, and the sole income provider for his family who live in a heavily mortgaged, modest property. He had no health insurance and had only recently taken out a private pension scheme. His average salary over the last three years was £17,500 gross per annum (basic salary of £12,000), based partly on commission. The family had amassed £850 savings towards their first family holiday. They are now deeply in debt and may soon lose their home.

His wife and friends rallied around but his care needs require periods of specialist nursing care and his wife needs respite care help. The children have had no help. The CICA received a detailed application some time ago from his solicitors but the CICA has postponed making a final award and wishes to argue the man is best placed in the care of a local authority home for disabled people. His family and solicitors will challenge this and pursue an award for independent living and a structured award at an appeal hearing soon. Due to defence representative delays, it now eighteen months since the man was attacked and he has not seen his attackers since they tried to kill him.

My statement for court and CICA
In Strictest Confidence: CICA Reference Number AE / 679 543 03

On 14 July 2005, at about 2.30 p.m., I had just completed a successful meeting and was pleased with the outcome and the preparations involved in what would be a large work contract. It was the culmination of two months' negotiations and I returned to my car, tired but elated. My car was parked in a multi-storey car park; I was half-dreaming about the prospect of my family having a well-earned holiday and I was mulling over the meeting when I felt a terrible thud to the back of my head, as I was placing my briefcase on the back seat of my car. What happened after was petrifying and savage as I was kicked, knocked and beaten with objects. I pleaded with the gang to take my money but they simply laughed and continued to kick me around like litter and beat me with what looked like baseball bats. It was impossible to try to protect myself because I was being attacked from every angle and with fierce severity. When they dragged me across the car park, I prayed it was all over but as they continued to beat and pin me down my nightmare became worse – still impossible to believe. They were laughing as I struggled while they threw petrol over me, and a sense of agony and dread took over me. I thought I was going to die there and I remember thinking of my wife and children and that I would never see them again. In what seemed like seconds they pushed me half up the car park ledge, set me alight and tossed me hurtling down four flights onto a road. It happened so fast I tried to put my hands out as my head was going to hit the ground first and I could feel intense pain and burning in my legs. Then, a pain I cannot describe and dread to remember consumed me and everything was dark. Everything was dark and then nothing. Apparently it was two weeks before I became conscious, since when everything has been extreme pain, confusion and humiliation. I am told the attack went on for about twenty minutes – it felt like it went on forever.

Before being attacked I would consider my life average in many ways. I worked hard and had a successful marriage and two beautiful children succeeding in school. I had never encountered violence as a child, was against capital punishment, nor did I believe in physical punishment of my children. I had never aspired to go to college and had never been out of work, was proud of our achievements and was a sociable and active man and father. I was an ordinary man with ordinary hopes.

Without others, I cannot live. I am alive by virtue of brilliant professionals and my brilliant wife but I do not feel I have a life and I want to know why. Why did these people do what they did? Do they care they were not just destroying me but my family and my sense of safety in this world?

What violence has done to me – physically

1. I cannot convey the physical pain I am constantly suffering. Words fail me.
2. If I move, I am in pain, and if I stay still too long, I am in pain.
3. It has affected my attitude and I know my family has suffered because of me.
4. I cannot accept that I cannot do basic things although the attack happened eighteen months ago and this leaves me feeling degraded and useless.
5. At all times, the NHS staff have been brilliant, in and out of hospital. But, I cannot cope with being a baby in a half-dead man's body, e.g. having to have my genitals washed by a stranger, toileted, having a paper read for me; to lose bodily control. It reminds me only of what happened and how I cannot get out of my hell.
6. I cannot mow a lawn, and can barely sit in our garden without assistance.
7. I cannot play any sport; I once enjoyed football in an amateur team, and golf.
8. It is more than a grief not being active because a grief can pass.
9. I cannot take part in a natural conversation and find the impatience of family and friends must show while I fumble for words or have a blank – leaves me angry and ashamed. So, when not trying to mock myself I remain silent.
10. It is hard to adjust to learning to try and use my left-hand as I was right-handed before the attack.
11. I am unable to write or use a computer – I am trying to adjust to disabled equipment by using voice machines on my computer, but it is hard.
12. My injuries mean I cannot speak confidently for myself, e.g. to sort out this victim statement I have had to disclose intimate personal details to a Dictaphone that was typed by someone I have never met. I am grateful but it has left me feeling useless and embarrassed.
13. It seems like I am a useless flesh ball of pain, like a big baby unable to look forward to development and wholly dependent on others for so much.
14. Being fed by my wife in front of my children with a spoon is degrading (and confusing for my children).
15. To be unable to play with and cuddle my children due to physical restriction and pain breaks my heart.
16. Nothing I do is spontaneous; everything requires planning and discussion with others to help me most days and nights, e.g. toileting, eating, washing, reading a paper.
17. It is cruel that I am unable to sleep with my wife due to my needs; and changes to our living room are required so that it can be fitted with disability adaptations.
18. It is cruel that, due to loss of physical feeling and injury, I am unable to enjoy many sensations or have sex with my wife.
19. Periodic physiotherapy is tough to handle and reminds me all the time of how I came to be what I am.
20. What is left of my energy and body gives no hope without extreme pain and dependency.
21. It seems I cannot do anything except receive help from and rely on others.

What violence has done to me – mentally

1. *My wife is a remarkable and unique woman who has never complained about anything that she has lost in me.*

2. *This leaves me privileged and also feeling useless as she deserves much more and I cannot do much to change matters.*

3. *This leaves me angry, frustrated and frightened because she should move on for her sake and the children but without her I have no reason to live. It causes great mental turmoil for me.*

4. *I cannot handle pain if I am exhausted and I have not had proper sleep since the attack.*

5. *It does not feel like I am what I have become and I deeply dislike what I must face what I have become.*

6. *Sometimes, without reason, I find myself sobbing and trying not to let anyone hear.*

7. *I feel I have failed my wife and children.*

8. *My children have definitely changed since the attack, and for the worse. They are almost beyond the control of my wife. They were not like this before.*

9. *There is nothing I can do and my eldest child when angry said he'll do what he wants and that I was 'stupid', and he kicked me to press the point. This led me into a deep depression I am not sure I can come out of because in a way he is right.*

10. *After this incident, I tried to be upbeat and not complain but my moods can be extreme, e.g. for ten days I would not speak and hardly ate after my son kicked me. I think I wanted to die.*

11. *I have ceased to be a useful and effective parent, adding to the burden of my wife and family.*

12. *Every physical move reminds me of all the events of the day my life was battered and set on fire.*

13. *My mind is like an endless video recording constantly replaying every scene of what happened. It seems whether I want to think about what happened or not – memories crush my head.*

14. *When I can sleep I remember the laughing and mocking of the gang and the terror of it all. In sleep, when I can get it, I remember, as though it is really happening again, the terrible anguish and pain as I hit the ground. So, I try not to sleep.*

15. *The NHS services have been great to me and my family and I have been told I have PTSD and they have explained what is happening to my mind and why. It does not make it go away or feel easier.*

16. *Between physical pain and mental terror I feel trapped and tormented. It seems I am in a prison in my body and mind.*

17. *My life has no privacy or mystery.*

18. *My old football friends and family are good people and they do everything they can. But, I cannot join in conversations easily and hearing about sport depresses me.*

19. *I am helpless, angry and devastated – it is all too much. I feel trapped in a body and mind I do not recognise or want.*

20. It seems I cannot do anything except receive help from and rely on others.

What violence has done to me – aspirations and socially

1. Whenever possible, I try get my wife to go away on her own with friends while other family care for the children. She has no life and not the life she planned.

2. My speech embarrasses me since receiving a head injury and makes me feel too self-conscious to be very social. It reminds me of what has happened.

3. Our family have never had the holiday we planned but the children have been away with my wife while I had respite care.

4. The gang have injured more than just me and some friends have backed away and a few have remained loyal.

5. I have no hopes any more.

6. It seems my injuries may stabilise and after a period then steadily go downhill.

7. It seems I cannot do much but be grateful, which I am, but I am angry that the life I have is of no value to me.

8. All attention revolves around my needs as though I am a baby and this has affected the children and I fear they will grow into reckless adults and resent me for what they have lost – if they can remember.

9. It seems our home will be repossessed and our social worker will try to find an alternative home if in law it is seen we did not make ourselves 'intentionally' homeless.

10. I want my children to return to the normal people they were and not get worse.

11. In time I hope to be able to meet other disabled people and find how they cope and what they do.

12. My work is to endure a morning or afternoon without ranting, and sobbing and my dream is to erase the constant memories of what these people did and have made me become.

13. My dream is to have one day without extreme pain.

14. I want the CICA to stop making my life more painful with delays and questions that make me feel like I am a liar or criminal and at fault. I want compensation to equip my home and provide the things I need to do the best I can.

15. I want to feel safe in my skin and outside world again.

16. Although my wife will not accept this I think she should move away with the children and find the good life she deserves, if only for the children.

17. My aspiration is that justice is seen to be done. I need to hear why these people did what they did and if they are pleased with what has happened.

18. My aspiration is to see justice take control when I was given none and can never have none.

What the sum total of violence has done to me

1. It will never be possible to be what I once was or find the physical, mental or financial means to reflect the kindness and skill of those who have kept me alive. This will take me a lifetime to understand.

2. In destroying most of me, the gang destroyed most of my family.

3. They have destroyed my dreams and those of my wife and companion.

4. They have destroyed my children's innocence and safety in this world.

5. My children have been robbed of a loving and active father.

6. I have lost the sense of safety in life.

7. I have lost all independence to make and act on decisions or desires in my life.

8. It is not even possible to give voice to all my feelings.

Brian Smythe – 2 October 2007

Giving evidence

If you are required to give evidence, it is essential to state the truth. However, in being confined to questions that are constructed and posed by an expert defence team, you will be offered limited scope to offer fully factual answers; don't expect a defence team to treat you well. Why would they? They are out to win – this is what's meant by our adversarial legal system. It may come to be that the defence bring people from your past to cast doubt on your character to detract a jury from the 'issue' (i.e. violent injustice). Be prepared to be left feeling humiliated and degraded, even though you have done nothing wrong. It is important to prepare yourself and experts like the police and trauma specialists can effectively help you develop techniques to best handle such situations. Like the ritual of saying goodbye to the remains of a loved one, the ritual for justice requires planning how you will cope and be heard.

A few tips

- Re-read the section about slow, rhythmic breathing and practise this before, during and after the trial – especially if giving evidence.
- It may be that you are expected to look at 'scene of crime' photographs and if you have not had appropriate expert help this could be difficult for you in court as well as bring back raw feelings. Ensure you have secured the expert professional help you deserve long before the trial. When seeing the images they will take your breath away, but the impact will be lessened if you have prepared; if you have been in denial, and not had appropriate expert help, the impact will be more severe.
- Be prepared to feel a sense of being back in the event. Partly, as stated, this is the requirement of the court process and partly about matters about trauma and common sense.
- Be aware of how you wish to be seen by the public, jury and judge. Take some time and plan what you will wear and how you will convey your dignity and loss.

- Do not be worried about looking at the jury: they have a great influence over the outcome of how you will adjust in the future. Do not be afraid to try to look at the face of the accused. Try to avoid rapidly looking all over the courtroom – focus slow and clearly. Work out how you will maintain your breathing during the difficult questions that may go on for what seems like ages.
- It is natural to weep. Especially if you are being attacked by a defence team or being asked to recall memories of anguish. Do not hide from crying. If you cry, it is because you mourn and the situation you are in adds to the grief. Do not use tissues, which disintegrate, but take a handkerchief.
- Take a small momento that is precious to you, whether it be a dead loved one's former possession or something you own and treasure (e.g. a photograph, a ring). If things get nasty and tough during the trial, hold it tight and let it give you strength.
- Wear some fresh perfume or aftershave and rub onto your wrists before going onto the stand. Again, if things get nasty, you'll have something pleasant with which to counter the ugliness.
- Drink liquids (like water or tea) to help ease the acid of anxiety and help moisten your throat. If you drink water while in the witness box, do not worry if you shake. Many people prefer not to use cups, etc. while giving evidence, as it becomes another hurdle. The shaking itself is a distraction, which makes them feel more self-conscious.
- Before giving evidence, maybe before the trial starts, ask the clerk of the court to secure permission from the judge for you to suck mints. These will prevent your throat from drying up completely and becoming sore and hoarse with anxiety. Two double-strength mints will help to produce saliva and help to maintain your ability to do the best you can and clearly.
- It is acceptable to ask the trial judge whether you can have questions repeated or worded in a different way if you do not understand. It is acceptable, if you believe you are being spoken to in an inappropriate tone by counsel, to ask the judge to request the defence person to change their tone.
- If you need to use the lavatory, or believe that you cannot take any more questions – if this has been going on for a long time, it is reasonable to state this to the judge. Most judges will do everything within their means to make the experience as tolerable for you as possible.
- Once you have given evidence and may not be required again, you will have offered your best in the pursuit of justice. It is then that your exit and escape plan needs to be put quickly into action.

The jury's verdict – the sentence

Generally, people do not believe they see justice done within the court hearing, whether in relation to a jury's decision or the sentence that the judge passes on an accused. For example, a judge may pass a life sentence for a murder, but the murderer only serves a minimum number of years before a Parole Board reviews the sentence. Often, with 'good behaviour', this sentence may become shortened and suggests that the lengthy investigations, the huge legal bill for providing prison facilities, defending the criminal and paying his defence team and the judge have left the people with another loss. This makes trying to progress and rebuild a life even harder if a primal confrontation (revenge) and social need (justice) are thwarted. Inevitably, it leaves injured or grieving people wondering at the sense of a publicly funded system that allows this to happen – also, the fact that there seems to be insufficient punishment before rehabilitation. It trivialises the life or loss of the victim. It is the government's current policy to review which existing criminals may be released early due to severe overcrowding in British jails, which is a concern for many people.

The trial verdict may be challenged by you or the defendant, which will mean a possible appeal or retrial and prolonging the fight for justice. You must, therefore, continue to take extra care of every aspect of your life. Do not let any CICA or court process consume you to a degree where you have lost sight of your right to be given tenderness, and continue take care of yourself.

The summing-up by the judge will, it is hoped, reflect the tragedy and reasons for the type of sentence passed down. When the hammer comes down, the case is in one sense over. A sense of sudden finality – like the ritual of the funeral – often envelops people. After months, it suddenly and abruptly has come to an end. Again, people often feel aware that their loved one is not coming back and a sense of violation remains.

After a trial

If a retrial or appeal is to be pursued, avoid giving interviews to the media, even if a sense of raw rage is engulfing you. It will only hinder a potentially fair appeal or retrial. It remains a healthy practice to retain as much privacy as you can and reclaiming this can include providing the media with written statements delivered by your solicitor or the police. The grief or anger you have is private before it passes into the public domain. Remember, if you agree to speak to the media for money this must be made plain and the amount taken into account in any future CICA application. It will reduce the amount that the CICA will award.

It is important to have preplanned how and where you are going to be immediately after the trial. You should not be alone; preferably, you should not be at your usual home. This is not just because of the unwanted attention of the media, but because it is common for people to collapse totally. It is as though all the anticipation, pressure and dread have been released by the ending of the trial. Often this coincides with the departure of agencies that you had grown used to and liked – the FLO and others. This is where family, friends and other agencies can help by finding a secure place for you that will assist recovery. It will take much more time before you can make real plans. These should be in place and somewhere confidential, away from the media, for you to grieve, rest and recharge. It is hoped that services may have organised a charity to fund a break or provide a temporary safe location. Four weeks is a realistic time to be away. This is a time when it is easy to self-reproach, so it is best spent taking exquisite care and recharging. Take matters very slowly, one day at a time. The ritual for justice was a way for fighting for a dead loved one or fighting back for yourself – you have done your best, the power of decision lay with others. It is time to concentrate on moving on and it's going to be a long, tough road.

Victim liaison schemes

These schemes are quite new and are supposed to alleviate long-term worries people affected by violence often have. The idea was to make victims after the trial have a sense that they have not been forgotten. The service has evolved from the Victims' Charter 1996 and more recently the Criminal Justice and Court Services Act 2000. It extends the 'entitlement' and rights to access about information or consultation for victims of sexual and other violent crimes where criminals received a prison sentence of more than one year. The Act also specifies the actual offences where the victim liasion service requirements apply. It defines what violence means for the probation services.

Limitations of rights

Unfortunately, as many people affected by violence often encounter, justice is not readily given and the new legislation has created a sort of league table of offences. These offences, regardless of the impact upon a person's life, define what, if any, information the probation service is obliged or 'inclined' to offer a victim. It is remarkable that this service is only offered to victims of offences named in the indictment. If several victims are killed or physically injured, but only one victim's name was on the indictment, then it would be only that one victim or, in the case of death, the victim's family where the service requirement applies. The requirement only applies in cases where death or actual physical injury is either caused, intended or likely.

This is something that the police must make clear from the onset to those affected by violent crime. Also, reviewing whether all people affected should automatically be cited to ensure victims affected are treated with dignity is necessary. The current government's habit of providing veneer, in place of dynamic social justice and services, in this case of victims' rights actively undermines the practice of justice for those genuinely affected. Many probation services attempt to meet the enquiries of 'non-required victims' as far as possible, and individual probation services have the power to extend the service beyond that covered by 'requirement'. Unsurprisingly, this is also about resources and requires sufficient staff to respond to enquiries. To create significant restrictions on the rights of people in these circumstances is, far from assisting rehabilitation or justice, tantamount to secondary victimisation. The service cannot inform a victim about which prison the criminal is held in, nor state the exact release date, nor the criminal's release address.

Playing with numbers ...

The Home Secretary... called on everyone to do their bit, urging the public to join the 'chain of responsibility' and take up the fight against crime in their own communities. 'We all carry responsibility for the society and communities in which we live. The government takes its responsibilities seriously to prevent and reduce crime and to build stronger communities. But others have to do the same. That means everyone from government to police and the wider criminal justice system, family, individuals and the wider community,' he told a Sheffield residents group.
'All of us have responsibility for the society we live in. I accept mine on behalf of the government, but nobody else should be passing the buck either. Only by combined endeavour can we change the communities in which we live.'
More controversially, Blunkett sought to put public perception and media coverage in perspective, arguing that official statistics show crime rates to be at their lowest level for two decades.
'Anyone reading recent reports would think that crime, and violent crime in particular, is now spiralling out of control. The reality is very different. There is a growing problem with street robbery and mobile phones in particular, as the figures we released earlier this week showed. But overall crime is now falling and has been for some time,' he said.
Shadow Home Secretary Oliver Letwin said: 'His claim that people are safer than before sits uncomfortably with the government's own figures, which show that the level of violent crime has soared since Labour came to power'.
'Figures show that in the last three years, violence against the person has increased by 20 per cent and robbery by 42 per cent. Total violent crime has risen by 21 per cent. Despite government promises, and their highly vaunted Anti-Social Behaviour Order Scheme, anti-social behaviour continues to create fear and insecurity on our streets. These orders have proved to be a bureaucratic failure,' said Letwin.

Speech to a Sheffield Residents Group, 11 January 2002, from Internet News:
Bruno Waterfield: *Tackling crime and the fear of crime*

Flesh on numbers – not the same as the Home Secretary's

- March 2000–March 2001: 600,900 recorded violent incidences.
- Represents increase of 3.4% from previous year.
- Most serious incidences rose by 4%.
- Largest increase 15.8% (12,500) were racially motivated violent crimes.
- Wounding up 18.2% (3,200).
- Highest age group of victims were between 14 and 19 years old.
- Suspects were four times as likely to be male.
- Female rape rose by 1.5%.
- Male rape rose by 10.7%.

Home Office: *Statistical Bulletin for England and Wales,* July 2001

The Victim Liaison Service includes :

- Information about sentencing and custodial processes and how they apply in the individual's case.
- Information on key events during the time the offender is serving sentence, e.g. appeals, absconding/escape, recalculation of sentence dates.
- Opportunity for victims to be consulted in relation to temporary release.
- Opportunity for victims to have their concerns and views taken into account in relation to release licence conditions and to be informed of agreed licence conditions.
- Information on the month of the offender's release date and the area where the offender will be living on release.
- Information on key events during the period offender is on licence in the community, e.g. recall.
- A point of contact for victims if they are concerned about the offender's behaviour, e.g. unwanted contact from the offender.

At the end of this section – see Useful addresses – is a contact point for your nearest probation and victim liaison services.

Released prisoners' information – victims of sexual and other violent offences

This leaflet explains that, under the Criminal Justice and Court Services Act 2000 and the Victims' Charter (see below), the National Probation Service will contact you to find out if you want to know what happens to an offender after he or she is sentenced to prison.

You can expect a member of the probation service to contact you if one of the following applies to you.

- You have suffered a sexual or violent offence for which the offender has been sentenced to one year or more in prison or a young offenders' institution. (In this leaflet, all references to prisoners or prisons apply equally to young offenders or young offenders' institutions, or similar institutions.)

- You have a close relationship with someone who has suffered this type of offence and who is vulnerable, for example, a child or elderly relative, and you are acting on their behalf.
- You had a close relationship with someone who has died as a result of this type of offence.

The National Probation Service can also offer this service if you have been a victim of other serious offences, for example, if you are afraid the offender may try to find you. However, the National Probation Service is not able to offer this service where the offender has been sentenced to less than twelve months in prison.

These procedures apply where the prisoner is sentenced to be held in a prison in England or Wales, and is being released to an address in these countries. They do not apply where an offender has been sentenced to be held in hospital, although the government is considering ways in which the victims of these offenders may also receive or provide information.

Nor do these procedures apply where a prisoner receives a number of sentences, for different offences, which add up to more than twelve months in total, unless one of the sentences is for twelve months or more for an offence against you.

How long will the prisoner be in prison?
Under the current law, prisoners do not usually serve the whole of their sentence in prison. When a prisoner is released will depend on the length of their sentence, how much time they spent in prison before they were sentenced and whether they have passed a risk assessment for being released on licence or home detention curfew (which involves wearing an electronic tag to check where the wearer of the tag is after a certain time at night). The period of supervision on licence is an important part of a prisoner's sentence. The National Probation Service supervise all adult prisoners who were sentenced to twelve months or more after October 1992 for a set period after they are released. All young prisoners are released on licence and are automatically supervised for a set period. There are more details on these arrangements below.

The National Probation Service works with prisoners and prisons to draw up a plan for supervising offenders after their release. This includes approving where a prisoner will live, and whether any restrictions will apply to them after their release. The Probation Service then supervises prisoners when they return to the community.

Life-sentence prisoners
There are special rules for life-sentence prisoners, who may not be released at all if they are considered to be a danger to the public. The National Probation Service supervises all life-sentence prisoners on a life licence. Even after their release, life-sentence prisoners can be sent back to prison at any time during the rest of their life if their behaviour gives serious cause for concern.

Other sentences of twelve months or more
Offenders who are sentenced to twelve months or more fall into two other main categories.
1. Automatic conditional release
- Offenders serving a sentence of twelve months to four years will usually be considered for release on a home detention curfew two months before the halfway point of their sentence. Serious sex offenders cannot apply for a home detention curfew. Decisions about other prisoners are based on careful risk assessment. If they are refused a home detentioncurfew, these prisoners must be released at the halfway point of their sentence. The National Probation Service always supervises these prisoners after their release. How long the National Probation Service supervises prisoners varies depending on whether they were released on a home detention curfew or not, but can last until the end of their sentence for

some sex offenders. If an offender breaks any of the conditions of curfew or supervision, that offender could be sent back to prison. Also, if the offender commits a new offence at any time before the end of the sentence, they could be sent back to prison until the end of his/her original sentence, and also have to serve any new sentence for the new offence.

- For offenders who commit a sexual or violent offence, the courts have the power to say they must be supervised for even longer after they are released, if the court considers that this is needed to prevent them from committing further offences. These offenders are released under the arrangements set out above, and serve the extended supervision period on top of the period they would be expected to serve on licence. Licence conditions apply for the whole supervision period, and offenders may be sent back to prison if they break these conditions.

2. Discretionary conditional release
- Discretionary conditional release applies to offenders who are serving a fixed sentence of four years or more. These prisoners become eligible for release from prison (known as 'parole') at the halfway point of their sentence, and may be released on parole at any point between the halfway and two-thirds point. Parole decisions are based on careful risk assessment. If a prisoner is refused parole, he/she will be released when he/she has served two-thirds of their sentence. Whether prisoners are released on parole or after having served two-thirds of their sentence, the National Probation Service would still supervise them until three-quarters of their sentence has passed. If the offender breaks any of the conditions of the supervision, he/she could be sent back to prison. Also, if the offender commits a new offence at any time before the end of the sentence, he/she could be sent back to prison until the end of the original sentence, and also have to serve any new sentence for the new offence. If you would like to know more about the sentence that the prisoner in your particular case will serve, you can ask the victim liaison officer when he/she contacts you.

Contact by the National Probation Service

If you are in the group of people listed in paragraph 1b, the National Probation Service will normally write to you within two months of the offender being sentenced. They will offer to meet with you for the following purposes.

- To give you information about prison sentences in general and how prisoners can proceed through the system.
- To ask you whether you would like them to contact you at key stages in the criminal justice process and tell you when the prisoner is being considered for final release.
- To check whether you have any concerns which you would like them to take into account when they are considering the conditions for the prisoner's final release.
- To give you the name of someone you can contact at the probation office which covers your area.
- To explain how they will use any information you provide.
- To tell you about any other services that may be able to help.

Your choices to give and receive information

You have the following choices

- You can choose to be told about stages in the prison sentence (when decisions might be taken about temporary or permanent release), and give your views about conditions that will apply when the prisoner is released or other matters.
- You can choose to be kept informed about stages in the prisoner's sentence, but decide not to give your views about conditions that will apply to the prisoner's release.
- You can choose not to be given any information. In this case, tell your victim liaison officer.
- You can change your mind, at any time, about being contacted. But if you do, or if you change your address, you will need to let the victim liaison officer know immediately.

What happens if you give information?

If you want to be kept informed and to give information or express your views or concerns, you should tell the victim liaison officer at your first meeting. The following will happen if you do this.

- The National Probation Service will tell you when the offender is being considered for release.
- The National Probation Service will discuss your views and concerns with you before the prisoner is released. They will also give you the opportunity to give your views about the conditions that will apply when the offender is released.
- Before the offender is released, the National Probation Service writes an assessment report in which they give their recommendations to the authority considering the conditions of the offender's release. The National Probation Service will consider your views when recommending any conditions.
- The National Probation Service will give you the choice of knowing what is written in any assessment report about you and your views. This report is written before the offender is released. They will also tell you about any extra conditions of release, relating to your concerns, which they are recommending.
- The prisoner will normally have the right to see the assessment reports, except in certain circumstances. The victim liaison officer will be happy to explain this to you before you give your views.
- You also have the right to give information to the prison governor or parole board, but the prisoner will normally have the right to see this information. You can discuss this with the victim liaison officer.
- Once the parole board or prison governor has decided about the offender's release, the National Probation Service will tell you whether the offender will have to keep to any conditions after they are released. If so, the National Probation Service will give you details of any conditions which relate to contact with you, and any other information they consider appropriate in your case.

The National Probation Service should contact you within two months of the offender being sentenced. However, if it has not been in touch, you can contact your nearest probation office, which should be able to give you more information. (The address and phone number will be in the local phone book under 'probation service'.)

Types of legal representatives
Solicitors

There are many types of solicitors; some specialise in corporate banking, marital and family work, medical negligence on personal injury and some have a small general knowledge in various fields of legal practice. A privilege enjoyed for centuries by barristers was done away with by Parliament in the Legal Services Act 1990, and this has allowed, in special circumstances, solicitors to secure the right to audience in the higher courts before judges. Solicitors continue to take instructions from their clients and in turn instruct barristers, who generally lead proceedings in high-courts. At the present time there are approximately 55,000 practising solicitors in England and Wales, who generally work in groups called firms – of which there are approximately 10,000 within England and Wales.

Legal executives

A legal executive is a type of junior solicitor who works within a firm of solicitors and takes on many forms of legal work, but, unlike a solicitor or barrister, has no rights of audience in court. They do have the power to make applications in barristers' chambers. Legal executives are members of the Institute of Legal Executives (ILEX) and this institute regulates their conduct.

Barristers

Until 1990, barristers had the privilege of ancient and exclusive rights to speak in all superior courts – the High Court, the Court of Appeal and the House of Lords. The training of a barrister requires having achieved a degree in law and completed a vocational trainee barrister training course that takes place at the Inns of Court Law School in London, or one of the designated Bar vocational course training centres around the country. Upon completion of the vocational training a trainee barrister will be called to the Bar and at this stage must undergo a further year of pupillage – during this time watching and learning from another barrister referred to as 'pupil-master'. In Scotland, the equivalent of barristers are legal experts known as advocates who have a very similar training.

All barristers belong to a professional body called the Bar Council, and there are approximately 7,000 practising barristers in England and Wales, and two-thirds of these practise and work in London. The remainder practise in various trial centres such as Leeds, Birmingham, Liverpool and Norwich.

After a barrister has practised at the Bar for at least ten years they are regarded as a senior barrister and at this point in their career it is possible for some to be invited by the Lord Chancellor to become a Queen's Counsel. This is familiarly referred to as 'taking silk' because this material is used in the making of the robe a barrister becomes entitled to use, and a Queen's Counsel is entitled to use the letters 'QC' after their name. Under the old criminal compensation scheme – the Criminal Injuries Compensation Board – all award decisions were made by medical experts and barristers and Queen's Counsel.

Crown Prosecution Service (CPS)

The CPS was born out of the Prosecution of Offences Act 1985 and its role is to undertake criminal prosecutions. Solicitors and barristers who specialise in assessing cases and procedures that will lead to prosecutions and carrying out further court functions staff the Crown Prosecution Service. For example, they have the power to make an application in a magistrates' court to have bail denied. The CPS is often justifiably criticised for failing to proceed with prosecuting alleged criminals. If a criminal trial takes place at a Crown Court, the CPS instructs counsel (barristers) to act on its behalf. It was reported (*Daily Telegraph*, 11 May 2000) how a report commissioned by the CPS after the Commission for Racial Equality stated it would launch an investigation if the CPS failed to produce an investigation itself into racism within the CPS. The service was condemned for institutional racism within its own service and its treatment of its own staff. This cannot inspire confidence from tax-paying citizens in Britain, including those people from ethnic minorities.

Director of Public Prosecutions (DPP)
The DPP is the head of the CPS and has responsibility for taking decisions whether to prosecute in cases of great importance or if a case is deemed politically sensitive. The DPP is appointed by the government of the day and has a role to advise about matters on criminal law and be a reference point for harmonisation for Chief Constables to ensure legislation is implemented throughout the country in the same way.

Attorney-General (A-G)
The A-G is the government's senior legal officer and is appointed by the Prime Minister of the day from within the ranks of MPs who were practising barristers before they were elected to the House of Commons. The A-G represents the Crown – the government's interests in important legal cases.

Lord Chancellor
The Lord Chancellor of the day is the most senior appointment in the whole judicial system and the Lord Chancellor will be an eminent legal practitioner. On becoming the Lord Chancellor he will be a member of the government's Cabinet. It is a highly powerful, political and prestigious job. The Lord Chancellor has three major roles: the speaker of the House of Lords (for the government of the day), the head of Britain's judiciary and the role of Lord Chancellor. The power and scope of the Lord Chancellor's role is extensive and he is the only Cabinet member to play an active role in three essential areas of government and policy. The Lord Chancellor advises the Queen on the appointment of the judiciary – the appointment of senior judges.

Judges
The judges are among the most senior practitioners of law, and preside over the running of any case that appears in the higher courts requiring a judgment. In Britain, there is a reasonable argument about how old some

judges are; in the main, the majority strive to achieve justice alongside implementing well established practices for a just and legal outcome with each case before them. They will command a significant level of legal experience.

Judges hold enormous power and privilege and they are the most important characters in the court because it is the judge who oversees the practice of law and assists a jury. A judge does what their title suggests – they judge. What informs making a judgment and a sentence on an alleged criminal is a juggling of both sides' legal arguments, the evidence, that together we have to call justice. They ensure legal representatives present cases within the law (to try to keep manipulation of jurors to a minimum), assist jurors with complex legal terminology and direct the jury in the key issues before they go away to debate and decide the case on trial and reach a decision about innocence or guilt, and keep the media under control. The judge will determine the severity of a sentence after the jury has reached its decision about innocence or otherwise.

When a judge is presiding over a trial and the case has presented anomalies that require a new basis for decision in the court where the case is being heard, the decision is called a precedent. The precedent will stand as active law unless and until overturned by a higher court – hence common law going back centuries and influencing the present. This precedent is active only within the court's jurisdiction and status. A judge's summing-up, 'reason for deciding', is a very short statement or sentence, considered to be the heart and essence of the point of a case or legal issue the judge has sought to secure through juggling ancient and modern law.

Different types of courts

In Scotland
District courts
The district court is at the bottom end of the court hierarchy in Scotland. It only deals with summary criminal matters. The district court can impose a prison sentence of up to 60 days and impose a fine of up to level 4 (presently £2,500). The most common types of offences to be dealt with in the district court are breach of the peace, assault, vandalism, theft (but not theft by housebreaking), speeding, TV licensing offences, electricity fraud and miscellaneous road traffic offences.

The district court is a lay court where a justice of the peace who is a lay person sits with a legally qualified clerk (in some areas justices sit in threes).

The only exception is stipendiary magistrate courts in Glasgow where the stipendiary magistrate sits on his or her own and is legally qualified and has the same powers as a sheriff who is sitting summarily. The difference between summary procedure and solemn procedure is that in summary procedure the judge sits on his own.

Sheriff Courts

These courts are the next highest level in the court hierarchy and managed by the Scottish Court Service. The courts deal with summary cases involving criminal matters where up to a three-month or £5,000 fine can be imposed. Sheriffs are solicitors who do not practise law upon becoming a sheriff. In 'solemn' cases a sheriff will hear a case with a jury and has authority to impose a maximum prison sentence of three years.

Supreme Courts

The Supreme Courts have two branches. One deals with civil cases. The other (High Court of Justiciary) deals with serious violent crimes such as rape and murder and has the authority to impose a maximum prison sentence of life. The cases are led by advocates and Queen's Counsel and usually heard before a jury.

Court of Criminal Appeal

If an appeal is lodged it goes before three judges who will be advocates or Queen's Counsel and if a new point of law is presented a further two judges may be included to reach a decision about an appeal.

The Scottish Court Service and Scottish Executive Justice Department Courts Group have several excellent publications (many that are free) about various courts and their duties. For information contact:

> **The Scottish Court Service**
> **Hayweight House**
> **23 Laurieston Street**
> **Edinburgh**
> **EH3 9DQ**
> **Telephone: 0131 229 9200**
> **Fax: 0131 221 6890**
> **E-Mail: enquiries@scotcourts.gov.uk**
> **Website: www.scotcourts.gov.uk**

In England and Wales

Magistrates' court

At the present time, there are approximately 700 magistrates' courts all over the country. However, this number is likely to be significantly reduced by the changes that are currently underway in PM Blair's government. Magistrates' courts are presided over by three judges called justices of the peace (JPs) and these individuals are appointed by the Lord Chancellor and are the closest that the general public – not legally qualified – get to playing a role in our legal system, as they can become JPs. There is another form of magistrate called a stipendiary: these magistrates are qualified solicitors and they deal with more complex and serious matters. Stipendiary magistrates sit alone in judgment. JPs work part-time and are paid expenses and a nominal sum for loss of earnings and are assisted on matters of law and procedure by the court clerk. The clerk sits immediately in front of the JPs. The clerk will be a qualified solicitor or barrister.

The type of offence that a person is accused of determines in which court the case will be tried – the magistrates' court or the Crown Court. Because of this, all offences are divided into three categories:

1. **Summary offences:** these are tried only within a magistrates' court, for example, driving issues or common assault.
2. **Either-way offences:** these are tried in the magistrates' court or the Crown Court, for example, theft, burglary or dangerous driving. These are 'either way' because where the crime is sufficiently serious, i.e. where the offence carries a probation sentence, suspended sentence or heavy fine and where an alleged criminal's reputation and freedom are at stake, that individual has the right to ask for trial by jury. The current government is reviewing many of these either-way offences along with other areas of the criminal justice system.
3. **Indictable-only offences:** these can be tried only in the Crown Court, e.g. robbery, rape or murder. For readers of this book affected by serious violent crime, the Crown Court will be the most probable venue for trial.

Crown Court

The Crown Court will try all indictable-only offences and those either-way cases transferred from the magistrates' court. The Crown Court will also sentence defendants sent to the Crown Court by the magistrates' court after a trial of an either-way offence where JPs take the view that they do not have the sentencing powers that reflect the crime.

A trial in the Crown Court is by judge and a jury and it is the role of the judge to be the arbiter of law, whereas the jury decides on the facts of the case. At this present time a jury consists of twelve citizens who have the power to decide upon the guilt or the innocence of the defendant and the judge has the responsibility to sentence the defendant when the jury concludes that the defendant is guilty. The issue of whether to continue using juries and for what type of cases is currently under review by PM Blair's government.

The Crown Court has the powers to hear appeals from a defendant convicted in a magistrates' court against a sentence imposed by the magistrates if the individual pleaded not guilty. A prosecution party has no right of appeal to the Crown Court. Decisions made within the Crown Court do not bind any other court.

Court of Appeal
The Court of Appeal's main function is to hear appeals about Crown Court decisions. A defendant, as of right, may choose to appeal as a matter of course against the conviction – where the appeal involves a question of law. If it involves a question of fact, or a combination of fact and law, then leave is required. If the appeal is against sentence, leave of the Court of Appeal is required. The head (President) of the Criminal Division of the Court of Appeal is the Lord Chief Justice who, in reaching a decision, is assisted by several Lords Justices of Appeal. Decisions of the Court of Appeal bind all inferior courts.

A prosecution cannot appeal to the Court of Appeal against the acquittal of a defendant, or against the sentence imposed upon the defendant. It is within the powers of the A-G, if he perceives the sentencing of an individual to be unnecessarily lenient, to take leave of the Court of Appeal and refer the case to the Court of Appeal for review of the sentence.

House of Lords (HL)
The HL is the final court of appeal in England, Wales and Northern Ireland but excludes Scotland in criminal cases. There is a requirement, if an appeal is to be heard by the HL, that the appeal must involve a significant point of law of general public importance. The title given to the five so-called Law Lords is 'Lords of Appeal'. There is only one court and consequently very few cases reach the HL. A decision from the HL is binding on all other courts. If a point on European law comes before the HL and the parties concerned cannot agree on interpretation or its application then the HL must refer this point to the ECJ for a final decision (Article 177 EC Treaty).

Court

European Court of Justice (ECJ)

Increasingly, British citizens are turning to the ECJ to pursue the justice that, regrettably, the UK system is failing to provide. This does not mean going to the ECJ (in Luxembourg) literally, as EC law is often enforceable directly in our national courts. In 1973, the UK became a member of the European Community (EC) and consequently the UK is also subject to EC law, which is presided over by fifteen judges – one for each member state. These judges normally sit in smaller chambers – in plenary only for matters of significance.

The purpose of the ECJ is to ensure that the treaties are interpreted correctly and that EC law is applied uniformly across the member states. Its role is enshrined within the constitution of the EC (the Treaty of Rome). Once the ECJ has interpreted the issue of legal contention the case is then returned – in this case to the HL to pursue resolution; the HL must accept the decision of the ECJ, which is supreme in matters of EC law.

European Court of Human Rights (ECHR)

Increasingly, again, British people seeking justice are turning to the ECHR (in Strasbourg), because they cannot secure justice within the British legal system. In order for a person to make an application to the ECHR, they must first show they have exhausted all domestic legal remedies available to them – at this time that final stage is appealing to the HL. The decision as to whether you have a case for the ECHR to hear is assessed by the Human Rights Commission whose decision on the matter is final.

The ECHR decides upon alleged human rights abuses. Although it is not part of the EU, it is supported by the member states of the EC who signed the Convention on Human Rights, including Britain. These rights include: the right to life, the right to liberty and security of the person, the right to a fair trial, to freedom of expression, to education and to freedom of religion. The past decisions of the ECHR are now binding upon our domestic courts as we have incorporated the Convention into our domestic law: in the Human Rights Act 1998 (brought into force in Scotland in 1998 and in England and Wales in 2000).

Useful addresses

Websites

www.homeoffice.gov.uk this website covers a huge range of areas of Home Office work and other allied services like the Justice and Victims Unit and Probation Service. From this site the National Probation Directorate has a public enquiry e-mail facility that can be accessed for details of your nearest probation/victim liaison service.

www.hmprisonservice.gov.uk information about the prison service for England and Wales

www.scotland.gov.uk an excellent website covering many useful and well laid-out Scottish Departments with excellent up-to-date information on a wide range of criminal justice matters and statistics.

Court Witness Protection Schemes

Please see local telephone book or ask your FLO or social services for details about visiting and finding out about what this service offers.

Did you sweep us far from your feet?
Reset in stone this stark belief?
Salted eyes, and a sordid dye
Too many years.

But don't despair this day, will be their damnedest day
Ooh, if you take these things from me.

Did you feed us tales of deceit?
Conceal the tongues who need to speak?
Subtle lies and a soiled coin
The truth is sold, the deal is done.

But don't despair this day, will be their damnedest day
Ooh, if you take these things from me.

Undefied, no signs of regret.
Your swollen pride assumes respect.
Talons fly as a last disguise
But no return, the time has come.

So don't despair this day, will be their damnedest day ...

Ask your appointed police officer to make contact with the local social services to see you at home as a priority, or the hospital social worker if you are an in-patient. Most hospitals have social work departments and the police can liaise with hospital staff to make sure that they see you quickly. At the point of personal tragedy, it is better to secure a statutory and multi-agency combination of services to protect and assist you as they have the power, expertise and duty in law.

It is important to consider asking social services to see you, especially if you have urgent crises (e.g. relating to children, emergency rehousing or medical needs). If you choose to have an advocacy group act as a voice for you, it should be done when you want and you have chosen. As mentioned, in an unravelling crisis, making plans that will protect, create a level of control and safety should involve you in the planning. (See sections on police, pp. 22-53, social services, pp. 160-172, and proposals for the future for specialist teams, pp. 321-322.)

The way it is

Unfortunately, there are very few advocacy groups listed specifically for people affected by violent-related crime, and there are some groups who did not respond to invitations for inclusion here. There are a few groups which at this time it is not desirable to include. It is both ironic and disturbing that the criminal justice system exists because of victims, but so little qualitative or credible provision exists for victims of violence. It seems everyone fares better except victims – criminals receive free expert legal representation, psychiatric care and rehousing. The legal profession has a lucrative source of income. It is not balanced or fair, and those affected by violent crime deserve much more than ad hoc groups and inadequate legal care and protection. It seems that those affected remain an afterthought, to be made grateful for what is, too often, too little, too late.

An overview

Why refer to a small cluster of generally well-intentioned and fragmented but, again, generally, non-productive groups as the *victim club*? Although they communicate with one another, they also appear unable to work effectively with each other for the wider good of society. They have complex reasons for being involved and congregate in a cycle of unproductive 'conferences'. Yet they fail to galvanise local community interest or awareness. To say 'conferences' is to exaggerate the usefulness of what takes place and of the groups' importance. Sadly, they fail to ask themselves why they are not progressing; and generally, they show an alarming level of ignorance about the needs of how to help victims. This is highlighted by their failure to aid individuals effectively so that victims can transform their personal agony into progressive lives. The *victim club* does not generally attract volunteers with strategic or fundraising skills who wish to be associated with the *victim club*. The *victim club* assumes public money should be offered without proper accountability or good use.

These small groups – some have charitable status – have generally evolved out of genuine, personal, horrendous, violent experiences where the victims' needs were inadequately addressed. The absence of effective services is a recurring issue throughout many people's experiences. Genuine unmet need is a consistent beginning for any emerging social group pioneering for immediate help and long-term change. The dilemma the *victim club* appears to have is that it is 'stuck'. It is 'stuck' in that many of the key activists carry patently unresolved problems that directly get in the way of their own best intentions. No amount of funding will be enough to make such a group useful if they lack accountability and produce a service that is effective. Sadly, at this time, these groups fail to provide victims of violent crime with anything nourishing and useful. They appear to be stuck and this is due to a lack of objective distance from personal trauma, lack of skills and an inability to attract serious statutory funding or credibility.

There are many reasons that have led to this unfortunate state of affairs. It seems a common cluster of factors exist that make them undesirable to use when in deep crisis, including:

• general failure to attract well-trained volunteers;
• failure to attract well-trained volunteers fails to produce serious funding or volunteers;
• failure to provide developed and credible responsive strategies for developing themselves into inclusive services – some after ten years. For example, some of the *victim club* state that only those who are family and who have experienced murder can help those affected by murder. This is silly: many people live in unmarried lifestyles; many violent crimes take place within 'normal families'. Many families affected by murder state that they want experts to help them, and not another family, especially if they are 'stuck' in their personal grief and loss. Many victims of violent crime experienced violence within a family environment;
• they tend to exclude many sections and ethnic minority communities, gay people or single people who are not part of a family but remain in need;
• the institutional power that the Home Office and Victim Support control nationally for victims dictates the national awareness of the health, social and legal needs of a silent large minority of victimised people. Small groups cannot compete without support of the authorities, media and police. This goes against government talk about diversity or choice. There is no real choice for victims within this sector of groups and the *victim club* members are not the agencies to fill this gap at this point in time;
• within the *victim club* are some dysfunctional groups who appear unable to offer objective hope and change in the lives of victims. There is no power in the status of victim, nothing nourishing and productive to be trapped for many years as a permanently angry victim;
• to be a victim of violence is a horrendous experience – an event of life-changing impact, indeed – but need not mean that to be forever stuck as a 'permanent victim' can help people or is healthy. Some within the *victim club* cannot develop beyond the 'permanent victim' mindset, always out of control, always angry. No one benefits from this. The term 'victim' is not very pleasant and not a label that most victims wish to have pinned on them forever – people wish to progress and reclaim control and have nourishment in their lives, and to do more than survive. This is not to belittle physically raw and anguished horror: it means most people need to progress with quality help;
• some of the reasons for lack of diverse services for victims is that people affected by serious violent crime need expert statutory services;
• the *victim club* would not be trapped if people affected by violent crime were afforded the same automatic choice of expert services that violent criminals are afforded;

- the *victim club* needs to step back and look at what is its real motivation and for whom. To step back and review the remarkable communities that have endured centuries of abuse, stigma and prejudice and ask how and why have they transformed themselves. What is it that these communities have produced that the *victim club*, sadly – and, in all probability, for many years to come – will not achieve?;
- if these few groups looked intellectually and sought guidance from the disability movement, the gay movement and women's movement they would find a high level of organisational skill, education and knowledge. All these groups have a diverse set of members that specialise in specific areas and do not try to be everything that they cannot be. They avoid unproductive personality-power games in the higher pursuit of empowering members of their communities. It is not so long ago in Britain that the disabled, gay people and women were placed in psychiatric institutions for life simply for being different. These communities can act as markers of pride and education for the fragmented and angry victim club, as these communities have developed some of the greatest and diverse responses to social needs since the 1950s. They have also contributed to a large number of violently victimised people over many years. Our society owes these groups so much for transforming suffering into dignity and dignity into tangible and measurable services producing political public awareness – and change.

Why is it like this?

Human weaknesses get in the way of making services for victims work well. People start with good intentions, but the deep tragedy of their personal loss fuels the emergence of a group can become *the* same reason for blocking genuine progress; personally or for the group. In time, the 'issues' overshadow the unmet personal unmet needs and these will not go away until faced – privately. Important public issues become shadowed and lost by the wrong issues, especially if the group does not have enough strong people to deal constructively with a strong personality that is off-track. If strong-willed people with important contributions become somewhat lost because of a mixture of public concern, egoism, dominating personalities, lack of personal awareness or lack of democratic processes, then the group will collapse and sometimes this is the best end for a group.

This is common in these phases of evolution where there is no significant-sized group anyway. It is not uncommon for splinter and dissatisfied members to break away and start afresh and continue to maintain the goals that first brought them together. These are common phases for many in a group's development; individuals have to move away, or take a different task in a group for that group to progress or continue. This period of change can be stressful and is inevitable as a group matures, or disappears, and becomes more than a group reacting and responding to injustice and unmet need. It is the point when a group must decide whether it is going to be more than a neighbourhood support group or a regional, robust, managed organisation. A group's ability to have clear standards of practice, training and accountability is a marker of its ability to be of genuine use to a community. It is hoped that in future editions of this handbook there will be greater representation and existing groups will have time to mature and review their standards and practices for the benefit of all.

Right now, where are the violent crime victim-focused groups represented within the rapidly changing political forums and changes like the NHS Partnership Boards? How will the political and social care needs of victims find voice in the new arena of policy shaping? Inability to rise beyond the status of perpetual victim will never liberate ordinary people affected by violence to the prominence they need. Against this landscape and experience, it does not offer newly victimised people direct assistance or progress.

These are not new or radical assertions. Similar observations have been made by people in need and academics like Professor Paul Rock in his work, which gives an overview of policies for victims and development of groups in Britain and some of the 'tribal' clashes.

A few tips
- Until the cluster of unremarkable and undesirable victims groups evolve and mature into credible and inclusive organisations, they should be avoided.
- Discuss with your FLO, social services or some of the advocacy organisations if you feel the need for further agencies to help; establish what they should be able to provide you with. It is your nightmare and your life – select groups carefully. It is not good enough for a group to say 'we know what it's like' as sole reason for coming into your nightmare: what else can this group tangibly provide? The aim is to reduce turmoil, not have others increase it!
- It simply is not good enough for a newly traumatised person to be contacted by such a group purely because they have had someone dear who has been murdered or gravely injured. In itself, for you, as a bewildered and very vulnerable person, confused empathy simply is not good enough. They are more likely to need you than you are to need them. Be selective and say 'no, thank you'!
- If any group approaches you with offers of help and cannot prove they have successfully completed police checks, successfully completed a minimum of fifty hours' volunteer training, have a clear reason of what they are offering and you have not requested their visit – then politely avoid them. It is quality and expert help you deserve and require.

Victim Support
Victim Support is *the* largest and most widely known voluntary agency for victims of violence in Britain. Those who have contact with them appear to

have very polarised views on them. Many people in need are very pleased and grateful for their intervention. However, many people have had varying degrees of dissatisfaction about Victim Support, from being ineffective and failing to be aware of the complexity of victims' needs, to sometimes giving less than helpful guidance – albeit with the best of intentions. It is the latter that requires some comment and constructive attention for statutory services to address. Victim Support features for many of us as 'the people' who sort victims of crime out. This stems from our hearing their name on TV and from our general awareness of public services. It is as though Victim Support is a venerable elder that, by virtue of age and reputation, is not questioned or allowed to be criticised – even constructively. Generally, it seems many people and professionals regard Victim Support as better suited to dealing with minor crimes. Victim Support stands aside and aloof with its unquestioned government backing from the other fragmented members of the *victim club*. Structurally alone, while dominating the 'voice' for victims, it seems to pay the price for unconditional compliance and dependence upon government funding. In part, it makes Victim Support grandiose, unsure of its national genuine usefulness, but remains the founder of the *victim club*.

However, it is *the* dominant voluntary organisation that attracts the largest funding from the Home Office, has automatic invitation to government forums for review of victim needs and enjoys media support. Victim Support is *the* policy shaper and 'voice' of victims that government chooses to accept. But, does Victim Support really reflect the large number of citizens affected by violent crime? Should it wish to carry, alone, the significant burden of being the dominant single agency for speaking for a nation's victims?

Can Victim Support produce services well and embrace government policies for diversity? Will it remain exclusive without showing the real diversity of Britain?

Victim Support has paid staff while much of its work is undertaken by volunteers, and the skills and training vary considerably throughout England, Scotland and Wales. Some individuals, and local schemes of volunteers, do remarkable work, but, generally, and as a matter of concern, people's experiences of Victim Support consistently say it is ad hoc and that standards and accessibility vary. Many seriously injured people find Victim Support of little or no value. One of the more effective services that Victim Support provides is the Court Witness Scheme. (See section on going to court: pp. 208-241.)

Victim Support simply cannot deal with everybody's problems all the time – and nor is it wise for Victim Support to wish to monopolise service provision to the nation. Unfortunately, Victim Support appears to continue to wish to try to do this by continuing its monopoly as the only powerful agency for everything to do with people affected by violence. This is doomed to fail the people affected by violent crime and challenge its own future existence. It has mistakenly done this for years, which has fostered resentment and (some) fair criticism about how good Victim Support really is. It is a victim of its own failure to politicise victims' issues, political greed and policies for expansion. It cannot do everything and it is unhealthy for our nation to have only one large charity. In no other business or service sector would such a monopoly be accepted, so we must ask why this has come about.

Where does Victim Support come from?

Unlike other groups from the *victim club,* Victim Support did not evolve from individuals' unmet needs but directly from a government pilot project. This has characterised the image, practice and value of Victim Support and its service conflict between political activity and passive compliance. It cannot shake this fact and image and contributes to the wider cynicism it attracts from many places.

The idea for a service dealing with victims of violence in Britain was conceived by NACRO, a government rehabilitation organisation for offenders' service, in the early 1970s. In 1974, a pilot scheme for victims in Bristol became a success and expanded with government aid into a national association of victim schemes in 1979. By the late 1980s, Victim Support, as it had been renamed, and distanced from the Probation Service, had secured permanent government funding and become *the* primary victim service to be used for referrals by Home Office dictate by police forces and other statutory services. Victim Support in a short time acquired the status of *the* 'voluntary' voice of the victim, whether victims wished so or not. If we look at Victim Support historically, in the 1970s and the massive social and political changes of that era, it was, from its inception, government led. It was not like many other organisations, e.g. services for battered women and later services for people with HIV, created and led by the people in need where politicised public pressure was placed to push for government concessions – it was not people led. Victim Support was the creation of a government agency – was this a means of controlling a potentially vocal and politicised community unlike groups, say in North America? The problem then – as now – is that the voice and the social, health and political aspects of real people affected by violent crime are muted; moreover, nor is it politicised or really user led. It provides a convenient election soundbite for successive governments to say – 'look how we help victims'.

Successive governments bestowed compliance with funding. However, with this also came access for Victim Support to other government agencies with a small but significant level of power within the machinery of the criminal justice system – a niche. Like an ancient aunt expecting a favourite chair to be reserved unconditionally, Victim Support is disinclined to sit anywhere other than where it is currently placed.

But, who does Victim Support really speak for – its funders, the people or government policy whims, or all of these? There are double binds littered throughout, making good intentions flawed. Several factors conspire against Victim Support reforming, including the turbulence of our times and Victim Support's inability to be dynamic. The state of play will continue: Victim Support will hold the same sway and hold government attention as society increasingly disintegrates. Our world is more fragmented and violent.

> But in these cases we still have judgement here –
> that we but teach bloody instructions,
> which, being taught, return to plague the inventor.
> This even-handed justice commends the ingredience
> of our poisoned chalice to our own lips.
> He's here in double trust ....
>
> ... And Pity ...
>
> William Shakespeare: *Macbeth*, Act 1, Scene 7

Power plus passivity

Fortunately, Victim Support is reviewing its practices and services. Locally, smaller schemes may have been undertaking reviews and we must hope that they will develop more confidence in being receptive to change and emerging as competent groups without domination. Victim Support will remain important as it has so much power from government and media support, e.g. the BBC's *Crimewatch* programme. But the quality of service that you receive will depend on the area and training of the local scheme. This is in part due to Victim Support having too much work to do – albeit by its choice – and of course the increase in violent crime.

Victim Support is seen nationally as stifling service alternatives and real diversity. However, in the absence of good-quality monitoring about how people experience it – statutory agencies say 'where's your proof?'. Quite. Where is it? The proof is changing the lack of diverse services for victims' needs and the overdue monitoring of what Victim Support users think of what they get. This is what the government claims to want from all services when talking about inclusivity and diversity. Many police forces have not requested that Victim Support provide service monitoring, which reflects how unimportantly victims are perceived.

This is unhealthy overall because, until very recently, Victim Support did not even monitor service users' comments about how effective and useful its services were even though recently it received £24m from the Home Office. In Scotland, service user comments were formally identified as an important quality marker for reviewing services – this started in November 2001; plans are afoot to introduce this in England and Wales in 2002. Approximately half of local groups have been collating services user comments for some years, but these have never been pulled into the national office for reviews. Victim Support's national headquarters is slowly changing and becoming more reflective about its services and, it is hoped, that it will encourage the Home Office to be constructive in aiding new groups and charities throughout England, Scotland and Wales. Despite good intentions and good work in areas, and with good individuals on board, Victim Support has not broken its unquestioned power and relationship with central government departments.

Past or present – where are they going?

This old academic observation by Claire Corbett and Mike Maguire continues to have a service and pressing political resonance today:

> a consequence of the new funding may be that allocation only to VSS and not to any other organisations concerned with victims, helps to give the former a status akin to a monopoly position within the 'victims' field'... The success of the government's victims policy now depends so much on the performance of this one organisation and will ensure that its profile remains high in the media and in official publications. NAVSS will become increasingly well known as the central source of information and comment, and perhaps, a focal point for campaigns to improve the way that victims are treated. Similarly, the police will be encouraged to attach higher priority to referrals to Schemes, and more victims will become aware of their existence and purposes.
>
> [...] however one consequence could be that the police, who are the chief repository of information about recent victims, come to regard VSS as the only organisation with which they need to communicate on any problem involving victims, and hence become reluctant to co-operate with others, particularly more radical and less compatible groups such as Rape Crisis Centres ... It is not difficult to imagine such attitudes forming part of a more general trend, whereby an 'orthodox version' of the 'victim problem' and its solutions is gradually created, based almost exclusively upon the philosophy, values and practices of the Victim Support movement.

Claire Corbett and Mike Maguire: 'The value and limitations of victim support schemes' in *Victims of Crime – A New Deal*

At worst, this adds a form of secondary institutional victimisation that does not benefit people affected with complex needs resulting from violent crime. Very few large organisations heavily funded by a government department would be allowed not to provide routinely comprehensive evidence of service users' comments and evaluation or place the services out to tender for best value for taxpayers' needs and money. Whatever their future changes hold, whether in the form of NHS trust-type financially 'independent' but not *really* independent regional groups, unless the culture at headquarters in England and Scotland is fundamentally altered, future changes will be like rearranging chairs on the Titanic. Britain needs more than one major victim service, which is developed in the section on setting up groups (see pp. 338–363).

For details of your local Victim Support scheme, check your local telephone book or check their website address for details.

First, remember to secure statutory service help. Voluntary and ad hoc voluntary help will not be an adequate replacement for the expertise of qualified social, legal, health and police services.

Useful reading

After Homicide – Practical and Political Responses to Bereavement, *by Professor Paul Rock,* published by Clarendon, 1998. A good overview of government policies for victims; historical development of victim groups in Britain.

Violence in Society – the Reality Behind Violent Crime, *by Alix Kirsta,* published by Century, 1998. A good self-help guide.

Hidden Volunteers – Evaluating the Extent and Impact of Unrecognised Volunteering in the UK, published by Community Services Volunteers, January 2000.

Community Futures – Local People's Hopes for Improving the World on Their Doorstep, October 2001.

The State of the Volunteering Nation – Why We Need to Open the Doors of the Public Services, published by Community Services Volunteers, April 2002.

Community Services Volunteers have many publications and reports stimulating opportunities for people to take activity in the life of their community:

The CSV Press Office
Telephone: 020 7643 1338
E-Mail: pressoffice@csv.org.uk
Website: www.csv.org.uk

Unresolved anger is a costly burden. It keeps traumatic material highly charged and in active memory. It keeps us chained to the past, in bondage to a heavy load that we carry around each day, a load that erodes peace, happiness and eventually health.

Resolving anger from a serious offence or trauma is not easy. It does not usually happen quickly or all at once. Rather, it is a process that may not progress until considerable healing has taken place.

Glenn R. Schiraldi Ph.D. – 'Unfinished Business' in *The Post-Traumatic Stress Disorder Source Book – A Guide to Healing, Recovery and Growth*

Nothing about life after violent crime is easy and nothing in this handbook is easy to achieve, nor does this handbook attempt to suggest it is anything other than what it is: a profoundly raw process. If a life is to have meaning after tragedy, all the issues highlighted in this handbook, including progressing through huge grief and many other harrowing obstacles, must be overcome. An additional burden in coming to terms with violation is adjusting to what it has taken from you; how you will progress to a stage where you can not only survive but, indeed, live with self-progress. It must begin with facing the fact that nothing can be the same. It begins with not denying the impact and, as a wise counsellor observed, when such tragedies crash into our lives it forces a confrontation about every aspect of our being. It involves our attitude to ourselves, the provision of services and resources and the political will properly to address the compensation and human rights of victims of violence. It is about everything – and it takes time. It takes time to make private sense of the intolerable; it takes time to seek out and accept as much professional guidance as we can. At some stage, and this will vary from individual to individual, a progressive way has to become a goal to unlock the intensity of what has taken place in order to begin to live life with meaning and achievement.

What is 'it'?

If, all the services are doing their part, what is 'it' that those who suffer must do to aspire to their greatest level of progress? To achieve such a fantastic goal may, even after many years since the tragedy, seem too overwhelming; walking away may seem all we can do. Without letting go of the power of the raw anger and hurt, it will not be possible to progress. It is the case that some people cannot move to a stage of progress and good living and so the suggested reading list highlights a few remarkable men and women who, against the odds, have succeeded. This is not to diminish the suffering of others, but it is about not allowing a criminal to add further casualties to their lists; perpetual raw grieving would not be the wish of those loved ones who are gone. The people listed are there to remind us of real hope and progress. They should be seen as the masters of the near-impossible, as they have moved forward in their lives. The journeys of these people trace a common path from the road of tragedy to surviving and progress. In order to progress, they had to face their rage and the totality of loss – with help! This is what 'it' is.

How?

Nothing is easy! In the process of transformation, what people feel is like a sense coming back to life, because when people emerge they will have changed. Nothing about life, or adjusting to injury, can allow people to be the same. Physically and mentally, change was inflicted and how to progress and live a life with new meaning involves making room to live with, and around, everything that is lost. This time, a slow change with your determination is required – one that you control and learn to master. There is no hierarchy of 'my loss is greater than yours' – profound suffering is real for those it affects. To find yourself talking and feeling like this will not help you.

This requires new ways of taking care of yourself. These include diet and exercise and breaking the silence violence creates in victims – an unhealthy and non-nourishing silence. It requires accepting, with courage, that no one can transform his or her life after such agony without expert help and legal guidance. It also calls for some painful soul-searching: what has this event done to you? It requires learning to talk about who and what you are – not just about the tragedy but about who you were before; to learn to make connections within your past and present life – and your inner and outer world; for example, the people you know and how you live and where. Maybe these were fine once, but are they enough now? Do they bring you harm, or nourishment and a slow, confident peace in your new life? Simplify your life in every way you can, or must. What is going to be your trick for successful rehabilitation?

Making connections ...

To help us make connections about living and our needs, it is useful to look at a theory of working with the terminally ill. Dr Elisabeth Kübler-Ross, who broke the Western taboo on discussing non-violent death, established a useful theory. In her work, she broke the silence and focused on the stages of dying and the needs of those dying from medical conditions; she compassionately brought this out into the open. Her influence in the care of the dying has had a huge benefit on how people understand the stages of dying, and it has educated certain professionals. As her work concentrated on those dying from anticipated illnesses like cancers and HIV/AIDS – conditions where time allows those affected to make time to adjust – it does not fit with unpredicted violent loss. However, her work does have some value in guiding those who must carry on in relation to adjusting to missing physical remains of people, adjusting to disability and adjusting to trauma brought about by violent crime.

Dr Kübler-Ross's gift was to locate the basic emotions people must find within themselves – both those directly affected and those indirectly affected by dying and death; the importance of facing up to the rawest feelings and trying to make sense of the intolerable; and because it goes against the human ego to cope with the sense that life is not forever. For those affected by violent crime, some aspects of the theory have value in terms of helping make sense of the emotional conflict. Her theory sits best in making connections with the mental trauma of the differing violent losses and how we may best make sense, adjust – and progress.

In her work, five core reactions to dying and death were identified. These are very helpful for people adjusting to violent loss because, rather than relating to the reactions of a conventional death (which remains a deep loss), these core elements relate more to the psychological trauma and struggle to adjust. The five reactions are: denial and isolation; anger; bargaining ('maybe they have the wrong person?', 'what if she went on holiday and hasn't told anyone?', 'maybe a retrial will prove it is not my friend?'); depression; and acceptance.

Acceptance is the theme of this section: the long, turbulent, private path towards a life of greater control, dignity, safety and fulfilment. If you refer to Professor Horowitz's list of trauma symptoms, you will see how these relate to the five core elements; see pp. 104–113. The list will not be a cure, but may help to provide foundations for facing the intolerable – to make sense in order to progress.

It is ...
Not smooth or easy! It is lonely and sometimes feels terrifying and littered with guilt, hate and self-loathing and the primal need to drown the hyper-feelings that must be resisted. It is not easy! Do not pretend the turmoil is not there or hope that with help and the passage of time all will revert to as it was before. You will find a way of handling pain as it becomes more manageable and the intensity and sore reminders ease.

It is about accepting what this tragedy has cost you and means, without becoming permanently 'stuck'; to find the state of connectedness with oneself or being where one's head, heart and environment flow – like a river. This is the trick and the goal. Events, smells or anniversaries will recharge raw feelings, and it is ultimately a tough decision not to become 'stuck' – but to let go. To flow emotionally against the odds, against 'flashbacks', panic, people crossing the street from embarrassment or turning one's home from one extreme of making your home a shrine to another extreme of throwing out every reminder. Find a new balance. A balance where a river of inner dignity and mental acceptance directs each action in changing beyond victim to survivor; to a 'marked' and renewed person.

It is the significant reduction in anguish and distress through self-responsibility and time that requires good-quality services and good people. It is to accept the totality of everything. To know within the deepest dread and terror that with time passing a real potential for achieving progress and good living exists. It is, to put it another way, to become a friend of the dread and how a merging of feelings changes a person with time so the hurting is less debilitating and becomes part of you. It is in the nature of love and loss to mourn. Without facing everything – everything the tragedy has brought about – nothing nourishing and stable will come to be.

Make realistic goals

If personal success in surviving violence is to become a nourishing reality, then you will have to change, as will those around you. Again, this is not easy. For some, it will mean learning to break a long habit of silence; for others, learning humility; for others, it will mean leaving destructive relationships behind. Realistic goals are important because it is tempting to make 'promises' that may be well intentioned but unrealistic, placing far too much pressure upon you. This will cause an added sense of failure when you need to remember the experience of winning. It will heighten depression and feelings of unworthiness and maybe it is you who needs to receive – and not give.

In time, slowly, very, very, slowly, begin to build nourishing and easy relationships. The crime changed you and everything that has come afterwards. In time, you will come to realise how strong and remarkable you are to have reached this point. You are no longer the person you, or others, once knew. There will be new crises as well as mundane matters ahead. This is in the scheme of ordinary living. They are enough! It is enough, and you have had enough. Enough! Move on.

The old pen-pal club ...

You will have amassed a pile of documents and solicitors' letters over the years. Do not throw documents away: they may be needed in the future and they could be important legal documents. Also, they lay testament to some of the practical effort, fear, rage, desolation; within your written lines is the proof of your struggle and the absence of grace. These cost you greatly and should not be a preoccupation but left as part of your heritage. So, for the time being, put them away – somewhere safe, in a bag.

Be open to good opportunities ...

A flower has opened in my heart ...
What flower is this, what flower of spring,
What simple, secret thing?
It is the peace that shines apart,
The peace of daybreak skies that bring
Clear song and wild swift wing.

Heart's miracle of inward light,
What powers unknown have sown your seed
And your perfection freed? ...
O flower within me wondrous white,
I know you only as my need
And my unsealèd sight.

Siegfried Sassoon: *A flower has opened in my heart*

To be realistic requires looking at everything, including those within your life and whether they bring power and safety, or drain you of either. To look at what your physical, mental and environmental needs are and to commit yourself to progress for yourself and those who are no longer with you is good. This may include looking at:

- People – greater desire to communicate and value the good relationships with others, to be assertive and cease to allow yourself to be 'wound up' by petty irritations or insignificant people.
- Personal – to understand how to know the meaning of 'enough'! To value the chance to make your life good. Maybe, after a lot of time recovering, to help people in need – but not too much of your time and maybe not with people affected by violent crime. What has happened in your life has made you a member of a growing minority and unwanted club – there is wisdom you have acquired and which enables you to do something for others.

- Opportunities – to learn to be open to new opportunities. Some profound changes have been violently forced upon you – now it is your time to find a new life, interests and skills. Use them!
- Time – violence forces a meaning about the value of time that will never be forgotten. Avoid futile people and events; surround yourself with people who use time as you wish to – avoid the ignorant. Ignorance is a bit like flu: it has an alarming ability to spread.

Place your personal matters in order and give sufficient time and practice to learn how to have fun without guilt – to live as well as you can with good fun. Strange as this may sound, you have a right to find this in your life.

Where to find the best ...
When violent trauma crashes into our lives, for many people, and for the first time in their adult lives, they have (un)wanted time. These are a few tips about constructively filling the void that initially is very menacing and empty. Try to find the energy and interest to search for as much information about your particular circumstances and interests as possible.

Libraries
Our libraries are generally under-resourced and facing closures, which is an indictment of our governments. While they exist, use them for somewhere to go to read newspapers and use reference libraries for details about legal aspects or special-interest matters beyond law. Libraries hold access to a lot of free information and the calm of a library can bring its own sanctuary and ensure that, in the early stages of adjusting, you get out and about. Libraries will save a lot of money, especially if you wish to seek out and select a solicitor, using a reference library to look through listings. If you are disabled, a mobile library service can still secure listings for you.

Websites
Some libraries allow free use of their computers to access the Internet if you want to check any of the web addresses. It will be up to you to find the best of all that is available for progressing your life and also to find the best ways not to become isolated from what is going on. Be cautious of all groups you may come across on the Internet and never part with private, financially related information; never let young people access the Internet without clear rules and guidance – e.g. check they have blocked access if going online. The Internet is a world-wide advertising board. Some people are selling information that is great and a lot more are selling deceit and worse.

The Internet is not adequately regulated by law: this is due to its rapid growth – the law has to catch up. Also, the Internet is world-wide, which is another headache for the law. Always check if groups are properly accredited with any agency. The web's greatest benefit for people trying to progress their lives is providing access to a huge range of people and organisations. Increasingly, services and individuals share skills and raise social issues through the Internet but common sense and caution are necessary.

Adult classes

Libraries can provide information about learning many skills, free of charge if you claim social security, on a great range of subjects, including basic computer skills, building a website or learning a language. Try to find the means to join two adult classes that are unrelated to violent crime and seek out good people – who do not have to have been affected by horror – to be good company. If you are in the early stages of adjusting and dealing with agencies and cannot afford a computer, then, certainly, learning a basic level of competence on computers gives confidence and control and will save a lot of time.

Useful reading

The Legacy of Rachel Nickell – The Last Thursday in July, *by André Hanscombe,* published by Century. A powerful story from a remarkable family. A source of strength, transformation, power and dignity for us all to learn and take strength and courage from.

Josie's Journey, *by Dr Shaun Russell,* published by BBC Worldwide, 2000. The powerful story of the remarkable Russell family; matches the above publication's qualities.

Victims of Violence, *by Joan Jonker,* published by Fontana/Collins. One woman's story of campaigning for victims of violent crime. Generally available from reference libraries.

Victims – Surviving the Aftermath of Violent Crime, *by Alix Kirsta,* published by Century, 1988. A self-help guide similar to this work but references to CICA are very outdated, as are references about some services, which is inevitable with any directory-style book. A book written for victims of violent crimes, their families, friends and colleagues, it offers advice on life after rape, assault or burglary, where to turn to for help, how the legal system works, understanding the long-term symptoms of shock, how the CICA scheme works and practical ways to protect yourself. Not readily available but libraries can order for you.

Narziss and Goldmund, *by Hermann Hesse,* originally published by Penguin and recently published in 1997 by Peter Owen using a different translator and entitled Narcissus and Goldmund. Ideally, the first edition is preferable and its translation by Geoffrey Dunlop is more lyrical. For those struggling with adjusting to grief and change, this book provides fantastic prose and comfort. This fictional work is a masterpiece and worth seeking out through a library. It is a story of longing and transformation and what is found and lost along the way of a boy moving into adult life. It is set in medieval Europe; the writing is simply beautiful.

© Alex Thorn 2003

Legal

Lady Bracknell: 'How old are you?'

Jack: 'Twenty-nine.'

Lady Bracknell: 'A very good age to be married at. I have always been of the opinion that a man who desires to get married should either know everything or nothing. Which do you know?'

Jack (after hesitating): 'I know nothing, Lady Bracknell.'

Lady Bracknell: 'I am pleased to hear it. I do not approve of anything that tampers with natural ignorance. Ignorance is like a delicate exotic fruit; touch it and the bloom is gone. The whole theory of modern education is radically unsound. Fortunately, in England, at any rate, education produces no effect whatsoever. If it did, it would prove a serious danger to the upper classes, and probably lead to acts of violence in Grosvenor Square. What is your income?'

Oscar Wilde: The Importance of Being Earnest

Finding a solicitor who is competent in criminal compensation or medical negligence is not easy. But take heart: there are many fine men and women practising law if you know where to look and if you ask around! To make your search easier, this handbook lists some of Britain's most dynamic solicitors with the relevant experience.

Undertaking criminal injury cases is not particularly attractive for solicitors as it involves a considerable amount of work dealing with an aloof and difficult agency, i.e. the Criminal Injuries Compensation Authority (CICA), for little profit. This is especially the case since the introduction of the Criminal Injuries Compensation Act 1995 and its cost - or tariff-based, injury-scoring system. The Act is a controversial one which, sadly, the present government wishes to keep.

The relationship you have with your chosen solicitor will be one of the most important relationships you will have in your life subsequent to the tragedy that has occurred. It will define the practical, emotional and legal consequences of the tragedy and afford you the financial means with which you can progress in life – with dignity, independence and the freedom to choose services. The compensation for the injuries you sustained, or those that affected another person in your life, will depend on the solicitor's aptitude, their ability to integrate legal knowledge with your individual circumstances plus medical evidence and their capacity to work dynamically. An indication of the calibre of the prospective solicitor will be indicated, in part, simply by the manner in which he or she answers your early questions.

It is important that you take responsibility for finding the best service available. Do not choose a firm just for its proximity to your home – much of the work will be done by correspondence anyway. If you find the expertise you need is 100 miles from your home, you should consider what is more important to you: the convenience of a local firm or your long-term goal of finding the best legal representation available to secure justice for your future. The relationship that will develop is a professional one which, while costing you money, will provide expert guidance and action. It is a relationship that requires your patience and trust in the solicitor and his/her ability to evidence tangible respect for your needs in order to pursue the best outcome with the CICA.

No matter how much you respect your solicitor, or personally like him/her (which should be near the bottom of your scoring system), if you wish to have a smooth working relationship that is cost-effective and as pleasant as possible for both, then a letter of terms as to what work is to be done is necessary. After a couple of months, the exchange of information should be less frequent as the solicitor should be in receipt of all the unresolved issues and have a firm grasp of how to proceed. Remember, every piece of work the solicitor does will cost money. Therefore, you may wish to consider asking your solicitor to send you a monthly update on all aspects of what work has been done on your case and what specific problems, if any, still exist. Remember, if you have significant injuries, or complicated fatal-loss issues, resolving your application could take years. This is unlikely to be the fault of your solicitor.

Which firm – where to begin?

Do not assume it will automatically follow that, because a firm has many branches, it will deliver a better, more experienced service or, most importantly, it is going to give your particular case more time and attention. Draw up a table, as illustrated on page 263, and include the names of six to ten firms with their phone numbers.

Contact with a solicitor

Remember, you will have only a one-hour free consultation with one solicitor. So take your time to reflect upon how you have assessed the firms you contacted before using this important free legal advice session – if you decide it is necessary to meet. The one-hour free session is referred to as

'Legal Help' and is the only free legal aid from the Legal Services Commission (LSC) you will be entitled to, so use this time to agree formally what work you are asking a solicitor to take on.

You will see that the table on page 263 provides you with an easy reference from which to make telephone calls to prospective solicitors. This will enable you not just to assess your gut feeling about the person you are speaking to, but also to analyse any variations to answers to the same question. Here are a few questions you may wish to ask a prospective solicitor. It is recommend you ask at least six firms before short-listing to three or four.

Questions

1. How many criminal compensation claims have you personally dealt with?
2. How many criminal compensation claims, with my specific injuries, have you dealt with?
3. Realistically, in your experience, how long do you think my claim will take to be resolved?
4. Realistically, in your experience, what type of final award am I likely to secure?
5. What options for payment of legal fees do you offer, e.g. per hour, or a percentage of the final award?
6. Have you taken claims to the old CICB or through the CICA Scheme? If you were successful please say in what specific way?
7. Are you a member of any professional body? If so, which one and would you object to me confirming this membership?
8. Have you attended any specific training courses for Personal Injury solicitors with legal institutions or charities?
9. How do you keep clients up-to-date with developments concerning claims? Do you write to them once a month in writing, or phone every two weeks?
10. What information would you require to start my application with the CICA?

Choose a scoring system and stick with it like glue! For example, use a system from 0 to 5 where 0 = seriously awful, 1= only if desperate, 2 = unremarkable, 3 = maybe just about OK, 4 = sounds good, 5 = brilliant, clear, thorough! Brilliant = totally dynamic, willing to listen, clear grasp of your problems in law, upfront, not shallow or sickly, not patronising, no-messing answers, no sales pitch and a clear explanation of fees! Do not use half points! Do not start to add totals until you have finished speaking to the

Scoring Solicitors

Firm	Phone Number	Scores										Total Score
		Q1	Q2	Q3	Q4	Q5	Q6	Q7	Q8	Q9	Q10	

Scoring Solicitors: 0=seriously awful 1=only if desperate 2=unremarkable 3=maybe just about OK 4=sounds good 5=brilliant, clear, thorough!

Q1. How many criminal compensation claims have you personally dealt with?
Q2. How many criminal compensation claims, with my specific injuries, have you dealt with?
Q3. Realistically, in your experience, how long do you think my claim will take to be resolved?
Q4. Realistically, in your experience, what type of final award am I likely to secure?
Q5. What options for payment of legal fees do you offer, e.g. per hour, or a percentage of the final award?
Q6. Have you taken claims to the old CICB or through the CICA Scheme? If you were successful please say in what specific way?
Q7. Are you a member of any professional body? If so, which one and would you object to me confirming this membership?
Q8. Have you attended any specific training courses for Personal Injury solicitors with legal institutions or charities?
Q9. How do you keep clients up-to-date with developments concerning claims? Do you write to them once a month in writing, or phone every two weeks?
Q10. What information would you require to start my application with the CICA?

© T.S. Duckett 2003

263

whole batch of prospective firms. Try to remain detached and analytical, without any sense of commitment at this stage. Telephone the prospective solicitors over a period of a few days, while the impression they each make is still reasonably fresh, but do not be *too* hasty to short-list. If you remain unimpressed with all/many of your candidates, choose some more and repeat the process.

Making a decision

When you have found a few solicitors to short-list, see which have the highest scores and why. If a firm stands out a mile, then you have a winner. If two or three firms come very close, does something stand out to give one the edge over the others? If so, you may wish to contact the short-listed firms again or write to them, 'without obligation', to discuss the general issues of your claim – but there is a problem here. Many firms will not communicate 'informally' beyond an initial telephone enquiry or letter and will expect formal payment, per hour, beyond the initial brief question and answer and 'Legal Help' one-hour session. For some solicitors, it is a method to try to rush prospective clients into making a decision to use their firm. If you come across such a firm, erase them from your short-list. The solicitor's willingness, at this early stage, can help your final decision because this is an indication of how a solicitor responds to a demand being made of them.

Why are you drawn to one firm over another? This is what you must keep asking yourself, and stick to the table you have designed. It is very, very important that you make a good decision as early as you can after the incident. If possible, try to choose a good solicitor within the first four weeks of your initial tragedy. Legal excellence is what you must concentrate upon securing. If you are in London and you come across an outstanding firm in Manchester or Plymouth, so be it! This must be the firm for you. Differences exist between Scottish and English law, so it is best to look within your country's own legal jurisdiction. If you live in Wales, it is recommended to consider English solicitors and vice versa if in England.

Now that you have made the best choice possible, having asked all the pertinent questions you can think of (in your current position), selected a diverse number of firms (and not for geographical convenience), stuck like glue to your scoring system and taken a few days to mull over all the information given by prospective solicitors … mull things over for one more day! If you are still comfortable with your choice, call the chosen solicitor and ask to make an appointment, if you agree that a meeting is necessary, or agree, in writing, the terms for that solicitor to resolve your criminal compensation claim (solicitors call this 'taking instructions').

Once you have made your decision

What a stressor – well done! This is not an easy process at the best of times – and to accomplish making this decision at a time of intense stress is no mean feat. This decision must be made from a cold analysis of scores based on a set of objective questions – with a little recognition for instinct and intuition when speaking with the solicitors. The first session – agreeing initial terms – should be provided for within the Legal Help scheme. The solicitor will ask you to provide as much original medical and police detail as possible. When you both agree the terms, there should not be very many new areas to surprise you or the solicitor. This is because the core elements of your selection process should have provided specific details about what you want – so the solicitor should be able to make an informed commentary on your situation.

Initially, it will help the solicitor if you send all documentation necessary:
• police crime number;
• hospital reports and addresses;
• all injuries/people affected;
• whether you have already requested a criminal injuries compensation application.
See the CICA section about what documentation a solicitor will need to forward to the CICA for possible awards for injury, pp. 290–295.

It is important to have, in writing, a copy of the agreed terms and to let the solicitor know, promptly, if something is missing or wrong. Matters such as: how you wish to be kept up to date, the issues that need to be addressed immediately, the mid-term issues requiring attention and a termination clause if there is any dissatisfaction with the solicitor's performance. This dissatisfaction cannot be because they did not get the exact sum of money sought, but rather if the final award is unreasonably low, due to their failure to provide the CICA with all relevant documentation, or through a sub-standard service generally.

If matters go seriously wrong

It is always important to make sure you have tried every means possible to sort out any problems, or dissatisfaction, openly and clearly. To lodge a complaint is a serious matter and a draining, and sometimes costly, process, so be sure to try to make every effort to avoid the need to complain by being constructive and direct. As the months turn into years, the pressures can feel too much – and they may not be the fault of your solicitor.

Within legal institutions, there exist bodies that investigate complaints about negligent work practices, exorbitant fees and other substandard practices. As with lodging any complaint in Britain, the initial burden of cost lies with you and you will need to provide mountains of paperwork to prove effectively that you are telling the truth. All avenues to resolve a complaint should be exhausted directly with your solicitor. If you cannot resolve the matter with the actual solicitor, then submit in a letter the specific points of complaint to the firm's senior partner before lodging an external complaint. If this produces no acceptable resolution, then the following bodies exist to investigate.

Office for the Supervision of Solicitors (OSS)

The OSS was established by the Law Society in September 1996 and, although it has independent powers, it remains accountable to the Law Society. The OSS's responsibility is to investigate allegations of professional misconduct and inadequate legal service, but it does not provide legal advice. Through the Remuneration Certificate procedure, the OSS is able to express a view about whether a solicitor's charges have been fair and reasonable. In extreme cases, it can investigate complaints of gross overcharging as this comes within its responsibility.

Although the organisation is in its infancy, it continues to provide a vital service with enthusiasm, though it is underfinanced. The OSS has been inundated with requests for help as it continues to strive for justice for the public against corrupt solicitors. Yet, a seemingly regressive notion was aired by its director who expressed serious concerns about the volume of complaints in his second Annual Report (1999). He alerted the public that the increasing number of complaints received by the OSS is "jeopardising our ability to protect the public ... we must change our strategy if this problem is to be solved. We must shift the emphasis of our role away from direct investigation of every complaint ... the profession, at a local level [the firms people will be complaining about], must become the primary complaints handlers, enabling us to concentrate our resources less on dealing with individual complaints and more on a supervisory role".

If this proposal is enacted, it will mean even less opportunity for people to secure justice within the legal system, but also begs the question: what is the OSS really aiming to achieve? These proposals are self-defeating. They are cost-cutting measures that will *not* help people and will diminish the honourable objectives of the OSS. The OSS is an essential, if under-resourced, supervisory service confronting criminal and sub-standard solicitors. It requires greater funding to continue its work and meet the ever-increasing referrals.

Choosing a Competent Solicitor

The failure of the OSS lies in not making known publicly the names of criminal and sub-standard solicitors, which allows these individuals to resurface elsewhere and often repeat whatever misdemeanours they previously committed, knowing their professional body implicitly protects them. We saw what horrors the GP Dr Shipman, and his professional governing body's failure to act, produced.

Useful addresses

Office for the Supervision of Solicitors
Victoria Court
8 Dormer Place
Leamington Spa
Warwickshire
CV32 5AE
Telephone: 01926 820082/3
Fax: 01926 431435
HELPLINE: 01926 822007/8/9: Monday–Friday 9.30am–4.30pm
Remuneration Enquiry Line: 01926 822022

The Office of the Legal Services Ombudsman
22 Oxford Court
Oxford Street
Manchester
M2 3WQ
Telephone: 0161 236 9532
Fax: 0161 2362651

General Council of the Bar
3 Bedford Row
London
WC1R 4DB
Telephone: 020 7242 0082

Solicitors' Indemnity Fund (SIF)
100 St John Street
London
EC1 4EH
Telephone: 020 7566 6000

The Law Society for England and Wales
113 Chancery Lane
London
WC2A 1PL
Telephone: 020 7242 1222
Fax: 020 7320 5964
Website: www. lawsoc.org.uk (general)
Website: www.solicitor-online.com (listings of names of solicitors only)

The Law Society holds a complete list of solicitors for England and Wales but declines to make recommendations about any firm. It is also a regulatory body.

In Scotland

The Law Society for Scotland
Client Relations Office
26 Drumsheugh Gardens
Edinburgh
EH3 7YR
Telephone: 0131 226 7411
Fax: 0131 225 2934
Helpline: 0845 113 0018
E-Mail: cro@lawscot.org.uk
Website: www.lawscot.org.uk

A very useful Internet link to a broad range of Scottish legal agencies (owned by book publishers) is: **www.butterworthsscotland.com**
The Crown Office and the Procurator Fiscal Service are headed by the Lord Advocate, who is assisted by the Solicitor General for Scotland. They are the Scottish Law Officers and members of the Scottish Executive. The Procurator Fiscal Service is divided into areas, with an Area Procurator Fiscal for each area.

Argyll and Clyde – at Paisley
Ayrshire – at Kilmarnock
Central – at Stirling
Dumfries and Galloway – at Dumfries
Fife – at Kirkcaldy
Glasgow
Grampian – at Aberdeen
Highland and Islands – at Inverness
Lanarkshire – at Hamilton
Lothian and Borders – at Edinburgh
Tayside – at Dundee

Within the areas there is a network of forty-eight Procurator Fiscal offices – one for each sheriff court district.

The Procurator Fiscal Service for Scotland
29 Chambers Street
Edinburgh
EH1 1 LD
Telephone: 0131 226 4962
– for regional offices contact Head Office or visit website
Website: www.procuratorfiscal.gov.uk

In England and Wales

The Bar Pro Bono Unit is able to select individual cases in which it chooses to appoint an experienced barrister to represent a client for no fee, for example, a grievance or complaint with the CICA or an NHS trust. It is naturally inundated with requests, and contact is best made in writing before requesting an application form that is the basis for a decision to help. This application must be completed before a decision about assisting can be made.

> Co-ordinator
> The Bar Pro Bono Unit
> 7 Gray's Inn
> Gray's Inn Square
> London
> WC1R 5AZ
> Telephone: 020 7831 9733
> Bar In The Community: 020 7841 1341
> Fax: 020 7831 9733
> E-Mail: enquiries@barprobonounit.f9.co.uk
> Website: www.barprobono.org.uk

Association of Personal Injury Lawyers (APIL)

APIL was formed in 1990 by a group of solicitors and barristers representing injured people. They were dedicated to the improvement of services provided for victims of personal injury, promoting the interest of key opinion formers (central government and key policy-makers) and working for its members. The political lobbying to promote the needs, in law, of victims of violence by the APIL continues to be excellent. In 1999, APIL's objectives were to:

- promote full and just compensation for all types of personal injury;
- promote and develop expertise in the practice of personal injury law;
- promote wider redress for personal injury in the legal system;
- campaign for improvements in personal injury law;
- promote safety and alert the public to hazards whenever they arise;
- provide a communication network for members.

APIL was one of the most rigorous and vocal organisations to criticise the Conservative Government and its introduction of the Criminal Injuries Compensation Act 1995. In opposition, the current Labour Government was advocating the repeal of this Act – if it came into power. APIL continues to lobby for reforms to the current system and has formulated a Charter for Victims of Injury.

APIL is regularly contacted by victims of violent crime seeking details of the best law firms to approach for advice and herein lies a significant conflict between ordinary people's needs and APIL's policy not to recommend one particular firm over another. This is a difficult bind for an organisation, but it is an even worse bind for a layperson who needs to know where to start. That is why this handbook includes a list of firms that readily provide evidence of their experience and ability – see Directory for listings.

What APIL can do is the same as the Law Societies do for England and Wales for Scotland, and by sending enquirers a list of APIL members in their district. It remains the responsibility of the enquirer to pursue and select a firm. This sometimes leaves the victim of violent crime in a distressing circle because what he/she needs is the security of a professional body that guarantees excellence. APIL has a code of practice for its members. To be a member of APIL, applicants must be law students, practitioners or academics. It does not guarantee specialist competence in CICA claims, however – merely in personal injury law in general.

To get more information about the work of APIL, or to obtain a list of its members in your area, contact:

> **Association of Personal Injury Lawyers (APIL)**
> **33 Pilcher Gate**
> **Nottingham**
> **NG1 1QE**
> **Telephone: 0115 9580585**
> **Fax: 0115 9580885**
> **E-Mail: mail@apil.com**
> **Website: www.apil.com**

Listings of solicitors can be found in the Directory. Many of the firms listed there were found in the directories produced by the Spinal Injuries Association and Headway, which contain many more listings. Many of the firms listed in this book's Directory will also be found in *Chambers' Guide to the Legal Profession* and *Legal 500* and are definitely worth referring to in reaching a decision. These will be available from any large reference library with a good law section, or may be requested.

There have been restrictions. Victims' compensation may be refused or reduced if they have criminal convictions, even if these are unrelated to the current incident; the Criminal Injuries Compensation Authority, like the Committee, appears to consider that some victims are 'undeserving'.

But a social contract of this kind should surely include all citizens unless they are implicated in the crime that caused the injuries. The scheme has also been restricted by the imposition of a lower limit (currently £1,000) below which the victims receive no compensation, under the 1995 scheme an upper limit of £500,000.

This is not based on principle, but saves money. A case could be made for excluding awards amounting to less than their administrative costs, but no such limit restricts the prosecution of offenders, so there is no logical reason why it should be applied to victims.

> Martin Wright: *Justice for Victims and*
> *Offenders: A Restorative Response to Crime*

The way it is

We arrive at the section that shares the title of this handbook. For innocent victims who wish to survive and progress to the best of their abilities, quite often they will have no option but to seek government aid – state criminal compensation. No one likes charity, above all those who have already lost so much in their lives. Governments and administrators say the scheme for compensation is society's way of showing sympathy – but is this what is really happening? No victim wants sympathy, but they do want justice. Nor do victims wish to be made more vulnerable by having to pursue compensation, as it reminds them of their sense of loss of independence and the continued impact of the crime in their lives. Money is a highly emotive subject and, without it, people cannot progress their life and health. The scheme for allocating money is not generally perceived or administered as sympathetic, efficient or fair by people who deal with it.

It is strange how we treat victims of violence in our society. Sometimes, it seems as though we quietly believe it is their own fault: scroungers–cons or 'each to their own': 'sort your own life out'! It seems to be like this, until some tragedy affects that individual, then everything is different. We seem to treat people affected by violent crime as the Victorians treated the poor – that it was their responsibility to sort themselves out. The poor were made to feel cheap and low, being forced to enter the workhouse, which would be mean, meagre and demoralising. The price for entry was destitution.

There is much that is positive about taking control and responsibility for our lives and this we must all aspire to do. This is also making a contribution to your community in some constructive form and, when vulnerable, it involves receiving provision for needs, if we are to be a really civilised society. The slow and drawn-out process administered by the aloof, expensive, one-way service run by the CICA for many is as degrading and traumatic as the violent crime itself. But, for many, there will be no choice but to pursue a claim from this monopoly, and degradation will have to be endured. This is a sad reflection on any government that chooses to treat innocent, vulnerable citizens in such a way.

People will say: the CICA's better than nothing, would you rather we did not have it? But the question is redundant: the real issue is what would happen if all the victims of violence in need were not provided with compensation. They are likely to become a forceful political lobby, among other things. It should be noted that many choose not to apply as well. The issue is not about distributing money for money's sake and should never be so; it is about the unmet needs from injury and loss for those victims affected by violence. For such people, to be provided with a dignified service as part of a free legal service, which offered realistic amounts of compensation, would be an expression of real sympathy. Regrettably, applicants must pay all legal fees, usually from their compensation, unless they have other means such a trade union.

It is easy to criticise a service that has hard decisions to make and where money is limited – all exacerbated by emotive associations. But, after years, it is hard to come across a legal expert, public service worker or individual who has anything positive to say about the CICA. Unsurprisingly, the CICA, the Home Office and detached academics find the service very good overall – but, as a witness said during the 1960s Profumo trial – 'they would!'. Assessing long-term needs is complex work requiring competent and qualified people who are not shrouded and protected within cynical legislation. The work of the CICA is not easy, but is made even more difficult by the legislation that makes it clear what its principal goals must be. The compensation process is a one-way street determined at each stage by the CICA Scheme. But, while the work of the CICA is tough, if the aim of awards is to make a gesture of sympathy and support for victims, then it has failed, as the process achieves neither effectively. A better and more dignified way has to be found for all concerned.

We are a very wealthy nation and we must choose, through how we vote and how we become involved in our communities, what is more important

– the personal opportunity for self-reliance or the democratic distribution of wealth and resources. It seems healthy, well-educated, well-resourced public services are the foundations of a decent society that will produce more decent people. We ought to provide those affected by violent crime with realistic compensation as a sensible reflection of loss. As Britain increasingly becomes less committed to a well-resourced welfare state, the need for realistic criminal compensation will increase as a means for victims securing basic health and social care. The problem is that a huge criminal justice budget is allocated, but only a tiny amount goes specifically to victims.

> The global figure – including NHS care for victims, social care, everything – the annual cost of crime in Britain is £60 billion a year according to a four-year study by economist David Anderson.
>
> *The Aggregate Burden of Crime* – in *Journal of Law and Economics*
> Tony Thompson in *The Observer,* 23 April 2000

Anderson's study was inevitably criticised, but what was fascinating and helpful was to see where the Treasury allocates money and where victims fit into the allocation. Anderson's study broke down every single factor, e.g. accident and emergency, hospital care, social services and legal services. For example:

- each prison costs around £1.9bn a year to run
- salaries for staff £930m per year
- the police force £7bn
- the Legal Aid Board (now Legal Services Commission) £1.4bn
- average annual CICA parliamentary vote has been including expenditure by the Criminal Injuries Compensation Board/Scheme/Appeal Panel
  1996–1997: £231m
  1997–1998: £222.4m
  1998–1999: £130.5m
  1999–2000: £137.1m

The CICA is a non-departmental public body and is referred to as an Executive Agency. It has its general working of the Scheme reviewed by the Home Secretary (Michael Howard's wish to detach himself from direct intervention) – via the Justice and Victims Unit within the Home Office and the Criminal Injuries Compensation Act 1995 makes the Home Office 'Sponsor' of the CICA. A sort of 'just get on, do not bother us and keep them quiet' attitude.

The way it was

There has been state compensation in one form or another – aside from state welfare benefits – since 1964. For many years, the system was administered under the Criminal Injuries Compensation Scheme 1990 by the Criminal Injuries Compensation Board and, incredibly, solicitors are still resolving cases within this 'unlawful' system although the Criminal Injuries Compensation Act 1995 did away with the Board. Provisions for giving the common law scheme statutory effect had never been developed within the Criminal Justice Act 1988 – until Michael Howard (the former Home Secretary) decided to change matters.

The Law Lords' concern about the Home Secretary's position was that it would go against the 1988 statute, which envisaged (among other issues) that it would remove a Home Secretary's role and powers for review and discretion (section 171) to allow direct intervention (ss.108–117 of the Criminal Justice Act 1988). This meant there existed a contradiction between the then government's future intentions of the executive scheme and the declared intentions of Parliament, i.e. Michael Howard's proposed Act was illegal. For him to succeed in pushing through the future legislation with alarming speed, he dismissed the House of Lords' judicial review (by a 3:2 majority) ruling that he was acting illegally by repealing ss.108–117 of the Criminal Justice Act 1988. His government's response was that the Bill was introduced on 8 November 1995, it was placed before Parliament on 16 November 1995 and enacted on 12 December 1995 – coming into force on 1 April 1996. Many politicians, professionals such as APIL and members of the House of Lords and trade unions, vigorously challenged the Home Secretary.

> The British taxpayer [who is also victim] is happy to pay out more than any other in the world to compensate victims. It is the duty of the government to make sure the money is well spent … Britain has the most generous compensation scheme in the world, providing more money than the USA and more money than the rest of the EU put together.

Michael Howard: *Press Release 11 May 1995: 103/95* [comment in bracket is the author's]

As taxpayers, we still await clear criteria about how this statement and running of the Scheme can be judged adequately. Under the old Board Scheme, payment of awards had been made under an *ex-gratia* system and this caused concern among applicants and legal experts about the limited areas for challenging decisions and areas that appeared arbitrary in the *ex-gratia* assessment method. It is hard to see how the Scheme has improved this process for securing a reasonable objective award. If one looks at the Directory for solicitors and how, on appeal, awards are significantly increased, it begs the question whether the CICA makes initial 'arbitrary' awards, hoping people will quietly fade away.

The CICB was administered by civil servants and applications were assessed by highly qualified barristers, QCs and medical professionals for decisions about awards based on common law practices. The awards generally mirrored what a person would receive in a court hearing in other types of court action. This was expensive because future health care *is* expensive. The old system was very slow and lacked technology to process applications and effective communication with other agencies for proof and decisions. These expert Board Members did not come cheap, either.

It is referred to as the 'unlawful' system simply because since 1964 the CICB had become an agency working without legislation and it was necessary for a change that formally brought the system into law. The tragedy is, that when the opportunity came to make provisions lawful, the Home Secretary who rushed through the controversial legislation, Michael Howard, was driven by ideology and cost-cutting. So changes, in fact, were about saving money and the individual needs of victims' injury and loss were less than significant. This was to be done via the introduction of the tariff-based scoring system for injuries within the Criminal Injuries Compensation Act 1995. The Treasury hoped that, with the introduction of this Act, within the first five years of its implementation, it would save £700 million – at the expense of victims. The Act came into force on 1 April 1996 and is how all future claims are now administered alongside minor amendments of the 2001 Rules for the Scheme. Unlike the old system, the new Scheme has a top compensation award of £500,000 – regardless of the applicant's individual injuries and loss. This ignores the individual nature of injury, denies justice to victims and does not seem to reflect the type of sympathy from society the public would expect.

The CICA wanted £86.50 per hour from this author to answer basic questions, and the Justice and Victims Unit also failed to assist research constructively. From the little gathered, over 10,000 outstanding CICB claims are still awaiting decisions, and over 65 per cent of applicants are obliged to secure expert legal advice to deal with the CICA. The Scheme, as the new 'lawful' system is referred to, is not really a compensation scheme, despite the name. In reality, it is an administrative clearinghouse obliged to seek ways to reduce overall costs. It is a remote, one-way application street with very limited recourse to appeals and change and is best regarded as an executive social security service, but without the ability, skill and efficiency of a local social security office. This is not a way of expressing society's sympathy or approaching the level of justice a victim needs. Within the whole policy of compensation is the assumption that, what applicants do not receive in direct compensation, they will be entitled to with state welfare benefits – another form of compensation. But this is not the case, as some people who cannot return to work due to the severity of injuries must repeatedly reapply for benefits and in a climate of cost-cutting lose these benefits. Meantime, calculations for awards implicitly make up the rationale for a final gross award – before deductions for means-tested state benefits.

> The tariff-based scheme was introduced with the aims of slowing the increase in overall costs, making those costs more predictable and controllable, making the scheme simpler to administer.
>
> Comptroller and Auditor General: *Compensating Victims of Violent Crime: HC Session 1999–2000*

Service standards of the CICA

Readers should be mindful that the following CICA service standards bear very, very little, or no, relation to the service they are likely to experience in reality.

> CICA states an application will be dealt with courteously and confidentially. CICA will write with a decision regarding an application as quickly as the time it takes other organisations to respond to the CICA enquiries.
> CICA aims to respond to any correspondence within two weeks.
> CICA aims to acknowledge an application and send out all routine enquiry forms to the police and medical authorities within two weeks of your application.
> When the CICA receives all replies, it aims to write with a decision within four weeks.
> If you are dissatisfied with the CICA decision and ask for a review, the CICA will acknowledge your application for a review within two weeks of receipt.
> When reviewing a CICA decision, the reviewed decision will be made within 4 weeks of written request. If further enquiries are needed, the CICA will write with a decision when they have the information they want within two weeks.
> If a CICA decision is accepted, or that agreement is found at the appeal stage, the CICA ensures that payment is made within four weeks upon confirmation from the applicant or appeal panel.
> Once a decision has been made at the appeal stage, the decision is final and no further action is possible.
>
> CICA: *Service Standards, Aims and Objectives*

The Criminal Injuries Compensation Authority (CICA)

Complaining about the CICA

If dissatisfied with the manner in which the CICA has handled the administration process, a complaint may be lodged *in writing* and sent to:

> Operations Manager
> Criminal Injuries Compensation Authority
> Tay House
> 300 Bath Street
> Glasgow
> G2 4JR

The letter must *state the complaint* and *include your CICA reference number.* Complaints are considered by a senior worker who will reply in writing within four weeks of receiving the complaint. If you remain dissatisfied it is possible to write to your MP with all the correspondence relating to your complaint. Only by writing to your MP may you approach the final option for complaining. The MP can choose not to support your complaint.

If the MP agrees to support your complaint, he/she will contact the Ombudsman – the Parliamentary Commissioner for Administration. The Ombudsman has limited powers to investigate the quality of administration. The process is very long and no intervention is possible beyond writing a report recommending change and commenting on maladministration. It cannot change any award decision.

No further options or measures exist.

The Criminal Injuries Compensation Authority (CICA)

Report crime to police and receive a crime reference number

It is your responsibility to decide whether to request an application and assessment for compensation – write to CICA for an application

Applicant accepts or rejects decisions or award

Applicant can accept or reject review decision in writing in set period of time

Applicant can request within set period an appeal

CICA
Assesses your application and sends a reference no. which should always be quoted

Makes award decision – maybe to make no award

Within set days written request for a review of decision. This new decision can be upheld or changed

Decide whether it will accept request for an appeal

CICAP appeal decision is final. Previous decisions may be overtuned and awards reduced or increased

Applicant has no further recourse to review or appeal after this stage. No further action by the CICA

If applicant wishes to complain at any stage about the manner in which their case is dealt with by the CICA. 'Independently' means internally by the CICA Headquarters

There is no appeal against any complaint decision reached

If the applicant is dissatisfied with CICA's *administrative* conduct in dealing with the application, e.g. losing papers or ignoring information that affected the way their application was dealt with, they can write to their MP and ask him/her to write to the Parliamentary Ombudsman

The Parliamentary Ombudsman will require the paperwork and has the decision whether they will accept the complaint or not. The Parliamentary Ombudsman does not change the award, only investigates the standard of how the CICA did their administrative tasks. They will write a report that is forwarded to the government offices and may make recommendations about the CICA *administrative* standards

Decision of the MP and Ombudsman will be *the* final avenue to persue. Nothing further can be done if you remain dissatisfied

© T.S. Duckett 2003 *CICA: Application, Assessment, Awards and Complaining*

278

The Criminal Injuries Compensation Authority (CICA)

Useful reading and addresses

Generally, law books are extremely expensive and you may wish to use your reference library rather than purchase these books; you can track down articles on the Internet.

Guides to the Criminal Injuries Compensation Scheme, *issued by CICA.* There are two guides, one of which should be relevant for you.

Victims of Crimes of Violence – A Guide to the CICA Scheme 1996–31 March 2001. This is the booklet needed if you received your injuries between the dates stated. Details about fatal injuries are included within this information.

Victims of Crimes of Violence – A Guide to the CICA Scheme 1 April 2001 to the present. For criminal injuries received after the above date. Details about fatal injuries are included within this information.

European harmony?, *by Richard Scorer* in *Personal Injury Law Journal,* August 2002.

Claiming Compensation for Criminal Injuries *by Dennis Foster.*

The Criminal Injuries Compensation Act 1995, published by The Stationery Office (see below).

Compensation for Criminal Injury, *by Professor Desmond Greer.*

Compensating Crime Victims – A European Survey, *(ed) Professor Desmond Greer.* Written just before the implementation of the 1995 Act, this remains a vast, accessible and fascinating analysis of European compensation schemes. Published by Freiburg im Brisgau.

Compensation for Victims of Violent Crime – Possible Changes to the Criminal Injuries Compensation Scheme: A Consultation Paper, published by The Stationery Office (not known if findings were publicly released).

Personal Injury Practice, *by J. Hendry, M. Day and A. Buchan,* 2nd edn, published by Legal Action Group.

Criminal Evidence and Procedure – An Introduction, *by Dr Alastair N. Brown,* published by Butterworths Scotland. Excellent text on procedure and evidence. Written for law students.

Atiyah's Accidents, Compensation and the Law, *by Peter Cane,* 5th edn, published by Butterworths. A vast, academic analysis of the use of law, provisions and arguments to justify compensation.

Recovering Damages for Psychiatric Injury, *by Michael Napier and Kay Wheat,* published by Blackstone Press. Excellent legal guidance, descriptions and case examples; very outdated directory of PTSD experts.

Tort Liability for Psychiatric Damage, *by N.J. Mullany and P.R. Handford,* published by Sweet & Maxwell. Excellent legal volume written for legal experts.

Forensic Psychiatry, Clinical, Legal and Ethical Issues, *by J. Gunn and P. J. Taylor (eds),* published by Butterworth-Heinemann. Excellent collection by various experts.

Essentials of Forensic Psychological Assessment, *by Marc J. Ackerman,* published by John Wiley. Useful guide for psychologists on what they need to be mindful of when assessing and treating clients.

CICA
Tay House
300 Bath Street
Glasgow
G2 4LN
Telephone: 0141 331 2726
Fax: 0141 331 2287
Website: www.cica.gov.uk

CICAP (Appeals)
11th Floor
Cardinal Tower
12 Farringdon Road
London
EC1M 3HS
Telephone: 020 7549 4600
Fax: 020 7549 4643

CICA
Morley House
26–30 Holborn Viaduct
London
EC1A 2JQ
Telephone: 020 7842 6800
Fax: 020 7436 0804

The Stationery Office Bookshops

71 Lothian Road
Edinburgh
EH3 9AZ
Telephone: 0870 606 5566
Fax: 0870 606 5588

18–19 High Street
Cardiff
CF1 2BZ
Telephone: 029 2039 5548
Fax: 029 2038 4347

123 Kingsway
London
WC2B 6PQ

Parliamentary Ombudsman
Office of the Parliamentary Commissioner for Administration
Millbank Tower
Millbank
London
SW1P 4QP
Helpline: 0845 015 4033
Fax: 020 7217 4160
E-Mail: opca-enqu@ombudsman.org.uk
Website: www.ombudsman.org.uk

Parliamentary Ombudsman
Office of the Parliamentary Commissioner for Administration
28 Thistle Street
Edinburgh
EH2 1EN
Helpline: 0845 601 0456

Parliamentary Ombudsman
Office of the Parliamentary Commissioner for Administration
Fifth Floor
Capital Tower
Greyfriars Road
Cardiff
CF10 3AG
Helpline: 0845 601 0987

> Public feeling demands that innocent victims should be able to maintain a reasonable standard of living compared with that which they enjoyed previously, but this does not extend to compensating in full from public funds the loss of earnings incurred by very highly paid employees.
>
> Comment on whether it is fair that very highly paid citizens should receive the full award available, from Peter Cane: *Atiyah's Accidents, Compensation and the Law, 5th edition*

Note: Do not complete an application form on-line. The facility on the CICA's website to download an application form and print it out must never be confused with the possibility of completing and then sending while on-line. Do not even think about it!!

The CICA allows a victim two years from the date of a reported violent crime to forward an application. In exceptional circumstances, such as sex abuse of children, it generally extends this time limit. Take time to find yourself a sound agency from whom to get initial advice. For good-quality initial advice an exception to the rule about non-qualified legal experts is the Citizens' Advice Bureaux who have the talent to assist in completing a 'rough' application and gathering a list of what matters you need to consider when applying. This also means the 'Legal Help' time with a chosen legal expert can be used dynamically and productively. Before sending an application, it will be essential to seek expert professional legal guidance in completing the application and assistance in dealing with the CICA. Expensive as this will be, it will be better than accepting being poorly advised, and struggling with the consequences, or trying alone to make sense of an extremely complex process. It is best to view the payment for expert legal services as a means of long-term investment for justice and personal progress. Later in this section, we look at small but significant ways of preparing and gathering documentation that will assist your legal expert, and reduce some costs and time.

In most circumstances, applicants should not seek help from people who do not have formal qualifications and expertise in this field. If they do, it will probably prove to be a source of further loss.

Things to do

• Make a request for the right application form by telephone via the CICA Helpline, or by writing to the Headquarters or downloading an application form from the CICA website.

• Make several copies to use for 'rough' applications before sending a completed application after securing excellent expert guidance. If the CICA has sent a form, use this one as the original to forward to the CICA. Always use the reference they give.

• Remember to request the booklet about the procedures and to read it slowly.

• When you receive your application (which is long), you will receive a CICA reference number. Every communication, medical report and police report must have the CICA number.

• Make sure the application is returned within the set time stated. Your claim is based on the contents, so take advice, and time in completing.

• Buy an address book specifically for dealing with all the agencies that are going to be in contact with you.

• Buy a large ring-binder folder and some folder dividers as you are about to become a stationery office: to survive you must maintain order in what you do. In the ring-binder with dividers, write titles for the following:

> CICA letters
> my replies
> solicitors
> medical reports, appointment cards and letters: (a) physical; (b) mental
> employment matters
> social services letters
> housing matters
> financial matters, e.g. state benefits or savings

• Keep all correspondence within this ring-binder.

• Keep the most recent correspondence on top and in the right place.

• From this time you must photocopy every letter and report sent or received and keep on file and ensure your solicitor has originals of everything. It is often easier to request that all correspondence be first sent to your solicitor and then copied to you.

• Find yourself a very good solicitor if you have not already. Have a clear 'shopping list' of matters like needs and injuries you need to clarify, e.g. 'non-recorded injuries'.

• The 'Legal Help' free one-hour session may be used to take the application along with all the relevant proof, addresses and reference numbers and ask your solicitor to complete the CICA form for you. The CAB may have helped you prepare a good 'rough' copy application.

• Agree with your solicitor who is to make contact with the CICA – remember, each call the solicitor makes and every letter read about you will cost you money. It is recommended the solicitor is nominated as the key contact for everything to do with the CICA and you supply whatever is required to the solicitor.

- If you try to secure as much original medical, employment and related documentation, this should reduce the need for either you or your solicitor as you can contact the CICA. (See section on hospital, pp. 4–21.)
- Try to learn/improve IT skills and have access to a computer. It will give you a sense of control and allow you to survive the process better and reduce the clutter in your home.
- Communicate simply with your solicitor and agree how often and in what way you will be updated or attend medical assessments. Everything is going to be billed, so you may decide to ask for bi-monthly updates in writing unless a pressing matter arises.
- It is important to understand that the application submitted by you, or on your behalf, will be the basis on which your application is assessed. Make sure everything is listed clearly including every injury, such as back conditions, some may not be the primary injury but may develop into a significant injury in the future.
- It is reasonable to use a volunteer from a large group or the skills within the Citizens Advice Bureaux to help you write the letter requesting an application and 'rough draft' – but only in this matter.
- Take some time to gather all the documentation to include with the application.
- If it is necessary to communicate with the CICA, always do so in writing via a solicitor.
- Allocate specific days when you deal only with CICA matters. It will be one small area of self-care over which you have some control. Place the CICA ring-binder and related matters away in a cupboard on the days when you are not working on your application. Keep your survival a priority!
- Maintain, or start to take great care of, yourself because this application process is going to be lengthy, repetitious, often degrading and extremely stressful. Do not let the CICA process take over every aspect of your survival and progress.
- Everything within an application must be honest and independently backed up if necessary.

Things not to do

- Believe you must rush to complete the CICA application as soon as you receive it.
- Pretend this is anything other than a raw necessity to survive, to bring safety and well-being back into your life. It is not a lottery.
- If you have significant to catastrophic injuries, do not think your application will be resolved quickly or without requiring a review or an appeal.
- Become obsessed with 'when the compensation comes' – easily done when economically vulnerable.
- Resort to well-meaning but chaos-creating individuals unqualified to complete the application with you. Some large groups claim to have a lot of expertise in this area. A few individuals may; most know a little and many offer the wrong advice.
- Think you will achieve more by not instructing a competent good solicitor. They charge a lot, but you can be assured of the best possible result in return for your future well-being.
- Act like a victim by being silent when you need to speak.
- Never lie to the CICA or your solicitor under any circumstances.

Applying

In the CICA guidelines, it points out there is no legal definition of the term for violence, so the CICA must judge every case on its circumstances. To quote the guide, 'crimes of violence usually involve a physical attack on the person... e.g. assaults, wounding and sexual offences ... or the threat of violence'. However, you must ensure certain matters are fully cooperated with and documented. It is up to the individual to make an application and it *must* be in writing. The application must be written within two years of the violent crime taking place.

The CICA reasonably expects that the crime was reported to the police or a responsible agency such as a social or health services.

There are two types of forms and you must state in your letter if you are requesting a *personal application* – for yourself or on behalf of someone. The other form is for where a criminal death has left a spouse or children without a significant adult or carer. In these circumstances you must request a *fatal application*.

Homosexual relationships are recognised as being as valid as heterosexual relationships if a couple have lived together for two years or more (para. 38 2001 Scheme).

For children and young people, please also request the leaflet called 'Child abuse and the Criminal Injuries Compensation Scheme'.

If you are applying because of injury or death caused by a motor vehicle, the CICA can only assess an application if it can be evidenced that the motor vehicle was used as a weapon to cause criminal injury. In other circumstances of injury, applications in writing should be made through the driver's insurance company and, if the driver was not identifiable, through:

> **The Motor Insurers' Bureau**
> **152 Silbury Boulevard**
> **Milton Keynes**
> **MK9 1NB**

The CICA considers only applications resulting directly from a violent crime or threat of violence and this includes where you were, or the person on whose behalf you are applying was, directly injured by the incident.

Applications for a street mugging where no significant injury took place would not be accepted.

Applying requires that personal and/or mental injuries have left you incapacitated for more than twenty-eight weeks.

The criminal injury must have taken place *within* Britain.

If you are a victim of violent crime living in Northern Ireland, it is not possible to secure an award under the Scheme, but you should apply in writing to:

The Compensation Agency
Royston House
34 Upper Queen Street
Belfast
BT1 6FD

Useful contacts and reading

Read directory entries in section about social security for Citizens' Advice Bureaux, pp. 00–0.

Read section on solicitors, pp. 260–270.

Read suggested contacts and reading in section on CICA, pp. 271–280.

Criminal Injuries Compensation Authority FREEPHONE: 0800 358 3601.

See Criminal Injuries Compensation Authority's guidelines.

See CICA website: www.cica.gov.uk

The Legal Aid Board has an Investigation Board to investigate firms suspected of defrauding the Legal Aid Fund, alongside the Police and Office for the Supervision of Solicitors. In 1997, they managed to convict three solicitors of fraud and in 1998, they convicted two solicitors all of whom have been struck off the roll by the Solicitors' Disciplinary Tribunal.

Solicitor A was convicted of fraud for the sum of £14,000
Solicitor B was convicted for fraud in excess of £1,000,000
Solicitor C was convicted for fraud for £30,000

Legal Aid Board: Report 1999

Four law firms specialising in immigration advice have been closed for malpractice after investigation of 100 companies, a report by the Legal Aid Board says... a sharp rise in the cost of legal aid for immigration in the past twelve months from £36 million to £48million... the Chief Executive said... The investigators found outrageous behaviour at one end of the scale while the other firms were highly competent.

Daily Telegraph, 18 May 1999

A teacher unable to work since suffering a nervous breakdown because of a 'bullying' headmistress has won a £300,000 settlement from his council employers ... the father of two has been on psychiatric medication since 1996 following a year-long series of confrontations with the headmistress he questioned ...the deteriorating atmosphere began affecting Mr A's mental and physical health ... he began suffering insomnia; he became obsessive about work and could think and talk about nothing else; he lost interest in his own children; he lost interest in his appearance.

Daily Telegraph, 11 May 2000

Legal Aid is to be provided to the families of twenty British children who claim they have been burned by hot coffee served by the burger chain McDonald's ... McDonald's says its customers like their drinks hot – and points complainants towards a nannyish warning on its cups.

London Evening Standard, 2002

Two internal frauds committed against the Authority (CICA) were identified in 1998. They involved the submission of fraudulent applications on behalf of fictitious clients supported by forged police and medical reports. One fraud, an employee of the CICA obtained £52,000 with applications worth a further £100,000 submitted before the fraud was detected. The employee and her husband were convicted of obtaining money transfers by deception. In the second, a member of staff, an ex-member of staff and two others were convicted of obtaining a money order by deception and conspiracy. The members of staff were dismissed. (No figure submitted)

The Comptroller and Auditor General: *Compensating Victims of Violent Crime: Report Session National Audit Office 1999–2000*

An application will not be considered if it is assessed that you, or the person you are applying for, actively engaged in a way that created the injuries; including using provocative language, and starting a fight.

In order to apply for assessment for an award, an alleged offender does not necessarily have to have been apprehended by the police or found guilty in a court.

For an application to be assessed, it is necessary to be assessed that you personally report the crime at the very earliest opportunity to the police – or another statutory agency, which must contact the police. At some point it is expected that you personally contact the police.

A police crime reference number must be available and quoted in the application.

If not by you – because of age, mental health or injuries – the police must be notified at the earliest point by someone on your behalf. You must be willing to cooperate fully, including being a prosecution witness. If you do not, the CICA will rightly withhold or reject your application. Fear of reprisal by cooperating with the prosecution is not generally accepted. This is rightly to ensure against fraudulent applications and equally to ensure that violent crime is rightly dealt with.

The CICA generally expects that a person who causes criminal injury does not benefit in any manner from any award. (Contentious in domestic and sexual violence applications, this point requires expert legal guidance.)

The CICA sometimes decides in cases of children to invest any award until that child has reached 18 years and is regarded as an adult 'free of exploitation' and not living in the same home or district as an offender.

The CICA's claim officers can reduce or withhold an award if they are dissatisfied with the conduct of the applicant before, during or after the incident, if they believe making an award is inappropriate.

For adults, such as in domestic violence cases, the CICA would not accept an application if the victim remained in the household or in connection with the offender; even if the applicant/victim cooperated with the police and the prosecution.

The CICA will reduce or withhold an award if persistent evidence shows a failure to comply with CICA requests for any information or attending medical examinations. Rightly, the CICA must satisfy itself that public money is being awarded appropriately.

Previous criminal convictions

The CICA has the right to reduce or deny an award if you have a previous criminal history. It uses a table of years spent in prison and penalty points that will influence its decision but will ignore convictions that are spent under the Rehabilitation of Offenders Act 1974. The application for mental trauma by the birth father of the late Billie-Jo Jenkin was rejected following the murder of his fostered teenage daughter, who was allegedly bludgeoned to death by her foster father while under the responsibility of social services and courts.

Ms Crawford booms at Ms Davis: 'You wouldn't be able to do these awful things to me if I weren't still in this wheelchair!'

Ms Davis retorts: 'But 'cha are ... ya are in that chair!'

From the film *Whatever Happened to Baby Jane*

The Scheme does not use learned barristers, advocates or Queen's Counsel. They remain in place to complete outstanding applications made under the old CICB rules and so these cases will be assessed under those rules. The new assessors are Civil Service administrators called claims officers and attempts made by the author to see a job specification for a claims officer's post were, sadly, denied.

A claim officer's job

The Criminal Injuries Compensation Act 1995 states claims officers are responsible for deciding, what awards, if any, should be made in individual cases and how they should be paid, i.e. they can choose to delay payments, make full awards or ongoing series of interim awards.

If applicants appeal against decisions made by a claims officer, they will be open to review determined by an adjudicator.

A claims officer has the authority to waive time limits in exceptional circumstances if this is considered to be in the interests of justice.

A claims officer can make directions about conditions of an application as he/she considers necessary.

A claims officer has authority to require applicants to attend medical examinations. In these circumstances the CICA *may* pay for reasonable travel costs.

The Act states: the *standard of proof* to be applied by a claims officer in all matters before him will be the *balance of probabilities*.

When injuries are significant or catastrophic, it is common for the CICA to request that the applicant be examined by one of its appointed medical experts. This generally causes very long delays and distress in producing reports.

What you need to provide for assessment

- In order for a claims officer to attempt an assessment effectively, the standard of proof of injury and loss is on the balance of probabilities, meaning that it is essential you secure expert legal assistance.
- In doing so there exist ways to reduce time and legal costs and take some minor control in a process that provides very little control for an applicant.
- When there is significant to catastrophic loss, it will save a lot of time if, in discussion and agreement with your solicitor, you take it upon yourself to provide the following and any other documentation they require. All documentation you may receive must go directly to your solicitor as part of his/her gathering a request for an amount of an award. The solicitor needs all the information in writing that is available, to help you.

Remember, the sole basis for the outcome of an application for compensation will be made – often at a review – purely on the quality of proof and the *balance of probabilities*. The latter is rather ambiguous and open to interpretation and legal debate but, generally, mean, in all likelihood the overall impact of the injury, loss and future losses and needs. The application form is the basis for all assessment and decision.

Documentation

It will assist you and save both time and some costs if you take it upon yourself to secure honest and accurate documentation in the areas below. All documentation must be original and it is good to keep at least one spare copy in your own ring-binder folder. It should always be addressed to your solicitor. The solicitor must receive a copy of everything so they can forward to the CICA complete documentation of all related application matters. It provides good practice and reduces the waste of time for all concerned.

Injuries: Loss

Request in writing early cooperation from your consultant physicians in providing a full report about all your injuries at the time of the violent crime and any conclusions they have about future illness, including deterioration. This applies to physical *and* mental injuries. The physician may not offer you a copy, but the solicitor can expect one. It is important that the consultant physicians include your CICA reference number and any hospital number. The CICA will write to them anyway, but it does no harm to prompt them. (See section about being in hospital, pp. 4–21.)

If you have taken (dated) colour photographs of injuries while in hospital, forward these to your solicitor as part of a package of documents. These are relevant where an injury previously appeared minor or less significant and becomes more significant.

290

Care needs

Sometimes, when significantly injured, a measure of future loss and needs will have to be quantified. Also, it helps include what was wrong in the early stages of injury. How independent were you? Are your injuries likely to alleviate in the short term? Or have injuries deteriorated in the mid- to long term? Will it get worse or slightly easier?

What you can do is write letters to convalescence agencies that may have provided care, as well as to family and friends as appropriate. They will need to be very specific, for all concerned, as to the type of care provided and the duration. Again, these should be sent directly to your solicitor. If it is family and friends, they should state in the letter that the information is true, print their names, sign and date. Remember to request that they include your CICA reference number. (See table opposite for guidance.)

Employment

If you work, it is a good idea early on to write to your employers for a detailed reference. It should include information about the work you carried out and your ability to do the work and the likelihood you would have been promoted in the future (but for the incident). It should state what they believe *in all probability* to be the highest position you might have achieved pre-injury. (Remember to request that they include your CICA reference number.)

It will also be productive to have in writing previous employers' references to prove your work record and the type of work you undertook, or tutors' or teachers' reports if you are quite young.

If you are over twenty-one years old, it is worth including your curriculum vitae (CV). The CICA will want proof of everything you have done and whether you stayed in a job for a long or a short time.

Your statement: what injuries and what you have become

This is something that will be important for your CICA assessment and can be based upon the statement you present to the court at a trial – if there happens to be one. The current name for it is a 'victim's statement'. The suggestion here is to make it a full chronicle about the entire impact the violent crime has had upon you, from the incident, hospitalisation, after hospital and how you envisage your future in every way. Equally, if it is a fatal loss, to detail all its consequences in a similar way. Also, what it has done to you – its continuing effect on you. It is a valuable document, in your words. Just as the CICA will require that every nuance of your life be examined, this is one area in the one-way process where you may

Need	Carer / Relationship	Frequency	Date	Current Involvement	Frequency / Hours

It is not possible to give specific levels of future need as the professionals have been unable to provide much of a prognosis. From how matters stand and from what physicians have stated I should expect to experience a greater degree of dependency upon carers from around the age of fifty years, regardless of two hip replacements or not, and that my condition is degenerative with restrictive mobility will follow and has been evident since 2005. CICA Reference Number AE / 679 543 / 03 constructively assert the experience and needs of yourself as they are for you. Remember to include your CICA reference number and spend a lot time in preparing the statement before sending it to your solicitor; ideally, it should continue from any court statement. (Please see section about going to court and the importance of a victim statement, pp. 208–241.)

What your solicitor will be doing...

'I cannot but remember such things were, and were most dear to me' –
In vain would Prudence, with decorous sneer,
Point out a cens'ring world, and bid me fear:
Above that world on wings of love I rise:
I know its worst and can that worst despise –
'Wronged, injured, shunned, unpitied, unredrest;
'The mocked quotation of the scorner's jest' –
Let Prudence' direst bodements on me fall,
Clarinda, rich reward! o'erpays them all –
As low-borne mists before the sun remove,
So shines, so reigns unrivalled mighty Love –
In vain the laws their feeble force oppose;
Chained at his feet, they groan Love's vanquished foes;
I dare not combat, but I turn and fly:
In vain religion meets my shrinking eye;
I dare not combat, but I turn and fly:
Conscience in vain upbraids th'unhallowed fire;
Love grasps his scorpions, stifled they expire:
Reason drops headlong from his sacred throne,
Thy dear idea reigns, and reigns alone;
Each thought intoxicated homage yields,
And riots wanton in forbidden fields –

By all on High, adoring mortals know!
By all the conscious villain fears below!
By, what, alas! Much more my soul alarms,
My doubtful hopes once more to fill thy arms!
E'en shouldst thou, false, forswear each guilty tie,
Thine, and thine only, I must live and die!

Robert Burns: *Passion's Cry*

Your solicitor will be gathering all the information cited above and placing it into a document in readiness to forward to the CICA. When that time comes, the solicitor will prepare a schedule of special damages that carefully evidences the proof of different losses and the amount of award requested.

In a case involving serious injury, it is essential to secure the guidance and involvement of very good solicitors within the fields of compensation and/or medical negligence. The solicitor's role is to:

- compile all relevant information about your claim – with your assistance;
- advise on all related matters;
- assist you in completing and submitting the application form;
- obtain the necessary evidence;
- deal with the CICA/CICAP, including representing you at a CICAP oral hearing if necessary;
- advise you throughout on the status of your application, the prospects of a successful award and whether any award made is reasonable within the rules.

The rules of the CICA Schemes are highly complex. As already stated, it is crucial to your future to get this right. You must obtain clear and reliable advice about:

- which scheme applies to your claim. There are currently three schemes still in operation: the old CICB Scheme, the 1996 CICA Scheme and the 2001 CICA Scheme;
- whether you are likely to be eligible for an award, i.e. have you been the victim of a 'crime of violence' within the meaning of the rule?;
- whether you are outside any of the relevant time limits or other provision, e.g. reporting to the police, and whether any remedial action can be taken;
- whether any award is likely to be reduced or disallowed, e.g. by reason of the circumstances of the crime or by reason of your own criminal convictions;
- what can and cannot be claimed, i.e. 'heads' of claim. This varies according to which scheme applies;
- how awards are quantified under each 'head of loss';
- what evidence, e.g. medical evidence, lay witness evidence, other types of expert evidence, are necessary in order to maximise your award, and where they can be obtained;
- deductions, e.g. state benefits past and future which will be deducted from loss of earnings/special expenses;
- whether any award made by the CICA should be appealed to CICAP, the independent appeals panel.

The CICA's Job – Assessing your Application

What solicitors include in the schedule
The documents, medical reports and other written evidence cited above will be submitted as part of the application. This will take some time depending upon your injuries and the cooperation of those who need to communicate with the necessary people. Gathering proof and evidence is essential to any claim and the accuracy of the solicitor in preparing the schedule of special damages becomes an essential means for legal persuasion and argument for evidence of asserting the *balance of probabilities*. This is why the application must be timely, full, honest, accurate and unambiguous.

Delays in forwarding a claim by a solicitor should not be because of competency or attitude – if you choose well. It will, more likely be because of a need to understand how your injuries and general loss 'even out' over months, plus expert medical advice. This is a stressful time, as some injuries require a period to settle to find an average pattern of injury, need and loss. This also requires public services providing good early care to relieve injury and help assess need. The CICA may have different reasons and make very different interpretations. To make a premature claim may pre-empt the onset of other specific criminal injuries and it will undermine your chances of securing the fairest claim. Also, people with multiple injuries may be subjected to a series of independent examinations by the CICA before a final award is offered.

Heads of damage
The schedule contains what are referred to as 'heads' – these are the main areas on which the CICA assesses the eligibility of your application. These refer to Levels (25) and bands of tariff-fixed standard amounts per injury. 'Heads' is a term for the areas of loss, injury and need.

The heads are: the CICA tariff-based criminal injury, earnings, special expenses, care costs, future loss. The outline about heads can be found within the 2001 CICA Scheme Rules in rule 38 paras 30–34 and special expenses paras 35–36.

The 1995 Act and the 2001 CICA Scheme Rules do not make provision for other relevant losses like clothing, travelling for medical treatment or loss of care services.

Multiplicands and multipliers

In cases involving serious to catastrophic injury it is often the case that the victim will suffer financial losses in the future, e.g.:

- Loss of earnings – if the victim cannot work as a result of the injury, or is restricted by reason of injury in the sort of work he/she can do.
- Costs of care and assistance.
- Costs of special equipment required by reason of the injury.

Any lump sum, i.e. a one-off compensation award, as far as possible, should reflect these future costs and financial losses. The 'multiplier' and the 'multiplicand' are used by solicitors to calculate the lump sum that should be paid to compensate for future financial losses.

The *multiplicand* is the annual loss. For example, if the victim was earning £10,000 net per year at the time of the assault and, as a result of the assault, is permanently unable to return to work, the *multiplicand* for future loss of earnings is £10,000.

Deciding the right multiplier

The *multiplier* is the amount by which the *multiplicand* is multiplied in order to calculate the relevant lump sum payable.

If the victim suffers injury at 45 years, and is permanently incapacitated from work because of the injury, it might be reasonable to assume he/she would have worked until age 65, which would be twenty years' loss of earnings.

On the face of it, one might think in order to calculate the relevant lump sum payment for future loss of earnings one would multiply the *multiplicand* (say, £10,000) by a *multiplier* of 20, giving a total figure of £200,000 (20 x £10,000).

However, if the victim is compensated now for loss of earnings which, but for the injury, would have been payable in future years, then the victim is, in effect, receiving earnings earlier than would have otherwise been the case. This is called 'accelerated receipt'. The victim can invest the lump sum now and earn interest on it. Therefore, the *multiplicand* is 'discounted' to reflect accelerated receipt. Justice is not willingly given.

The amount 'discounted' takes into account the contingencies of life, i.e. events which might in any case have interrupted the victim's earnings, even if he or she had not suffered a criminal injury. Also, the level of interest the victim might be expected to earn if his or her compensation award is prudently invested. For example, for a twenty-year period of loss, the appropriate *multiplier* might be 13.

As can be imagined, deciding the multiplier can give rise to a great deal of argument in civil claims. However, under the CICA, the applicable *multipliers* are set out in Table A on page 19 of the detailed rules of the 2001 CICA Scheme. In these rules, Table A specifies, the *multiplier* 'converts an annual loss over a period of years into a lump sum payable at the beginning of that period'. This one-way street will be played out on your behalf by an expert solicitor.

Fraud by patients

Patient falsely claimed over £2,500 a year in travel expenses to an out-patient clinic.

Fraud by pharmacists

Conspiring with a GP - a pharmacist submitted bogus prescriptions for reimbursement with a value of over £1 million.

Some pharmacists made significant amounts of money substituting an expensive drug with a cheaper alternative but claiming payment for the more expensive one.

Fraudulently generating fees for emergency opening, one pharmacist claimed to have been called out over 400 times in a month. (No figure given)

Fraud by GPs

A doctor refused to see his patients at his surgery only to claim £150,000 in night visits at their home.

A dispensing GP issued bogus prescriptions for residential home patients over several years with a value of more than £700,000.

Fraud by hospital consultants

A senior specialist falsified employment agency timesheets while working full-time for an authority generating £46,000 in fraudulent income over five years.

A consultant recorded private patients as NHS patients in order to avoid making appropriate payments to the hospital. (No figure provided)

Fraud by NHS staff

Investigation at one NHS trust revealed over £380,000 in claims for duty payments and hours worked with no evidence the work had been done.

A travel claims officer submitted false claims – replicating genuine claims and BACS payment details into his bank account – the loss totalled £60,000 over four years.

Fraud from patients' income

A community living scheme manager stole over £12,000 from two disabled patients whose finances he was responsible for managing.

Fraud by research

a senior consultant fraudulently claimed to have performed a pioneering surgery, and computer records were tampered to falsify results. This type of fraud is important because medical knowledge is developed in part on the published results of previous research work. (No figure provided)

Prescription fraud alone is estimated to rob the NHS of £150 million a year
Alan Milburn, Minister of State: *Countering Fraud in the NHS,* 1998

The Different Types of Compensation

One of the most controversial aspects of the introduction of the Criminal Injuries Compensation Act 1995 was the introduction of the cost-cutting tariff system. This allocated a fixed band of money for specific injuries regardless of age. With the increase in violent crimes, governments succeed in their aim of saving significant amounts of tax payers/victims' money. As mentioned earlier, this was a major motivation of government and radical shift away from how the previous CICB schemes operated that allowed individual need to be assessed. Please see section on CICA, pp. 00–0. It shows beyond doubt the real value of 'buzz phrases' and political 'spin' and how importantly victims of violent crime are really regarded by government.

The 1995 Act and the 2001 CICA Scheme Rules have a fixed number of levels of injury and numerous body parts that are costed and fixed. It remains unclear how often these are reviewed to keep in place with rates of inflation and the future value of any awards when the pound is devalued upon joining the Euro currency.

Maximum award

Of major concern and controversy is the 1995 Act and 2001 Rules' stipulation of a maximum award of £500,000 regardless of individual loss and incapacity. This has a huge bearing upon the means by which significant and catastrophic applications reflect real loss and long-term need and is extremely inadequate, e.g. for people with severe brain damage or major paralysis.

Interim payments

These reflect the CICA's acknowledgement that some applicants in serious need may require interim payments to meet existing health needs while awaiting a final decision about an award. The negative aspect of interim awards is these may become a pattern of failing to reach a just decision in reasonable time and drawing out a final award with real 'value'.

Heads of damage

See pp. 295–297 assessing on heads of damage.

Structured settlements

When a large award is made, in the order of the maximum £500,000, solicitors can negotiate a structured settlement. These can provide tax-free structures for receiving annuity payments. Structured settlements can be paid in stages, to the applicant directly or to an appointed person or legal representative. For young people, the structured settlement allows for an award to be held in trust. The important aspect of settlements is the income is not subject to income tax as the applicant's income. Advice can be taken from a solicitor or a financial adviser as to the most beneficial annuities to be purchased.

Only those who have lost a loved one at the hands of a murderer can begin to understand the pain and grief suffered by bereaved families. The impact can affect not only the immediate family, but also friends, colleagues and neighbours. For all too many, the repercussions can last for the rest of their lives ... Many families of murder victims – and many other victims of crime – feel neglected by the criminal justice system and a great deal more needs to be done to meet their needs. I can assure the House that this Government will take action to redress the balance of the criminal justice system in favour of victims, while maintaining the interests of justice.

Alun Michael, former Minister of State for the Home Office,
1.14 p.m., 21 May 1997, House of Commons

A claims officer has the authority – even if an interim payment has previously been made – to reconsider the basis of eligibility for any further award.

A claims officer can reconsider a claim at any time before actual payment of a final award where there is new evidence or a change in circumstances. This cannot happen once adjudicators have made a direction and decision at appeal.

However, after the appeal panel has made a decision, and before an award has been paid, if a claims officer believes that a change in circumstances or new evidence justifies questioning whether an award should be withheld or changed, the CICA will request that the adjudicators for appeal have a rehearing.

If a claims officer directs a reconsideration, the applicant will be notified in writing and must reply in writing within thirty days, providing any evidence to be added to the reconsideration.

Regardless of whether an applicant sends a written statement of evidence, the claims officer will write with notification of the reconsideration with a reconsidered decision about the application.

Reopening cases

A decision reached by a claims officer or appeals panel and accepted by an applicant is generally regarded as final.

A claims officer may re-open a case where significant change in the material state of the applicant's medical condition exists such that injustice would occur if an original assessment were allowed to stand. This relates to an applicant's subsequent death resulting from criminal injury.

An application will not be re-opened after more than two years after the final decision. However, if the claims officer is satisfied on the basis of new evidence presented to support re-opening a case, it may be accepted, if there is no need for extensive enquiries.

CICA reviews
A senior claims officer who dealt with your case will assess all applications for a review.

If a review against a claims officer's decision is wanted, it must be made in writing within ninety days of the date of the decision to be reviewed. Good reasons must be stated, along with any additional information.

Exceptions to this limit may be considered in exceptional circumstances by a senior claims officer if it is decided that there are good reasons or it is in the interests of justice.

The reviewing officer will reach a decision in accordance with the provisions of the Scheme, on the basis of the original application. The officer can review the full original application on any aspect, e.g. eligibility, award offered.

The senior claims officer's decision will be sent as a written notification stating the reasons for the review decision based on the original application or award.

The senior claims officer may choose to invite, in writing, the applicant and the legal expert to an oral hearing to review the decision and evidence before the CICA.

The reviewed decision can be accepted or rejected. If rejected, and you wish to pursue your application, you must lodge a request for an appeal.

Oral hearings
A member of the appeal panel may refer an application for an oral hearing against a decision taken on a review.

If a member of the appeal panel chooses *not* to refer an appeal for an oral hearing, it is referred to another adjudicator. The adjudicator will refer the appeal for determination on an oral hearing on the evidence available.

The adjudicator considers whether the review decision was to withhold an award on the basis that an injury was not sufficiently serious to qualify for an award equal to least to the minimum payable under the tariff.

The adjudicator will review an award if a different decision would have been reached had a dispute regarding material facts been known.

The adjudicator may request an oral hearing if the material evidence does not provide the ability to reach a decision without a hearing.

Where an appeal is not referred for an oral hearing, the adjudicator's dismissal of an appeal is final and the review decision stays the same. The dismissal is given in writing to the CICA and applicant.

Oral hearings of appeals

If a member of the panel has made an appeal referral for an oral hearing, that adjudicator will not take part in a hearing. The members of the panel who will determine an oral hearing will number at least two.

Written notice of twenty-one days is normally given prior to a date for a hearing.

Applicants are allowed to bring a friend or legal representative to the oral hearing. The costs for this will not be met by the CICA, although the members have some discretion to direct the panel to meet reasonable travel expenses.

At the appeal, witnesses from both sides may be called by the claims officer or medical experts and may be cross-examined. This takes place in private although in some cases, with the permission of the applicant, the panel may give permission for observers, e.g. the media. The identity of the applicant throughout in these situations remains confidential.

Adjournment of a hearing may result in the panel directing an interim payment and giving whatever direction to the claims officer they see fit.

If they believe the appeal was vexatious or frivolous (wasting their time), the panel members may reduce the amount of the award as they see fit.

Determination of the panel members is normally made at the end of the hearing, or soon afterwards in writing.

> True generosity consists precisely in fighting to destroy the causes which
> nourish false charity.
> False charity constrains the fearful and subdued, the 'rejects of life', to
> extend their trembling hands.
> True generosity lies in striving so that these hands – whether of individuals
> or entire peoples – need be extended less and less in supplication, so that
> more and more they become human hands which work and, working,
> transform the world.
>
> Paulo Freire: *Pedagogy of the Oppressed*

An adjudicator is normally an expert from the world of law, commerce, medicine or psychiatry and only appointed by the Home Secretary. They will become a members of a panel known as the Criminal Injuries Compensation Appeals Panel and the Home Secretary will appoint one of the panel as the chairman.

The Home Secretary will also be responsible for appointing administrative staff to support the work of the panel with appeals.

The panel has responsibility for advising the Home Secretary on matters he requests and the other direct work of determining and reviewing evidence. These include other types of appeal.

> The Panel's aim is to support victims of crimes of violence by hearing their
> appeals promptly and deciding them impartially and fairly.
>
> CICA Appeals Panel: Business Plan 1998–9

If an applicant is dissatisfied with a decision reached at a **review**, that applicant may appeal against this decision in writing to the Appeals Panel on a form provided by the CICA.

The statement of appeal must provide strong reasons for an appeal, along with any **new** additional documentation that should be submitted for assessment. The written request for appeal and completion of the **appeal form** must be received by the Appeal Panel within **thirty days**.

If the applicant brings a legal representative, the CICAP will not pay travel or related expenses.

If a CICAP worker considers, in very limited circumstances, it is in the interests of justice to do so, an extension of the thirty-day time limit may be granted.

If an applicant requests an extension of the time limit and the CICAP worker has refused to grant this, the applicant must write directly to the chair of the CICAP, requesting an extension and stating the reason. The chair or another member will make a decision about the request, which will be made in writing.

The *standard of proof* in all matters to be applied by the panel is the same as that for a claims officer. It is the burden of the applicant or legal representative to put as strong a case as possible before the panel as to why the review decision or related matters is/are not appropriate.

The panel has authority to request that the applicant be re-examined for the status of any injuries or related matters. Reasonable expenses incurred will be met by the CICAP.

Appeals about time limits and reopened cases

The chair of the panel or another member/adjudicator will determine any appeal against a decision taken on **review**.

If the appeal concerns a decision *not* to reopen a case and the application for reopening was made more than two years after the date of a final decision, the panel member must be satisfied that a renewed application does *not* generate extensive enquiries by the CICA, which is the same criterion used by a claims officer.

If a panel member allows an appeal to proceed, he/she will direct the CICA about the conditions and terms of reference.

If the panel member **dismisses** an appeal, this will be stated in writing, with reasons. This decision is final and no further options exist.

> The panel's budget 1998–9
> £2,800,000
> £986,000 – staff salaries
> £435,000 – panel member fees
> £750,000 – accommodation, travel subsistence
>
> CICA Appeals Panel: *Business Plan 1998–9*

Appeals about awards

A worker from the CICAP may refer for oral hearing any appeal against a decision taken at a review.

It is possible for a worker at the CICAP to refer a determination to a panel member if that worker does not refer for an oral hearing.

The panel member may make a referral for determination about any aspect of contention or dispute.

Refusal to proceed with an appeal by a panel member, i.e. a dismissal, is final and reasons will be stated in writing. This decision is final and no further options exist.

Rehearing of appeals

If an appeal is determined in the applicant's absence, the applicant may apply in writing for a rehearing of the appeal, stating reasons for non-attendance. This request must be received within thirty days of the notification of the outcome of the hearing that the applicant failed to attend.

A worker from the CICAP may waive the time limit if it is in the interests of justice.

If the worker does not, the same procedures apply as in appeals about awards (see above).

In such circumstances, the decision will be referred to the chair or another panel member for determination and written notification of the decision with reasons provided.

If a worker believes good reasons exist for a rehearing, these will be put forward.

At the **rehearing**, different panel members will hear the application.

The decision reached will be final and no further options exist. Please see chart in the section about the CICA on page 278 that outlines the process.

If it were done when 'tis done,
then 'twere well it were done quickly.
If the assassination could trammel up the consequence,
and catch with his surcease success –
that but this blow might be the be-all
and the end-all! – here!
But here, upon this bank and shoal of time, we'd jump the life to come.

But in these cases we still have judgement here –
that we but teach bloody instructions,
which, being taught, return to plague the inventor.

This even-handed justice commends the ingredience
of our poisoned chalice to our own lips.
He's here in double trust …

… And Pity …

William Shakespeare: Macbeth

The Criminal Injuries Compensation Authority said the award reflected how the scheme worked. Howard Webber said: 'Ms Z's case highlights that no amount of money can make up for the suffering caused by such horrific events. It cannot reward her for the heroism she showed. But £50,000 can provide real help for people to rebuild their lives. The scheme lets society show its sympathy for victims and recognise their suffering. You cannot compare it with awards in the courts where a guilty party compensates the victim'.

Daily Telegraph, 7 February 2001: Howard Webber, Chief Executive, CICA,
referring to award made to Ms Z who survived attempted murder

… And Pity …
I have no spur to prick the sides of my intent but only
Vaulting ambition which o'erleaps itself
And falls on the other.

William Shakespeare: Macbeth

It is easy to attack any agency, especially if it cannot publicly defend its record on individual cases. This handbook is not about victimising and that extends to the CICA even though it is so obstructive and oppressive. The old Scheme was not perfect. It was incredibly slow, but applicants knew decisions were taken by legal experts and broadly within common law damages limits. It meant an award would be sensible – not lavish, but sufficient that victims could rebuild their lives. If victims of violence had a lobby group of powerful politicians and legal experts, it would be interesting to test the validity of the Criminal Injuries Compensation Act 1995 in relation to the Human Rights Act 1998. However, it is really tough to find any positive comments about such a remote, degrading and drawn-out process. If the CICA were a privately run company, it would simply grind to a halt and cease to be functional for failing to promote good work, efficiency and quality.

The important development was placing within legislation the issue of criminal compensation, but this was overshadowed by the motives of the Conservative Government to find a means to save money. The current government has no intentions of repealing the 1995 Act.

Pride should indeed be taken that Britain has a state compensation scheme, but this should not entertain arrogance or complacency. It does not square because Britain 'pays more compensation than all the European countries put together' that reducing and tightening eligibility criteria is the solution, or an example of 'effective expression of government sympathy'. Britain is one of the most violent countries in Europe, with the largest prison population in Europe.

Britain should be generous in its compensation because it is one of the wealthiest nations in the world – reputedly fourth, in fact – and we claim to be a democratic and compassionate society. Clearly, we are not! Of course there is not endless money, but survivors of violent crime must be seen to be a priority and currently are not, because, historically, they are a numbed and silent growing minority who have not campaigned or sufficiently mobilised themselves. However, this is changing.

Regrettably, and not so churlish as it may seem, nearly everything about the CICA is wrong! Its existence, the CICA's main objectives, the one-way processes applicants must react to – all make depressing and oppressive reading. To experience the service is the stuff of nightmares – regardless of the CICA's claims to efficiency. Trade unions, people affected by violent crime and statutory agencies find the CICA a resource that is cumbersome and draining; a dreaded, non-departmental executive public agency. Directory listings of solicitors evidence how dysfunctional administratively the CICA appears to be and not analytical in decisions. It seems to pull a small award out of the air. This, when challenged, is significantly altered, at cost to the applicant. Applicants often state they find the CICA process as debilitating and traumatic as the violent act – this is what is wrong with the

CICA Scheme. Applicants do not require sympathy: they are members of the public and taxpayers and, if allowed, the wider public would not object to sensible levels of compensation being awarded. We must all expect more from government to demand that the CICA respectfully and effectively deal with the broken lives of people. It is a basic necessity and a basic marker of a civilised, wealthy society.

The 1995 Act

This is a one-way process with extremely little leeway for applicants or their expert legal advisers. Nothing is made easy for applicants at any stage. It is a victimising one-way street.

The legislation is inflexible and intended to be so; as a result, it fails to allow individual applicants to be treated on the basis of their individual injuries and loss.

What is wrong with the CICA is it exists to save money over the appropriate compensation of people affected by violent crime. It is the legislation and the non-skilled, aloof administrators and lack of openness that compound its revulsion and derision for those who encounter the CICA.

There is no dignity or reflection in the process or legislation.

Injuries are fixed on set bands of potential award, thus constituting an unfair system for compensating injured people and carers. This is not a beacon of sympathy, generosity or justice.

The legislation allows this executive public service a dangerous level of autonomy and alarming lack of robust accountability and independent public scrutiny, which one would expect to see in a contemporary democratic society and service.

Legislation says the Home Office is sponsor of the CICA and will not involve itself in the day-to-day operational running of the CICA. This has allowed the CICA excessive power and insufficient accountability.

Lack of free expert legal representation victimises applicants. If alleged violent criminals are guaranteed expert representation, then, automatically, it should be available to known innocent victims of violent crimes.

What is Wrong with the CICA?

The 1995 Act should be repealed; the tariff system is unjust. The government is committed to keeping the ruthlessly implemented 1995 Act it once opposed alongside the House of Lords and others. Is it a prelude to dismantling state criminal compensation?

Accountability

The Scheme lacks sufficient public scrutiny and accountability and the legislation made it so. The Scheme does not produce a more efficient service – one of the justifications for the tariff-scoring scheme. Of major concern is that the decision to place emphasis on cost-cutting over proven expert need is an injustice. The replacement of expert legal and medical persons with claims officers who are responsible for the running and decision-making is unsatisfactory. This is shown in the number of cases where a first offer for an award is declined, and the applicant has to go through lengthy and costly appeal processes. It seems the CICA shows a disturbing lack of good administrative practice, and is a very expensive process for applicants where huge legal bills reduce the value of awards for specific health care and the amount is not adequately reflecting care needs, cost of living or reflective of inflation.

Money – the tariff-based way

So there is a paradox. The criminal justice system depends heavily upon victims for the reporting and detection of offences and for the provision of evidence in court. Yet, it does not appear to value the victim. The system is not geared to the perspective of the victim. The decision-making is one-way [...]

The Scheme decides who is eligible and what expenses may be claimed in each case, according to the guidelines used to set it up. There may be no consideration of what harm victims do suffer, or whether the compensation scheme is meeting any need expressed by victims. State compensation is given from the state to the victim, according to rules devised by the state. This ignoring of the expressed needs of victims is strange [...]

If we never look at the reactions of victims, how can we discover whether suffering is alleviated, expenses or losses recompensed, moral status restored, or cooperation with the criminal justice system increased? ... we may find that public statements about the worth of victims, which are later shown to be hollow, may rebound on any who set up such ineffective schemes.

Professor Joanna Shapland: *Victims, the Criminal Justice System and Compensation*

Inadequate awards and implicit reliance upon a disappearing welfare state to justify the decision of low awards do not work. These social security payments can be means-tested and thus deducted from a gross award and they are not 'protected' benefits that are guaranteed for life – although they are calculated into an award.

Our society has a diminishing welfare state and realistic awards are a necessity, not a luxury. Failure to upgrade tariff values annually in keeping with current inflation, failure to promote debate and realistic review in keeping with national needs all compound to make the CICA award tariff system meagre and cynical.

The assumption that a welfare state exists to replace what the CICA award does not offer financially is misleading. What is really left of welfare provision?

Review of the awards' value is needed for when Britain joins the Euro, otherwise we will slump further into muted discontent as a society.

When the IRA attempted to slaughter the entire Conservative Cabinet in a bomb attack, Lady Tebbit sustained horrific debilitating impairment, among other injuries, and received an appropriate award under the old Board Scheme. A few years later, her husband's party, the Conservatives, welcomed the massive reduction in awards to save the Treasury money. One wonders how long Lady Tebbit's claim took to be finalised? And, as the wife of a high earner, one wonders how Lady Tebbit would fare under the new CICA Scheme?

Administration

The CICA must be computer literate and up to speed with new technology; in the twenty-first century, with all the IT we have, there is no justification for the time taken to reach decisions.

Independent expert reports must be forwarded to the CICA much more promptly and a reduced payment penalty introduced for slack and lazy expert independent assessors. Applicants' lives are at risk due to substandard administrative delays.

The CICA needs to make the skills base of claims officers and others known and easily available to the public. It is shrouded in mystery.

The purpose of the CICA is to recognise criminal damage in the lives of those affected, but too often treats applicants contemptuously and as if they were criminals.

The CICA says reviews and appeals take place generally because of the change in details provided to them. It is more probably the difficulty for applicants knowing where to access expert assistance and the objective of the CICA to find any means to reduce any award, together with applicants' fear of debt. The CICA encourages applicants to seek assistance in completing CICA forms from a victim's charity where skills are very diverse. The advice given is often poor and wrong.

The CICA is a glorified, remote social security service but cannot function as efficiently as a local DSS office, or an average supermarket. Complaints should be published in the annual report and broken down into type, outcome and time of resolution.

The complaints process needs to be administered without bias by an independent tribunal like those operated by the DSS. Currently, too much power resides with an agency with too little effective and open accountability.

Why doesn't the CICA, in keeping with contemporary best-practice methods, issue questionnaires to applicants upon completion of an assessment for quality assurance and service feedback. What might applicants say?

Insufficient understanding about the importance of submitting a thorough application, trauma and inability to know the outcome of many needs makes an early application without expert guidance extremely hard.

The rigidity of the tariff-based system negates inevitable health changes and individuality, which under the old Board Scheme expert legal practitioners were better capable of assessing – albeit without cost-cutting concerns. Then, emphasis was about realistic reflection for obvious needs and future loss.

For a better future ...

- Whatever system is to be considered in the future, it must reflect the practical loss and obvious financial needs of applicants within European and human rights values.
- People affected by violent crime should no longer be treated like criminals.
- Repeal and replace the Criminal Injuries Compensation Act 1995 and the 2001 Rules.
- Return legal experts and common law as the appropriate response of public service within sensible, unfettered government interference and ideology.
- Use a system where, after a trial, a judge is allowed to use common law criteria to set a figure within a month of a trial pending all necessary reports.
- Consider the implementation of the Netherlands model where three judges make an early decision.
- Disband the CICA and replace with a tribunal such as an employment tribunal structure working with broad and flexible bands of assessment for injuries and loss. This, combined with guidance from actuaries or the learned Judicial Studies Board, has a lot to offer as an alternative. DSS staff work within an enormous and stressful workload and generally produce a better-quality output and decision-making service: specialist dedicated DSS teams could be brought in to assist administering the system, e.g. the Disability Living Allowance Service.
- Introduce the Alabama (America) model where a victim sits on a panel with equal power with other panel members to determine appropriate levels of compensation.
- Staff from the CICA should have external trainers take them through what it is like to be on the receiving end of their service and should meet periodically with user groups.
- CICA staff must have their job specifications made open to the public.
- CICA should make public the salaries of postholders.
- Abandon the mono-victim industry of subcontracting Victim Support. The CICA procedures and its internal work culture merely serve to amplify the unmet need for early expert legal guidance when completing an application form.
- Review the usefulness of the Justice and Victims Unit and assess whether the savings would better be utilised elsewhere.
- Review the composition of inspection members when the Audit Commission undertakes reviews.
- Penalise inept and poor administrative independent expert report assessors. Delays should not be to the detriment of applicants for a CICA medical report. Four weeks is ample time.
- The CICA takes note of applicants who state that medical records are incomplete.
- Free life health care, transport and housing for significant to catastrophic injuries.
- Cessation of deduction of means-tested welfare benefits in calculating a gross award.
- Welfare benefits should not require reapplication and should remain protected and ring-fenced money for life – that is not the current case. (Even though eligibility for benefits is part-assessment and calculation for award.)

314

- Free expert legal advice for any applicant throughout the entire process as a basic right – like that afforded to an alleged violent criminal.
- Replace the CICA's work with specialist teams recruited from social services, the police and private business by regional or city-wide bases to make quarterly inspections. All are familiar with producing a more efficient and effective manner and service and are familiar with many areas of law and dealing with agencies and issues currently dealt with by the CICA, but much better.
- National Lottery money should be available immediately to support best practices through diversity of where/how victims access help. After all, did Eton College need £12m or the National Opera House £21m? Government could focus on assisting the Inland Revenue to recoup many millions of pounds of tax lost in avoidance by corporations and relocate them to a compensation scheme and specialist social and health rehabilitation schemes.
- Fledgling survivor/victim charities fail to receive Home Office recognition they deserve and require, e.g. MAMAA and SURVIVE. Funds should be immediately channelled into the best groups, to avoid a mirroring of the problems found in the general poor quality currently available from the *victim club*. Those ineffective victims groups should be known to the public and denied charitable status and public funding. Expert knowledge can never be reduced to ad hoc second-rate chaotic 'help'.

It was as though the world turned upside down.
When the shock had worn off,
When, in spite of everything – in spite of terror ... and of the habit,
developed, through long years, of never complaining,
never criticising, no matter what happened.
There was nothing there now except a single commandment.
It ran – All animals are equal but some animals are more equal than others.

George Orwell: *Animal Farm*

Legislation says the Home Office is sponsor of the CICA and will not involve itself in its day-to-day operational running. It was the will of the Conservative administration under the then Home Secretary, Michael Howard, to distance government from the workings of the CICA: see pp. 271–280 on the history and motives of the then Conservative Government in this respect.

People affected by violent crime are still waiting for justice to be seen in the shape of proper care and provision and a new approach to confronting the shortfalls of the few agencies victims are offered and those of the CICA. Recent trumpeted fanfares from government about new recognition for victims falls a long way short of what is needed right now. 'Spinning' too much can cause a sick feeling as well as disorientation! This government continues in its failure to robustly meet the needs of victims of violent crime. This has to include repealing the Criminal Injuries Compensation Act 1995, failing to liaise with the Department of Health about good-quality provision for people affected by violence, failing to empower our police force with adequate training and resources. The Home Office continues to fail people affected by violent crime. It has left people affected by serious violence feeling they are institutionally, secondarily victimised.

Questions ...

What was the global amount allocated 1999–2000, 2000–01 and 2001–02 by the Home Office for all criminal justice system issues, e.g. prisons, policing, remand centres and contributions to local authorities in provision of violent criminals?

What was the gross amount of money allocated by the Lord Chancellor's Department, for the same period towards defending violent crimes?
What was the gross amount of money allocated by the Crown Prosecution Service, for the same period, towards prosecuting violent crimes?

How much is spent in the provision for violent criminals from police investigation, free expert legal representation, prison service, after-care rehabilitation services including housing and access to statutory and voluntary services funded by government?

In contrast, what is spent specifically for those affected by violent crime?

It is hard to find accurate answers to these basic questions. They are basic service questions that relate to use of the money of tax payers many of whom are, or are related to, people affected by violent crime. They are basic compared to the expensive route of trying to pay legal fees to deal with the CICA and absence of willing statutory services. The Treasury and the Scottish Executive along with the Lord Chancellor's Department positively tried to assist in addressing these questions. Oddly, it proved confusing to secure the answers one would expect the Home Office to know. In part, many aspects to these questions are complex from the position of service delivery, but they should all be easily answerable as they are within the Scottish Office and its excellent website. After all, the money comes from one source and it is reasonable to expect that source to have simple access to where that money is used. The Scottish Office has succeeded because it separates successfully the 'variables' of services and can add up the varying departments costs. It is a fact that costs and services do actively interlink and it is difficult to show variables and specifics. Nevertheless, it is important that professionals actively show how much free expert legal representation and the criminal system cost in comparison with what is specifically allocated to victims of violence.

Answers ...

The total estimated spend on the criminal justice system for 2001–02 was £14.3 billion, including the Home Office, Lord Chancellor's Department, CPS, Serious Fraud Office and local authority grants to police (Treasury for England and Wales, 2002).

Trying to break down specific costs to estimated defence-only costs shows, including all the legal aid costs advice and assistance, allowance for the duty solicitor scheme, magistrates' courts costs, Crown Court were: 2000–01 £152.6m; 2001–02 £201.2m. These figures do not include appeals against sentence or conviction (Lord Chancellor's Department, 2002).

Unanswered questions ...

What are the global costs for prosecuting violent crime for the last three years in England and Wales?

After speaking with some twenty civil servants – many positively trying to help within the Lord Chancellor's Department, Home Office and Crown Prosecution Office – they all insisted the other should have the information required. This does not include written requests. After one year, I concluded that the information would not be volunteered, mainly due to the fact no single government agency is correlating data to one source (even though it derives from one source). Obstruction was a factor among some workers. Different government departments correlate fragmented specific areas of global costs that affect their department, but no one agency appeared able, or willing, to give the sum total in context. This would not happen with the running of a small business and fails to offer what legal processes cost the taxpayer. It would be fair to assume that the Home Office or Treasury would wish to see value for taxpayers' money and to guide future provision. It seems costs to prosecute and explain defence of violent crime are less important than finding ways of itemising ways of reducing money for victims of violent crime or providing equally expert legal presentation to deal with the CICA. Also, to some degree, the public would not like the amount known regarding what prosecuting violent criminals costs each year – and their defence. These figures should be easily available within a democratic society with an open government but they are not. They make the costs of victims' care placed out of context with those of who are freely defended and prosecuted.

In Scotland ...

In Scotland, costs, sentencing and compensation have been broken down to show: police service £727m; Scottish Prison Service £178.3m; criminal legal assistance £85.6m; criminal injuries compensation £27.8m; Crown Office and Procurator Fiscal Service £46m; criminal justice social work £37.1m; Court Service £22.8m; district courts £3.9m; and secure child accommodation £2.4m. Also, advice and assistance in criminal matters £7.5m; representation £2.6m; Duty Solicitor Scheme £.9m; appeals £1.5m; six months in prison £13.4k; average cost of probation order £1.4k (Scottish Executive,1998–99)

> More than £80 million a year is wasted by unnecessary delays and adjournments ... allowing offenders to evade justice ... 60, 000 cases a year 13% of the total are discontinued when they get to court.
>
> Audit Commission: *The Route to Injustice*

318

The Justice and Victims Unit (J and VU)

The Justice and Victims Unit has many sections and this part is specifically referring to the section that works with Victim Support and the CICA. The Justice and Victims Unit (formerly known as the Victims and Procedures Unit) is responsible for monitoring the work of the CICA. The difficulty the Justice and Victims Unit has is in part the wording of the legislation that prevents involvement in day-to-day operational running of the CICA. This is compounded by a historical difficulty in showing a satisfactory detached perspective and capacity to promote change from the CICA or to encourage the Home Affairs Select Committee to review areas of performance. It would be healthier to see a wholly independent agency scrutinise the working of the CICA. The Audit Commission does inspect the functioning of the CICA but it has yet to urge for review of the repealing of the 1995 Act and all that goes with it. It can only be hoped that, in this new century, a new culture and quality of staff are encouraged to become genuinely more open to accountability about who they are and what they do. The Justice and Victims Unit is not sufficiently detached from the CICA to act robustly in the pursuit of best practice, inspection, natural justice and implementation of confronting the CICA and its substandard practices.

This results in great injustice and distress in the lives of many applicants who suffered violent crimes. An independent body should replace the Justice and Victims Unit and quarterly inspect the efficiency, types of complaint and general inspection of the CICA performance. New Care Teams as proposed on page 322 would largely reduce the need for the Justice and Victims Unit.

The Home Office is failing to place effectively the wider social, health and legal needs of victims of violent crime. The government has access to several learned reports about need, services and recommendations, mostly ignored because they require social policy shifts in priorities – and money. It is failing to ensure that people in need are promptly located into statutory services where needs will be best addressed, as they are in the case of violent criminals. People seriously affected by violent crime are waiting to see justice with dignity for what they have suffered, and without being subjected to a dreadful and demeaning compensation process. The Home Office must cease its unconditional biased and flawed support for Victim Support that negates people's needs for choice and negates government's wider 'spin' about diversity and inclusivity.

The Home Office

Useful addresses

Note: See also sections on choosing a competent solicitor (pp. 260–270). For details about the CICA please refer to pp. 236-237 and the Scottish Office website for Scottish-related government departments and websites.

Home Office website: www.homeoffice.gov.uk
This site has information about all aspects of the criminal justice system and victim liaison duties among other services.

www.homeoffice.gov.uk/rds
useful site about the various Home Office areas of duties and research work.

www.open.gov.uk
A useful website that takes you to several government departments and varying types of information.

Home Office Pack: Information for Families of Homicide Victims. A not very useful cluster of leaflets and addresses. Written by Victim Support, Home Office and SAMM – an affiliated agency of Victim Support

How to Understand an Act of Parliament, *by Dr D. J. Gifford and John Salter,* published by Cavendish, 1996. A really good text about how to make sense of Acts of Parliament; get a copy in your reference library.

For a better, dignified service model

> A man may see how this world goes with no eyes.
> Look within thine ears – see how yond justice rails upon yond simple thief.
> Hark in thine ear!
> Change places, and handy-dandy, which is justice, which is the thief?

William Shakespeare: *King Lear*

What real excitement and hope existed on that glorious, hot May morning in 1997, with the massive mandate the people of Britain gave the new Blair government. How far away that feeling seems now. How sadly, and rapidly, people sensed betrayal and disappointment. What a disappointment for our society and what a privileged opportunity to do something dynamic and honour pledges made in Opposition! Opposite is a straightforward model that would ensure that the needs of people in need are statutorily addressed. It allows existing structures to remain while developing new teams under the directorship of regional police chiefs to provide qualitative long-term social and health care. This is in keeping with new legislation and government rhetoric and ensures that those in need are positively placed within institutional services from the onset. The make-up of the new teams should come from within the NHS, the police and social services and thereby avoid the ad hoc and inadequate voluntary 'help' of the *victim club*. The model mirrors how criminals are treated and if undertaken will see that the broad and complex needs of people in need are legally protected. Funds should be redirected from the Department of Health due to the absence of provision of adequate services and failure to provide a good use of laws, care and protection currently allocated to social and health services. This will be a fresh and exciting use of public money and will effectively deal with the needs of people properly and win public support – the same people who place power in the hands of politicians and who can remove this power from politicians.

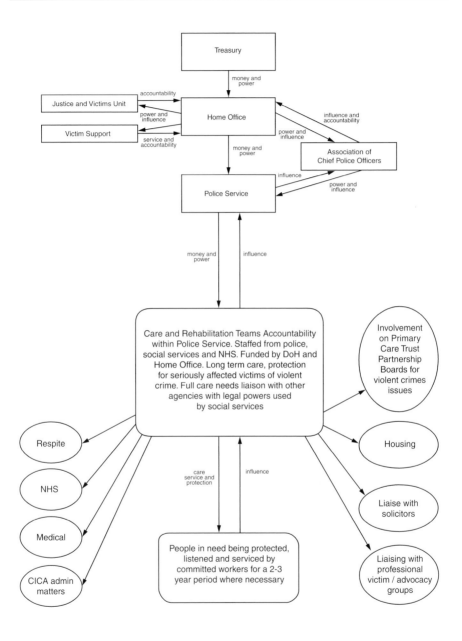

Treasury

money and power

accountability

Justice and Victims Unit

power and influence

Home Office

influence and accountability

Victim Support

service and accountability

power and influence

money and power

Association of Chief Police Officers

influence

Police Service

power and influence

money and power

influence

Care and Rehabilitation Teams Accountability within Police Service. Staffed from police, social services and NHS. Funded by DoH and Home Office. Long term care, protection for seriously affected victims of violent crime. Full care needs liaison with other agencies with legal powers used by social services

Involvement on Primary Care Trust Partnership Boards for violent crimes issues

Respite

Housing

NHS

care service and protection

influence

Medical

Liaise with solicitors

CICA admin matters

People in need being protected, listened and serviced by committed workers for a 2-3 year period where necessary

Liaising with professional victim / advocacy groups

© T.S. Duckett 2003 *Old and New: Power, Influence for Service Provision*

Midway, this way of life we're bound upon
I woke to find myself in a dark wood,
Where the right road was wholly lost – and gone.

Aye me, how hard to speak of it,
That rude and rough and stubborn forest,
The mere breath of memory stirs the old fear in the blood!

But when, at last, I stood beneath a steep hillside,
Which closed that valley's wandering maze,
Whose dread had pierced me to the heart root deep.

Then I looked up, and saw the morning rays
Mantle its shoulder from that planet bright,
Which guides men's feet aright – on all their ways.

Dante Alighieri: *Divina Comedia*

A reason ...

It seemed important to provide evidence to explain why a handbook like
this was justified. People who had experienced violent crime and related
victim services were invited to say what they felt about the manner in which
they had been treated. Various victim groups and solicitors were
approached; Victim Support declined. Agencies were asked to forward to
their clients a set of general questions and how they answered them was
entirely left to the individual. Only a few people responded and here are a
few people's comments, unaltered. These people welcomed a chance to
break the silence.

Dear Sir/Madam

Thank for your letter. My injurie of crime affected me mentally. It affected me in
finding employment with men. Victim Support was not really helping but
reassuring someone to talk to. My claim taken 1 year to be assessed I believe I got a
fair award. I did not have any problems with the CICB/A.

© Suffolk 2003

Dear Simon

Victim of Circumstances

I was a victim of a violent unprovoked attack, by three persons, whilst on my way
home from work one evening in November of 1995, to which a charge of attempted
murder was made.

I sustained a fractured jaw, several damaged front teeth, requiring various forms of treatment, hair torn from my scalp and stabbings to my head using a household kitchen fork, along with other cuts and bruises. As a result of this I have lost my left-sided nasal sense of smell, suffer severe tinnitus in my left ear, and have to live with frequent migraine headaches. My biggest problem has been my inability to overcome the whole incident, with thoughts and flashbacks haunting me on a daily basis.

I have had various forms of treatment, some provided by the National Health Service, involving a clinical psychologist, an occupational therapist and a psychiatric social worker. I have also undergone private treatment by a qualified trauma/stress counsellor and critical incident debriefer.

The National Health Service treatment I was given was most disappointing and left me feeling let down on numerous occasions, it was my opinion conducted in a totally unprofessional manner. The private counselling I received was handled far better, but to no avail unfortunately with me continuing to suffer from post traumatic stress disorder as had been diagnosed.

I have felt totally excluded and distanced by the CICA/B from day one, in putting in a claim for compensation. I feel that it is essential to enlist the services of a reputable solicitor and I see this is a vital part of the compensation claim, one with whom you are able to stay in contact with, for updates concerning your claim if I hadn't sought there help and advice, I feel I would have felt even more isolated and at a greater disadvantage.

It seems to me that although this scheme exists, to help victims of violent crime, payment is almost given out grudgingly, if at all, and with no real representation of the horrific violent crimes people are suffering.

My own incident happened in November of 1995 and I am writing this in August 2000. I have had two small interim payments, from the CICA/B, to assist funding of my private counselling, but this time delay in making a final payment is only continuing to fuel my ongoing problems, of not being able to shut the door on this part of my life.

This incident has changed my life dramatically, from once being outgoing and sociable, with many friends and having had various interests and hobbies and enjoying just being alive, to becoming introverted, reclusive, nervous and fearful having almost no social interaction at all.

My six year relationship with my partner ended with her not being able to cope with the dramatic changes to my personality that had taken place with bouts of depression and moodiness, fits of frustration anger and hatred, directed at her and society's failure in dealing with the causes and issues brought about by violent crime. This eventually destroyed our happiness together and our plans of marriage, and starting a family ended, three years after my assault.

I hope that one day I can learn to lead a normal life again, trusting and having faith in my fellow human being. But all this seems a distant dream at the moment, with continuing reports in the media, both local and national, of increases of violent crimes throughout the country and the powers that be seemingly unable to stop this growing culture, we now seem to accept as being part of everyday life.

I haven't really made any significant progress in recovery, be it with medication or counselling, and see my life as having been ruined with no sense of purpose in anything I do at present, and having nothing to look forward to, for the future. I feel isolated in my own world, cut off from the rest of society wishing I could just turn the clock back.

© Norfolk 2003

To Whom It May Concern

I was involved in a much-publicised arson attack at a cinema in London and hospitalised for a week because of the effects of smoke-inhalation; (my throat and lungs were badly affected). I was told that if I had been in the building for one more minute I would not have survived and was also diagnosed as having Post Traumatic Stress Disorder.

About a dozen people died and an unknown number were injured. So far as I am aware no-one is sure of the number of people hurt or traumatised as there has been no co-ordinated attempt made to help victims and their families. I was trapped in a hot, dark, smoke-filled room for about an hour before being rescued by the Fire Service. The horror of being in that room – it felt like I was being roasted alive in an oven; the screams and cries of those with me in the building; the crackle and smell of burning as the fire got closer; the shock of being dragged to safety over a dead body; my first gulps of fresh air when the fireman who saved me sat me on a second-floor window ledge, are all memories that never really leave me.

I received enormous support and help from the Roman Catholic Chaplains at the Hospital whilst I was an in-patient and from my GP afterwards. After being discharged, I was off work for about five weeks to begin the long process of recovery but felt like a marked man as deeply personal aspects of my life had been exposed to my colleagues, and, indeed, to my friends and family.

The first weeks after the fire were very difficult. I was glad to be alive, of course, and relatively unscathed physically, but I lived in a nightmare of flashbacks, panic attacks, grief, coping with family and friends (always supportive even though they were traumatised themselves at finding out what I had been through), and the realisation that my whole life had been ripped apart, and my future changed, by the vicious act of a complete stranger! I felt I had no control over my life.

Before I was discharged from hospital I was referred to where, I was told, there was a centre of excellence for the treatment of Post-Traumatic Stress which would be able to help me to cope with the situation. I felt hugely relieved and hopeful, especially as I was offered an appointment very quickly. So I went there optimistically, although I had no idea what my visit would involve.

Initially, I was disappointed at finding a rather dismal clinic – too obviously 'Freud-meets-Habitat' in inspiration, but my 'session' was okay. I got a lot off my chest and felt better at the end of it. I returned for a second session about a week later and was told that I was coping well (this was about a month after the fire, when I was still numb in many respects), and that I should contact them for another appointment when I felt that I needed one.

A few weeks later, when the full horror of what had happened was beginning to dawn on me and I felt as though I was falling apart, I 'phoned as instructed but was told that I could not be seen as I had only been funded for two sessions. No discussion! Rejection! It seemed to me that I must have been seen by them on sufferance; I was not a worthy recipient of their and effort like, say, the 'pc' Kings Cross survivors (their treatment of whom is loudly trumpeted). They had judged me and found me wanting! Of course, it was another trauma – but this time delivered by supposedly caring liberals.

I saw my GP who referred me to the counsellor attached to the GP practice and I saw him regularly, probably for about eighteen months and received very kind, non-judgemental help and support. Without that input, I think that my life may have fallen apart. As it was, I found working-life and living in London to be increasingly difficult but was fortunate enough to be able to move away.

I applied to the CICB shortly after the fire, through my solicitor. The procedure was professional, as one would expect – but icy and very protracted. It took a very long time for things to happen and even the necessary reports were not carried out until 1997. There seemed to be no sense of urgency on the part of either the CICB or my lawyer, the fact that I needed a rapid response, at least initially, to enable me to begin to re-build my life seemed to be of no importance. This sloppiness was in itself stressful and added to my legal costs (not reflected in the award, so far as I am aware). Perhaps they were simply following their usual procedures – I have no means of knowing – but the officials gave me no indication of either sensitivity, or an appreciation of my case. It was not "professional detachment" – we were talking about a massacre, after all – I believe that moral judgements were made early on as to my presence in a cinema on a Saturday evening.

The fact that I was the victim of particularly horrendous attempted murder was pushed aside. In fact, I recall the Board Member actually implied, in his evidence at the subsequent trial, that the survivors who were pursuing compensation claims were 'in it for the ride!'. That kind of callous ignorance is especially horrible when spewing from the mouth of public servants and does nothing to aid a victim's recovery. I was given a small interim payment but my claim was not finally settled until 1998. The amount finally 'agreed' was niggardly, bearing in mind my career was in tatters. But the flint face of respectable bureaucracy (which I had also experienced at the Middlesex Hospital) really seemed to be telling me to go away – I was lucky to be alive and my injuries were not 'pc'! The whole CICB process seemed to drag on unnecessarily and I am of the view that this is intended, although perhaps subconsciously, in the hope that applicants will either die, go away or accept whatever is offered without a fuss – which is what I did.

My life has changed in so many ways since that dreadful day. I no longer have a job; I have emotional and social difficulties; I am more cynical than before. All I can say is that the real help received has come from the Church, my GP practice, my family and friends. The agencies set-up to look after people like me – failed.

© Lancashire 2003

Our son was a decent, talented and innocent 15 year-old boy when he was butchered and our lives fell apart. There was no one to help us. What else could we do but close our doors and cry?

Each day, outside, was a big sorrow and if we met anyone we knew all they had to say was 'sorry' and our tears would flow. We would avoid anyone we knew – walking around with a pretend smile. Once the doors were closed, inside, we would think of the day our child was murdered from start to finish. The whole horrific nightmare from being badly treated by the Police, the hospital, the press, the farce of justice – everything behind our doors crashed around in our heads and in tears. Our child was slaughtered and we were not there to fight and protect him. Sometimes, we wish we couldn't remember but we forget nothing! Walking behind *our* child's coffin – you would never think your child would die before yourself. I pray to God 'let this nightmare be over' and let us live again. I myself have a sleep disorder, my husband has a total memory block of his lifetime and all that goes through his mind is constant thoughts about our son.

My oldest son is drinking himself to death; my second eldest has gone deep into himself and says nothing in case he hurts us. And my daughter, she just cries from the time she opens her eyes till she goes to sleep and then the nightmares start. What life have we got – none! But, our son's murderer served four and a half year and got out on 'good behaviour'. We got the life sentence not him. The law is cruel! I have never asked for anything in my life from anyone, but life is a full circle and I hope this man gets what he deserves.

Nothing is easy and nothing's the same. Nothing feels safe. Nothing is safe. Our experience with the Police to this day has not been good whether it was the way they refused to tell us about our son being dead in the hospital, the aggressive way they did instruct someone to come and identify 'the body', the way we were treated at

Court. The Police seemed ignorant and aggressive and didn't care. It was like we were 'dirt' to them and still are, even when the killer's mates desecrate our son's grave. These things break us down further and the Police have failed us badly. We didn't get any professional help and we know we need it and Victim Support were no use whatsoever. It doesn't make sense! We are suffering and the killer receives help and sympathy – it seems even from the Police – why? What have we done wrong?

Our son had a disability and was cornered by a known vicious attacker and butchered with a hunting knife that had a history of attacking people with knives and had tried to kill others the day he cornered our child. Our son was caught when he was entering a fairground. He had no chance of escaping. Our son was repeatedly stabbed and knocked to the ground. He got up, and ran 100 yards into a field lay down on the ground and bled to death all alone like a wild animal, and I was not there to say goodbye. This especially breaks my heart as a mother and his father and family. Our child, alone and terrified dying – what agony and fear he must have known and what courage he showed to try and fend-off his killer. I can't say here what the killer did to our child's body. How can someone who did what he did be released on 'good behaviour'?

I have phoned the Police and told them my son's murderer is living and walking about where we live as he is still on licence till 2004. He is not allowed to come in this area till then but they want proof, what do the police want his head on a plate? What more must we suffer? Why do we have to do the work of the Police? They say time is a great healer – no it's not! Everyday is a clawing heartache; my other three children keep asking me 'does this heart ache ever go away?' I tell them 'no you just get use to the hurting'.

If this country is civilised it needs to show it! It can start by helping people who are affected by violence because at the moment we are all treated like dirt. Criminals seem to get a good deal and in some cases killers do change for the better. But, they cannot undo slaughter and the endless agony they leave for those left to struggle with – endlessly. The killer of our son will kill again and another family will be crushed forever and the Police will probably be no better to them. People like us need proper professional help and protection and the Police need to do their job properly and not the way they do around here. We deserve and need respect.
We need professional practical help if we are to start to cope with what it means to have a good young man slaughtered. No service has helped us at any time. It seems victims could do with some justice in this country and not patronising politicians, or gloating media people watching our grief while indifferent to justice. There is no end, no justice and no one on our side – we are the last on the list for everyone. We are alone. Why?

Is this not a crime to destroy a whole family to be left in limbo? To sit and wait for a knock on the door and say "I'm home mam!". We are all in God's hands and we pray for God to take us so we can be with our son. They say there is no reason and they say that time will heal. But neither time nor reason will change the way we feel for no one knows the heartache that lies behind the smile. No one knows how many times we have broken down and cried.

To our lost child we speak these words.

There won't be any doubt you are so wonderful to think about and hold in our hearts, but;
It is anguish, so hard to be without you.
We cannot bring the old days back when we were all together,
The family chain may be broken now, but your memories, our love will live forever.

© Tyne and Wear 2003

Advancement
and
Community Action

It's not
what you thought
when you first began it
you got –
what you want
now you can hardly stand it, though –
by now you know

it's not going to stop
it's not going to stop
it's not going to stop
till you wise up

you're sure
there's a cure
and you have finally found it
you think
one drink
will shrink you till
you're underground and living down
but –

it's not going to stop
it's not going to stop
it's not going to stop
till you wise up

prepare a list for what you need
before you sign away the deed
cause –

it's not going to stop
it's not going to stop
it's not going to stop
till you wise up

no, it's not going to stop
till you wise up
no, it's not going to stop
so just …

We are a society that is very unhappy with itself. We want to believe we are democratic, but citizens across the nation know we are an increasingly fragmented and angry society. We are not a society that appears to be comfortable with looking at itself seriously. We are a society that has deluded itself for centuries that it is the 'mother of democracies' when we know your socio-economic start in life will have great bearing upon how others, especially those in authority, will treat you. Who you are, what you do and where you live does impact on the services you receive across the nation. It has always been this way. It is just in the last twenty years that we have seen a serious social downturn we have not experienced since the 1930s. This state we're in – this state we have all contributed towards by voting or failing to vote – is steadily sliding towards an abyss of social and racial violence. Ask any public sector worker and look about you: from Motherwell to Margate, we are witnessing a polarising and seething social disintegration. The only beneficiaries of a society in decline are a government with transient values, racial supremacists, other irrational groups or individuals who seek to find any excuse to act on violent ignorance.

Why is our society so violent and why can't we even participate in sport like football without excessive violence from players and spectators, requiring policing at taxpayers' expense? Why do people in our society believe it is acceptable to go to foreign countries and urinate into the food people are eating on boulevards, create violent confrontations with peaceful holidaymakers, fight on aeroplanes, and riot and brawl in the streets of Europe? Why is it we are in the state we're in? As citizens, we all have a responsibility to do more than our national pastime of moaning like tethered, angry miserable people. It is time we all did a little more and wise up and expect a little more from ourselves and from those in power.

We are in a state that chooses not to provide basic public services to a good and uniform standard, if at all. There is nothing to be proud about being a wealthy nation that accepts it has public service 'waiting lists' when there should be none. All the services referred to in this handbook are services those affected by violent crime need. We are losing essential public sector workers through poor resources, constant government undermining and switching of policies, lack of workers through poor salaries and low morale. We are losing talented men and women from the skilled police, education, fire, health and social care services that are opting for a totally different source of employment or leaving the country. The state we're in cannot afford to lose talented workers. They leave behind a vacuum of newly qualified workers and top-heavy management structures and growing unmet needs of citizens. Losing skilled talent will be to the detriment of all in society.

We are in a state that provides expensive expert legal representation freely to alleged violent criminals. However, we subject victims – who are dependent upon state criminal compensation to fund their applications from their own compensation. Legal representatives command high fees to deal with the CICA. Approximately 65 per cent of applicants are represented by trade unions or solicitors (CICA Headquarters 1999). The assessment process we know is degrading, and many find almost as dreadful as the violence to which they were subjected (directly or otherwise). The state we're in fails to reflect individual need and loss with realistic compensation and services. We are in a state that affords wider provision to criminals than those affected by violent crime. It is fair to say our society is in a sad state!

Our media are seriously disinclined to help progress the long-term social, health and economic needs of victims. Sometimes they do their job well. Regrettably, they generally misuse victims 'in the public interest' and adopt an almost titillated or voyeuristic stance on the latest 'news' of one more 'tragedy' devastating yet one more family's life. The police recently had some responsibility in colluding with this when in the summer of 2002 in Cambridgeshire two schoolgirls were murdered. The use of traumatised parents in television 'appeals' has become common practice but how effective is it in getting criminals to release their victims? In this tragedy, the decision to use the families with the media was unnecessary and ill judged. The media generated a deplorable frenzy of coverage that manipulated a public response similar to that following the death of the late Diana, Princess of Wales – killed, lest we forget, while fleeing the media. The private tragedy of the schoolgirls and their families rapidly swept out of the control of their families, denying them the opportunity to privacy, let alone rehabilitation. What is missing in the lives of people in our society that creates a desire to act in this way? The public behaved like a manipulated frenzied mob, coming to the home town of the Cambridgeshire children in their thousands – why? Where was the humility in swamping a town to sit in graveyards, eating fish and chips? What does this tell us about ourselves? What is missing in the lives of people in the state we're in and would they wish to be treated in the same way? Where was the respect for the grieving families who faced the most horrendous of challenges? As a society, how well have we served these families, suffering incredibly and forced to adjust to the impossible? Equally importantly, the media saturation also placed at risk the possibility of the legal process being free to progress properly and allow the families confidence that justice would seen to be done. The pursuit of wealth for media owners outweighs a genuine relationship with the public that reflects constructive reporting about social need and genuine public interest issues. They decline to report sensibly the consequences of the state we're in. Nor do they wish to help the public make important connections between their lives, television and social injustice and the ballot box. It is as though beyond reactive titillation the media seem to enjoy private horror as 'news'. The media are disinclined to assist our state in making connections with the long-term daily struggles and appalling misery and loss violence causes. Our media have the power but not the will to pressure government for significant changes for victims. Why did the media not connect, translate and relocate public issues about the Cambridgeshire schoolgirls to encourage the public to come together in a massive demonstration in our major cities for better provisions for victims, as groups such as SURVIVE and MAMAA have championed for years? Why did the media not suggest leaving the families alone and encourage a positive gesture, e.g. linking arms from Glasgow to Whitehall in London, or organise candlelit demonstrations through cities? The 2002 media-induced saturation coverage, as we have seen before in the 1990s with the Bulger and Russell families, was intrusive and sensationalist. Public ambivalence has not helped the state we're in.

As an academic once observed, the media show power without responsibility and this makes them dangerous. A few years ago, for a couple of days, the disappearance of a little schoolgirl in the north-west of England became medium-level 'news'. The wording of the reporting made reference to her being from a large single-parent family living in social security bed and breakfast accommodation. The little girl had gone to a nearby chip shop. Her body was found a few days later and there was no huge public outpouring and wave of reaction from the media or public – was this little girl's life of less value because her family were poor? Maybe it is time the media were further bound by law and regulated. The media could do so much to help, so much more to educate the public and apply pressure on government if they wished.

> We know that a man is not a thing and is not to be placed at the mercy of things … we know that a baby does not come into the world merely to be the instrument of someone else's profit. We know that democracy does not mean the coercion of all into a deadly – and, finally, wicked – mediocrity but the liberty for all to aspire to the best that is in him, or that has ever been.
>
> Angela Davis: *If They Come in the Morning*

When horror enters our lives we cannot be prepared for what follows. It starts with the incident of being victimised and progresses to a series of secondary and institutional victimisation. Much of this handbook has explained what to do when you are treated badly by services, some of which are specifically created to assist victims of violent crimes. How can a person progress his/her life if he/she is treated meanly and grudgingly by aloof and cynical services within a one-way state system? How can anyone get beyond the daily status of victim and aspire to progress life with purpose if he/she is constantly devalued by ambivalent politicians, powerful media and the lack of public will to demand change for those affected by violent crime? How can an innocent person profoundly affected by violent crime survive if he/she is institutionally treated day by day like a criminal?

The final part of this handbook shows how to go about progressing the political and campaigning issues for people affected by violent crime and how to awaken our unhappy society. These final sections are about how to make this society a place that shows effective strategies for social and political responses to help survive and progress after violent crime. To make a contribution that does not offer pity, but the means to aspire to be much, much more.

Where do we go from here?
As a society, we cannot go much lower before social strife spills into sustained social unrest. Globally, we are living through an awesome era. Together, we must make a decision and find politicians with values that are not transient and shallow; who will champion the traumatised and growing minority of victims of violent crimes. Some academics debate whether there should be any criminal compensation, so if we disband compensation what is likely to happen? If such politicians were violated, would they apply for compensation? If there were no compensation or CICA, it is likely we would find a far more politicised and robust victim lobby evolving rapidly, and maybe this would be better, as we have seen in other countries that have successfully placed victim's needs within their legal and social care framework. In mainland Europe, what is not provided within a sum of compensation is genuinely provided in 'protected' welfare benefits and services. Has your MP ever done anything for victims of violence? Your vote does have some power. Use this well.

In the section on the Home Office (pp. 316–322), a sensible model for changing the place victims are given institutionally is made and is easy to establish – if the media and public will could be encouraged to make this happen. It would make victims' needs positively and institutionally addressed; it would place the charities, or lack of specialist victim charities, in a clearer context for being part of real diversity for surviving violent crime.

If we are to get beyond our cultural habit of 'moaning without responsibility' we must be prepared to change and progress our lives and make our society a safe place to live in and a place of which we can be proud. If we want this, then we must confront the injustices and inequalities in health, education and, for the purposes of this text, the attitude of the state towards victims of violent crime. Unsurprisingly, where we do see community and social change taking place it is largely spearheaded by women actively doing something. They are not moaning. They are eloquently and powerfully articulating and responding to those in crisis; they do so without appropriate funds – look at MAMAA or SURVIVE. The politicians will change when the powerful mass media machine and public will decide they have had enough.

Change is never easy or comfortable, but we have a choice to make – sooner rather than later. Do we care, really care, what happens to people affected by violent crime – or not? One day, these people might be your family and friends, and possibly, one day it may be you – and what would you need?

The importance of diversity for survivors

It is ridiculous that one large nation of approximately 60 million people has one dominant victim charity. Moreover, ours, as we know, is a violent nation. The dominance enjoyed by one victim charity does not make for diversity or choice for people in need; nor can one charity meet the supply–demand of so many differing types of people and injuries.

As discussed earlier, it seems a significant obstacle to encouraging diversity is our own attitude towards the issue of victims, and the way Victim Support, as a government-created and funded body, is regarded as *the* unquestioned agency for people by statutory agencies like the police, social services and the media. All these powerful services and government have areas of influence in the national and regional provision of services about victims' needs and providing practical and financial support. Fledgling groups trying to attract Home Office approval and funding are often greeted with a blanket – seemingly unquestioned – response that Victim Support is *the* voluntary provider of victims' services, regardless of ability or suitability to deal with complex legal and personal matters. The fact that Victim Support has only recently properly started to gather better service-user feedback after thirty years is something, albeit overdue. Very few large organisations heavily funded by a government department would be excused from providing clear, reliable service-user feedback. Government funded organisations normally need to evidence this for renewal of funding, and be submitted to independent scrutiny that routinely includes the comments of service users. The National Audit Office reviewed Victim Support's services and a report was due in 2002. Let us hope this leads to a cessation of Victim Support's monopoly.

Only the police service appears to address victims' legal, social and emotional needs robustly. How has it come to be that victims have failed to attract motivated wealthy sponsors, priority and dignified care and constructive media attention from society? It is easy to see how victims can become trapped in self-destructive rage and disintegration while being made effectively invisible. And yet, how many of us have not been directly or indirectly affected by violence? Why are victims treated the way they are?

Communities from which victims can learn

Government responsibility is only one factor that is required for making change and compelling statutory agencies to do their work thoroughly and willingly. It is up to victims and survivors to take control and positively change the public view of victims and their lives. This takes time, talented people and groups that are dynamic and work well together. We have excellent role models to help steer and provide guidance in two very different communities: the gay community and the learning-disability community. Two very different groups that once were heavily stigmatised and treated deplorably and who have secured significant social and political recognition over the decades. They succeeded in forging change by actively taking responsibility and control of the 'needs' and political agenda and had articulate people taking up issues from political lobbying, direct help to fundraising. Two groups within these communities give victims and survivors of violence hope and guidance to force the tempo and agenda for governments to change: Stonewall and MENCAP. The former is the gay and lesbian lobbying group that influenced many legal changes. The latter, for people with profound learning disabilities, has been extremely influential. Another service and public issue the government and media ignored, but which dynamic gay men and women in the Terence Higgins Trust forced to change, was educating us about HIV/AIDS. Change for the good of society can happen!

The needs remain unmet and many people find existing victim groups inadequate, to say the least; moreover, we have a marker of what not to become through the worst-practice methods of the *victim club* (see pp. 242–251). We also have a tiny selection of advocacy groups and organisations providing examples of best practice like the Women's Aid Federation, SURVIVE and MAMAA. Here are some tips about setting up groups of differing types that use best practices as their foundations, which you may wish to start one day.

©Jacob Epstein: *Day*. Reproduced with the generous permission of the London Transport Museum.
Not for recopying without prior written consent of the owners

337

Setting up a group

There is a lack of diversity in the groups and organisations that exist for people affected by violent crime: we must work out some basic ground rules. What do you want to do? How will you go about getting what you want? How will you prove what you do is needed? What type of structure will the group have, e.g. will it become a large group with charitable status or a small, community, informal self-help group?

A self-help group

A small self-help group tends to be local and casual. Possibly, a group like this begins through a shared community tragedy where many in the neighbourhood are affected directly or indirectly. Initially, people may meet in one another's homes, or hire a religious centre or school in which to meet weekly. In time, such a group will find itself with maybe a small informal number of members or the group simply finishes because the reasons no longer bring people together. Alternatively, such a group may find it has a two-tier number of people, like a group who want to arrange meetings and lobby MPs and others who will lend practical support or only want to take what the group offers.

If the group remains casual and informal, e.g. meeting for a meal, going to a pub, taking children on a picnic, it remains good practice to agree that confidentiality of expressed feelings, addresses and names is respected. Many individuals and groups fall out with one another because the heady mixture of grief, anger and abrupt sense of insecurity have prevented agreement on some basic house rules. These house rules can be whatever the group wants, but they must respect confidentiality for one another and be clear what it is they want to do. These rules can always change, but they need to be clear and agreed. If a self-help group starts to become more interested in being active in victim and survivor issues, i.e. to want to help others, they will need to have an agreed purpose. Many members of the *victim club* are disastrous because they are trying to be everything to everyone, which is unachievable and self-defeating. They serve no usefulness. They lack real purpose and fail to get motivated, quality volunteers onboard; this is, in part, because the ground rules are not used well, if they exist at all. If there are more than twenty regular members of your group who are committed to wanting to be a group, then writing down what you are, how you are going to achieve your goals is worthwhile. It does not have to be complex or long, but being clear about what you are doing *is* important.

Setting up services

If a significant need exists in your area, or you wish to campaign about a particular issue that's relevant to victims of violent crime, then this is more than an informal self-help group. It is essential you have clear, simple structures and a system in place. A trap many aspiring groups make is the failure to create transparent structures that reduce power-crazed egos; where errors get out of control. No matter what size of group you might choose, it is important that the power of the project is democratically established.

Don't!

- assume that because your need and issue are valid you should automatically become a charity (expanded elsewhere);
- assume that because your need and issue are valid you will automatically deserve or get government or charitable donations.

These assumptions are consistent flaws among dysfunctional groups because they have failed to 'prove' the need in various ways. We are also a society dismantling our welfare state and we will do better to look at how groups get established in the USA and in mainland Europe. It is a hard slog and uphill battle to emerge into a credible and productive service-providing group, which requires clear accounting for any donations, trained and police-checked volunteers, clear structures of accountability and proof that what you do actually benefits people.

Own goals ...

The other trap many fledgling groups make is the failure to attract competent volunteers, as without a core group of trained and fit volunteers a group aspiring to become large, i.e. represent victims in a region, will fail. Many groups are created to respond to unmet needs and these individuals without strong guidance forget in the campaigning and struggle for justice that their needs and grief still need to be addressed quietly and professionally. If you do not have a solid group of healthy and articulate volunteers, you cannot play in the game because you do not have a team! It is not enough to know what is needed: if you wish to set about making a change, then this is exactly what you need to show you are doing with best practices. Many groups fail through charismatic people who have forgotten their own wounds are a very long way from healing. Such people do not help the social and political agenda and they have in common the tendency to 'project' rage onto others. To put it another way, they act like abusers! It diminishes their personal integrity and personal needs and trivialises the aims of the group and repels funders and talented volunteers. Self-care is a responsibility for all.

Structures – the trick!

Another serious trap fledgling groups repeatedly make is to assume that money should be provided automatically. We live in a cynical and angry society where the *victim club* runs around chasing the same sources of funding and invariably fails. A strong argument is needed to justify any funding, and this is as it should be. Unfortunately, within a dwindling welfare state and increasing social deprivation, funding becomes an even rarer commodity. Without clear, solid, strategic policy and written structures with reliable people in place within trustee committees, management committees and cell-groups for specific service volunteers, why should anyone wish to fund a group without good order? The trick for any group is to create excellent structures from which to work. Summarised in this section are some tricks and tips that may be of assistance. It will be seen how all of the parts are interconnected, which is a marker of a group functioning well.

The following is an outline for a group that wishes to provide a wide range of services and so will be of a significant size and have a respected level of knowledge and cooperation with other services. Let us imagine they have existed for five years and have successfully provided voluntary services and have outgrown the temporary premises they have used. Although this group is national, it mainly responds to people living within the south-east of England.

An example of an expanding group

This is an outline of a proposed group this author has established on the Internet and is worth looking at for its structure. It also acts as a self-contained advertisement and poster for newspapers or a website. Please note, no services will begin until a large body of trained volunteers are in place with management structures and private funding. Note also how the areas reflect social responsibility, law, equality of opportunity, practical services and independent funding sources. This has a clear starting point. It is setting out with a wide range of services to complement other services – or the failure of others to deliver.

DIGNIFY!

Greater London Group

Diversity Creates Positive Competition
Positive Competition Through Creation of Resources
Stimulates Opportunity
For Better Quality Services For Those Affected By Violent Crime
This Constructively Confronts
Some of the Social Despair in Our Society

Do Something – Use Your Skills and Help DIGNIFY!

DIGNIFY! feels it's time that we did more than just complain! It is time to get beyond being trapped permanently like a victim, either personally or in our community.
DIGNIFY! says if you want to be part of a new, robust support response within Greater London for people affected by violent crime and do something that will make a positive change – we welcome you warmly!
DIGNIFY! hopes to start recruiting and training realistically during the next year. In the meantime, initial meetings with DIGNIFY! will create structures – management committees, plans, etc. for encouraging fundraising and recruiting volunteers to help.
DIGNIFY! starts from a solid foundation of unity, purpose, skills and trained volunteers.
We especially welcome expertise in any of these areas:

- ☐ IT
- ☐ fundraising
- ☐ telephone help line
- ☐ legal advice/representation
- ☐ interpreters
- ☐ campaigning/education
- ☐ social and health services
- ☐ general office assistance
- ☐ home care
- ☐ befriending

When sufficient people have applied to become involved with DIGNIFY! and completed a volunteer application, training sessions will be organised and people contacted. It is important to make realistic offers of support and understand and accept the importance of why police checks on all applicants are necessary; and why a selection process is important, especially when working with vulnerable people.
DIGNIFY! supporters will reflect the diversity of our multiracial and multicultural Greater London and will welcome applications from all communities of our vibrant and diverse city, especially people with any of the skills abovementioned.
If you want to register interest and consider becoming involved with DIGNIFY! please leave your name and address.

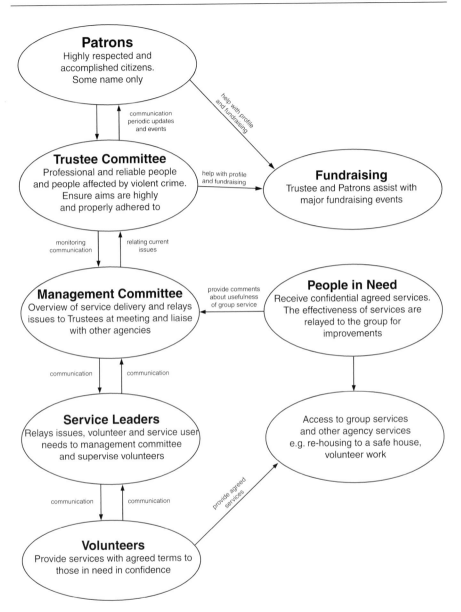

Patrons
Highly respected and accomplished citizens. Some name only

communication periodic updates and events

help with profile and fundraising

Trustee Committee
Professional and reliable people and people affected by violent crime. Ensure aims are highly and properly adhered to

help with profile and fundraising

Fundraising
Trustee and Patrons assist with major fundraising events

monitoring communication

relating current issues

Management Committee
Overview of service delivery and relays issues to Trustees at meeting and liaise with other agencies

provide comments about usefulness of group service

People in Need
Receive confidential agreed services. The effectiveness of services are relayed to the group for improvements

communication

communication

Service Leaders
Relays issues, volunteer and service user needs to management committee and supervise volunteers

Access to group services and other agency services e.g. re-housing to a safe house, volunteer work

communication

communication

provide agreed services

Volunteers
Provide services with agreed terms to those in need in confidence

© T.S. Duckett 2003 *A Functioning Group or Charity*

342

Volunteers

To repeat, quality volunteers are essential: which means they are trained, police checked and supervised. Volunteers do have goodwill and skills, but they are not qualified statutory workers, nor can they replace certain care issues, so groups that state only those who have been affected by murder can help others in the same position are, frankly, self-defeating and ridiculous.

If you are more than a local self-help group that meets informally to go away for country walks or meet to have a party occasionally, then you will need competent and emotionally healthy volunteers and group structures. Here is a sample volunteer application form you may find has questions you may need to have answered by interested people. Taking care of trained volunteers is part of best practice, as these people are offering time and skills. They will also require good supervision. When working with people in need, it is important that an agreed understanding of specifically what is wanted and offered is mutually adhered to by all. Police checks must be undertaken by all applying to become involved with your group.

DIGNIFY! – Volunteer Application

Welcome and thank you for applying to become a volunteer with DIGNIFY! We want from the onset to impress upon you our gratitude for your support and equally to ask you to remember to be honest at all times when answering questions and to be realistic about what amount of time you can really spare to support us. It is important for us all to be realistic as to the amounts of support offered in a practical way – even if you wish you could offer more time! Please bear this in mind throughout when answering questions and please ensure all questions are answered; be aware questions regarding criminal history and agreement to a police check must be completed for any assessment to proceed. Thank you! We will contact you to confirm that your application has been accepted and state when the next training sessions will take place.

This Information is Held Within the Strictest Confidentiality

Personal Matters

Full name – *please include any different names you may use or may have previously used*

Please tell us your date of birth

Home address

Telephone

E-Mail

Employment – *please say what you do and your employers' address*
if unemployed, please say what you do with your time

How would you describe your physical and mental health?
It is important we know of any restricting levels of physical or mental illness and whether these will inhibit your intentions and our needs.

Practical skills matters

Part of being a volunteer is about not being misused or having unfair demands placed upon you or being unrealistic about what you don't like or cannot do, and at DIGNIFY! we try to ensure that people are placed within the area they are interested and have skills to make your time stimulating as well as worthwhile.

In which area are you offering support to DIGNIFY! as a volunteer?

☐ **IT** – Using computers to assist in designing related work such as monitoring calls, fundraising, developing a database.

☐ **Fundraising** – This is a specialised area and we always welcome people with experience or means that allow DIGNIFY! to secure greater service delivery and strategic stability. It will require skills in making exciting ideas happen within the DIGNIFY! remit such as regional day awareness, local fundraising initiatives, large fundraising events like concerts appealing to our diverse population in the north.

☐ **Education/Campaigning** – This requires a lot of regional travelling alongside DIGNIFY! management or trustees in schools, private industry, colleges, religious centres, community centres and may involve working alongside the social services or police. It will be embracing DIGNIFY!s goals and work, and our implementing government policies in community involvement, encourage people of all ages to discuss or support awareness and action in the impact of violent crimes within families and communities. It will of course have an ancillary role to promote new volunteers and funding opportunities.

☐ **Interpreter** – This is a highly specialist and important role, requiring highly competent linguistic skills, an awareness of confidentiality, listening skills and accurate translation.
Please state what your languages are and how you have acquired fluency (e.g. from family, travel or education)

☐ **Telephone Helpline** – This will require specialist training in listening and advice skills and accessing people for appropriate services. Specific training and selection will take place because of the intense nature of this work. A database is being developed for helpers to assist callers and DIGNIFY! is working alongside statutory agencies on a special referral system for those in need following violent crime. This is not about becoming someone's friend but guiding people to the very best of services known and taking practical distress away by making necessary calls to others – such as a friend or the social services or police. Commitment to a schedule and timetable will be essential for the efficient running of this service so requires a strict routine and this work requires planning and consistency.
☐ **Home Help Services** – This may involve doing things like managing to ensure

people's property is secure if in hiding, taking a break or away attending court. It may require taking children to and from schools or helping them when visiting a loved one possibly in hospital. It may mean redecorating a damaged home or walking a dog. It will require some direct contact with people in distress and need and therefore requires particular selection and specific training in working with distressed people and your role as a volunteer.

☐ **General Office Help** – This involves helping with general administration work and involves some contact with confidential data and so, as with all volunteers, a code of strictest confidentiality will be expected.

☐ **Befriending** – Specialist-trained befriending and support.

What is the realistic amount of time you can offer DIGNIFY!?
Please do not answer this question until completing the rest of this form. Please be realistic when doing so.

Between 1–2 hours every week ☐
Between 1–2 hours every other week ☐
Between 1–2 hours every month ☐
Between 2–4 hours every week ☐
Between 2–4 hours every other week ☐
Between 2–4 hours every month ☐
Between 4–6 hours every week ☐
Between 4-6 hours every other week ☐
Between 4-6 hours every month ☐
Between 6–8 hours every week ☐
Between 6–8 hours every other week ☐
Between 6–8 hours every month ☐
Between 8–10 hours every week ☐
Between 8–10 hours every other week ☐
Between 8–10 hours every month ☐

Equality of opportunity matters
This part of the application helps DIGNIFY! regularly monitor its practice and membership and equality of opportunity for recruiting within our diverse communities of northern England. It also assists DIGNIFY!'s evaluation and monitoring data.

Do you consider yourself to be disabled?　　　　Yes ☐　　No ☐
Please tell us why and to what degree of severity

Please say how you would describe your racial and ethnic identity, e.g.; African, Asian, black British, white British, black other, white other, Chinese, Jewish, coloured mixed race, white mixed heritage, other European or do not wish to answer.

Please say how you would describe your sexual identity e.g.; bisexual, heterosexual, homosexual, unsure or do not wish to answer

Please tick whether your gender is

female	☐
male	☐
transsexual	☐

Have you personally or has someone close to you been affected by violent crime?
yes ☐   no ☐
myself/someone close
if yes, please tick description that is most close to you:

very recently	☐
quite recently	☐
about 1 year ago	☐
about 2 years ago	☐
about 5 years ago	☐
a very long time ago	☐

It is in the nature of whatever area of valued help offered to DIGNIFY! that you will directly or indirectly have contact with highly distressed and vulnerable people, possibly from within your own smaller community. Violence affects all communities and ages and DIGNIFY!'s work is about advancing justice for people affected by violent crime and we ask within equality of opportunity, what, if any, criminal history you may have.

I have never had any form of criminal record ever   yes ☐   no ☐

The information provided here is honest and I am happy for DIGNIFY! to write formally to the police and request a police check for any criminal convictions, as is the standard process for all potential volunteers

Please sign agreement for DIGNIFY! to forward an enquiry to the police about any criminal convictions here

Full name

Signature

Date

Location of form completion

Thank you! We will contact you to confirm your application has been accepted and state when the next training sessions will take place.

To become a registered charity, or not

If your group has become quite active and useful and is responding to people's needs and the group serves a purpose, it may decide it is worthwhile to apply to become a registered charity. Contrary to many people's understanding, it is very easy to become a charity and the governing agency – the Charity Commission – has generally little regard for the performance of charities unless they are a major charity misusing funds. It has conferred charitable status on some dubious groups that does not help advancement. The Charity Commission's objectives are to:

- give public confidence in the integrity of charity [also to]
- ensure charities are able to operate for their purposes within an effective legal, accounting and governance framework
- improve the governance, accountability, efficiency and effectiveness of charities
- identify and deal with abuse and poor practices
- maintain a register of charities
- investigate misconduct and abuse of charitable assets, take or recommend remedial action
- give advice to charity trustees to make administration of their charity more effective; and
- where necessary, make schemes and orders to modernise the purposes and administrative machinery of charities and give trustees additional powers.

Charity Commission: *Booklet on Guidance*

The Charity Commission is concerned to see that the constitutional matters and systems of a charity are in place, and its accounts. It rarely intervenes in complaints about a charity's service delivery and effectiveness to the detriment of charities working within best practice. This is very much the case with the *victim club* where many have charitable status and deplorable standards on the whole. The fact they have charitable status clouds their need to exist with the protection of the title charity so in this area the Charity Commission has consistently failed to meet its objectives.

The benefit of becoming a charity is it brings some tax benefits and allows people to acquire a registered number. The less beneficial aspects lie in the extra paperwork involved and a charity cannot become as political as it may wish to be. This explains a lot about the state we're in overall. However, if a group is to become a credible and robust service, at some stage reviewing whether to become a charity or not is a good idea. Whatever course of action is decided for your group's status, the highest standards and individuals are needed alongside a proven usefulness for society.

Useful addresses

Charity Commission for Scotland
Inland Revenue Charities Department
Meldrum House
15 Drumsheugh Gardens
Edinburgh
EH3 7UL
Telephone: 0131 777 4040
Fax: 0131 777 4045
Website: www.charity-commission.gov.uk

Charity Commission for England and Wales
Harmsworth House
13–15 Bouverie Street
London
EC4Y 8DP
Telephone: 0870 333 0123
Minicom: 0870 333 0125
Fax: 020 7674 2300
Website: www.charity-commission.gov.uk

Also, depending upon location, at:

2nd Floor
20 King's Parade
Queen's Dock
Liverpool
L3 4DQ
Telephone: 0870 333 0123
Fax: 0151 703 15555

Woodfield House
Tangier
Taunton
Somerset
TA1 4BL
Telephone: 0870 333 0123
Fax: 01823 345 003

National Council for Voluntary Organisations (NCVO)
Helpdesk: 0800 279 8798
Telephone: 020 7713 6161
Minicom: 0800 018 8111
E-Mail: helpdesk@ncvo-vol.org.uk
Provides information, advice, support and publications to voluntary organisations in England

Council for Voluntary Service (CVS)
For information about your nearest branch contact
Telephone: 0114 278 6636

Wales Council for Voluntary Action (WCVA)
Cyngor Gweithredu Gwirfoddol Cymru

Telephone: 029 2085 5100
Represents interests of and campaigns for voluntary organisations in Wales providing advice, information and training

Directory of Social Change
(Books) Telephone: 020 7209 5151
(Research) Telephone: 020 7209 4422
(Training) Telephone: 020 7209 4949
Publishes books and provides training for voluntary organisations and co-organises a national charity fair in London

Companies House
Telephone: 029 2038 0801
Provides information to the public on companies (status, solvency, etc.)

Association of Charitable Foundations
Telephone: 020 7422 8600
Website: www.acf.org.uk

The Almshouse Association
Telephone: 01344 452 922
Fax: 01344 862 062
Provides advice and assistance to almshouse charities in the United Kingdom

You know what you do – how do you plan what to do?

Without structures, trained and police-checked reliable people – and no matter how tragic or noble your cause may be – your group will be of no social value if you cannot provide unprejudiced services and monitor what you do. People in need do not need chaotic, dysfunctional groups, which only heightens the sense of anguish and loss of control. A dynamic group reduces chaos with agreement of people in need and knows how to communicate and refer people to other services. It must be willing to be seen to do work - and equally hold itself willing to service accountability and inspection. Fundraising has to start from ground level upwards. For example, a group has to be prepared to share premises, ensure documentation is secure and people affected by violent crime offer consent and know what exactly is held on computer about them. A group must show the ability to undertake the hard slog of gathering small fundraising incomes from seasonal balls, local discos, and so on. The Terence Higgins Trust (for people affected by HIV), started without media and government interest and functioned for some years from people's homes, providing high standards of diverse services. Groups flying about with nothing but ignorant emotions are everywhere and if you wish your group to be known to be different,you must prove this! These are some of the structures and social issues that may relate to what you wish to achieve. Try to keep everything simple: avoid the temptation to use jargon unless it seems necessary. A strategic plan is the blueprint for how your group will develop – it becomes a mirror for why and how you exist. (See strategies and policies in section on police, pp. 27–28.)

Keep the strategy plan simple and make sure it reflects what the group says it intends to do. It helps to break up the different parts of what you do, what you want and what you offer. Opposite is a blank sheet that is useful for deciding your group's services and goals and on the subsequent pages are suggestions for a five-year development plan for a group called DIGNIFY! Please note how they reflect law, personal and practical needs and community action and how the group will make each issue come to be. The important matters that require discussion and writing down are within the headings and laying them out in this way helps potential funders make sense of your goal.

> It seems to me like this. It's not a terrible thing – I mean it may be terrible, but it's not damaging, it's not poisoning to do without something one really wants …

As before, let's imagine that DIGNIFY! has reached a stage in its development where it has secured good working relations with agencies, is providing useful services to people in need and has outgrown its tiny premises. It is hoping to secure funding to get larger premises, set up a convalescence home in partnership with agencies for children and adults affected by violent crime, employ minimum paid workers and involve itself further in schools and community action. It has the respect and support of the media and civic leaders and continues to generate 75 per cent of its own income

---

							Issue
							Need
							Action
							Result
							Who
							Cost

Issue	Need	Action
The status quo Unmet needs –	DIGNIFY! exists to fill unmet needs – emotional, financial, environmental and political due to failure of statutory services. It is the only regional dynamic and cohesive agency responding to growing unmet needs of people affected by violent, long-term horror.	The south-east region requires a fresh and realistic independent agency that responds to growing social unmet needs resulting from violent crimes. DIGNIFY! exists and does effectively respond and now requires dynamic recognition and resourcing without being fettered to obstructive and redundant agencies failing to grasp statutorily their duties or funding constraints.
Past, present and future	Statutory agencies continue to reject their legal, civic, moral and humane duties to provide comprehensive strategies, policies and services for people affected by violent crimes. DIGNIFY! fills this gap – still	A new multi-agency committee to meet with DIGNIFY! to agree and oversee a regional strategy and implementation
DIGNIFY! has outgrown its current premises and service resources, unstaffed service from private homes against all odds. In order to continue and develop a comprehensive plan and realistically funded programme are required.	DIGNIFY!'s work must continue; it is needed and now must function with assistance that does not diminish or constrain its core function, objectives or autonomy	Review of DIGNIFY!'s internal and mid-term objectives. Development of a strategic plan and guidance. Accept guidance from voluntary/statutory sector experts
Immediate needs – premises, training venue for increased volume of volunteers, funding		

Issue	Need	Action
Capital costs Premises	DIGNIFY! supplements statutory services without full recognition or realistic funding, or reflection of saving to taxpayers for service delivery. Peppercorn, permanent secure-rented premises are urgently needed. Government initiatives of multi-agency and community-led civic duties are being flouted – to the detriment of the north of England – and lives	
Development of services	DIGNIFY! has outgrown its fledgling role and urgently requires premises that allow DIGNIFY! to progress meeting diverse needs of people affected by violent crimes	Social Services, Housing, Leisure and Recreation Departments must radically review priorities, resourcing and funding in keeping with crime prevention alongside police and DIGNIFY!
Multi-agency involvement

(continued) | DIGNIFY! wishes to advance its growing collaborative work and social response alongside statutory agencies – the police, social services, law agencies, housing, psychological, welfare and allied voluntary agencies. Key surgery services from one base are essential | Police, health authority – hospital and GP, social and housing, welfare and legal services on a committed rota basis to assist in establishing specialist advice and referral sessions for those in need |

Issue	Need	Action
Fund-raising – see also Education and public education	A bold, sustained fundraising plan will be activated once sufficient volunteers and strategic agreement is achieved. This will generate improved resources, service delivery, profile, financial independence and education Regrettably, the stark reality is that the UK has no diversity of how and where people receive responsive and effective assistance. DIGNIFY! exists to redress this growing problem and will start monitoring needs	Local fundraising initiatives and media appeals. Initiate discussions with The Media Trust and REACH Public demand, absence of dynamic and flexible skilled services for victims of violent crime demand DIGNIFY! develop its telephone, practical, emotional and educational services.
Emotional and practical assistance DIGNIFY!'s attention to individual needs results shows a need for increased communication and smooth referrals to statutory services	Many victims decline, or are sent away from, established agencies/statutory services or choose to seek support from DIGNIFY. Reduced access to services means no diversity for complex needs	DIGNIFY! wishes to address diverse unmet needs without unnecessary duplication. To secure and accept expert guidance and support
Status quo	DIGNIFY! is directly contacted by people affected by horror – untreated and ignored by taxpaying public service workers	Statutory agencies to facilitate via DIGNIFY! sustained cognitive behavioural therapy in groups. Community psychiatric nurses are unacceptable and insufficiently qualified for this unmet need and not to be considered viable.

Issue	Need	Action
Outreach PTSD Group Behavioural Cognitive	Qualified Consultants in PTSD are required to provide sustained group work for DIGNIFY! members that can directly channel people into statutory services. Unmet trauma places extended long-term expenditure and service need upon the region	DIGNIFY! and police to pioneer social services, develop universal priority intervention plans of highest-quality services and assessment for anyone/family affected by violent crime as the first base for any agency involvement as a routine standard following violent crime. This requires thorough planning and agreement, multi-departmental and agency cooperation, These protocols to be endorsed by senior committees & DIGNIFY!
Social services	Social services must be compelled to follow through their legal duties and commit to a policy for dealing with people/families in crisis	
Volunteers Recruitment of volunteers	Since 1997, DIGNIFY! succeeded in existing largely via self-generated and regulated funding. This has reached a situation where our demand and public wish to become involved means DIGNIFY! justification has outgrown its status quo DIGNIFY! wishes to find people also unaffected by violence to join its work for those suffering injustice and trauma	A massive recruitment campaign will take place for volunteers in various specialist capacities. Within this we hope to attract experts from key service areas. All age groups and races will be encouraged including specialist degree students and people not affected by violent crime. Specialist colleges to be approached for teaching; volunteers and access to premises e.g. law, social work, psychiatry, welfare benefits; housing, fundraising and marketing Media will be used to advertise and recruit

Issue	Need	Action
Supervision of volunteers and planned training in service areas	Recruitment of experts from various fields will be called upon to plan training and supervision. A new Steering Committee will be formed	Various groups of trained volunteers to improve groups in education, helpline/emotional and practical support, social and health services, legal matters, fundraising and marketing
Educational videos	DIGNIFY! requires an educational video to be made for its promotional work and for training of its volunteers. DIGNIFY!'s history, people's needs & stories, areas of volunteer service areas	Initiate discussions with media departments within universities to assist in making of video(s). This may be discussed as part of a Masters/PhD thesis.
Equality in recruitment	DIGNIFY! welcomes people from all sectors of society to be trained as effective volunteers and equality policies will be developed	Volunteers will be recruited from local and regional canvassing and talks, training will take place at pre-planned weekends at a local college. Selection and police checks will follow as will contracts of confidentiality
Training of volunteers	Specialist trainers will be used for specialist issues e.g. bereavement, PTSD, social/health services, compensation law, listening and basic counselling skills	Nominal fees and expenses will have to be provided in some cases as well as funding for training venue
Supervision of volunteers	DIGNIFY! recognises the role of volunteers and to negate exploitation and reduce stress and advance personal stimulation monthly group supervision would aim to be offered	To secure expert volunteers to facilitate supervision in groups to reduce costs and maintain a degree of work intimacy, equal opportunities and high standards

Issue	Need	Action
IT equipment and training	IT is necessary to continue DIGNIFY!'s development and especially for volunteers to access a database for the helpline	IT equipment, training will form part of development and service and involve better monitoring of services and need
Additional quarterly training	DIGNIFY! is committed to equality of opportunity and service and recognises the pivotal role volunteers play, personal generosity of time and skills	DIGNIFY! is committed to providing quarterly one-day seminars to keep volunteers appraised of developments in the varying areas of work
Community education Crime prevention alongside police	DIGNIFY! has sound links with the police and education departments and civic leaders. These need to be developed into the wider region and communities	Work programmes in all school-levels, re violent crimes and prevention, fundraising initiatives for DIGNIFY!
Implementing Home Office initiatives, policies and responsible citizenship		
DIGNIFY! responds to victims/survivors of violent crimes in an immediate manner and provides a public voice for the vulnerable and trivialised suffering. This work remains valid and part of DIGNIFY!'s educational work in keeping with government policies and civic duties		Pursue more specialist campaigns and sustained media and fundraising coverage, to liaise with local and Police authorities for designing campaigns in schools especially with 9 to 18 year olds. To require the media henceforth to provide a minimum fee of £75 per request for statements or £250 per TV appearance, for DIGNIFY!'s senior volunteers to conduct some campaigns

358

Issue	Need	Action
Sanctuary emergency premises	Unmet need exists for an anonymous property in the region for those unable to return to a scene of violent crime, emergency family care, holding centre for statutory agencies to mobilise effective resourcing, media-free or for court witnesses who must travel very long distances	DIGNIFY!, social services, housing, health services to draw up plans for premises that must remain anonymous and wholly free of media invasion
Mid and long-term plans Convalescence/respite centre	A need exists to allow traumatised victims a safe recovery environment. A country environment needs to be acquired – fully equipped	Develop negotiations with DoH, private sector, housing corporation and strategic health authorities
Specialist child centre	A specialist child centre for convalescence is urgently needed	
Regional and civic responses	DIGNIFY!'s work is in the region and communities. This needs to be administratively integrated into civic policies, government polices and DIGNIFY's! plans to help people share the horror and solutions to violence	Creation of gardens of remembrance in civic centres with CCTV – criminals to be named, fined, photographed. A place of open space for remembrance and stone of names of murdered, injured people. Place for fundraising events – concerts solely focused on violent crime, peaceful events and recognition. In keeping with EU and govt policies on greening urban areas

©T.S. Duckett 2003

What's terrible is to pretend that the second-rate is first-rate. To pretend that you don't need love when you do; or you like your work when you know quite well you're capable of better.

Doris Lessing: The Golden Notebook

This is a sample of what part of a detailed strategic plan would need to consider. Agencies exist to help to prepare plans, which should also be used as it is good for emerging groups to seek out experts with skills in this area to become members of their group.

Underpinning any group's potential are two final pieces of administrative structure that are also our foundations for best practice. They reflect the connections between what is said, what is done and by whom. First, monitoring the work that is undertaken is essential, whether a charity or not, because, ideally, you will be wishing to reach out to as many diverse members of society affected by violence as is possible. Second, the equality statement is the underpinning guide to the integrity and attitude you create within your group. It should reflect the foundations for justice and a respectful society. These are some of the tricks to successful building of diverse groups providing fresh attitudes and services that are thought out. These are some of our challenges! These are the connections that make real unmet needs and give our communities a chance to find strength, dignity and safety and this is a good place to finish this handbook.

EQUALITY MATTERS

Monitoring Form To Be Completed for Each Call AFTER CALLER states/receives whatever help is needed or available

Need	Crime	Action	M/F	District	Ethnicity	Disability	Unmet Need	Time VOL

All headings will have to be coded e.g. Crime: rape 2, murder 1.This will require coding for all matters
Need: Someone to talk to 4, Immediate medical attention 1, Statutory services referral immediately or next morning 2 etc
District: have 25/30 districts with eg London as 1 – use police or county boundaries for further numbering.
Disability: Did caller have disability as defined under Disability Act? - answer Y/N - if yes 1 = hearing, 2 = sight, 3 = other unmet need
Code unmet need: e.g. caller without access to statutory help 1, without informal help 2, problem in agency helping 3
Ethnicity: do alphabetically – see data from Commission for Racial Equality for headings or contact the NCVO

© T.S. Duckett 2003: *Monitoring form*

Our mission statement

JUSTIFY! exists to make a substantial change to the way that victims are treated in Britain. JUSTIFY! will achieve this by making a lasting impact, ensuring the public's support for the victims and how they are cared for by their community and within the criminal justice system. We will change society's ambivalent attitude towards crime and fight for the better treatment of, financial support for, and promotion of legislation in favour of, any victim of crime.

Aims

JUSTIFY! aims to

• support and empower victims with whatever means are at our disposal;
• educate the public about the importance of the prevention of crime;
• coordinate awareness through the introduction of specific projects that will benefit and enhance the quality of life for the victim;
• provide an information and referral service to appropriate statutory and voluntary services; and
• stimulate change within the criminal justice system for greater compassion for the victim.

To make our mission and aims remain pertinent, dynamic and receptive, JUSTIFY! maintains the following standards and values as common to all people who contribute service to JUSTIFY! and whoever receives any level of service from JUSTIFY!

Values

• **Dignity:** the universal recognition of the intrinsic value of each individual's life regardless of circumstances by respecting their uniqueness, their strengths and weaknesses, their needs and providing services with immutable respect.
• **Privacy:** the universal right of the individual to be left alone, or undisturbed and free from intrusion or unwanted public attention into his/her affairs, subject to his/her own safety or that of others.
• **Independent justice:** the service offered will always promote the independence of the citizen and avoid condescension by always maintaining the advocacy role for a victim and survivor within their individual crisis, and in the pursuit of natural justice, pursuit of optimum individual rehabilitation and personal independent fulfilment.

• **Respect:** the services accessed will ensure respect for every citizen through being responsive, respecting different lifestyles and enhance and encourage every citizen affected by crime to reach their optimum potential in life.

- **Security:** acknowledging the immutable right of every individual to secure the tangible human objective and subjective desire to be safe. Where possible, assist in the process of this value being made an everyday reality for all.
- **Right of citizenship:** through direct engagement with citizens and other institutions we will strive for all victims to have the same rights and access to justice as other citizens. Simultaneously, in our development of services we will remain committed to being as accessible as can be achieved to all citizens that reflect the abundant cultural and racial diversity of contemporary Britain.
- **Choice:** the importance of achieving our aims will be through the campaigning and promotion of improved provisions for citizens affected by crime, in part, through individual awareness of choice of access to services and rights within legislation.

How those working in JUSTIFY! and our service delivery will be sustained and measured

- **Workers:** whether salaried, or working for no income as volunteers, will be treated with respect for their individual and collective contributions towards the mission, aims and values within the everyday work of JUSTIFY! Their skills, knowledge and involvement is needed, valued and respected as is the quality of effort in which workers give of themselves.
- **Quality in services:** will always remain a pertinent means of measuring the justification and existence of JUSTIFY! as many citizens who become victims of crime make contact with us before statutory services. Quality also exists within our mission, aims and values. We endeavour to maintain the highest of standards in all aspects of service delivery and monitor and record the type of work we deal with. This will include the people affected and where they live, the quality of statutory service response and unmet need as well as planning and funding data such as how grant aid and donations are specifically utilised.
- **Openness:** JUSTIFY! prides itself and will continue to take a non-complacent pride in its organisational openness. This will be maintained and measured by developing and remaining open-minded and open-hearted to the citizens who use JUSTIFY! This openness will include accessibility to inspection by grant-providers of public monies, production of accurate and certified accounts and periodic reviews of policy procedures and distribution of a biannual newsletter to members

and service-users.

- **Service-user involvement:** JUSTIFY! exists to promote the equitable resolution of unmet and ongoing needs and issues of citizens who become victims of crime. We will continue to monitor and review effective measures that maintain unfettered and sustained communication with citizens who are service users. They will, in time, determine and strongly influence the planning and wider strategic path of JUSTIFY! These will be best served in the structure of periodic forums, ongoing monitoring of services, our external independent complaints procedure, annual meetings, time-limited representation and proportional service-user representation on our management committee. It will also embrace the common pursuit of dignity and equality of opportunity.

- **Equal opportunities:** JUSTIFY! recognises that equality does not exist universally and the pursuit and securing of it is an ongoing objective and desire to make equality a reality for citizens who are affected by crime. The notion of equality must therefore remain the prerogative for those with power, privilege and sometimes prejudice. It is for the knowledgeable person, in the genuine public, to turn his/her personal troubles into social issues, to see his/her relevance within the community and, in turn, help his/her community see the issues' relevance for others. JUSTIFY! exists to pursue the end of inequalities within the personal injustice, social and legislative mechanisms that prevent equality of justice for victims of crime and to redress inequalities within other manifestations and consequences of inequality.

- JUSTIFY! continues to try to meet this challenge within its mission, aims and values. This is enshrined within each aspect of our work by lending voice, knowledge, skills and services to abused, disadvantaged citizens by using any mechanism at our disposal to empower, enrich and make tangible equality-based change within the lives of victimised citizens. In challenging specific discrimination against citizens who are victims of crime, JUSTIFY! endeavours to ensure discrimination or disadvantage caused by race, disability, gender, age or sexual orientation is confronted, and will not, and does not, affect the right, access, quality or priority of service offered.

Directory

This final section has a few of the outstanding firms of solicitors dealing with personal injury and mental health specialists dealing with trauma. Naturally, there are many more about and these are a few who welcomed this project and being involved in it. In Scotland, there are far more NHS specialists in trauma who either stated they did not want to attract further work or were unresponsive. Unfortunately, in Wales, at this time, there is only one heavily over-worked consultant psychiatrist specialising in trauma.

All agencies were responsible for writing their own entries to show readers exactly what they do. Always remember to request evidence of agencies having been vetted by the police, especially when dealing with charities.

Emergency

Emergency services should only be called if a genuine and immediate crisis is affecting direct safety.

If you feel your safety is in immediate and direct threat, contact the police using the emergency number.

If it is a crisis that can wait, contact the police on a non-emergency number or social services. Social services provides an out-of hours service and its offices can be found within local directories.

Advocacy Organisations

Edinburgh Association for Mental Health – Greater Edinburgh

EAMH is a voluntary organisation that addresses mental health needs and issues, through the provision of services and information and by developing new ways of meeting needs through research and partnership working.

EAMH has undertaken extensive research into the mental health needs, care and treatment of adult survivors of childhood sexual abuse and provides the following support services for abuse survivors.

> Contact: Edinburgh Association for Mental Health (EAMH)
> 40 Shandwick Place
> Edinburgh
> EH2 4RT
> Telephone: 0131 225 8508
> Fax: 0131 220 0028
> E-Mail: eamh@freeuk.com

Our Services
Oasis is a support project for women run by EAMH and covers the Greater Liberton area of Edinburgh. Both one-to-one counselling and group support are available for female survivors living in the local area. Self-referrals and agency referrals are both welcome and should be directed to:

> Oasis Team Leader
> Telephone: 0131 225 8508 or 0131 666 1606
> Mobile: 07980 487656

Directory

Counselling – EAMH's counselling service provides open-ended counselling for people experiencing mental health problems. A significant number of the counsellors have specific expertise in working with survivors of childhood sexual abuse. Self-referrals only are accepted and should be directed to:

Volunteer Services Team Leader
Telephone: 0131 225 8508

Publications
EAMH conducted a two-year research project examining the mental health needs, care and treatment of female survivors of childhood of sexual abuse. This was managed in conjunction with the University of Edinburgh. The research was undertaken by Dr. Sarah Nelson, who has over 20 years' experience in researching and writing about childhood sexual abuse.

The research examined the views and experiences of survivors who had used mental health services and of the professionals from both statutory and voluntary agencies who provided

services accessed by survivors. The resulting report, *Beyond Trauma*, was launched at a national conference in June 2001. Copies of both the summary and full report are available from EAMH.

A second publication, *Beyond Trauma: Implications for Social Workers and their Practice*, developed some of the themes from the main report. This report is also available from EAMH.

Women's Aid Federation of England – All England

Women's Aid Federation of England was founded in 1974, although its beginnings are hard to establish. Informal safe houses for women have existed in Britain and America from the late nineteenth century and probably long before. The first Women's Aid refuges were set up in response to women's desperate need for a place of safety to stay with their children and were run entirely on the voluntary labour of committed women, activists and survivors. Today there are over 250 locally based Women's Aid organisations running over 400 refuges and support services throughout England. In a year, over 50,000 women and children stay in refuges to escape domestic abuse. Our National Domestic Violence 24-Hour Helpline expects to receive over 70,000 calls in the coming year.

Areas of Expertise
  • Co-ordinating a national network of refuges and advice centres
  • Working with the government to develop legislation relating to domestic violence.
  • Protecting women and children through our network of over 400 refuges and organisations.
  • Giving support through our 24-Hour National Domestic Violence Helpline and Women's Aid Website.

Address: Women's Aid Federation of England
  PO Box 391
  Bristol
  BS99 7WS
  24-Hour National Domestic Violence Helpline: 08457 023 468
Telephone: 0117 944 4411 (Office)
Fax: 0117 924 1703
E-Mail: info@womensaid.org.uk
Website: www.womensaid.org.uk

Please contact either Myra Johnson or Teresa Parker

- Every minute in the UK, police receive a call asking for assistance with domestic violence.
- On February 8th 2000, 2045 women and 2745 children were living in refuges in England.
- One in four women experience domestic violence at some stage during their lives. (British Medical Association, 1998)
- Two women are killed every week by current or former partners. (Home Office/Cabinet Office, 1999).

'It took me ages to get the courage to leave. Three times I went for a divorce, twice he talked me out of it. How could I leave? I was stupid, fat, ugly, no one would believe me, he would kill me, I would not be allowed the children, the list goes on and on. I was made to feel that I only lived because of him. Of course everything was my fault and if I did as I was told it would all be okay. It was not.'

Carol, 37

'In fact, when I got pregnant it (the abuse) was even worse. As a result I lost our first child, but didn't dare tell the hospital what he had done. He kept telling me if I was a better wife it would stop.'

Debbie, 31

'I now know that we are lucky to be alive. I feel like I can breathe again. Me and my kids are safe. I know that we still have a long journey to go on before we can find a place of our own, but the refuge are helping me to build a future. It has been wonderful to be with other women like me and share my experiences. I don't know what I would have done without Women's Aid, I dread to think what might have happened if I had stayed with him. I hope that one day I will feel really safe and won't be constantly thinking that he will find us.'

Delia, 26

'Knowing that you have helped a woman escape is empowering – even more so when children are involved and you know that they will no longer have to live in a violent environment.'

Helpline volunteer

Women's Aid is constantly working to end domestic violence against women and children.

Women's Aid Federation 24-Hour Domestic Violence Helpline: 08457 023 468

---

safe The Domestic Abuse Quarterly
The UK's first dedicated journal on domestic abuse

safe aims to provide a national multi-agency forum and information exchange to support and promote the development of effective responses to reduce domestic violence.
For details of subscription to 'Safe: The Domestic Violence Quarterly' please write to Women's Aid, PO Box 391, Bristol, BS99 7WS, telephone on 0117 9444411 or email info@womensaid.org.uk.

Mothers Against Murder and Aggression – National
Registered Charity No: 1074817

Mothers Against Murder and Aggression, MAMAA, was established in 1993 in the aftermath of the tragic death of Master James Bulger.

Directory

Ordinary everyday parents united with the initial aim of establishing a National Child Safety Awareness Campaign. This has successfully been achieved by constructive communication with professional bodies such as MPs, police, doctors, coroners and counsellors.

Our biggest development to date is the support we are able to offer bereaved families throughout the country. These are people that have lost children and other loved ones through the violent act of murder.

MAMAA can be contacted at: Wales: Dee Warner: 0791 996 5476
England: Lyn Costello: 0795 106 2398

What MAMAA Will Make Real
MAMAA wants to see and run a 'Retreat' where families and friends can go for safety, counselling and respite.

Increase the quality of communication between all parties affected by horror.

Educate the general public and professional bodies about the needs of homicide affected families.

What MAMAA Wants
Commitment to fight for justice for victims of violent crime.

Provide an unfounded volunteer 24 hour helpline to those in need.

Make real unmet needs for safe retreat and sanctuary, respect for victims, services for recovery without prejudice.

MAMMA Knows
A 15 year-old daughter was stabbed to death at school. A year later their 15 year-old son killed himself. He needed retreat then – they need retreat now!

A 15 year-old son was stabbed to death because of his colour. Death threats were made against the family. It was the local police service collected enough money to send the family away until the trial. They didn't have their fare home!

Arriving home from holiday to find their 27 year-old son stabbed to death on their kitchen floor. When the police team finished, they were left to scrub the blood from the tiles. They cannot sell their house. Where will they go to escape the constant nightmares?

What MAMAA Does
Offer common sense, unpatronsing practical and emotional help with support wherever possible

'We came home to find our 12 year-old daughter strangled in our living room.'
The house became a crime-scene. They had no friends in this country and had to walk the streets with their 5 year old son.

'Forty years on she still walks the moors looking for the body of her 12 year old son'
Every time his killers sneeze, the press hound her.

'Their 18 year-old daughter was raped and murdered on Christmas Day. They cope all year, but where do they go on the 25th December?'

'Their nine year-old daughter was snatched while playing. They campaign tirelessly and now they're falling apart without the help they deserve and need.'

'His 5 year old daughter was shot to death with 14 more of her classmates. Three years later he had a breakdown.'

'The police knocked to tell her they had found parts of her nine year-old son. She had to cook tea for five other younger children.'

These people need, deserve, to dignify their terror – our society needs to provide, retreat, good services with dignity without prejudice

MAMAA's Funded
We fund ourselves from donations from our own pockets.

MAMAA's 'RETREAT' Appeal
Families and many others desperately need a 'Retreat' – a place they can safely find respite. Respite means, in most cases, the ability to escape the unwanted attentions of the press. People need to be somewhere quiet and away from where the murder has taken place, to create the opportunity to receive expert needed counselling and legal advice that is generally not readily accessible.

A 'Retreat' exists in Australia, and funded by the Government, unfortunately our government does not share the same proof, level of compassion or indeed foresight in recognising the overwhelming unmet basic requirement.

MAMAA intends to launch a 'Buy a Brick' campaign to generate the urgent funding required to make sense and sanctuary of people's need and help transform the impossible. If you, or your company, can help in any way with sponsorship, printing or indeed the purchasing of 'bricks', please contact us.

MAMAA's Respected
This initiative is backed by agencies like NACRO, The Zito Trust, Child Bereavement Trust and The Police Federation.

Will You Help MAMAA Grow?
We welcome your practical expertise and financial support. We welcome any professional and committed voluntary assistance to make surviving the impossible bearable. We welcome genuine help to progress living with safety and dignity. We welcome genuine help.

We welcome financial support to progress and make real what those in need deserve because to find common sense, compassion and justice costs money. We welcome any fundraising experts and donations and we thank you! Kindly please make cheques payable to:–

MAMAA
HSBC
Account no: 312 835 53
Sort Code: 40-46-20

Thank you for your support and we wish you health and justice!

368

Directory

PETAL – Scotland
The support group for those experiencing trauma and loss

PETAL was formed in October 1994 by a group of people with the personal experience of the loss of a loved one through murder to provide practical and emotional support. Since then, it has expanded to include those affected by losses through suicide and through fatal road accidents.

PETAL provides supervised counselling, support by trained volunteers, support groups for adults and children, and telephone support.

PETAL also provides practical help through the provision of information, home visits, and visits to court. There is a 24 hour Helpline and all messages will be answered within one working day.

PETAL workers network with all relevant statutory and voluntary agencies, and make referrals to other agencies if this is requested.

PETAL provides a safe and confidential environment where those experiencing traumatic loss can talk to trained volunteers or meet with others in similar circumstances to share mutual thoughts, feelings, and experiences.

PETAL provides help and comfort for as long as any individual or family wishes.

PETAL is a registered charity with no affiliation to any religious or political party and is open to all sections of the community.

If you want to know more about PETAL's services, the training offered to volunteers and outside bodies, or any other item related to trauma and loss, please contact us:-

Telephone: 01698 324502
Fax: 01698 323724

Funding Sources
PETAL is supported by funding from North and South Lanarkshire Councils, charitable trusts, and members fund raising.

Inquests and Coroners

INQUEST – England and Wales
INQUEST was founded in 1981 by the families and friends of people who had died in custody, to campaign against such deaths and for changes to the way they were investigated.

INQUEST works directly with the families of bereaved people facing a Coroner's Inquest. We provide legal and other advice and work with families and their lawyers. Our main area of expertise is deaths in custody – in police custody, prisons, immigration detention centres, psychiatric and special hospitals – as well as the investigations held into them, though we can provide general advice in relation to all inquests. INQUEST aims to raise public awareness about controversial deaths, and campaigns for the necessary changes to improve the investigatory process, increase accountability of state officials and avert further deaths.

Contact:
Title: Caseworker
Address: INQUEST
    Ground Floor
    Alexandra National House
    330 Seven Sisters Road
    London
    N4 2PJ
Telephone: 020 8802 7430
Fax: 020 8802 7450
E-Mail: inquest@inquest.org.uk
Website: www.inquest.org.uk

Areas of Specialism
- Coroners' Inquests
- Deaths in custody

Services Offered and Catchment Area
Please see our aims and work above and geographical areas

Other Areas of Important Work
Campaigning for reform of Coroner's Inquest system

Donations and Volunteers
INQUEST campaigns to pursue justice and help vulnerable people and we welcome donations and volunteers. Please contact us if you can offer assistance.

Publications

Recent Publications and Developments In Inquest Law (both for Lawyers Group members);

INQUEST News (newsletter for members);

Annual Reports (which contain detailed articles on casework and campaigns);

A Short Guide to Inquests; Case reports, policy reports, Parliamentary and UN submissions etc – please see website or contact INQUEST for details.

Children

ChildLine
Founded: 1986

Description of Service:
ChildLine is the UK's free helpline for children and young people in trouble or danger. It provides a confidential phone counselling service for any child with any problem, 24 hours a day, every day. It listens, comforts and protects. Trained counsellors provide support and advice and refer children in danger to appropriate helping agencies.

ChildLine also brings to public attention issues affecting children's welfare and rights.

Directory

Chief Executive: Carole Easton

Information for directory and database entries

Address for children: Childline
Freepost 1111
London
N1 0BR

Telephone: Helpline: 0800 1111 (24 hours, every day)

Special Services Helpline: 0800 884444 – 'The Line'
A special helpline for children living away from home
(Mon to Fri, 3.30pm to 9.30pm; Sat and Sun, 2pm to 8pm)
0800 400222 – Minicom
(Mon to Fri, 9.30am to 9.30pm; Sat and Sun, 9.30am to 8pm)

Address – Admin: ChildLine
Studd Street
London
N1 0QW

Contact: Public Relations Department

Admin telephone: 020 7239 1000

Admin fax: 020 7239 1001

Website: www.childline.org.uk

E-Mail: NB: we are not currently able to answer E-Mails about problems or offer online counselling.

ChildLine Scotland

18 Albion Street
Glasgow
G1 1LH
Tel: 0141 552 1123
Fax: 0141 552 3089

ChildLine Cymru/Wales

9th Floor   Royal Alexandra Hospital
Alexandra House   Marine Drive
Alexandra Road   Rhyl
Swansea   LL18 3AS
SA1 5ED   Tel: 01745 345111
Tel: 01792 480111   Fax: 01745 345333
Fax: 01792 480333

The bullying line is open Monday to Friday 3:30pm to 9:30pm 0800 44 1111

CHILDREN 1ST – All of Scotland
Registered Charity No: SC 016 092

For over 100 years, CHILDREN 1ST, the Royal Scottish Society for Prevention of Cruelty to Children, has been working to give every child in Scotland a safe and secure childhood.

Today, CHILDREN 1ST supports families under stress, protects children from harm and neglect, helps them recover from abuse and promotes children's rights and interests.

Throughout Scotland our staff and volunteers use their skills to help children overcome difficulties in their lives and rebuild trust and confidence.

Contact
For information about CHILDREN 1ST services please contact us at:

> **Telephone: 0131 337 8539**
> **Fax: 0131 346 8284**
> **E-Mail: info@children1st.org.uk**
> **Website: www.children1st.org.uk**

Areas of Specialism
CHILDREN 1ST has projects throughout Scotland for children's needs

Our Abuse Recovery Projects help children and young people who have been physically, sexually or emotionally abused. We also provide support to families and carers of children who have been abused.

Our Family Support Services works with children and young people who have social, emotional or behavioural difficulties.

Supporting parents is also an important part of our work. We work closely with parents both alongside and/or in addition to our work with children.

Our Helpline for parents
ParentLine Scotland is the free confidential helpline for parents in Scotland. You can call about anything at all, large or small. ParentLine Scotland is for all parents and anyone caring for a child. The Helpline offers information, emotional support and a listening ear.

Are you worried about a child?

- If you are worried about a child and you want to talk through your concerns you can call ParentLine Scotland
- If a child is in danger contact the police or your local social services immediately.

Telephone ParentLine Scotland on Freephone 0808 800 2222

Other CHILDREN 1ST services
- Children and Young People's Rights Workers
- Family Group Conferences
- Young Carers Project

Directory

Publications

The Huge Bag of Worries – a story book aimed at under 9s encouraging them to share their worries.

Hands Off! – a magazine to raise awareness among 12–17 year olds of the nature of sexual abuse, that it is never their fault and advising on what to do to prevent and stop sexual abuse.

Tips to Beat Stress – a leaflet to help parents identify and cope with stress.

Please send a SAE for one copy of any publication. If you require further copies please telephone 0131 337 8539 or look up our website.

National Society for the Prevention of Cruelty to Children (NSPCC)
England, Wales and Northern Ireland

The NSPCC is the UK's leading charity specialising in child protection and the prevention of cruelty to children and has been protecting children from cruelty for over 100 years. The NSPCC is the only children's charity with statutory powers enabling it to act to safeguard children at risk. It is authorised under the Children Act 1989 to apply for care, supervision and child assessment orders in its own right. As well as providing a wide range of specialist services to help abused children, the NSPCC also runs a number of public awareness campaigns around the issue of child abuse. All NSPCC projects, including the National Child Protection Helpline, are staffed entirely by professionally qualified staff.

Address: NSPCC
　　　　　Weston House
　　　　　42 Curtain Road
　　　　　London
　　　　　EC2A 3NH
Telephone: 020 7825 2500
Fax: 020 7825 2525
E-Mail: infounit@nspcc.org.uk
Website: www.nspcc.org.uk
www.there4me.com (special service – see details below)

Helpline Details

24-Hour National Child Protection Helpline: 0808 800 5000
Text-phone (for the hard of hearing): 0800 056 0566
Welsh Language Helpline (Mon-Thur 11.30am–6.30pm): 0808 100 2524
Asian Helplines (Mon-Fri 11am–7pm):
Bengali　　0800 096 7714
Gujarati　0800 096 7715
Hindi　　　0800 096 7716
Punjabi　　0800 096 7717
Urdu　　　0800 096 7718
Helpline Service E-Mail: Help@nspcc.org.uk

Areas of Specialism
A 24-Hour National Child-Protection Helpline that provides counselling, information and advice to anyone concerned about a child at risk of abuse. The NSPCC Helpline can provide specialist advice on child welfare or protection. If we believe a child is at risk of significant harm, we will take appropriate action.

The NSPCC provides a specialist Helpline for Welsh speakers and helplines in five principal Asian languages, Bengali, Gujarati, Hindi, Punjabi and Urdu. These services are available at specific times (see above for details) but any calls received out of hours are diverted to the central Helpline service.

The Helpline also provides support and advice for adult survivors of child abuse

NSPCC Teams and Projects
The Society also has over 150 projects throughout England, Wales and Northern Ireland whose work varies from area to area but can include –

- Investigations into allegations of complex child abuse
- Assessment, counselling and therapy to repair the damage to children and families caused by abuse
- Consultations and advice to professionals and organisations
- Educational and advisory services
- A wide range of preventative projects working with parents and children to promote good parenting and positive outcomes for children.
- The NSPCC Training and Consultancy provides expert training and consultancy services to professionals working within child welfare and related areas.

Our Referral System
The vast majority of NSPCC projects do not charge users for services, however they mainly only take referrals from local agencies such as social services and police forces. For information on NSPCC services in your area please contact your local NSPCC team (if unsure, details can be obtained from NSPCC national centre on the number listed above).

There4Me
There4Me is an interactive website designed for 12–16 year olds where any young person with access to a computer can make contact with an NSPCC advisor. Its target audience is the two thirds of young people who have been abused who do not take advantage of current services to speak about their abuse.

The service consists of a wealth of static information including an agony aunt page where young people can send or read e-letters, and an interactive feature called Got a Problem? This allows young people to answer a series of prompted questions that takes young people to a specific piece of advice on the site. The purpose is to help young people find their own solutions to their problems. Young people can also post messages to each other on the Message Board, that we hope to develop to consult with young people about a range of issues. All the messages are checked by an NSPCC advisor before they are posted, to ensure Internet safety. Young people can also contact an NSPCC advisor by logging on to their private in-box, where they can either send an E-Mail or chat directly to an advisor in 'real time'. For extra security, these parts of the site are coded so that no-one else can read someone else's conversation. The site is located at www.There4Me.com.

Directory

Treatment Offered

Therapeutic services can be appropriate for children and young people aged between 3–17 years. As a first step, therapeutic services aim to provide a service to children and young people in local authority accommodation as these may be the most vulnerable, isolated and severely abused children. Referrals will also be received directly from children and young people themselves. The third priority is the provision of therapeutic services to children and young people who have received NSPCC investigation services through Specialist Investigation Services.

Medico–Legal Reports

The NSPCC produces reports as expert witnesses in relation to care proceedings and for young people displaying inappropriate sexual behaviour who have come into contact with the criminal justice system. It also provides assessment reports in relation to adult sex offenders. The availability of these services varies from area to area.

Publications

The NSPCC has a large number of advice publications covering a number of topics relating to child protection. For a full catalogue please contact the publications dept direct on 020 7825 2775. We cannot single out specific publications.

Court and Prison Services

Scottish Prison Service (SPS) – All of Scotland

In relation to victims, SPS operates the Scottish Victim Notification Scheme in terms of which victims of serious crimes in Scotland can receive information relating to their assailant's release from custody. A victim can opt to join the Scheme where an offender has received a sentence of 4 years or more. If they do so the victim will be notified by letter of the offender's release, normally one month in advance. An equivalent scheme for England and Wales is operated by the Home Office.

The current Victim Notification Scheme began, initially on a pilot basis, on 1 April 1997. At present only victims of violent or sexual crimes whose assailants have been sentenced to custodial sentences of 4 years or more are eligible for inclusion in the Scheme. The Scheme does not apply where the offender was sentenced before 1 April 1997, and so victims are not automatically eligible for inclusion in such cases. However, applications for inclusion from victims where the crimes were dealt with before the start of the Scheme are treated sympathetically wherever possible.

Victims are eligible for inclusion in the Scheme if they were direct targets of the offence: for this purpose 'victim' includes the personal representatives and immediate family of a deceased victim or where the victim was a child. After establishing the eligibility of a victim in a particular case, the Procurator Fiscal writes to the victim asking if he or she wishes to join the Scheme and sending him or her registration forms. A victim will only be included in the Scheme if he or she registers by returning the completed forms to SPS.

Most victims who join the Victim Notification Scheme do so when first approached by the Procurator Fiscal. However, a victim who is eligible to join the Scheme can also do so at any time thereafter by application to SPS. We aim to respond to all applications within 2 days of receipt.

Where a victim has joined the Scheme, SPS will at the appropriate time issue a letter advising the victim of the offender's release. The normal target is to issue each letter one month before the offender is due to be released. However, in some cases it is not possible to achieve that target because the date of release is not known a month in advance. In such cases the aim is to issue the letter as soon as possible once the date of release is known.

Since the Scheme was established, a number of improvements have been made. These include development of good practice guidance for the administration of the Scheme; extension of the Scheme to include notification of when an offender has been transferred to another jurisdiction on an unrestricted basis, has died or has had his conviction quashed; and establishment of a diary system to ensure early notification to victims of the release of prisoners on parole or licence.

The existing Victim Notification Scheme is seen as providing a suitable basis for continuing notification to victims. However, from our own consideration of the Scheme and discussions with other interested parties a number of possible improvements have been identified which we believe can be implemented by SPS within the current framework of the Scheme.

These further improvements are as follows:

- computerising the existing Scheme database;
- ensuring that all enquiries from victims who are members of the Scheme are responded to within 20 working days;
- developing an automated system to provide a link to the Scheme database in order to support the administration of the Scheme; and
- extending the Scheme to include temporary release (such as home leave) of offenders from custody.

The aim in the longer term, as set out in the Scottish Executive Justice Department's Action Plan, is to extend the Scheme to all victims who wish to receive notification of their assailant's release regardless of the nature of the offence or the length of the offender's sentence.

The Scottish Prison Service (SPS) is an Executive Agency of the Scottish Executive Justice Department. It is responsible for operating the penal system in Scotland, which consists of 15 establishments (plus 1 privately-operated prison).

Its Mission is:
- to keep in custody those committed by the courts;
- to maintain good order in each prison;
- to care for prisoners with humanity; and
- to provide prisoners with a range of opportunities to exercise personal responsibility and to prepare for release.

A copy of the SPS Action Plan on victims issues was published in October 2001. It describes our current activity in more detail as well as proposals for extension of the Notification Scheme, and is available on our website.

Directory

Further information about the Victim Notification Scheme or about other aspects of SPS activities can be obtained from us as follows:

Address: Legal Policy Branch
          Scottish Prison Service
          Room 311
          Carlton House
          5 Redheughs Rigg
          Edinburgh
          EH12 9HW
Telephone: 0131 244 8670
Fax: 0131 244 8589
E-Mail: gaolinfo@sps.gov.uk
Website: http://www.sps.gov.uk/

HM Prison Service – England and Wales

The Prison Service operates a helpline for Victims. This is the only requirement on the Prison Service contained within the Victims Charter produced by the Home Office.

The number 0845 758 5112 is the point of contact for victims and the Prison Service, and is staffed by trained operators.

There are no other statutory requirements on the Prison Service with respect to victims of crime. There are provisions in other policy areas to withhold information provided by a victim from the prisoner, to protect the victim. These provisions are included in policies for Parole, Home Detention, Curfew, and Sentence Planning amongst other things.

Prison Service Aim

- Effective execution of the sentences of the courts so as to reduce re-offending and protect the public

Objectives

- Protect the public by holding those committed by the courts in a safe, decent and healthy environment.
- Reduce crime by providing structured regimes which address offending behaviour, improve educational and work skills and promote law abiding behaviour in custody and after release

What The Helpline Offers

- The line is open between 9am and 4pm. Answerphone and fax will be available outside these hours.
- Details will be taken of the caller (name, address, telephone number and connection to the prisoner) to deter the non-genuine.
- Details will be taken of the prisoner and the caller's areas of concern (e.g. harassment, possible early or temporary release etc.)
- The helpline staff will then seek to identify and locate the prisoner. The caller will be contacted by letter asking for further details if it has not been possible to locate the prisoner.
- The next step taken will depend on whether a prisoner is still in custody, already released, or under licence, but the concerns of the victims will be addressed and considered, and the caller will be advised on the action taken.

(Written by the Prison Service, London, with essential changes by author)

Definition of sexual or violent offences under the Criminal Justice and Court Services Act 2000

An offence is a sexual or violent offence for the purposes of s.69 of this Act if the offence is:
(a) a sexual or violent offence within the meaning of the Powers of Criminal Courts (Sentencing) Act 2000;

In this Act, 'sexual offence' means any of the following:
(a) an offence under the Sexual Offences Act 1956, other than an offence under ss.30, 31 or 33 to 36 of that Act;
(b) an offence under s.128 of the Mental Health Act 1959;
(c) an offence under the Indecency with Children Act 1960;
(d) an offence under s.9 of the Theft Act 1968 of burglary with intent to commit rape;
(e) an offence under s.54 of the Criminal Law Act 1977;
(f) an offence under the Protection of Children Act 1978;
(g) an offence under s.1 of the Criminal Law Act 1977 of conspiracy to commit any of the offences in paragraphs (a) to (f) above;
(h) an offence under section 1 of the Criminal Attempts Act 1981 of attempting to commit any of these offences;
(i) an offence of inciting another to commit any of those offences.

In this Act a 'violent offence' means:
(a) an offence which leads, or is intended or likely to lead, to a person's death or to physical injury to a person, and includes an offence which is required to be charged as arson (whether or not it would otherwise fall within this definition);
(b) an offence in respect of which an offender is subject to the notification requirements of Part I of the Sex Offenders Act 1997; or
(c) an offence against a child within the meaning of Part II of the Criminal Justice and Court Services Act 2000.

An offence is one to which s.69 applies if it is a sexual or violent offence for which an offender receives a relevant sentence i.e. one which is:
A sentence of imprisonment for a term of twelve months or more;
A sentence of detention in a young offenders institution for a term of twelve months or more;
A sentence of detention during HM's Pleasure;
A sentence of detention for a period of twelve months or more under s.91 of the Powers of Criminal Courts (Sentencing) Act 2000 (offenders under 18 convicted of certain serious offences); or
A detention and training order for a term of twelve months or more.

NPD list of offences which meet the 2000 CJCS Act's definition of a sexual or violent offence
Criminal offences which deal with 'physical injury or death' which might fall into this category include:

Common Law
Murder
Manslaughter
Assault (only to the extent where there was also a battery leading/likely or intended to lead to bodily injury)
Battery – where the offence leads to or was intended or likely to lead to physical injury
Infanticide Act 1938
s.1 – Infanticide

Directory

Offences against the Person Act 1861
- s.18 – wounding with intent to cause grievous bodily harm
- s.20 – malicious wounding
- s.47 – assault occasioning actual bodily harm
- s.21 – attempting to choke, suffocate or strangle
- s.22 – administering chloroform, etc. – where either the administering of the chloroform or the indictable offence committed leads or was intended to or likely to lead to death or physical injury.
- s.23 – administering poison, etc.
- s.28 – causing bodily injury by explosives
- s.29 – using explosives etc. with intent to do grievous bodily harm
- s.30 – placing explosives with intent to do bodily harm
- s.31 – setting spring guns etc. with intent to do grievous bodily harm
- s.32 – endangering the safety of railway passengers
- s.35 – causing bodily harm by wanton and furious driving
- s.37 – assaults on officers saving wreck
- s.38 – assault with intent to resist arrest

Robbery – where the manner of the offence involves death or physical injury to someone or was intended or likely to do so

Aggravated burglary – where the manner of the offence involves death or physical injury to someone or was intended or likely to do so.

Police Act 1996
- s.89 – assaulting a constable in the execution of his duty

Road Traffic Act 1988
- s.1 – causing death by dangerous driving
- s.3A – causing death by careless driving while under the influence of drink or drugs

Theft Act 1968
- s.12a – causing death by aggravated vehicle taking

Criminal Damage Act 1971
- s.1 – Arson
- s.1 – Arson with intent to endanger life
- s.1 – Arson being reckless as to whether life would be endangered

Criminal offences which come within the definition of sexual offences under paragraph (a) above are:

Sexual Offences Act 1956
- s.1 – Rape of a woman or man
- s.2 – Procurement of women by threats
- s.3 – Procurement of women by false pretences
- s.4 – Administering drugs to obtain or facilitate intercourse
- s.5 – Intercourse with girl under 13
- s.6 – Intercourse with girl under 16
- s.7 – Intercourse with defective
- s.9 – Procurement of defective
- s.10 – Incest by a man
- s.11 – Incest by a woman
- s.12 – Buggery

s.13 – Indecency between men
s.14 – Indecent assault on a woman
s.15 – Indecent assault on a man
s.16 – Assault with intent to commit buggery
s.17 – Abduction of women by force or for the sake of her property
s.19 – Abduction of unmarried girl under 18 from parent or guardian
s.20 – Abduction of unmarried girl under 16 from parent or guardian
s.21 – Abduction of defective from parent or guardian
s.22 – Causing prostitution of women
s.23 – Procurement of girl under 21
s.24 – Detention of women in brothel or other premises
s.25 – Permitting girl under 13 to use premises for intercourse
s.26 – Permitting girl under 16 to use premises for intercourse
s.27 – Permitting defective to use premises for intercourse
s.28 – Causing or encouraging prostitution of, intercourse with, or indecent assault on, girl under 16
s.29 – Causing or encouraging prostitution of defective
s.32 – Solicitation by men

s.128 of the Mental Health Act 1959
s.128 – Sexual intercourse with patients

Indecency with Children Act 1960
s.1 – Indecent conduct towards young children (includes gross indecency with or towards a child, under the age of 16, or someone who incites a child under that age to such an act with him or another)

Theft At 1968
s.9 – Burglary with intent to commit rape

Protection of Children Act 1978
s.1 – Indecent photographs of children

Sexual Offences (Amendment) Act 2000
s.3 – Abuse of a position of trust

Criminal Law Act 1977
s.54 – Inciting girl under 16 to have incestuous sexual intercourse
s.1 – Conspiracy to commit any of the offences above

Criminal Attempts Act 1981
s.1 – Attempting to commit any of the above sexual offences.
In addition:
Inciting another to commit any of these sexual offences.

Offences subject to the notification requirement under Part I of the Sex Offenders Act 1997 (other than those mentioned above).

Customs and Excise Management Act 1979
s.170 – penalty for fraudulent evasion of duty, etc. in relation to goods prohibited to be imported under s.42 of the Customs Consolidation Act 1876 (prohibitions and restrictions) – registration required only if the photographs included indecent photographs of those under 16

Directory

Criminal Justice Act 1988
  s.160 – Possession of indecent photographs of children under 16
In addition:
Any attempt, conspiracy or incitement to commit these offences.
Aiding and abetting, counselling or procuring the commission of any offence mentioned in Schedule 1 of the 1997 Act.

An offence against a child within the meaning of Part II of the Criminal Justice and Court Services Act 2000 (other than those mentioned above where they are committed against a child)

Children and Young Persons Act 1933
  s.1 – Cruelty to children

Child Abduction Act 1984
  s.1 – abduction of child by parent

Offences against the Person Act 1861 (not covered above)
  s.16 – Threats to kill a child

Sexual Offences Act 1967
  s.4 – procuring a child to commit an act of buggery with any person or a child
  s.5 – living wholly or in part on the earning of prostitution of a child

Misuse of Drugs Act 1971
  s.4(3) – supplying or offering to supply Class A drugs to a child, being concerned in the supply of such a drug to a child, or being concerned in the making to a child of an offer to supply such a drug

© Home Office 2002

Artwork and Document Design

Docutext Limited – London
Situated in central London, Docutext has been trading for over 10 years. During this time it has established a large customer base that has been built on offering clients the best service possible without charging extortionate prices.

When it comes to setting up a self-help group, or for established agencies in the statutory or voluntary sectors, Docutext can help by offering advice on the best approach to design and print of leaflets, newsletters and flyers as well as standard business and personal stationery.

Services offered:
  Document design and layout
  Black and White photocopying
  Colour copying
  Booklet making
  Binding
  Laminating
  Lithographic printing
  Printer and copier sales and leasing

How to contact Docutext:

Address: Docutext Limited
51 Westbourne Grove
London
W2 4UA
Telephone: 020 7792 1030
Facsimile: 020 7792 1258
E-Mail: admin@docutext.co.uk

Please ask for our specialists Adrian or Steve

Detection and Investigation
England, Scotland, Wales and International

Investigative Solutions

What We Do
Investigative Solutions provides a professional and cost effective investigation and research service to the legal profession, commerce and private clients. Our fees reflect the type of service and tasks required. We have many years of experience in conducting successful investigations with the highest of standards. This enables us to have a thorough and comprehensive understanding of the many problems faced by our clients. We are able to offer a complete investigation package tailored to specific needs and provide effective solutions with sensitivity and skills.

Unfortunately many of our clients are people who have become 'victims', having been cheated or tricked by the unscrupulous and dishonest individuals in our society. All too often the situation could have been avoided by some limited background investigation and objective analysis.

Investigative Solutions is able to undertake complex investigative work for companies, charities or individuals. We cover standard background and screening checks, for example for sensitive posts such as social services or charities working with vulnerable victims of violence to more large corporate matters.

Our Standards
We understand that confidentiality is of prime concern to many of our clients and we guarantee absolute discretion. There is no charge for an initial consultation and if we do not think we can be of assistance – we will tell you.

Who We Are

Jim Davies
Jim worked with the Metropolitan Police for 30 years, spent mostly as a Detective working at 'The Yard', where he became involved in investigations across the complete spectrum of serious and organised crime, including complex fraud.

Ian Forster
Ian is also a former Detective with the Metropolitan Police who worked in the busy West End and Central areas of London. While serving he was involved in investigations across the whole range of criminal activity.

Directory

Since leaving the police service both Jim and Ian have undertaken investigations, both nationally and internationally, working for government agencies, law firms, multi-national corporations as well as private individuals.

Full details of Investigative Solutions services can be found on our website.

    Address: Investigative Solutions
           5 Cricketers Drive
           Meopham
           Kent
           DA13 0AX
    Telephone: 01474 814552
    Fax: 01474 814552
    E-Mail: Enquiries@investigativesolutions.co.uk
    Website: www.investigativesolutions.co.uk

Our Accreditation Investigative Solutions is –

- Authorised to act as a Registered Body by Criminal Records Bureau
- Licensed by the Office of Fair Trading
- Registered with the Information Commissioner

A few case examples of Investigative Solutions:

Case 1

Our client was the family of a student who was very seriously injured in a 'hit and run' accident. Although the police had identified the driver of the motor vehicle they found he had left his address. Due to limited resources a warrant was obtained and the case left 'on file', with minimal enquiries being made to locate the individual.

Upon being instructed we were able to undertake more detailed enquiries and eventually traced the driver to his place of work. The police were informed and he was arrested and the family are taking civil action against the driver and his insurance company.

Case 2

As a result of the long term sickness of their Financial Controller a company hired a temporary replacement from a reputable Employment Agency. He was found to be very efficient – a person who went out of his way to be friendly and helpful. After he left they became the victim of numerous instances of fraud: large sums of money were transferred from various bank accounts by the use of forged documents.

An investigation of the Temporary Financial Controller's CV quickly revealed that qualifications were bogus and other details given were false or exaggerated. Following further investigation the police were informed and he was arrested and, together with accomplices, charged with fraud.

Neither the company nor the Employment Agency had undertaken any checks to verify his qualifications or background.

Disabilities
Changing Faces – National
This lay-led charitable organisation aims to create the conditions whereby individuals, institutions, and society at large, can face disfigurement with confidence. The Changing Faces Client Service provides psycho-social support for individuals affected by disfigurement. On a wider scale Changing Faces promotes public awareness, understanding and equal opportunities through work with health professionals, employers, schools and the media.

Contact: Ms Lorna Renooy M Ed
Title: Head of Outreach and Client Service
Address: Changing Faces
    1 & 2 Junction Mews
    London
    W2 1PN
Telephone: 020 7706 4232
Fax: 020 7706 4234
E-Mail: info@changingfaces.co.uk
Website: www.changingfaces.co.uk

Specialism
Psychological aspects of disfigurement due to any medical condition including scarring. At our launch in 1992 we concentrated on facial disfigurements, however we soon found that similar issues arise for people affected by disfigurement affecting any part of the body.

Services Offered and Catchment Area
The Client Service supports children and adults with disfigurements of any kind, as well as their colleagues, health professionals, teachers, friends and family. The majority of those who use the service live in the UK however we have contacts from all over the world via our website.

Referral Method and Funding Method
Changing Faces is funded by charitable donations. There is no fee for the Client Service although donations are welcomed. Clients contact us by telephone, letter and E-Mail. Support groups, and health and education professionals are asked to pay a small charge to cover the cost of booklets, study days and reading-lists etc., however telephone consultation is free. Employers negotiate market rates for in-house training courses.

Assessment Process and Waiting Time
Assessment takes place by telephone or face-to-face interview at our office near Paddington station, during office hours only. During busy periods you may have to wait a few hours or days for a detailed discussion of your needs with an Adult or Child Specialist.

Treatment Offered
Our salaried staff is made up of graduates in the social sciences, most of whom have additional professional qualifications in clinical psychology or counselling, assertiveness training, nursing, and teaching.
People with disfigurements can experience social anxiety, depression and low self-esteem. Behavioural problems, difficulties in making friends, forming relationships and finding work are common concerns. Research has shown that by acquiring good communication skills and coping strategies, combined with appropriate counselling and advice, many children and adults can very effectively overcome their self-consciousness and deal with difficult social situations, staring and hostility. This results in increased self-esteem and self-confidence, and a better quality of life. Changing Faces employs a number of specialists who are experienced in offering this sort of support through individual sessions and group workshops. The charity has

also developed a range of self-help booklets, and a video, for young people, adults and parents of children with disfigurements to develop their skills.

Medico-legal Reports
Provision of such reports is not a routine part of our service. We will usually advise you to seek an expert witness via your solicitor.

Publications
A complete list of Changing Faces publications is available free of charge by post. It is also on our website, where you can read a selection of our self-help booklets.

Changing Faces: The Challenge of Facial Disfigurement. *Written by James Partridge,* Founder Director

Self-help booklets covering practical skills for everyday life – titles include:

Facial Disfigurement – The Full Picture: A Comprehensive Guide To Facial Disfigurement.
Everybody's Staring At Me – How To Communicate When You Have An Unusual Face.
My Child Looks Different: A Guide For Parents.
Talking To Health Professionals About Disfigurement: A Step-By-Step Guide.
Making Your Face Work For You – A Guide To Managing Disfigurement In The Workplace.

Articles in Professional Journals – titles include:

An Evaluation of the Impact of Social Interaction Skills Training For Facially Disfigured People. *Robinson, E. Rumsey, N. & Partridge J. (1996).* British Journal of Plastic Surgery, 1, 49, 281–289.

Changing Faces: Taking-up Macgregor's Challenge. *Partridge, J. (1998)* Journal of Burn Care and Rehabilitation. 19, (2), 174–180.

Psychosocial aspects of Facial Disfigurement: problems, management and the role of a lay-led organisation. *Clarke, A. (2000)* Psychology Health and Medicine. 4 (2) 127–142

The British Council of Disabled People (BCODP) – Great Britain
BCODP was set up in 1981 by six groups of Disabled People who all wanted a national representative body. BCODP has grown to represent over 130 full member organisations. It is important to clarify whilst BCODP plays an active role in the political arena we have no party political interests and we seek only to address the issues which affect disabled people's lives.

Our role is to 'skill' individual disabled people through promoting the establishment and development of their own organisations. Local and regional organisations play a vital role in supporting, educating and empowering disabled people.

Why was BCODP set up?
- to support and promote the social model of Disability – the recognition that disability is caused not by a person's impairment, but by the disadvantage or restriction of activity caused by a society which takes little or no account of people who have impairments.
- to promote disabled people's full equality and integration into society
- to support the development of organisations of disabled people
- to act as the national representative voice of its member groups
Contact: The Information Office

Address: BCODP
       Litchurch Plaza
       Litchurch Lane
       Derby
       DE24 8AA
Telephone: 01332 295551
Minicom: 01332 295581
Fax: 01332 295580
Website: www.bcodp.org.uk

Or, for independent living issues, contact **National Council for Independent Living**

Contact: Information Officers

Address: NCIL
       250 Kennington Lane
       London
       SE11 5RD
Telephone: 020 7587 1663
Minicom: 020 7587 1177
Fax: 020 7582 2469
E-Mail: ncil@ncil.org.uk
Website: www.ncil.org.uk

Areas of specialism
  • campaigning on human and civil rights for disabled people
  • supporting organisations run and controlled by disabled people
  • information on independent living issues for disabled people
  • Disability Equality/Action Training

Referral method
Individual disabled people or organisations run by disabled people are welcome to seek information or support from BCODP, and if they wish become a member. Most services are provided free of charge, including individual membership for disabled people.

Volunteers
BCODP welcomes applications from disabled people seeking voluntary work, either within our Derby office or on one of our committees. For further details please contact our Information Office in Derby.

Donations
BCODP is a registered charity and is reliant upon grants and donations to carry out its work. If you are interested in making any form of donation please contact Paul Matthews at the Derby office.

Our Publications
Making our own Choices – Written and compiled by disabled people with direct experience of controlling personal assistance support services. Published 1993.

Cashing in on Independence – Published before the introduction of Direct Payments Legislation. Outlining the argument for the need for direct payments to enable people to control their own personal assistance services. Published 1994.

From National to Local – This research looks at the quality of service given by national information providers. It shows that they need to make significant improvements if they are to remain useful to local groups. A 'MUST' for information providers. Published 1995.

Demolishing Special Needs – A study which looks at how effective disabled people have been at accessing appropriate housing under 'Care In the Community'. This is a major report on what is regarded by many (including Government) as the 'cornerstone' of independent living. Published 1995.

Everything You Need To Know About Getting & Using Direct Payments – replaces **Controlling Your Own Personal Assistance Services.** A practical guide on all aspects of employing and controlling your own personal assistance services, including where and how to get the funds. Written by disabled people with direct experience. Free to disabled individuals on receipt of an A4 SAE, with stamp value of 72 or 54 pence. For everyone else please contact NCIL directly.
Note: This publication is only available directly from NCIL (see contact details opposite)

The Way Forward – a BCODP Resource Pack – A folder containing booklets on various practical aspects of running a group of disabled people, including lists of useful publications and organisational contact details. Published in 1997, currently being updated. Limited number available free of charge. Charge is to cover postage and packing.

User's Ability to Manage Direct Payments – Training pack to help people think about issues involved in assessing a user's ability to manage direct payments. Focuses on people with the learning difficulty label, but of wider application.

Notes on the Disability Discrimination Act as at April 2000 – A close look into the rights of disabled people using successful past cases. Written by David Ruebain and Joanna Owen from David Levene & Co Solicitors. David has been a popular speaker at our Human Rights Seminars.

The Disabled Living Foundation – United Kingdom
The Disabled Living Foundation (DLF) is the UK's leading disability charity in the field of information and advice on equipment solutions to independent living issues. It seeks to ensure that people are able to take advantage of the greater independence, easier living, and enhanced opportunities that can be found through full access to equipment and technology. It has a local-rate telephone Helpline, a letter and email enquiry service, an Equipment Demonstration Centre, training courses, an informative website, and numerous publications.

The Foundation produces DLF Data, the most comprehensive database of disability-related equipment in Europe. It is available on subscription in a paper-based format (the Hamilton Directory), as well as on CD Rom. It is also available on subscription on-line via the DLF's website. DLF Data is used by local health services and social services throughout the country, as well as by other disability and advisory bodies (and, of course, by DLF staff when assisting enquirers).

Where We Are –

Address: Disabled Living Foundation
380 – 384 Harrow Road
London
W9 2HU
Telephone: 020 7289 6111 (office) Helpline: 0845 130 9177
Textphone: 020 7432 8009
Fax: 020 7266 2922
E-Mail: dlf@dlf.org.uk or advice@dlf.org
Website: www.dlf.org.uk

Our Helpline

The DLF Helpline is open 10am to 4pm every weekday for anyone who wants impartial information or advice on assistive products (aids and equipment) and solutions to daily living issues (such as cooking, bathing, leisure activities, sleeping, mobility, and so on). The Helpline, which deals with around 25,000 enquries a year, is on 0845 130 9177 (textphone 020 7432 8009). A letter and email enquiry service is also available for those who prefer to write in with their queries. Letters should be sent to the address given below, while emails should be sent to advice@dlf.org.uk.

Our Website

The DLF website gives details of all the Foundation's activities mentioned, as well as the challenging and fun Events Programme (which includes running in Marathons and Road Races, walking the Great Wall of China, and Dogsledding in the Arctic Circle; call 020 7432 8008 for the Events brochure for details). The site also gives linked access to hundreds of websites of other disability-related organisations and suppliers of disability equipment, a discussion forum, and free access to DLF's fact sheets. The DLF website also hosts the up-date section for those who have purchased its specialist 'Handling People Pack'. Please log on to www.dlf.org.uk for full details of all that the Disabled Living Foundation's site has to offer.

Equipment

DLF's Equipment Demonstration Centre is one of the largest Disabled Living Centres in the country, with hundreds of items available to try out with the assistance of an Advisor. Appointments to visit the Centre can be made on 020 7432 8015, or email centre@dlf.org.uk. The DLF does not sell any products itself, but it can give full details of the products that are available from other organisations and commercial companies.

Publications

The DLF produces a wide range of publications, including factsheets related to choosing specific items of equipment; examples include *Choosing a chair, Choosing household equipment* and *Choosing a bath and bath accessories.* There is also *With a Little Help,* which outlines the types of equipment available across a range of products and gives general background information. Other publications include: *Equipped for Living* a detailed guide to equipment designed for older or disabled people; *Handling People* an information pack on moving and handling legislation and equipment; *A Garden for You* a guide to tools, equipment and garden design for disabled people; *A Kitchen for You* a guide to kitchen layout and equipment; *Flying High* a guide to air travel for disabled people; and *Dressing Made Easy* which gives advice on choosing and adapting clothing, and equipment to help with dressing.

A full publications list is available on request.

Training

DLF Training Courses cover a variety of areas, mainly targeting health care and social care professionals to assist their work with disabled clients. Examples include 'Introduction to Stroke', 'Seating and Positioning', 'Moving and Handling People Workshop', 'Equipped to Enable Children' and 'The Law and Practice of Equipment Provision'. A brochure giving full details of all the courses is available from the Training Administrator on the DLF telephone number given below (extension 244) or E-Mail: training@dlf.org.uk.

Where We Get Our Money

The DLF receives just 8% of its funding from the Government; the balance of the £1.3 million needed each year to provide its services comes from the sale of DLF Data and publications, its training courses, and private fundraising and we welcome any donations from interested companies or agencies.

RADAR – National

The Royal Association for Disability and Rehabilitation (RADAR) came into being in July 1977. A merger of the Central Council for the Disabled and the British Council for the Rehabilitation of the Disabled formed RADAR.

RADAR, The Royal Association for Disability and Rehabilitation, is a national pan disability network of, and for, disabled people. RADAR works to support the disability lobby and create an environment in which disability organisations can effectively campaign. RADAR also represents the spectrum of needs, views and wishes of over 8.6 million disabled people in Britain. With a membership of over 450 disability organisations, RADAR is a highly effective lobbying force for change.

Unfortunately, we are unable to offer assistance to victims of violent crime in any form regarding the crime. This is a specialist area and requires the expertise of those organisations that work in this field and we recommend you seek guidance from the police or social services.

Contact: Information Department
Address: RADAR – Royal Association for Disability and Rehabilitation
Telephone: 020 7250 3222
Fax: 020 7250 0212
E-Mail: radar@radar.org.uk
Website: www.radar.org.uk

Our Specialism

RADAR's Team of information support workers offer information and advice about a variety of subjects to RADAR members, disabled people, their families and friends, voluntary organisations, and any other group or organisation working in the field of disability.

The information the Department can provide includes details about the National Key Scheme (NKS) key and guide to accessible toilets throughout the UK; an annual guide to accessible holidays in Britain and Ireland; a series of fact sheets aimed at access groups; a guide for the needs of disabled children in school; a guide to services for disabled children; and an overview of the Human Rights Act 1998. The Team has access to a wide range of information resources and will provide further advice where possible. Other services available include a quality sign-posting service and detailed information about other organisations working in the field of disability.

The Department is open Monday to Thursday between the hours of 10am and 4pm.

Services Offered and Catchment Area
Letter, E-Mail and telephone enquiry service.

Who Can Contact Us
Open access – anyone requiring information relating to disability can use our service.

Areas of Important Work
As well as providing information, RADAR's Influence & Change Team includes members of staff who specialise in the fields of:–
- access
- transport
- social security
- housing and community care

RADAR has been successful in lobbying government, both in Parliament and with Whitehall, on behalf of its members in significant areas.

Funding
RADAR receives a percentage of its funding from the Government. The majority of RADAR's income comes from donations, membership subscriptions and the sale of RADAR's publications.

Some of our publications

Holidays in Britain & Ireland – a guide for disabled people
If Only I'd Known That a Year Ago – a guide for newly disabled people, their families and friends
Leisure Time Series: Arts and Creative Activities and Sport & Outdoor Activities
Children First Series: A Guide to Services for Disabled Children and A Guide to the needs of Disabled Children in School

Please contact us for a full publication list or kindly visit our website – thank you!

Headway: the Brain Injury Association – All United Kingdom
Registered Charity No: 1025852

Headway exists to promote understanding of all aspects of head injury and to provide information, advice and support to people with a head injury, their families and carers.

We have a network of over 100 local groups around the UK and over 50 run Headway House day care centres.

Headway also operates a helpline service open Monday to Friday 9.00am to 5.00pm. This provides information and support on issues concerning brain injury.

Contact:
Title: Information Officer
Address: 4 King Edward Court
King Edward Street
Nottingham
NG1 1EW
Telephone: 0115 924 0800
Fax: 0115 958 4446
Minicom: 0115 950 7825
E-Mail: information@headway.org.uk
Website: www.headway.org.uk

Areas of Specialism
Network of local groups and branches, across the UK, providing support, advice and services to people with head injury, their families and carers. To receive details of your nearest Headway group please contact Central Office (0115 924 0800) or look on the website.

Confidential helpline service open Monday to Friday 9.00am to 5.00pm. Provides information and advice on many aspects of head injury.

Publications
Headway produces a range of publications covering all aspects of head injury, for example:

- **What is Head Injury?**
- **Memory Problems after Brain Injury.**
- **Psychological effects of Brain Injury.**
- **Driving after Brain Injury.**
- **Skill Development after Brain Injury.**
- **Claiming Compensation after Brain Injury.**

Headway also produces a directory of solicitors experienced in running brain injury compensation claims. This is updated annually.

Spinal Injuries Association – National
The Spinal Injuries Association is the leading national charity for spinal cord injured people and all those concerned with their well-being. Established in 1974, with HRH The Princess Royal as its Patron, SIA offers information, advice and on-going support to spinal cord injured people on all aspects of living with their disability.

SIA's Services Include –
A Helpline providing information.

Advice
Peer support scheme to assist those undergoing treatment in Spinal Injuries Centres

A range of expert publications, including a bi-monthly magazine, addressing a wide spectrum of issues of interest and concern to spinal cord injured people.

Membership of SIA is open to all.

Contact details:
Address: Spinal Injuries Association
76 St James's Lane
Muswell Hill
London
N10 3DF
Telephone: 020 8444 2121
Fax: 020 8444 3761
Helpline: Freephone 0800 980 0501 (9.30am to 4.30pm)
Website: www.spinal.co.uk
Hours: 9.30am to 5.30pm – Monday to Friday

Royal National Institute for the Blind (RNIB) – United Kingdom

There are around two million people in the UK with sight problems. RNIB's pioneering work helps anyone with a sight problem – not just with braille, Talking Books and computer training, but with imaginative and practical solutions to everyday challenges. We fight for equal rights for people with sight problems. We fund pioneering research into preventing and treating eye disease. If you or someone you know has a sight problem, RNIB can help.

Specialisms
• RNIB run two specialist rehabilitation and skills development centres for people who have lost their sight as adults or whose sight has deteriorated. Both aim to give you the skills and confidence you need to cope independently at home, college, work and in the community. Courses are tailored to your individual needs and include assessment; vocational rehabilitation and training; independent living skills; job-seeking skills and/or skills updates to help you keep your existing employment. Our vocational advisory service gives guidance on further education and training and employment/self employment.

Both centres offer accommodation on site and please contact Centre managers for a full prospectus.

RNIB Manor House
Middle Lincombe Road
Torquay
Devon
TQ1 2NG
Telephone: 01803 214523
Fax: 01803 214143

RNIB Alwyn House
3 Wemysshall Road
Ceres
Cupar
Fife
KY15 5LX
Telephone: 01334 828894
Fax: 01334 828911

• RNIB also runs two further education colleges that offer rehabilitation programmes. Please contact the colleges directly for a full prospectus.

RNIB Redhill College
Philanthropic Road
Redhill
Surrey
RH1 4DG
Telephone: 01737 768935

RNIB Vocational College
Radmoor Road
Loughborough
LE11 3BS
Telephone: 01509 611077

• RNIB's Helpline gives information, support and advice for anyone with a sight problem. It can: put you in touch with specialist advice services; send you free information and leaflets; give you details of support groups and services in your area.

RNIB Helpline
Telephone: 0845 766 9999
Monday to Friday 9.00am – 5.00pm
Calls are charged at a local rate.
E-Mail: helpline@rnib.org.uk

General contact details:

Royal National Institute for the Blind
224 Great Portland Street
London
W1W 5AA
Telephone: 020 7388 1266
Fax: 020 7388 2034
Website: www.rnib.org.uk

RNIB Cymru
Trident Court
East Moors Road
Cardiff
CF24 5TD

RNIB Northern Ireland
40 Linenhall Street
Belfast
BT2 8BA
Telephone: 02890 329373
Fax: 02890 439118

RNIB Scotland
Dunedin House
25 Ravelston Terrace
Edinburgh
EH4 3TP
Telephone: 0131 311 8500
Fax: 0131 311 8529

Health Supplements

Optima Health – United Kingdom

Optima Health has been in existence since 1979, a family owned company that began selling vitamin and mineral supplements locally in the North of England.

Today, Optima Health has over 700 products in its vast range of supplements that are sold throughout the entire UK. Optima Health have a wide variety of vitamins and minerals that are an excellent source of nutrition, especially for those who are convalescing or looking to rebuild strength after having been the victim of a violent crime or accident.

Optima Health also has a wide range of herbal products, many of which are tailored to restoring health following injury or trauma. Products like Glucosamine, Chondroitin, Aloe Vera and Devils Claw are excellent for those who need to build strength in their joints following broken bones or fractures. Tea Tree Oil is probably the most effective natural antiseptic in the world that can be used on cuts and open wounds.

Optima Health has products that can be of assistance mentally and not just physically. Mental problems such as depression, anxiety or problems with the nervous system are often encountered in tandem with physical difficulties; to combat this products such as St John's Wort, Kava Kava, Ginkgo and Ginseng are just a selection of herbs which can help alleviate such problems.

Optima Health
Binbrook Mill
Young Street
Bradford
West Yorkshire
BD8 9RE
Telephone: 01274 360000
Fax: 01274 542020
E-Mail: admin@optimah.com
Website: www.optimah.com

The benefit of using natural products comes from the thousands of years of use, combined with the natural efficacy of a vitamin, mineral or herb which looks to negate the cause of a particular problem and not just the symptom, as often found in the modern medical world.

Optima Health realises that there are hundreds of possible problems that people can encounter after an accident, trauma, or indeed crime. As such there are probably many different ways an ailment can be treated. After initial consultation with your Doctor, a health food shop would be more than willing to help you make an informed choice as to which supplement can help you.

Directory

If you are unsure of your nearest health shop please phone 01274 360000, if you require some general assistance in choosing a supplement please ask to speak to our technical department on the same number and they will be more than willing to help.

Just remember, your health is our business ...

Abuse

Survive – North Yorkshire region
Survivors of Child Sexual Abuse in North Yorkshire

Survive has developed quite significantly. Our constitution has been changed to include male victims of child sexual abuse - a massive redirection for us. We are still coming to terms with the implication of all this. We have received a great deal of help from the wider North Yorkshire Community and are now beginning to make progress. We have formed a steering group to look at the wider issues of an integrated service and this has been well represented by the police, probation, the prisons, mental health and voluntary organisations.

Survive is a York-based organization offering a service to women survivors of childhood sexual abuse. We grew from a survivor run self-help group that recognized the local need for services to survivors of sexual abuse. Since our development in the early 1990s, we have supported adult women survivors living in North Yorkshire. We are a women only group, run by women for women, that specifically focuses on childhood sexual abuse.

Survive can also advise male survivors where they may access help and information. We promote the philosophy of self-help and aim to assist survivors in empowering themselves in order to define their own needs and access the support that they require. Survive is committed to equality of access for all women, regardless of race, nationality, disability, sexual orientation, marital status, age, mental health history, criminal record, class or religious belief. Survive is working to eliminate all discrimination in service accessibility and delivery, recruitment of staff, the recruitment of volunteers and in the management of the organization.

> Contact: Margaret Brearley
> Title: Chairperson – Survive Trustee Group
> Address: SURVIVE
> 10 Priory Street
> York
> YO1 1EZ
> Telephone: Help line – 01904 642830
>   Office – 01904 638813

Referral method
The service is open to adult women. Women usually self-refer, although we receive referrals through mental health professionals, other agencies, private and public organizations. There are no charges to clients for the Survive services, although some clients choose to make donations.

Assessment process
On occasions we operate a waiting list for the counselling service.

Waiting time
While individuals are on the waiting list for counselling they can use the support of the help line and one-to-one meetings. The length of time on the waiting list can vary according to demand for the counselling service, so please check with Survive to find out how long you are likely to have to wait.

Services offered:

Helpline
Available on Thursdays 7.30pm–10.00pm and answered by a survivor. There is also a 24 hour answer phone which is checked regularly. All helpline volunteers are trained to a high standard.

Counselling
We offer free, open-ended counselling to women survivors of childhood sexual abuse. We are an organizational member of the British Association of Counselling and Psychotherapy and our counsellors work to their ethical standards. We request that any women seeking counselling contact Survive direct.

Advocacy
Recently, we expanded our service to include work with the Family Protection Unit in York. We can help with support if you wish to take legal action through the courts.

Self-help Groups
We run self-help groups in York and Selby, where women can meet other survivors for support. The groups last about 10 weeks and are facilitated by Survive until the participants are ready to organize the group themselves.

Book Loan Service
We have a specialist library of relevant books, plus a wide selection of other material for research. Books can be borrowed for up to a month free of charge. A list is available and books can be posted free of charge.

Support
We can arrange one-to-one meetings with another survivor for support, guidance and information. Our Frontline volunteers can help with support to mothers of abused children.

Training
All helpline and front-line volunteers are trained to a high standard by experienced trainers and receive regular support as well as opportunities for ongoing workplace development through seminars and training events.

We also offer training and consultancy to other helping professionals. For example, our recent successful training conference was attended by professionals from across the UK.

Funding Sources
Funded by donations from public and charitable organizations, including: National Lottery Charities Board, Camelot, City of York Council, York Fund for Women and Girls. We regularly hold fundraising events and receive donations from patrons of Survive.

Directory

Publications
Leaflets on Survive services are available; please telephone Survive office for details.

Donations
Survive warmly welcomes donations and offers of expertise – these allow us to continue and develop the work for our communities.

One In Four – London and South-East of England
UK Registered Charity No: 1081726

Run for and by people who have experienced sexual abuse
One In Four is a London-based organisation offering support and resources to women and men who have experienced sexual abuse. Founded in 1999, One In Four is staffed entirely by people who themselves have experienced sexual abuse. It is this status that offers a unique space that both recognises the experience of abuse and its impact whilst also holding true that we are all more than that experience.

One In Four is committed to the empowerment of survivors. We believe that services must facilitate healing and recovery in a way that allows the person behind the trauma to emerge and regain a sense of self. One In Four is actively opposed to all forms of discrimination on the grounds of Age, Appearance, Caring Responsibilities, Caste, Class, Gender, HIV Status, Marital Status, Nationality, Political Beliefs, Religion or Spiritual Belief, Immigration Status, Race/Ethnicity, Sexuality, Long Term Illness, Unrelated Criminal Conviction, Physical or Mental Ability or Trade Union Activity.

> **Contact: Colm O'Gorman**
> **Title: Director**
> **Address: One In Four**
> 219 Bromley Road
> London
> SE6 2PG
> **Telephone: Helpline: 020 8697 2112**
> **Office: 020 8697 8022**
> **Fax: 020 8697 6843**
> **E-Mail: admin@oneinfour.org.uk**
> **Website: www.oneinfour.org.uk**

Referrals
Most of the people who access our service self-refer. We do however receive referrals from other agencies. The service is open to any adult who has experienced sexual abuse. There are charges for therapy services but these are operated on an ability to pay basis.

Assessment
Upon referral a first appointment will be arranged to offer the client an opportunity to come along and asses the service and to decide how we might best support her/him.

Waiting time
As we do not restrict the number of sessions or time span for therapy we sometimes need to operate a waiting list. Other support services such as the helpline and open evenings are available whilst you wait for a therapy appointment.

Services offered:

Helpline
Our helpline is open on Tuesdays 5–9pm, Wednesdays 12 noon–2pm and Saturday 10am–2pm. Outside these times there is a 24 hour answer machine. We will always try to respond to any call or message within 48 hours.

Counselling
Our counsellors all have relevant professional training and are experienced both personally and professionally in dealing with issues around sexual abuse. Sessions can be booked for daytime and evening appointments. One In Four has a policy of total confidentiality; no material or information disclosed will ever be shared or used in any way outside of the session or group meeting. Therapy is not time limited i.e. there is not a set limit on the number of sessions offered.

Advocacy
One In Four is a 'needs responsive' agency; we are here to help our clients in whatever way might be necessary. As well as providing counselling, therapeutic and support services we also offer a dynamic advocacy service that works to meet individual need. We can arrange services through referral or co-operation with other agencies, provide access to legal services, make contact with social services and if appropriate the police. We can arrange meetings with the police or lawyers at our offices and the advocate will accompany the client to such meetings if the client wishes. We can source medical services that are sympathetic to the needs of those who have been sexually abused and seek any other service or resource that might be necessary in each individual case.

Our advocacy service has one simple and clear aim: to work for our clients in order to empower them by providing safe and clear contact with the necessary services. The client decides what steps to take and our advocates act only under their direction. Our role is to determine and discuss the options.

Group Therapy
Facilitated groups are available for those who have experienced sexual abuse; we offer a wide range of groups in order to meet particular needs, groups for women and men only as well as groups that are mixed. These groups offer the space to discuss and share our experiences in a caring, supportive environment. They are a powerful way to break silence and end isolation. All our groups are therapist facilitated and run initially for 10 weeks. After this time, the group decides how it wants to continue. It may continue as a facilitated group or as a peer-support group.

Open Evenings
Open Evenings offer a space that does not demand discussion, work or thought but is simply a space to be free to connect with others in similar circumstances. They allow an opportunity to talk about personal issues if appropriate or simply give a chance to be in an environment which holds these issues without requiring that they be dealt with in any way. These evenings offer a 'way in' for people considering confronting issues around abuse, an opportunity to feel safe and held. For those in therapy or some other process they provide a safe space that can both hold and offer respite from this work. Open evenings are held on the first Tuesday of every month, 7–8.30pm at One In Four.

Directory

Support Groups

Support groups work in different ways, depending on what people have requested and what fits the subject. For instance there is a Tai Chi group where the doing of the movement helps unstick the feelings, in a space where there is the chance to share the feelings.

Funding

One In Four is funded through our work. We are commissioned to undertake work by statutory agencies and clients make a contribution towards the services they access; this contribution is based upon ability to pay; we work to ensure no one is ever denied support based on cost or inability to pay. We also receive donations from individual and corporate supporters and have received funding through public and charitable organizations.

Publications

All of our leaflets and information are available through our offices and may also be accessed at www.oneinfour.org.uk

Donations

We very warmly welcome donations and gift aid. Please contact the office if you are interested.

Rape Crisis Federation – Wales and England

The Rape Crisis Federation, Wales and England was launched in October 1996 and exists to provide a range of facilities and resources to enable the continuance and development of Rape Crisis Groups throughout Wales and England. We are the national voice for female survivors of rape and sexual abuse. The Rape Crisis Federation represents the interests of its 48 member groups throughout Wales and England and promotes the best practice and standards of professional support and counselling for women and girls survivors of sexual violence. Rape Crisis services have been in existence throughout Wales and England on an autonomous basis for over 25 years.

Areas of expertise

- We are a referral service to individual women who are seeking advice and/or support around the issues of rape and sexual abuse/assault by putting them in contact with their nearest local rape and sexual abuse counselling service.
- We provide a networking and skills sharing function to our member groups providing advice and support to member groups, individuals and other voluntary/statutory organisations seeking information on the issues of rape and sexual abuse/assault.
- We work with the government to develop legislation relating to rape and sexual assault.
- We speak out about sexual violence and campaign on the issues.

Address: Rape Crisis Federation – Wales and England
7 Mansfield Road
Nottingham
NG1 3FB.
Telephone: 0115 934 8474
Fax: 0115 934 8470
E-Mail: info@rapecrisis.co.uk
Website: www.rapecrisis.co.uk

Kindly contact either – Director for Strategy and Resources or the Director Strategy and Training.

'Thanks ever so much, it's so good to be understood and believed without having to go over and over again and again as to why I hadn't fought back and why it had taken me so long to tell.'

'Thanks for all your support in helping me and my family fight for true justice and in getting a conviction for my daughter's rapist.'

Who We Help and How We Help

- In any one year approximately 50,000 women contact our member groups. The RCF is the largest provider of specialist services to women and girls who have experienced rape and/or sexual assault.
- Of those women 99% identified their abuser/s as male. This statistic highlights the gender specific nature of sexual violence and further supports the continued need for women only services.
- 56% of women and girls contacting member groups were survivors of childhood sexual abuse. The RCF is the largest provider of support services to adult survivors.
- The majority of rape crisis groups operate a small waiting list of up to three months. All member groups would like to operate a 'no waiting list' policy, however lack of adequate funding means women and girls survivors of rape and sexual abuse must endure further distress before gaining appropriate support.

Donations

46% of our member groups operate on an income of under £20,000 per annum and last year all of our member groups reported facing drastic cuts to funding for the forthcoming year. The net effect will be that waiting lists will inevitably increase and in worse case scenarios the services may cease in that locality. All donations will be gratefully appreciated and welcomed to allow us to campaign for appropriate levels of funding for rape crisis centres in order to ensure that direct services for women and girls are available.

Thank you!

Social Work Standards

The General Social Care Council – National

The General Social Care Council does not deal with individual complaints from members of the public.

The General Social Care Council was set up in October 2001 under the Care Standards Act 2000 to raise standards in social care. It will establish a code of conduct for social care workers and, starting in 2003, set up a register of social care workers. It will have powers to look into allegations of serious misconduct or malpractice. The council also regulates social work training and will accredit courses and monitors course standards at higher education institutions offering training for social workers.

The General Social Care Council will regulate the workforce by publishing Codes of Conduct and Practice for all social care workers and their employers and by registering the social care workforce. It will normally only deal with cases when employers have concluded complaints and disciplinary procedures and removal from the register or the setting of additional conditions on registration need to be considered.

The Code of Conduct for workers will set down the standards of conduct expected of social care workers. It will ensure that workers know what is expected of them and that the public know what standards of conduct they can expect from care workers. The Code of Practice for employers will set out how employers should meet their responsibilities for managing and supporting their staff and ensuring that they do their jobs well.

All social care workers will be expected to meet the code and any serious failure to do so will be dealt with by employers and in the case of registrants may lead to investigation and action by the General Social Care Council.

The Council will operate in a manner that recognises the rights and responsibilities of employers and avoids duplication of processes or procedures.

More information about the work that has been done to date to establish the General Social Care Council can be found at our website:

> Address: General Social Care Council
> Goldings House
> 2 Hay's Lane
> London
> SE1 2HB
> Tel: 020 7397 5800
> Fax: 020 7397 5834
> E-Mail: info@gscc.org.uk
> Website: www.doh.org.uk/gscc

Setting up Groups and Charities

REACH – United Kingdom

REACH finds voluntary opportunities for experienced managers and professionals

REACH matches skilled volunteers with voluntary organisations

REACH is the charity which offers a free UK-wide matching service for volunteers of all ages and backgrounds, with high grade management, business and professional skills, and voluntary organisations which badly need their career expertise. The opportunities with voluntary groups on our database are normally part-time or time specific short term projects The whole UK is covered by this placement service supported by a network of 28 local Area Managers, themselves REACH volunteers. Over 12,000 placements have been made since REACH was launched over twenty years ago. There are presently over 3,500 REACH volunteers actively using their skills to ensure voluntary organisations remain viable and sustainable.

> Address: REACH
> 89 Albert Embankment
> London
> SE1 7TP
> Telephone: 020 7582 6543
> Fax: 020 7582 2423
> E-Mail: volwork@btinternet.com
> Website: www.volwork.org.uk

REACH recruits people from all backgrounds and communities who have time to offer, whether retired, still working, between jobs or taking a career break. People with career skills and experience who can give time regularly or just occasionally are increasingly needed to make use of their knowledge and expertise in support of a worthwhile cause. There are no age

401

limits and the service is free of charge to both volunteers and voluntary organisations. The opportunities are many and varied and cover such areas as training, counselling, welfare, children, disability, health, the arts and the environment. Typical volunteers' backgrounds include accountancy, financial services, marketing, PR, engineering, law, medicine, teaching, journalism, sales, social work and I.T.

REACH currently has over 2,900 vacancies on its register for voluntary roles so there is a very good chance that individuals will find an opportunity which will challenge them and make full use of their individual managerial or professional career expertise. For further information please call REACH.

REACH – The Charity that finds voluntary opportunities for experienced managers and professionals, without charge!

In Kind Direct – National

In Kind Direct accepts donations of surplus goods from industry for re-distribution to UK wide deserving causes. For example, In Kind Direct has already obtained £15million in surplus value of primarily new, surplus goods from 450 companies. A broad spectrum of primarily new goods are offered from coloured printers and stationery to household appliances and cleaning supplies to toys, refurbished equipment including fax machines, photocopiers and Pentiums with Microsoft software – everything but ingested medicines and food. The donated supplies and equipment are efficiently distributed to an expanding network of thousands of voluntary organisations.

Charities stretch their budgets by accessing goods at a fraction of their usual cost. Ultimately, the monthly catalogue will be published on the internet making it easier for charities to gain access to the goods donated to In Kind Direct.

Voluntary organisations pay a registration fee based on income to receive the monthly Goods Available List. A handling charge is paid per item that includes delivery direct to the charity's premises.

> **Address: In Kind Direct**
> **19 Milk Street**
> **London**
> **EC2V 8AN**
> **Telephone: 020 7860 5930**
> **Fax: 020 7860 5920**
> **E-Mail: info@inkindirect.org**
> **Website: www.inkinddirect.org**

We welcome any enquiries about our work and registration enquiries

In Kind Direct
Registered Company in England and Wales No. 1052679
Company Limited by Guarantee No. 3155226
VAT Registration No. 685 2052 31

Directory

The Media Trust – National

Our Purpose
The Media Trust is a registered charity (number 104 2733) and we help charities with their communications. We do this by encouraging media professionals to volunteer their skills, time and resources. We work across the UK.

What We Offer
Working in partnership with the media to meet the communications needs of charities, voluntary organisations and community groups:

- Advice and support from media and communications professionals
- Videos and television programmes for and about the voluntary sector
- Volunteering opportunities for media professionals
- The Community Channel, a television channel for the voluntary sector

What We Will Need If You Want Our Support
If you need help, we will ask you to complete an application form which will allow us to assess that need. This may be through one of our introductory surgeries or workshops, or a one-to-one match with a media professional.

There is a small charge ranging from £25 for a surgery or workshop to up to £100 for a match depending on the size of your organisation. Video requires a larger budget. Prices accurate at the time of going to print – please check website for up to date prices.

Our Contact Details:
Address: The Media Trust
3–7 Euston Centre
Regent's Place
London
NW1 3JG
Telephone: 020 7874 7600
Fax: 020 7874 7644
E-Mail: info@mediatrust.org
Website: www.mediatrust.org
We also have a range of online guides and application details

Other services and skills include:

- **Videos for the voluntary sector**
Are you a charity that wants to make a video to help raise funds, to tell your supporters what you're doing or communicate with your staff? We make high-quality videos at competitive prices for all types of voluntary organisations.

- **Broadcast programmes and training videos**
The Media Trust is dedicated to producing easy to use training videos and broadcast productions for use by voluntary organisations. We are currently securing funding for a major series of learning materials for video, web and CD-ROM.

- **Production facilities**
We offer low-cost production facilities to help charities and voluntary organisations with their projects.

Our Funding Sources
We owe enormous thanks to all our funders and supporters, and to those individuals who have contributed their efforts, paid or unpaid, to support the continued growth of the Media Trust. A full list of our funders is available on our website.

Information requests
We welcome any question on all aspects of accessing and using media. Use our message board to post a question or get in touch directly.

> Telephone: 020 7874 7600
> E-Mail: info@mediatrust.org

The National Centre for Volunteering – England

Since 1973, the National Centre for Volunteering has been promoting excellence in volunteering, offering a range of services designed to support volunteer managers and volunteer-involving organisations in England.

Volunteers play a vital part in the life of many organisations, but they themselves need ongoing support. Managing volunteers isn't always easy and it can be hard to keep up with all the issues and aspects of good practice. The National Centre for Volunteering is here to help anyone involved in working with volunteers, and can offer a variety of services.

> Address: Regent's Wharf
> 8 All Saints Street
> London
> N1 9RL
> Telephone: 020 7520 8900
> Fax: 020 7520 8910
> E-Mail: information@thecentre.org.uk
> Website: www.volunteering.org.uk

Our FREEPHONE HELPLINE (0800 028 3304) includes a textphone service, or the team can be contacted by email at: information@thecentre.org.uk.

Some of Our Services

The Information Service
The Information Team at the National Centre for Volunteering offers a free telephone helpline service for anyone who would like information or advice about good practice in working with volunteers. We can offer help on ongoing issues such as recruitment and retention as well as with practicalities such as paying expenses. The team also offers:

- a wide range of information sheets and free publications, which can be obtained from the Centre's website (www.volunteering.org.uk) or sent by post or email.

- a policy review service, offering detailed advice and guidance for organisations drawing up written policies on volunteers.

- a fortnightly E-Mail bulletin, comprising advice on good practice, information about training opportunities, resources and awards and news about legal issues affecting volunteer-involving organisations.

Directory

- A specialist library, containing thousands of publications and press cuttings all relating to volunteering, which can be visited on weekdays.

Publications

The Centre publishes a range of titles that cover most aspects of volunteering and are excellent value for money. Our publications on good practice and managing volunteers are designed to give you all the practical advice and information you need to do your job, whatever your involvement with volunteers. Our research titles offer more in-depth information and comprehensive studies of particular areas of volunteering. We also publish a monthly magazine and a journal, as well as a series of free booklets, research summaries and information sheets which capture the essentials in a quick and accessible format.

Examples of current publications include:

The Good Practice Guide – 2nd edition – Covers all the basics you need to manage volunteers effectively, and incorporates the latest information on criminal records screening, benefits rules and volunteers' expenses.

Safe and Alert – The ultimate good practice guide on how to ensure the safe involvement of volunteers with vulnerable clients, looks at the key issues around safety and features case studies and sample documentation.

You can order all our publications online at www.volunteering.org.uk/publications or telephone 020 7520 8936 if you'd like us to send you our brochure of publications and services.

For the full range of services available to organisations and individuals, please see our website or ring 020 7520 8936 for a brochure.

Welfare Benefit Advice

Citizens Advice Bureaux – Scotland

Citizens Advice Scotland was established in 1975 as a separate umbrella body for all Citizens Advice Bureaux in Scotland.

Citizens Advice Bureaux in Scotland, as in the rest of the UK, offer free, independent and confidential advice to the public on a wide range of topics, including criminal injuries and welfare benefits. They also refer clients on to other agencies, where appropriate.

There are 70 CAB offices across Scotland and you can simply drop in or phone for an appointment with an adviser. Addresses and contact details can be found in the local telephone directory under 'Citizens Advice Bureau'.

Alternatively, you might access the CAB Service's online Advice Guide (www.adviceguide.org.uk) which offers easily accessible advice and information at basic level, and fully reflects differences in Scottish law.

Address: Citizens Advice Scotland (CAS)
Spectrum House
First Floor
2 Powerhall Road
Edinburgh
EH7 4GB

Telephone: 0131 550 1000
Fax: 0131 550 1001
E-Mail: info@cas.org.uk
Website: www.cas.org.uk

Kindly note, CAS does not itself offer advice or information to the public, but is active in collating case-evidence from its members and in using this to press for change in social policy and legislation.

A comprehensive information system is the cornerstone of the CAB service across the UK. CAS develops and maintains the Scottish dimension by providing monthly updates to the system. CAS is also responsible for updating Scottish information in Keynotes and Advice guide, the condensed paper and online forms respectively of our main information system. Both have been written for easy use by the public and other advice agencies.

For further details visit the CAS website

Citizens Advice Bureaux – United Kingdom
The Citizens Advice Bureaux Service was set up in 1939 as an emergency advice and information service during the Second World War and is now the largest independent advice network.

Citizens Advice Bureaux provide free, confidential and impartial advice on almost any topic from benefits, debt, and employment to housing, legal and family matters from over 2000 outlets across England, Wales and Northern Ireland. Bureaux belong to the National Association of Citizens Advice Bureaux (NACAB) that sets standards for advice, training, equal opportunities and accessibility. Bureaux in Scotland belong to Citizens Advice Scotland. All Citizens Advice Bureaux are registered charities reliant on the work of nearly 22,000 volunteers. NACAB uses CAB client evidence to campaign for changes in social policies and services.

To find your local CAB see your phone book or www.nacab.org.uk.

The CAB Service aims:
to ensure that individuals do not suffer through lack of knowledge of their rights and responsibilities or of the services available to them, or through an inability to express their needs effectively and equally.

to exercise a responsible influence on the development of social policies and services both locally and nationally.

Address: National Association of Citizens Advice Bureaux
115–123 Pentonville Road
London
N1 9LZ
Telephone: 020 7833 2181 (admin only, no advice on this line)
Fax: 020 7833 4371
Website: www.nacab.org.uk
www.adviceguide.org.uk
(provides CAB information on-line 24 hours a day)

Areas of Specialism

Citizens Advice Bureaux provide advice to everybody on benefits, housing, health, employment, legal issues, family matters, debt and money advice, Tax, immigration, consumer rights and many more. Advice is free, confidential and impartial. Face to face and email advice is offered, outreach sessions run in schools, workplaces, health centres, prisons and many other venues. CAB advisers are trained volunteers and can help clients solve problems through negotiating on behalf of clients, for example with creditors, representation at tribunals and signposting to other services.

CAB client evidence is used to campaign to improve policies and services that aren't working.

Volunteers

Citizens Advice Bureaux are reliant on the work of nearly 22,000 volunteers as trained advisers, administrators, trustee board members, and to support IT development, PR and fundraising. Contact your local CAB to find out about current opportunities available.

Publications

NACAB publishes regular social policy evidence reports using CAB client evidence. Copies can be downloaded at www.nacab.org.uk or ordered by contacting our Social Policy department at NACAB Central Office on 020 7833 2181.

Reports cover all areas of social policy but recent health and legal related reports include:

Unhealthy Charges – CAB clients experience of NHS charges

An Unfit Test – looks at flaws of the incapacity benefit fit to work test

Barriers To Justice – looks at failings in the legal system

Solicitors

Scotland: Edinburgh

Allan McDougall and Co

Allan McDougall has over 20 year's experience in dealing with claims for criminal injuries and a wealth of experience in handling all types of personal injury work from simple road accidents to the more complex life-threatening and fatal cases.

Allan McDougall has a specialist department that deals exclusively with personal injury work. The Personal Injury Claims department (PIC) is headed by a Partner who is a member of The Law Society of Scotland's Personal Injury Panel. Other members of the PIC department are members of the Association of Personal Injury Lawyers. Allan McDougall is also a member of Compensure and is able to offer an insurance based scheme to enable people to raise personal injury court actions.

Clients can be seen at any of our offices and we will endeavour to make home visits if necessary.
Allan McDougall and Co specialises in:–

- experience in dealing with all types of personal injury ranging from minor injuries to catastrophic and life-threatening injuries
- experience in dealing with fatal cases
- experience in pursuing claims through the CICA procedure including attending hearings
- experience in dealing with occupational illnesses e.g. asbestosis

We are able to deal with most claims on a 'no win, no fee' basis.

Address: Allan McDougall and Co
3 Coates Crescent
Edinburgh
EH3 7AL
Telephone: 0131 225 2121
Fax: 0131 225 8659
E-Mail: mail@allanmcdougall.co.uk
Website: www.allanmcdougall.co.uk

Please contact Damien White

In a year Allan McDougall and Co can be dealing with in excess of 30 criminal injury claims. We deal with all types of levels of cases from the straightforward to more complex claims that require assistance of expert witnesses e.g. head injury claims. For example:

Mr A was lying in bed when he was assaulted. He suffered a hammer blow to the head. Consequently, he suffered brain damage and epilepsy. Following an initial rejection of the award his appeal was successful after extensive enquiries were made by ourselves including obtaining of expert reports to calculate future wage loss and the obtaining of a Care / Needs report to calculate both past and future care costs.

Mr B was a victim of a road rage assault. He suffered multiple facial injuries. His initial application was rejected as the CICA believed Mr B provoked the road rage attack. After an appeal hearing the CICA accepted Mr B was not responsible for the assault and awarded him a five figure award.

Mr C was a bus driver who suffered eye injuries after his windscreen was smashed by a gang of youths whilst he was driving a bus. As a consequence of his injuries Mr C lost his PSV driving licence and was unable to continue his employment as a bus driver. An initial offer was made by the CICA and was rejected as it did not compensate Mr C for future wage loss. At the appeal hearing expert evidence was led from an employment consultant. This evidence persuaded the CICA to make an award for future wage loss and the applicant received a substantial award.

Mrs D was a school teacher who was assaulted by a 9 year old pupil. Mrs D developed post traumatic stress disorder. Her application was initially rejected by the CICA as they did not accept she had been assaulted in accordance with the legal definition of assault and Mrs D appealed. At the hearing Allan McDougall led legal argument to persuade the CICA an assault had taken place. The appeal was successfully argued and Mrs D received an appropriate award of compensation.

408

Allan McDougall
93 High Street
Dalkeith
EH22 1JA
Telephone: 0131 6637261
Fax: 0131 6635483
E-Mail: dalkeith@allanmcdougall.co.uk
Website: www.allanmcdougall.co.uk
Please contact Grant O'Connor

Allan McDougall
2 Lambs Pend
Penicuik
EH26 8HR
Telephone: 01968 675694
Fax: 01968 676546
E-Mail: penicuik@allanmcdougall.co.uk
Website: www.allanmcdougall.co.uk
Please contact Bill Brown

We welcome your enquiry and will strive to secure the very best!

Balfour and Manson

Balfour and Manson has extensive expertise in Criminal Injuries Compensation work, dealing with claims from all over Scotland. Our teams include Members of the Association of Personal Injury Lawyers, (one of our Partners is the Scottish Regional Co-ordinator), and two of our Partners are Members of the Law Society of Scotland Personal Injury Panel. We have extensive experience of head injury claims and are members of the Scottish Head Injuries Forum and the Spinal Injuries Association. One of our Partners is the solicitor for Edinburgh Headway.

We have experience of dealing with all sorts of Criminal Injury Claims including sexual assault, child abuse (including non-accidental injury to children), assault on teachers and other assaults, and with such a large department, we are able to deal with all types of claims from relatively minor cases to very high value personal injury and medical negligence claims. We also have extensive experience of multi-party actions.

As Members of the Law Society Personal Injury Panel we are able to undertake cases on a 'no win, no fee' basis under the Compensure Insurance Scheme that protects clients from any awards of costs against them. We are able to visit clients at home or in hospital if necessary.

Address: Balfour and Manson Solicitors
54–66 Frederick Street
Edinburgh
EH2 1LS
Telephone: 0131 200 1200
Fax: 0131 200 1333
E-Mail: maggie.neilson@balfour-manson.co.uk
Website: www.balfour-manson.co.uk

Please Contact Maggie Neilson – Head of Litigation Department

Mr A was assaulted while trying to prevent a robbery. Prior to the incident he had lost an eye due to unrelated causes. As a result of the assault the sight in the remaining eye was severely affected, rendering him registered blind and unable to work. An initial offer of £6,000 was made. This was rejected and ultimately an award of damages of £327,500 was made following an appeal hearing.

Mr B was awarded compensation of £1,500 after he was assaulted outside his girlfriend's home. He sustained minor facial scarring as a result of the assault.

Mrs C was a teacher and was assaulted by a pupil while in school. He pushed her and she sustained a broken finger. She was awarded damages of £2,500.

Mr D was sexually assaulted by a former teacher. It was not until his assailant was prosecuted that he felt able to approach solicitors to discuss the assault. An application was submitted to the CICA outwith the usual time limit but they were persuaded by us that the claim should be accepted, although late.

Mrs E was a teacher. She sustained serious psychological injuries triggered by a pre-existing condition, although the actual assault in school was a relatively minor one. Her employers disputed that the assault took place and an Employment Tribunal application was lodged which was successful, challenging the employers' denial of the assault. A CICA application was then lodged and was rejected by a single member as being of too low value. This was appealed and a hearing took place. The final award was £89,000.

Scotland: Aberdeen

Burnside Kemp Fraser
Burnside Kemp Fraser is a firm that specialises in civil litigation of all kinds. Both David Burnside and Sandy Kemp are members of the Personal Injury Panel in Scotland.

The firm have continuing experience in pursuing claims before the CICA, and have recovered six figure awards and settlements from the CICA previously. The firm are also pursuing a claim under the new appeal tariff system.

The firm's other areas of legal expertise include employment law, personal injury claims and matrimonial law.

> Address: Burnside Kemp Fraser
> 48 Queen's Road
> Aberdeen
> Aberdeenshire
> AB15 4YE
> Telephone: 01224 327500
> Fax: 01224 327501
> E-Mail: law@burnside_kemp_fraser.co.uk
> Website: http://www.scoot.co.uk/burnside_kemp_fraser/
>
> Please contact Alexander Kemp
> (Declined to provide examples due to confidentiality)

Scotland: West Lothian Regions

Keegan Walker and Co
Keegan Walker are one of West Lothian's largest firms of solicitors and have a specialist division, The Compensation Claims Centre, that specialises in all types of compensation claims.

Iain Nicol is the Partner in charge of The Compensation Claims Centre and is a member of the Law Society of Scotland's personal injury panel of solicitors. He also has a keen interest in medical negligence work.

Our aim at the end of a case is to ensure that a client receives all the compensation that they are awarded without any deductions for legal costs being made, where possible.

We are also members of the panel of solicitors for National Accident Helpline and have clients UK wide.

The following are the main types of claim which we deal with:–

1. Road Traffic Accidents.
2. Work Accidents.
3. Professional and Medical Negligence Claims
4. Claims against Local Authorities e.g. slipping, tripping

Keegan Walker and Co have experience of dealing with many other types of claims such as Gulf War Syndrome, Hepatitis C sufferers from contaminated blood products and Deep Vein Thrombosis sufferers due to long haul air flights.

Address: Keegan Walker and Co Solicitors
The Compensation Claims Centre
Torridon House
Almondvale Boulevard
Livingston
EH54 6QY
Telephone: 01506 415 333
Fax: 01506 416 116

Free first interview always provided and provide a full legal aid service

Keegan Walker and Co also deal with claims on a 'no win, no fee' basis under the Law Society recommended Compensure Scheme.

Here is a sample of cases we have successfully assisted:–

Mr A – injured in a road traffic accident, permanent neck and back problems, inability to work, required extensive care support. Total award in excess of £500,000.

Mr B – involved in an accident on an adventure training course. Lack of proper instruction by organisers resulted in significant disability and inability to work. Needed house adaptations and daily home help. Award of £560,000.

Mr C – taxi driver stabbed by passenger. Initial derisory award appealed. Panel at oral hearing awarded £100,000.

Miss D – due to negligent treatment in hospital, foetus was killed. £9,000 awarded for mother's psychological trauma.

Ms E – due to professional negligence on part of former solicitor, client lost the right to pursue accident claim. Awarded £35,000 as compensation for what she should have received if original claim had been properly handled.

Mr F – fell from electricity pylon, fracturing pelvis and sustaining some wage loss. Awarded in excess of £25,000.

Mr G – injured on badly rutted football pitch that had not properly been maintained by local authority. Knee injury, wage loss and services awarded at more than £33,000.

Scotland: Glasgow

Legal Services Agency

Legal Services Agency is among the most experienced organisations in undertaking criminal injuries compensation applications in Scotland. Legal Services Agency's staff pioneered criminal injuries compensation application for abused children in the mid 1980s. The Legal Services Agency has produced tens of thousands of leaflets on criminal injuries compensation and its staff have been involved in drafting the leading text book on criminal injuries compensation in Scotland: **Claiming Criminal Injuries Compensation** *by Paul Brown, Hilary Hiram and others LSA 1997.*

Legal Services Agency undertakes a wide range of criminal injuries compensation applications. This includes but is not restricted to:–

- Complex matters involving employment and pension loss.
- High value claims involving injuries of maximum severity.
- Sexual abuse including particularly relating to children.
- Family violence.
- Murder cases involving large numbers of relatives whether they are 'fatal' applications or secondary victims.

Legal Services Agency undertakes a wide range of lecturing on the area including to Victim Support, local authorities and solicitors in private practice.

Legal Services Agency prefers to be consulted right at the beginning but will undertake hearings where individuals cannot find representation otherwise providing there is some prospect of success.

For more information:

> **Address: Legal Services Agency Limited**
> **3rd Floor, Fleming House**
> **134 Renfrew Street**
> **Glasgow**
> **G3 6ST**
> **Telephone: 0141 353 3354 for an appointment**
> **Email: lsa@btconnect.com**
> **Website: www.lsa.org.uk**

> **Call in at the free drop-in surgery most Wednesday afternoons between 2 pm – 5 pm.**

Here are a few examples of the extent of our experience

(1) Young person aged 19 seriously physically and sexually abused as an infant. Claim initially rejected as the Criminal Injuries Compensation Authority was of the view that it had not been established that a crime of violence took place. Detailed research undertaken including establishing the subsequent criminal career of the perpetrator of the abuse involving similar offences. Award of £7,500 made on appeal.

(2) Secondary victim claim: wife saw her husband die of a heart attack after he had successfully extinguished a fire caused by arson in part of the family home. Wife deeply traumatised as a consequence. The Criminal Injuries Compensation Appeal Panel accepted that the heart attack was directly attributable to the crime of violence (the arson) and the wife qualified as a 'secondary victim' under the 1996 Scheme. Substantial award made.

(3) *Victim originally offered inadequate award based on injuries. At appeal it was substantially enhanced to take into account emotional injuries and delay in entering the labour market.*

(4) *Victim with learning difficulties seriously abused by teacher. Claim originally rejected as the Authority suggested it had not been established that there was no consent. Detailed psychological evidence submitted and a substantial award made at appeal.*

(5) *Victim came to LSA after a hearing had taken place that resulted in a nil award. A judicial review petition was initiated and the authority conceded that the appeal hearing had been unfairly conducted. New hearing set down and a satisfactory award made.*

Scotland: Greater Glasgow

Penmans
Penmans were established in 1987, and has three Partners and one solicitor and are a firm engaged in private practice. Penmans takes pride in providing a dedicated service and in trying to represent marginalized people in need of experienced legal representation.

One Partner at Penmans accredited by the Law Society, Al Gordon, is a specialist in the field of child law and over the years has dealt with a large number of personal injury claims. These include, in particular, a large number of claims for criminal injuries compensation particularly for children and also adults generally. He has also dealt with numerous claims for adult survivors child sexual abuse.

Penmans have developed specialist experience and skills in

- Criminal compensation work – all levels of compensation applications
- Child Law – child abuse, neglect, custody, criminal compensation, Curator ad Litem
- Criminal Law – defending alleged criminals
- Family Law – extensive family matters including, disputes of custody, child protection

Address: Penmans Solicitors
175 Saracen Street
Glasgow
G22 5JM
Telephone: 0141 336 6646
Fax: 0141 336 5936
E-Mail: algordon@connectfree.co.uk

Please contact Al Gordon

Here are a few cases we have assisted with:

(A) *Penmans raised civil proceedings against a relative who had sexually abused his nephew but against whom no criminal proceedings were taken. £100,000 court damages awarded.*

(B) *represented adoptive parents of child sexually abused while in the care of its birth mother. Considerable difficulties were experienced in obtaining any information and initial CICA application was refused. After investigating thoroughly we were able to secure criminal compensation award for the child despite the child had no memories of having been abused. The child developed into a fairly normal person with her adoptive parents.*

(C) client's daughter strongly suspected of having been abused by her father but never proven. This case presented huge difficulties. The police were entirely unsympathetic, the child too young to say what had happened and obviously no proceedings were taken against the alleged abuser. It was almost impossible to establish what happened to the child. After initial rejection of a criminal injuries claim, the matter went to an appeal and a modest award was secured.

(D) represented adoptive parents of a baby only few months old that had sustained a fractured skull, fractured femur and other injuries. An application for compensation was made and initial award was far too low and after appeal the award was almost doubled.

Publications

Contributing author in **Children's Rights in Scotland (1st edition)**

We welcome your enquiry and will assist with the best of our skills!

Scotland: Edinburgh

The Scottish Child Law Centre

The Scottish Child Law Centre was established twelve years ago and is an independent charitable organisation based in Edinburgh that serves the whole of Scotland. The Centre aims to promote knowledge and the use of Scottish law relating to children and young people under the age of eighteen years.

The only criminal injuries compensation work we deal with specifically relates to children and young people under the age of eighteen years.

The Centre currently does not represent clients and is intending to do so in the future. The Centre has a telephone service that provides information on all aspects of Scottish law relating to children and young people.

Our Areas of Expertise
• child criminal injuries compensation
• parental rights and responsibilities
• contact
• residence
• education
• social work
• criminal law and procedures
• children's hearing system

> **Address: The Scottish Child Law Centre**
> **54 East Crosscauseway**
> **Edinburgh**
> **EH8 9HD**
> **Telephone: 0131 667 6333**
> **Fax: 0131 662 1713**
> **E-Mail: enquiries@sclc.org.uk**
>
> **Please contact Fiona Miller – Principal Solicitor**
>
> **Freephone For Under 18 year olds: 0800 328 8970**

Our Current Opening Hours
Monday: 9.30am – 4pm
Tuesday: 9.30am – 4pm and 6pm – 7.30pm
Wednesday: 9.30am – 4pm
Thursday: 6pm – 7.30pm
Friday: 9.30am – 4pm

Other Areas of Important Work
In addition, the Centre produces publications on current issues, organises conferences, seminars and provides training

The Centre has a consultative and advisory function for such bodies as the Scottish Executive and Scottish Law Commission

Example of our work and expertise

Query – child Z awarded £10,000 for having been sexually abused. The CICA held the award in trust for the child. Child's mother called enquiring whether they could access the fund.

Answer – CICA hold the award in trust for children under eighteen years, but money can be accessed with CICA's consent for purposes that benefit the child.

Some of Our Publications

Your Rights If Stopped By The Police
Your Rights If Asked To Go To The Police Station For Questioning Or If Detained Or Arrested By The Police
Do The Police Have A Right To Search Me?
Drugs and The Law
Are You Worried You Might Be Pregnant Or Have Recently Found Out You Are Pregnant?
Right To Financial Help For Teenagers and Teenage Parents
Information For Teenage Parents – Your Rights and Responsibilities
Who's Minding The Kids?
Working Children
Children's Hearings and the Rehabilitation of Offenders Act 1974
Scottish Child Law Centre's Guide to the Children (Scotland) Act 1995
Representing Children, Listening To The Voice of The Child
At What Age Can I Go To The Doctor?
Your Views In Court
Young People and Alcohol

Scotland: Dundee, Arbroath, Forfar and Perth

Thorntons WS
With offices across Tayside (Dundee, Arbroath, Forfar and Perth), Thorntons WS offers the most comprehensive service locally in all matters relating to violent crime. With a team of lawyers dedicated to dealing with such matters, we can assist those who have suffered by easing the load and advising clients of the options available to them.

With specialists accredited by The Law Society of Scotland in both Family Law and Child Law, our team also offers specialist services to families who have suffered violent crime. Key players include Sandra Sutherland, Stephen Brand and Graham Harding.

Sandra Sutherland (Partner) is the only Specialist accredited in the field of both Family Law and Child Law in Tayside and is recognised – both by other professionals in this field and by the general public – for her expertise. Stephen Brand (Partner) and Graham Harding (Partner) are also Accredited Specialists in Family Law and the team are recognised for their skills in dealing with a wide range of family and child law matters including criminal injury compensation.

Scott Milne (Partner), a member of APIL (Association of Personal Injury Lawyers), also has a growing reputation for his work in the field of reparation. Dealing with a range of claims, Scott is involved in a growing number of criminal injury related matters.

How to contact Thorntons WS

> **Contact: Sandra Sutherland**
> **Title: Partner**
> **Address: Brothockbank House**
> **Arbroath**
> **DD11 1NF**
> **Telephone: 01241 872683**
> **Fax: 01241 871541**
> **E-Mail: ssutherland@thorntonsws.co.uk**
> **Website: www.thorntonsws.co.uk**

Areas of Specialism and Expertise
- experience of negotiating fatal and severe injury claims
- experience in the pursuit of compensation in 'no win, no fee' cases
- authorised to issue 'Compensure', the Law Society of Scotland recommended after the event insurance product
- experience of pursuing claims in the offshore sector
- team of specialists exclusively pursuing compensation for those injured in accidents at work and road traffic accidents
- growing caseload of general and criminal injury compensation claims
- child law and family law expertise
- wide experience of advising in personal injury claims

Services Offered and Catchment Area
- full range of family, child and criminal injury services across Tayside; Dundee, Arbroath, Forfar and Perth
- no win, no fee cases undertaken
- legal aid
- home and hospital visits available
- authorised to issue 'Compensure'

Examples of case work

(1) Miss X was sexually assaulted over a 4 year period by her stepfather who was a member of the same household as her. At the time the criminal injuries compensation application was lodged, her stepfather still lived in the same house and the claim was rejected on the basis that he may benefit from any award made. After presenting evidence from a psychologist to the Criminal Injuries Compensation Appeal Panel, an award of £6,000 was made.

(2) Mr N was sexually abused over a period of 2 years by his stepfather that included anal intercourse. Initially the claim was rejected on the basis that he had a long list of serious convictions that were

416

committed after he was aged 16 and which would normally render him ineligible for Criminal Injury Compensation. This decision was contested and eventually an award of £5,000 was made, which is half of the normal tariff.

(3) Twins X and Y were repeatedly sexually abused over a period by their father. An application was submitted to the Criminal Injuries Compensation Authority. One of the twins obtained an award of £17,500 whilst the other obtained £15,000, as the abuse in her case was for a shorter period.

(4) A boy of 5 years of age was shot in the eye by another child who was aged 14. He lost one eye as a result and obtained compensation of £25,000.

(5) Miss L was a passenger in a motor vehicle driven by a disqualified driver. This was a matter that required to be taken up with the Motor Insurers Bureau on behalf of the client. Initially all claims were rejected on the basis that the client knew of the driver's disqualification. Eventually a settlement of £850,000 was negotiated.

Additional information on the specialists at Thorntons WS

Sandra Sutherland
- Accredited Specialist in Family Law
- Accredited Specialist in Child Law

  Mail: Brothockbank House, Arbroath, DD11 1NF
  Telephone: 01241 872683
  E-Mail: ssutherland@thorntonsws.co.uk

Scott Milne
- Member of the Law Society Personal Injury Panel

  Mail: 50 Castle Street, Dundee DD1 2RU
  Telephone: 01382 229111
  E-Mail: smilne@thorntonsws.co.uk

Stephen Brand
- Accredited Specialist in Family Law
- Founding member, past convenor and now secretary of CALM (Comprehensive Accredited Lawyer Mediators)
- Founder member of Family Law Association
- Member of Scottish Society of Curators
- Member of Mediation Committee of Law Society of Scotland

  Mail: 50 Castle Street, Dundee DD1 2RU
  Telephone: 01382 229111
  E-Mail: sbrand@thorntonsws.co.uk

Graham Harding
- Accredited by Law Society of Scotland in Family Law
- Member of Family Law Association
- Member of Association of Children Curators

  Mail: 5 Charlotte Street, Perth PH1 5LW
  Telephone: 01738 621212
  E-Mail: gharding@thorntonsws.co.uk

Directory

Scotland: Glasgow, Edinburgh, Dundee and Glenrothes

Digby Brown

Digby Brown has earned a reputation as one of Scotland's foremost firms of personal injury specialists with almost 90 years' experience providing legal services. One of the leaders in the field in representing clients claiming compensation in accident, injury and disease cases, the firm is described in Chambers Bar Directory 1998 as a 'prominent firm… expanding rapidly'. With offices in Edinburgh, Glasgow, Dundee and Glenrothes the firm provides a strong geographical network enabling us to promote clients' interests at first hand.

Investment in the latest technology has further enhanced the firm's ability to deliver a high quality, cost effective service to clients. Permanent data links with digital voice lines amongst all offices, internet access from every desk and extensive use of CD Roms and on line services gives each solicitor access to the computer assistance needed to deliver a winning competitive edge to the client.

Address: Digby Brown
The Savoy Tower
77 Renfrew Street
Glasgow
G2 3BZ
Telephone: 0141 566 9494
Fax: 0141 566 9500
E-Mail: maildesk@digbybrown.co.uk
Website: www.digbybrown.co.uk

Please contact Robert Swanney

Case Studies

Mr A was assaulted and developed severe back pain. His previous Solicitors advised acceptance of an offer of £7,500 from the CICA. He instructed us. We fully investigated the medical position in great depth and after evidence was presented to the CICA, he was awarded £228,000.

Mr B was a student who was assaulted and sustained brain damage. This occurred before his final Degree examinations. As a consequence of his injuries, he took two further years to obtain his degree and failed to achieve an Honours Degree which he was expecting. We obtained expert evidence and were able to establish a continuing wage loss for the rest of his life as a result of not achieving an Honours Degree. He was awarded £206,653.

Mr C was a graduate who was assaulted sustaining brain damage prior to obtaining employment using his Degree. A claim was made in relation to the emotional, behavioural and other psychological injuries impacting on his employment prospects. Having heard evidence, the CICA awarded £285,050.

Ms D was assaulted by her husband, sustaining severe head injuries. The injuries were of the utmost severity. She requires continuing care to live in the community. She was awarded £1,100,000 with the appropriate deductions to the CRU.

Mr E was assaulted and sustained moderate brain damage. Psychological evidence was presented to the CICA and a final award in the sum of £44,886 was made.

Digby Brown	Digby Brown	Digby Brown
7 Albyn Place	2-3 Teviot Place	Royal Exchange
Edinburgh	Edinburgh	Panmure Street
EH2 4NG	EH1 2QZ	Dundee
Telephone: 0131 225 8505	Telephone: 0131 240 8800	DD1 1DU
		Telephone: 01382 322 197

418

Directory

For further information, please see the firm's website, www.digbybrown.co.uk, or contact Robert Swanney, Partner, on 0141 566 9502

All of Scotland

Quantum Claims
Quantum Claims have operated since 1988 and have offices in Aberdeen, Inverness, Glasgow and Dundee. Quantum Claims are not solicitors but a firm of claims specialists dedicated to handling damages claims.

Over the years we have handled some of the most complex and serious criminal injuries applications, dealing with all matters through to the final exhaustive Appeal stage, including consideration for Judicial Review. We believe that it is all too easy to under-prepare for Criminal Injuries Compensation Hearings and have on appropriate cases instructed Counsel to ensure the best quality of representation for our clients.

We handle all applications on a true 'no win, no fee' basis.

Other areas of expertise
We specialise in all matters of personal injury claims, including road traffic accident, accident at work, industrial disease, other accidents, etc. We also specialise in breach of contract cases, professional negligence cases and in the growing market of employment law claims.

Addresses:
ABERDEEN
Quantum Claims
70 Carden Place
Aberdeen
AB10 1UP
Telephone: 01224 641111
Fax: 01224 621773
E-Mail: gac@quantumclaims.com

INVERNESS
Quantum Claims
1 Tomnahurich Street
Inverness
IV3 5DA
Telephone: 01463 71674
Fax: 01463 715212
E-Mail: inverness@quantumclaims.com

GLASGOW
Quantum Claims
90 Battlefield Road
Langside
Glasgow
G42 9JN
Telephone: 0141 6494650
Fax: 0141 6491533
E-Mail: glasgow@quantumclaims.com

DUNDEE
Quantum Claims
1 South Tay Street
Dundee DD1 1Nu.
Telephone: 01382 206820
Fax: 01382 206406
E-Mail: dundee@quantumclaims.com
Website: www.quantumclaims.com
Please contact: George Clark

At any one time Quantum run in excess of 50 Criminal Injuries applications country-wide. Two recent examples include:

1. We are acting for a claimant who sustained serious head injuries as a result of an assault. The Board have offered less than £20,000 with no reduction for contribution. We are appealing this matter on the basis that they have failed to properly analyse the extent of the injury and have further failed to properly take account of loss of earning capacity and proper services assessment for past and future.

2. We are currently dealing with an Appeal for a person who was the victim of a cruel practical joke that involved placing super glue in a glass. The Board have rejected this as not being a crime of violence, but we have pursued the matter as a crime of violence in terms that it is reckless conduct, a crime in Scots law. We are having difficulty getting the Board, comprising an English Q.C., to accept that that is the position and the matter proceeds to Appeal.

West Scotland: Ayr

The McKinstry Company

The McKinstry Company was formed over 18 years ago by our current Senior Partner, Graeme McKinstry. The McKinstry Company was the first solicitors firm in Scotland to be accredited with ISO 9001 quality standard that it maintains to this day along with the Investors in People accreditation.

Our Litigation department is headed up by Alistair Murdoch who is a partner within the firm and also a Solicitor Advocate, which entitles him to appear in the highest civil courts. Alistair Murdoch is also a member of the Association of Personal Injury Lawyers and has considerable experience in pursuing claims through the CICA and all Scottish civil courts.

As a firm we have significant experience in the field of personal injury work and the ability to handle cases which include:–

- Fatal accident claims for relatives of the injured party
- Head injury claims involving loss of working capacity and ability to care and look after oneself
- All manner of injury categories ranging from offshore accident to car accidents and victims of violent crime.

We undertake work on a Legal Aid basis subject to each client meeting the eligibility criteria laid down by the Legal Aid Board and where Legal Aid is not available we are often able to offer the facility of no win no fee arrangements. We currently operate the Law Society approved scheme that is backed by Compensure legal expenses insurance.

Directory

Address: The McKinstry Company Solicitors
Queens Court House
39 Sandgate
Ayr
KA7 1BG
Telephone: 01292 281711
Fax: 01292 610206
E-Mail: amurdoch@mckinstry.co.uk
Website: www.mckinstry.co.uk

Please contact: Alistair Murdoch

Our litigation department handles a significant number of CICA cases on a continual basis that varies hugely in both the type of injury and their complexity. Examples of a few cases which we have completed recently include the following:–

Mr X – the victim of an attempted murder and as a result has been rendered quadraplegic and will require constant care for the rest of his life. His claim involved a number of different facets including future care, wage loss and injury compensation. He was initially offered £250,000 by the CICB to settle the matter. On our advice this offer was rejected and the case proceeded to a full appeal hearing which resulted in an award of over a million pounds being made.

Mr A – the victim of an attack outside a public house where he was beaten and robbed. The assailants were tracked down by the police and after a very swift decision by the CICA some four months after the incident our client received a substantial offer of compensation.

A relative of Mr Y was murdered and this was witnessed by Mr Y along with the aftermath of the incident. An application is currently ongoing for compensation for the post traumatic stress that he has suffered due to the death.

As a firm we constantly strive to provide the highest level of service to all our clients and we are confident that we will be able to meet your needs and provide you with all the help necessary to secure compensation on your behalf.

Wales: Cardiff

Hugh James Ford Simey

Hugh James Ford Simey has the largest Claimant Personal Injury Department in South Wales. With offices all over South Wales as well as Bristol and South West England, it has over 40 years' experience of acting for the victims of accidents and assaults. The Claimant Personal Injury Division consists of specialist lawyers who are members of the Law Society's Personal Injury and Clinical Negligence panels, the College of Personal Injury Law and the Association of Personal Injury Lawyers.

It is the only firm in South Wales with a specialist head injury unit which is managed by a Headway panel member, and staffed by specialist solicitors as well as highly trained support staff including a qualified social worker with extensive experience in the field of disability, qualified nurse executives, welfare benefit advisers and a medical records officer.

Other areas of legal expertise include –

- Head Injury Claims
- Sexual Assaults – female representation can be arranged in appropriate cases together with the services of the social worker case manager
- Child Abuse – Members of the Law Society Children's Panel
- Assaults – minor; racial; and homophobic
- Extensive experience of successful CICA applications, reviews and appeals
- 'No win, no fee' advice and representation; Free first interview
- Disabled access; Home and hospital visits undertaken
- All advice and representation offered in jargon free simple language

Address: Hugh James Ford Simey
      Arlbee House
      Greyfriars Road
      Cardiff
      CF10 3QB
Telephone: 02920 224871
Fax: 02920 388222
E-Mail: mark.harvey@hjfs.co.uk
Website: www.hjfs.co.uk

      Please contact Mark Harvey

Below are some examples of our work

• *Child L was the victim of a sexual assault. We assisted her and her mother with their application and then with their subsequent review of the damages awarded by the CICA, resulting in an increase of the initial award to £7,500.*

• *Mr R was assaulted late one night and in trying to flee the assault ran into the path of an oncoming car, suffering serious injuries. His initial application was turned down by the CICB and we represented him in his appeal, resulting in an acceptance of the claim and an award of £250,000 damages.*

• *Mr A was assaulted outside a nightclub, suffering a fractured nose cuts and bruising; we assisted him in his application as a result of which he received an award of compensation from the CICA of £1,000.*

• *Mr Z was the victim of a racially motivated attack. He suffered extensive facial injuries and developed a post-traumatic reaction. We obtained compensation for the injuries and his financial losses from the CICA of £22,500.*

• *Child Q was assaulted by her father and was severely brain damaged. The CICB was persuaded to award her £821,000.*

We will advise you quickly, simply and effectively at the first interview as to whether there is any reasonable of winning the case or successfully appealing an adverse decision. If it is unlikely that the case can win or to do so it would be uneconomic to use a lawyer, we will tell you.

Wales: Swansea

John Collins and Partners

John Collins and Partners has over 16 years' expertise in criminal compensation work and our successful and dedicated personal injury team in pursuing compensation claims. Each solicitor is a member of the Association of Personal Injury Lawyers with our department being under the control of three members of The Law Society's Personal Injury Panel and a member of their Medical Negligence Panel.

Other areas of legal expertise include –

We specialise in maximum severity cases

- extensive experience of head injury claims – Member of The Headway Panel
- experience of spinal injury claims – Member of The Spinal Injuries Association
- experience in dealing with sexual assault
- experience of dealing with child abuse
- able to undertake all types of claims ranging from minor injuries to those of maximum severity
- experience in pursuing claims through the full CICA procedure and successfully attending many hearings where liability is disputed by the CICA.
- no win, no fees cases undertaken
- disabled facilities
- home and hospital visits available

> **Address: John Collins and Partners**
> **Copper Court**
> **Phoenix Way**
> **Enterprise Park**
> **Swansea**
> **SA7 9EH**
> **Telephone: 01792 773773**
> **Fax: 01792 774775**
> **E-Mail: t.morgan@johncollins.co.uk**
> **Website: www.johncollins.co.uk**

Please contact Tanya Morgan

At any one time, John Collins and Partners has a caseload of approximately 50–60 criminal injury cases. Our experience in this field runs from less serious injuries through to those of maximum severity such as head injuries resulting in permanent brain damage. Here are some examples –

Mr A was assaulted outside a public house by one its employees. He sustained brain damage as a result. Following an initial rejection of the claim his appeal was successful after exhaustive enquiries were made by ourselves and detailed evidence presented to the CICA.

Mr B was assaulted outside a nightclub and sustained severe head injuries. He was initially offered £35,000 by the CICA; upon our advice this was rejected and he eventually obtained £410,000 at an appeal hearing.

C was a child who was physically abused by his father. He sustained a fractured skull and damage to his eyes. As a result of his injuries C has undergone and will require further corrective surgery. Given the nature of the injuries and the future surgery required an interim payment was first made by the CICA before his claim was finally determined.

Mr D was assaulted and as a result fractured his skull. He has been left with deafness, tinnitus and a lack of smell and taste.

Mr E was a victim of a severe assault that resulted in him being shot, stabbed and beaten. A claim was made in relation to both his physical and also psychological injuries. Applications were also made by four members of his family claiming post traumatic stress disorder as a result of witnessing the attack.

We are confident we can offer a fast, efficient and sensitive service to people applying for criminal compensation.

Smith Llewelyn Partnership
Smith Llewelyn Partnership has over twenty years' experience and expertise in criminal compensation and personal injury claims. Smith Llewelyn Partnership prides itself in providing clear and simple advice in an easy to understand language. We undertake considerable CICA work from assisting the client in completing application forms, assisting throughout the application process, representing clients in reviews and appeals and in some cases simply advising in relation to awards and appeals which have already been made. We are familiar with dealing with complex cases and have offices in the centre of Swansea and Carmarthen.

Other areas of legal expertise include –

- Personal Injury
- Immigration
- Housing
- Family and Child Care
- Clinical Negligence
- Particular experience in violent racist crimes
- Particular experience in homophobic crimes

We are panel members of Headway, The Law Society Personal Injury Panel and APIL members.

- We operate a 'no win, no fee' type scheme for applications to the CICA
- First interview is free
- Disability access
- Simple and easy to understand advice for victims
- Offices in Swansea and Carmarthen
- Medically qualified lawyers as well as our own in-house GP, mental health nurse and midwife Charges

Smith Llewelyn Partnership can assist people completing a CICA application form and offer guidance about any further evidence that may be required. No charge for this work is made if the claim should fail and at the point of possible review or appeal we would discuss realistic prospects of success and the charges Smith Llewelyn may make.

Examples of settled or ongoing applications include:

Middle-aged lady seriously injured in Soho pub bombing in London. Award – £127,000
Young man involved in unprovoked attack with machete – injuries resulted in impotence – application ongoing

Young gay man suffered brutal long-lasting internal injuries following gay hate attack on returning home from night-club. Ongoing application – due to be reviewed. Interim award – £25,000

Young girl hit by pellet gun – suffered mild scarring. Award – £3,500

Young woman jumped from 1st storey of her home to avoid burglars – fractured wrist and fractured spine. Ongoing application – Interim award £7,750

9-year old boy hurt in playground – lost front tooth and suffered blot clot. Award – £7,650

>   **Address: Smith Llewelyn Partnership**
>   **18 Princess Way**
>   **Swansea**
>   **SA1 3LW**
>   **Telephone: 01792 464444**
>   **Fax: 01792 464726**
>   **E-Mail: mainoffice.slp@virgin.net**

>   **Address: Smith Llewelyn Partnership**
>   **105 Lammas Street**
>   **Carmarthen**
>   **SA31 3AP**

North East England: Sunderland

Ben Hoare Bell
Ben Hoare Bell has four offices in Sunderland and carries out personal injury work including criminal injuries compensation applications throughout the North East region.

The department has members of the Law Society Personal Injury Panel and a member of the Law Society Medical Negligence Panel, Headway Panel (specialising in head injury cases) and the AVMA (Action for Victims of Medical Accidents) Solicitors Referral Panel.

The department has extensive experience of criminal injuries claims from minor injuries to catastrophic injury cases of great complexity.

We will not only advise people on their applications and the review procedure, we will also where appropriate represent people at Criminal Injuries Compensation Appeal Tribunal hearings.

We have significant experience in dealing with sexual abuse and domestic violence cases.

Ben Hoare Bell is franchised by the Legal Services Commission in the field of personal injury, clinical negligence and many other areas. We try to provide a holistic service to our clients and our experience in welfare benefits work and community care work is particularly valuable for

those who have lasting effects from serious injuries.
Ben Hoare Bell offers advice and assistance with criminal injuries claims under the Legal Help scheme and also operates a 'no win, no fee' policy.

Ben Hoare Bell will make home or hospital visits whenever required.

Ben Hoare Bell historically has a strong commitment to social welfare law and also has thriving practices in the areas of mental health, education, housing, immigration, family and criminal defence.

> **Address: 47 John Street**
> **Sunderland**
> **SR1 1QU**
> Telephone: **0191 565 3112**
> Fax: **0191 510 9122**
> E-Mail: **advice@benhoarebell.co.uk**
> Website: **www.benhoarebell.co.uk**

For advice on criminal injuries compensation applications please contact Adrian Dalton, Francis O'Neill, Elizabeth Maliakal or Simon Garlick.

Examples of cases we have represented –

A 17-year-old boy who lost an eye in an unprovoked assault was refused compensation on the basis that the CICA did not accept a crime of violence had taken place. We represented him on appeal when he was awarded over £20,000.

A man in his thirties who attempted to stop a thief stealing his car and was run over by the perpetrator, sustaining a badly broken leg, was refused any award on the basis of very old previous criminal convictions. At the appeal hearing we persuaded the panel to exercise its discretion in his favour and he received a substantial award.

An 8-year-old boy who lost an eye in a shotgun incident was awarded nothing by the CICA initially on the basis that the perpetrator – another small boy – had simply been playing and there was no crime of violence. On appeal he obtained over £20,000.

A teenage girl sexually assaulted in a classroom in the presence of a teacher who took no action. The CICA refused at first to accept that the injuries sustained were worth over the minimum award or that there had been a crime of violence. On appeal an award was made.

A young woman was assaulted in her home by an ex-partner. She sustained significant brain and orthopaedic injuries, necessitating complex expert evidence. She received a sum in excess of £250,000.

England: Newcastle-upon-Tyne

McKeags
McKeags have been established as a solicitors practice for over seventy-five years and have a dedicated personal injury/clinical negligence team. They have a Legal Aid Franchise in personal injury and clinical negligence and the department includes two members of the Law Society Personal Injury Panel and a member of the AVMA Referral Panel.

Directory

Other areas of legal expertise –

- Extensive experience in head injury claims – members of the Headway Panel
- Experience in dealing with sexual assault claims
- Experience in dealing with child abuse claims (both multi-party actions and CICA claims)
- Experience in dealing with claims of maximum severity
- Vast experience in dealing with CICA appeals both against quantum and in those cases where an award has been refused
- 'No win, no fee' available
- Disabled facilities
- Home and hospital visits available

Address: **McKeags**
1 Lansdowne Terrace
Gosforth
Newcastle upon Tyne
NE3 1HN
Telephone: **0191 213 1010**
Fax: **0191 213 1704**
E-Mail: **patrick.rafferty@mckeags.co.uk**
Website: **www.mckeags.co.uk**

Please contact Mr Patrick Rafferty

McKeags is always running a case load of 30 to 40 criminal injury cases at any one time. Some recent examples include:–

We are presently acting for one claimant who suffered severe cognitive impairment following an assault in the mid 90s. His case is shortly to be heard before the Tribunal. Our schedule of loss includes a claim for lifetime loss of earnings and past gratuitous nursing care. In this case, we have liaised with the Court of Protection and the claimant's parents with a view to setting up a support network and care regime which will give the claimant security for the rest of his life.

We recently acted for an individual who lost his leg following a shotgun attack. In this case, we were able to successfully convince an appeal tribunal that the claimant's criminal history should not be taken into account and a sum of £70,000 was awarded in respect of his general damages for pain and suffering. This award was in excess of the top limit set out in the judicial studies guideline for an above knee amputation for the period when the award was made.

We are more than happy to take on claims where the applicant has been dissatisfied with the advice provided by their former solicitors who have advised acceptance of an initial offer from the Board. In a case which came before the Appeal Tribunal approximately two years ago, we were successful in recovering over £100,000 for a claimant who had received an initial offer of £2,000 which her original solicitors had advised her to accept.

At McKeags, we pride ourselves in fully investigating the psychological/psychiatric sequelae that the victims of violent crime may suffer. In the case mentioned above, the physical injuries sustained by the claimant were minimal but she was unable to continue in her business as a seaside landlady after being assaulted by a number of her tenants. The psychiatric evidence obtained by the Board did not credit causation, i.e. they felt that her ongoing problems were not as a result of the assault but rather due to a history of mental health problems. We obtained our own independent psychiatric evidence and called the expert to give evidence at the Tribunal hearing with the result that the claimant obtained £98,000 more by way of damages than had been offered by the Board.

We are more than happy to run Criminal Injuries Compensation Authority cases on a 'no win, no fee' arrangements and an initial interview will, in any event, cost nothing.

North West England – Manchester

Pannone and Partners

For the victim of criminal injury clear and reliable advice from a specialist and dedicated personal injury lawyer is a top priority.

Pannone and Partners' personal injury department have a wealth of experience in advising and representing victims of serious crime. Our department has been ranked 'Number 1' in the north west for the past six years by both the *Legal 500* and the *Chambers Guide to the Legal Profession.*

Pannone and Partners conducted the very first structured settlement with the previous CICB. We were co-founders of the Association of Personal Injury Lawyers and the Association of Child Abuse Lawyers. We are active members of Headway and the Spinal Injuries Association. We are accredited by ISO 9000 and possess a Legal Services Commission franchise.

Our personal injury department is supported by a specialist trusts and probate department which advises on Guardianship, Structured Settlements, Special Needs Trusts and Investment of awards.

Pannone and Partners have a dedicated team of over 50 specialist lawyers and successful extensive experience of advising and handling:–

- spinal injury cases
- brain and head injuries cases
- sex abuse, assault and rape cases
- fatal injuries
- injuries to children

together with all types of smaller CICA claims.

'No win, no fee' and contingency fee agreements are available, also legal aid in appropriate cases

> **Address: Pannone and Partners**
> **123 Deansgate**
> **Manchester**
> **M3 2BU**
> **Telephone: 0161 909 3000**
> **Fax: 0161 909 4671**
> **E-Mail: carol.jackson@pannone.co.uk**
> **Website: www.pannone.com**
>
> **Please contact Carol Jackson**

Pannone and Partners have successfully assisted:–

A catastrophically brain damaged infant, severe shaking injuries inflicted by parents before client taken into care and instructed by adopted mother when child was 13 years old. Award £665,000 – poor prognosis as to life expectancy.

Directory

Head injuries to an adult male of 29 years at time of assault. 34 years at time of award: £310,000.

Brain damaged child with tragically short-life expectancy following severe shaking as a baby. CICB award £365,000.

Assault on a man now aged 52 years who sustained a very serious injury, formerly worked as a self-employed accountant. Award £759,000.

A soldier in his 30s sustained hemiplegia following a stabbing in Germany. Case is on-going and anticipated the award will achieve the ceiling of £500,000.

The partner of the client undertook advocacy and preparation of the case before the CICB. A 56-year-old man suffered a stroke after witnessing a robbery at a local post office, causing hemiplegia and severe damage to speech. Neurological evidence showed a pre-exiting vascular disease and therefore was likely to have a stroke within a 2–3 year period thus the claim was for acceleration of the injury/condition. Award general damages £17,500 based on 2.5 years of catastrophic injury attributable to the incident. Total Award for 2.5 years £29,500.

Case brought by a partner of client for PTSD following an assault outside a nightclub. Total Award reduced by 50% due to previous convictions to £85,000.

Assault on young man causing incomplete spinal cord lesion with mobility difficulties, depression, impairment of sexual, bowel and bladder function. General Award £400,000.

England: Midlands, Nottingham, Derbyshire, Grantham and Leicester

Nelsons
Nelsons is one of the largest firms specialising in personal injury claim work in the Midlands with more than 30 lawyers in offices in Nottingham, Derby, Leicester and Grantham giving the firm a truly regional presence. Each of the lawyers employed deals exclusively with claims on behalf of injured people, giving us an unrivalled breadth of knowledge, experience and expertise in this field, which is vital in ensuring that all our client's claims are prepared and presented in the best possible way.

Other areas of legal expertise –

- Claims for the victims of clinical negligence –
- Members of Action for Victims of Medical Accidents
- Broad experience of catastrophic injury claims, e.g. head or spinal injuries leading to severe disability. We have close links with charities and victims' support groups
- Claims for victims of industrial accidents and sufferers of industrial diseases, e.g. deafness, asbestos related illnesses and RSI
- Group product liability actions for multiple claimants injured by the same defective products
- Comprehensive expertise in road traffic accident claims – Members of the Motor Accident Solicitors' Society
- We offer a full range of funding options, including 'no win, no fee' and legal expenses insurance
- Free initial consultation and advice

Address: Nelsons
Pennine House
8 Stanford Street
Nottingham
NG1 7BQ
Telephone: 0115 9586262
Fax: 0115 9589144
E-Mail: mailbox@nelsons-solicitors.co.uk
Website: www.nelsonline.com

For those interested in making on-line communication Nelsons have on their website a form enabling potential new clients to make contact about queries.

Please contact Bruce Williams

Criminal Injury Experience
As a firm we have a caseload of in excess of 140 criminal injuries claims at a time, covering a wide range of injuries from the most severe to the relatively minor. Our extensive personal injury experience enables us to assess accurately the appropriate level of compensation and thus to advise on many successful challenges of CICA awards. We believe that handling claims of this nature requires a particularly sympathetic understanding of the needs of victims of violent crime. We are also committed to ensuring that victims are not placed at a disadvantage in dealing with a system that is often seen as unsympathetic and even uncaring. We recognise that to certain categories of victim the system can seem especially daunting, particularly those from ethnic backgrounds and children and that a special approach is required in such cases.

We have recently been involved in the highly publicised trials in a group action on behalf of a large number of claimants who were the victims of institutional physical and sexual abuse whilst in care. Our specialist team handles a large number of claims of this nature.

Examples of cases where we have successfully represented claimants include the following:–

A woman who suffered brain damage after being stabbed in the head with an ornamental spear. She was left partially paralysed down her left side, had a 20% loss of vision and was prone to epileptic fits. She needed a wheelchair to go out. She had poor memory and concentration and profound clinical depression. After a single member awarded £40,000 for her injuries we appealed and obtained an increased award for her injuries of £65,000. We also recovered compensation for care, future loss of earnings, household aids and housing alterations, giving a total award of £310,000.

A female security officer who was slashed across the neck by an assailant with a knife. She was left with severe scarring and also suffered psychological problems. After an initial award of £8,500, we recovered an increased award of £45,000 on appeal.

A male graphic designer and artist was attacked without provocation outside a pub. He suffered extensive brain damage, leaving his left side largely paralysed. He also developed epilepsy. As a result of his injuries he will never be able to work and will require domestic care and assistance for the rest of his life. As he was left handed, he will not be able to return to painting. He was a promising talent at the time of the attack, as is evidenced by an unfinished mural in a local hospital that now bears a plaque explaining why it will never be finished. We used comparison with his contemporaries on his course to quantify his prospective earnings and opinions from experts in the art world to achieve an award for him of £500,000.

Directory

We welcome your enquiry and have branches in the following areas –
Nelsons
Sterne House
Lodge Lane
Derby
Derbyshire
DE1 3WD
Telephone: 01332 372372
Fax: 01332 365715
E-Mail: mailbox@nelsons-solicitors.co.uk
Website: www.nelsonline.com

Nelsons
2a New Walk
Leicester
Leicestershire
LE1 6TF
Telephone: 0116 222 6666
Fax: 0116 233 7821
E-Mail: mailbox@nelsons-solicitors.co.uk
Website: www.nelsonline.com

Nelsons
29-30 Avenue Road
Grantham
Lincolnshire
G31 GTH
Telephone: 01476 591550
Fax: 01476 591552
E-Mail: mailbox@nelsons-solicitors.co.uk
Website: www.nelsonline.com

England: Leicester

Harvey Ingram Owston
We are one of the leading personal injury firms in the East Midlands, and have a team of specialists with vast experience in handling complex and serious claims.

Our aim is to assist victims of crime receive as high an award as possible, working within the parameters of the Scheme. We accept the Scheme has room for improvement, but we believe that our support and expertise will make the procedure simpler and less of a traumatic process.

We are members of the Personal Injury and Medical Negligence Panels of The Law Society, Association of Personal Injury Lawyers and Action for Victims of Medical Accidents.

We offer free telephone advice and initial interview.

Other areas of legal expertise include –
The breadth of expertise regarding clinical negligence and criminal compensation matters is vast within Harvey Ingram Owston –

- fatal accidents
- severe head injuries
- severe spinal injuries
- multiple fractures
- significant success with a variety of compensation claims that cannot be described as the 'run of the mill'
- rape
- minor assaults
- severe attacks
- advice to clients to appeal against decisions not only to refuse awards, but in relation to the size of awards

Address: Harvey Ingram Owston
          20 New Walk
          Leicester
          LE1 6TX
Telephone: 0116 254 5454
Fax: 0116 255 4559
E-Mail: sjb@hio.co.uk
Website: http://www.hio.co.uk

At Harvey Ingram Owston we take pride in the sensitivity we provide to each client's needs balanced with thorough legal knowledge of the workings of the rigid injury aspects by the CICA's tariff scheme. It is our experience that unfortunately the inability to recover legal costs does influence significantly how clients proceed with their applications and on occasions, despite our advice client's choose, for understandable but not necessarily informed reasons, to withdraw or accept first CICA offers for awards. This almost certainly has an adverse effect on the level of damages people finally recover.

So, if you are confused, or clear-minded, and want expert legal advice and services about how or whether to proceed with an application, to decisions, to refuse the size of awards or any other legal matter contact Harvey Ingram Owston.

UK: East Anglia – Abroad

Cunningham John
Cunningham John understands that victims of Criminal Injury need special care, understanding, sensitivity and patience.

We understand that thanks to Government attempts to reduce the costs of the Scheme, it is necessary to be proactive and whilst pressing for an early conclusion, obtain interim payments wherever possible.

We have a national reputation for high damage awards. In the last three-and a-half years we have recovered more than £40million in damages for our Clients.

We offer:–

- Free informal initial chat about your case
- No Win No Fee Agreements
- Cunningham John act for injured people throughout the UK and abroad and visit Clients wherever necessary
- Particular experience of Sexual, Spinal, Brain, and other complex injuries, plus special interest in fatal claims and claims for psychiatric injury whether on behalf of primary or secondary victims

Panel Members:–

- Action for Victims of Medical Accidents
- Headway
- Spinal Injuries Association
- Law Society Personal Injury Panel
- Law Society Clinical Negligence Panel

Cunningham John have recently successfully helped:–

Under the old CICB rules –

Mr P – Assaulted in a pub, serious head injuries. Interim payment of £250,000 to buy a bungalow and set-up a care package. Final award expected to be in excess of £1million.

Under the new CICA Rules –

Mrs D – Sexually assaulted and raped by acquaintance (2 separate incidents). No award for sexual assault. £7,500 awarded for rape. No award made for consequential loss of earnings, advised to appeal but understandably did not wish to. Accepted £7,500 as awarded.

Children A + B – sexually abused £1,000 each received £7,000 on appeal.

Mr B – 17 years old. Injured in an unprovoked attack that left him unconscious. The first offer was £17,000, we advised rejection, we represented Mr B at the full appeal hearing and the offer was increased to £91,000.

Mrs P – suffered PTSD after her child was abducted, raped and murdered. She was awarded £175,000.

The firm has 5 Partners specialising in personal injury cases. Simon John has over 35 years' experience of Criminal Injury Claims and is described as 'a leading light' and 'outstanding' by *Chambers Guide to the Legal Profession*. Chambers research describes Cunningham John as having:–

- 'Strength in-depth and expertise'
- 'terrific commitment'
- 'big players'
- 'head and shoulders above the rest in the region'

FREEPHONE 0800 616 299
Out of hours number 01842 752409

Address: Cunningham John and Co
Fairstead House
7 Bury Road
Thetford
Norfolk
IP24 3PL
Telephone: 01842 752401
Fax: 01842 753555
E-Mail: postmaster@cunningham-john.co.uk
Website: www.cunningham-john.co.uk – for a free online assessment

Please contact Simon John

You can also contact Cunningham John at:–

Address: Cunningham John and Co
Manchester House
113 Northgate Road
Bury St Edmunds
Suffolk
IP24 3PL
Telephone: 01284 761233
Fax: 01284 702225

Address: Cunningham John and Co
1 Norwich Road
Watton
Norfolk
IP25 6DA
Telephone: 01953 881994
Fax: 01953 883746

Fair compensation is no accident!!

England: East Midlands and Nottinghamshire

Barratt Goff and Tomlinson
'Barratt Goff and Tomlinson a well organised and "forceful" exclusively personal injury practice who move things along smartly and make life difficult for defendants' - *Chambers Guide to Legal Profession 1998–1999.*

Barratt Goff and Tomlinson is a specialist firm dealing only in personal injury and clinical negligence claims. The firm has a national reputation for dealing with in claims of the utmost severity and it is our aim to build upon this reputation. We have a particular interest in criminal injuries compensation claims – particularly for those receiving head injuries and serious physical injuries.

In 1995, the firm relocated to its present offices to allow for expansion and to provide a more pleasant working environment. The offices were specifically designed with provision for disabled access, toilet facilities in the firm's recognition and commitment to disabled people.

Address: Barratt Goff and Tomlinson
The Old Dairy
67a Melton Road
West Brigford
Nottingham
Nottinghamshire
NG2 6EN
Telephone: 0115 981 5115
Fax: 0115 981 9409
E-Mail: mail@bgtsolicitors.co.uk
Website: www.bgtsolicitors.co.uk

Please contact Edward Myers

Edward Myers recently successfully challenged the Criminal Injuries Compensation Authority's refusal to provide the information on which they based their decision to refuse criminal injuries compensation to a brain injured young man. As a result of this landmark case the CICA have had to revise their procedures – and provide much more information relating to the reasons for any decision to refuse.

Solicitors at Barratt Goff & Tomlinson have been involved in a variety of high profile cases including:

- Marchioness Disaster
- Ramsgate Ferry
- Kegworth Air Disaster
- currently representing some very seriously injured victims of the Soho pub bombing
- Sahara coach crash
- Ladbroke Grove/Paddington rail crash

We have had frequent recommendations in *The Legal 500, Chambers' Guide to the Legal Profession* and *Legal Experts*.

England: Hull

Stamp Jackson and Procter
Stamp Jackson and Procter have a long history of involvement with the former CICB and its replacement the CICA. The personal injury team is headed by one of the region's few Medical Negligence Panel Members, Mr Simon Ramshaw. There are also many members of the Law Society's Personal Injury Panel. Stamp Jackson and Procter are also members of the Association of Victims of Medical Accidents and the Association of Personal Injury Lawyers.

Other Areas of Expertise –

- Trusts – to administer and mange trusts on behalf of clients who have been awarded damages by the CICA
- Experience of dealing with sexual abuse cases
- Experience of dealing with severe head injury cases
- Child abuse cases
- Experience in attending full CICB/CICA appeal hearings on behalf of clients
- More than 10 years' experience of dealing with and pursuing claims through the entire CICB/CICA procedure

- Free initial interview at home or hospital if necessary
- Legal Help Scheme (Green Form Advice) is available
- 'No win, no fee' policy undertaken

Foreign languages spoken – French, Spanish and German

FREEPHONE 0800 328 8923

Address: Stamp Jackson and Procter
5 Parliament Street
Hull
Humberside
HU1 2AZ
Telephone: 01482 324591
Fax: 01482 224048
E-Mail: msl@sjp.demon.co.uk

Please contact Mark Slade or Simon Ramshaw

Stamp Jackson and Procter currently have an active caseload of criminal injury cases of approximately 100 files. We also have a number of maximum severity cases some of which are continuing under the 1990 Scheme with the CICB. Under the CICA Scheme we have a broad spectrum of cases ranging from minor injuries to permanent injury type cases. Here are some recent examples –

Mr L was assaulted by a neighbour, suffering severe head injuries. An initial award was rejected and the matter is now proceeding to an appeal hearing. Stamp Jackson and Procter have obtained medical evidence, employment evidence and psychological evidence in support.

Mr W was assaulted by an unknown assailant and left in the street with a broken ankle. After initially rejecting the claim we successfully appealed and were successful in securing an award for the client.

Miss F was stalked and assaulted by an ex-boyfriend. She suffered nasty injuries to her face and teeth together with psychological problems. After rejecting the initial award of £1,500 we appealed on behalf of the client and successfully increased the award to £8,000.

Miss C was injured when a landlord of a pub let off an emergency flare in his pub. The flare hit the client in her face and she lost the sight of one eye. Stamp Jackson and Procter successfully ran a civil claim and the CICB claim together in order to ensure the client was properly compensated. This case was reported in Current Law.

England: The South West, Plymouth and Taunton

Wolferstans
Wolferstans has many years experience in dealing with claims for Criminal Injuries Compensation. It has one of the largest Personal Injury Claimant Departments in the South West as well as members of the Law Society Personal Injury Panel. Further it has a team of 4 Solicitors dedicated to Clinical Negligence work, one of whom is a Panel Member of the Law Society Clinical Negligence Specialist Panel as well as being an Assessor for that Panel. The firm's involvement in these areas includes being on the National Headway Approved Solicitors List and in the Directory of Personal Injury Solicitors operated by the Spinal Injuries

Association and the AVMA Solicitors Referral Panel. We also have members of the Association of Personal Injury Lawyers.

In addition we are on the Panel of Solicitors of the British Motorcycling Federation and have a specialist unit at our Taunton Office dealing with such claims.

Our involvement in these areas is hands on, with members actively being involved in local Headway branches. For those clients who have been unfortunate enough to lose mental capacity as a result of serious injury we have the benefit of a partner who is a Panel Receiver on the Court of Protection's Receivers Panel who currently has about 30 active Court of Protection files in about 18 of which she is the Receiver.

Wolferstans apart from providing top quality across the board skill and experience in Personal Injury, Clinical Negligence and Criminal Injuries work also specialises in:–

- experience in dealing with catastrophic injuries and co-ordinating rehabilitation in the areas of Criminal Injury, Personal Injury and Clinical Negligence
- extensive experience in dealing with fatal cases
- experience in dealing with industrial accident and occupational illness cases
- experience in sex abuse work

Address: **Wolferstans Solicitors**
Deptford Chambers
60-64 North Hill
Plymouth
PL4 8EP
Telephone: **01752 663295**
Fax: **01752 672021**
E-Mail: **info@wolferstans.com**
Website: **www.wolferstans.com**

Wolferstans Solicitors
Level 4, East Reach House
East Reach
Taunton
TA1 3EN
Telephone: **01822 350650**
Fax: **01823 354724**

Please contact Andrew Warlow at our Plymouth Office and Michael Cummings at our Taunton Office
We are a firm that has the benefit of the Legal Services Commission Franchise in the areas of Clinical Negligence and Personal Injury. Furthermore we operate many 'no win, no fee' cases.

Although we have substantial departments with all the benefits that provides in ensuring full, consistent and active support in producing the best outcomes for our clients we pride ourselves on being approachable and are happy to make home or hospital visits as appropriate. We treat our clients as individuals and will tailor our approach to suit their particular needs. This is illustrated by the fact that the experts we use are carefully selected to ensure that the best advice is obtained, even if this means instructing someone from well outside our region.

Our offices are wheelchair accessible

We are currently dealing with over 30 Criminal Injury claims. These vary in scale and nature. Examples include:-

Mr A a self employed landscape gardener waiting for a taxi to take him home after a wedding reception was stabbed repeatedly, with tendons to his fingers being severed. An initial offer from the CICA was appealed and an award of about three times the amount of the original offer was made.

Mr B was assaulted by a night club bouncer and suffered a fracture to his jaw and a loss of a number of teeth. An award was secured in the region of £5,000.

Mr C an apprentice, was attacked and suffered severe head injuries that have left him needing a substantial measure of support for the rest of his life. After interim payments had been received a final award of over £1.6 million was made. We are continuing to assist in the care of this young man in providing advice and assistance through the Partner who is a Panel Receiver.

Ms D suffered injury to her knee when a vehicle was driven into her after a degree of provocation. Application was made to the CICA who rejected the claim on the basis that the incident was not a crime of violence. A Review was applied for and rejected and an Appeal was also rejected following which a civil action was proceeded with and a settlement of the liability issue agreed with insurers on an 80:20 basis in our client's favour.

Mr E an elderly gentleman, was assaulted and suffered serious head injury. A prosecution of the assailant was discontinued by the Crown Prosecution Service. An application for compensation to the CICA was initially rejected. On Review it was accepted and an award made of £16,125. This award is currently being Appealed, an interim payment having been secured.

England: South West

Slee Blackwell

Slee Blackwell's Personal Injury Team has extensive experience in pursuing compensation claims, including a proven track record in criminal compensation work.

The Department is headed by Partner, Lee Dawkins, who is a member of the Association of Personal Injury Lawyers and Chair of the North Devon branch of Headway.

Our expertise includes –

- experience in dealing with sexual assault and child abuse claims
- experience in claims worth from £1,000 up to £1,000,000
- specialist knowledge and support of head injuries
- full support provided by other Departments in advising on any queries arising out of any claim, i.e. Independent Financial Advisor, welfare benefits and highly experienced Will and Probate team
- experience in dealing with domestic violence.

A full range of funding options offered including our popular 'no win, no fee' scheme.

> **Address: Slee Blackwell Solicitors**
> **31 Queen Street**
> **Exeter**
> **South Devon**
> **EX4 3SR**
> **Telephone: 01392 213000**
> **Fax: 01392 494773**
> **E-Mail: sleeexeter@sosi.net**
> **Website: www.sb.Law.co.uk**

The bulk of Slee Blackwell's criminal injury claims are assaults giving rise to compensation of approximately £1,000 to £5,000. We therefore have a particular experience in dealing with the typical difficulties that arise in assault cases, including allegations of provocation. Slee Blackwell also has experience in more severe and complex claims such as:–

Ms C – Sexual Assault/Child Abuse. After a successful appeal to the CICA Appeals Panel Ms C was awarded £20,000.

Mr G – Assault having been attacked by being hit in the eye with a coin. Awarded £10,500

Ms M – Sexual Assault/Child Abuse. After a successful appeal to the CICA Appeals Panel Ms M was awarded £50,000.

We also have branches at –

Address: Slee Blackwell Solicitors
1 South Street
South Molton
North Devon
EX36 4AH
Telephone: 01769 573771
Fax: 01769 574207
E-Mail: sleem@sosi.net
Website: www.sb.Law.co.uk

Address: Slee Blackwell Solicitors
10 Cross Street
Barnstaple
North Devon
EX31 1BA
Telephone: 01271 372128
Fax: 01271 344885
E-Mail: sleeblac@sosi.net
Website: www.sb.Law.co.uk

Address: Slee Blackwell Solicitors
12 Mill Street
Bideford
North Devon
EX39 2JT
Telephone: 01237 425225
Fax: 01237 425985
E-Mail: bideford@sleeblackwell.co.uk
Website: www.sb.Law.co.uk

Address: Slee Blackweli Solicitors
2 South Street
Braunton
North Devon
EX33 2AA
Telephone: 01271 812019
Fax: 01271 814204
E-Mail: info@sleeblackwell.co.uk
Website: www.sb.Law.co.uk

England: Bristol

Metcalfes

At Metcalfes our specialist lawyers can advise on all aspects of personal injury claims including claims for compensation as a result of acts of violent crime.

We offer a free interview service to assess and advise those who have been injured and visits can be arranged at home or hospital if required.

Distance is no object in Metcalfes' wish to offer clients the best of our experience and expertise.

Metcalfes has several Members of the Law Society's Injury Personal Injury Panel and has experts able to deal with every variety of injury claim including head injuries and spinal cord injuries. Whether the claim is large or small, all our clients receive the same care and attention.

> **Address: Metcalfes**
> **46–48 Queen Square**
> **Bristol**
> **BS1 4LY**
> **Telephone: 0117 9290451**
> **Fax: 0117 9299551**
> **E-Mail: hfalconer@metcalfes.co.uk**
>
> **Please contact Helen Falconer**

An injury may affect a person's life in many ways and our experience enables us to provide more than just legal advice.

A sample of the work we have undertaken:–

Mr G was a restaurant owner who was attacked by intruders when he was locking up his premises for the night. He was hit over the head with an iron bar and sustained long-term head injuries. His business got into difficulties and he had to consider retraining for alternative employment. His case was taken to a hearing and he was awarded £95,000 net of repayable state benefits.

Mr W was attacked in a pub and was hit in the face with a beer glass, resulting in facial lacerations. He was awarded £3,500

Ms T was sexually assaulted as a minor. The claim was bought several years later and she was awarded £6,600 for the resultant psychological trauma.

Mr B was assaulted with an iron bar, resulting in a minor head injury causing concentration problems and difficulties with short term memory. His symptoms were exacerbated by a subsequent road traffic accident. Damages were awarded in the sum of £4,000.

England: Portsmouth, Southampton and London

Blake Lapthorn
We also have an office in Southampton doing personal injury work.
Blake Lapthorn has over 15 years expertise in criminal injury compensation work. Our specialist and expert team of Personal Injury Lawyers also handles a full range of claims from childhood sexual abuse to road traffic. Blake Lapthorn has 6 members of the Law Society's

Personal Injury Panel and a member of their Medical Negligence Panel. We have a large membership of the Association of Personal Injury Lawyers and a member of the Association of Child Abuse Lawyers.

Other areas of legal expertise include –

- many years' experience in successfully dealing with the CICB and CICA
- an extensive experience of head and spinal injury claims – we are members of the Headway Panel and Spinal Injuries Association
- successful experience in dealing with sexual assault
- successful experience of dealing with child abuse
- successful experience in pursuing claims through the full CICA procedure and success at Appeal Hearings
- ability and willingness to undertake all types of claims ranging from minor injuries to those of maximum severity
- Blake Lapthorn also has experience in wrongful injury claims against the Police, bullying claims against schools, assault claims against individuals and developing expertise in human rights work
- We are a firm recognised by the Legal Aid Board Panel (Legal Services Commission) endorsed to undertake Personal and Medical Injury claims
- We operate a 'no win, no fee' policy
- We can make home or hospital visits when required

All members of Blake Lapthorn have an active and strong commitment to securing justice for all our clients and the pursuit of equal opportunity for citizens and human rights. Within our team, Paul Fretwell is a Member of the Association of Child Abuse Lawyers and also has a strong commitment to human rights and working with matters relating to the Human Rights Act.

Our offices are designed for disability comfort and access.

Address: Blake Lapthorn
Harbour Court
Compass Road
North Harbour
Portsmouth
Hampshire
PO6 4ST
Telephone: 02392 221122
Fax: 02392 221123
E-Mail: PAFretwell@blakelapthorn.co.uk
Website: www.blakelapthorn.co.uk

Please contact Paul Fretwell

Any people living in the London area wishing to secure expert assistance please contact Paul Fretwell directly at Portsmouth and he will arrange a meeting for convenience at the London office.

At any time, Blake Lapthorn has a caseload of approximately 30 criminal injury cases. Our experience in this field runs from less serious injuries through to serious head injuries resulting in permanent brain damage. Here are a few examples –

Mr A was a doorman assaulted outside a public house. He sustained a minor head injury, making an excellent recovery apart from some on-going anxiety. An initial inadequate award was rejected and pursued through review to a full appeal hearing where the award was trebled.

Mr B a public house landlord, was assaulted and sustained jaw fractures and other minor orthopaedic injuries. Made a reasonable recovery but some on-going pain and restriction and psychological trauma. Suffered some on-going loss of earnings and pension. Awarded £94,000 at appeal hearing.

Mr C a childhood victim of the notorious Frank Beck in Leicestershire. Criminal injury award only £8,000 but Leicestershire County Council were successfully pursued in negligence, the case settling just before trial for £150,000.

Mr D now aged 56, savagely beaten and thrown through window in a nasty unprovoked attack. Left with years after, on-going injuries of dizziness, ear problems, elbow and back pain and very serious depression and trauma. Unable to work since in his self employed business and requires on-going therapy, support and assistance from family and others. After appeal at a CICA hearing he was awarded £350,000, a fair reflection of his suffering and loss.

> Address: **Blake Lapthorn**
> **Kings Court**
> **21 Brunswick Place**
> **Southampton**
> **Hampshire**
> **SO15 2AQ**
> Telephone: **02380 631823**
> Fax: **02380 226294**
> E-Mail: **Swheadon@blakelapthorn.co.uk**
> Website: **www.blakelapthorn.co.uk**

England: London

Prince Evans
Prince Evans is a broad-based West London firm with a strong specialism in personal injury work. The Partner in charge of the Personal Injury Department, Bryan Neill, is an acknowledged leader in the field of catastrophic injury claims including spinal and brain injuries (see *Legal 500* 'Who's Who In The Law' and *Chambers Guide To The Legal Profession* – 'Leaders In Their Field'). These include injuries caused by criminal assault, gunshot wounds etc.

Prince Evans has developed a national reputation for cases involving compensation claims for injuries at all levels, obtaining record high damages for clients.

Prince Evans is also able to offer advice to clients on post-receipt investment of damages and protection of funds, and can offer comprehensive tax and financial planning advice.

Bryan Neill is a member of the Spinal Injuries Association Solicitors Panel, Headway Solicitors Panel, Law Society Personal Injury Panel, Association of Personal Injury Lawyers, Association of Trial Lawyers of America, Australian Plaintiff Lawyers Association and the International Medical Society of Paraplegia.

Directory

- The Personal Injury Team handles hundreds of successful damages claims for clients each year.
- Criminal Injury Compensation Authority claims are handled on a 'no win, no fee' basis
- Prince Evans' offices are fully wheelchair accessible with disabled facilities

> **Address: Prince Evans**
> **77 Uxbridge Road**
> **Ealing**
> **London**
> **W5 5ST**
> **Telephone: 020 8567 2001**
> **Fax: 020 8579 0191**
> **E-Mail: bryanneill@prince-evans.co.uk**
> **Website: prince-evans.co.uk**

All telephone enquires please ask for Bryan Neill or Bob Connelly

Here are some examples of recent CICB and CICA awards:–

Mrs B – dragged behind a car by handbag snatchers. Spinal injury. Compensation award £1,114,658

Mr A – thrown from a pedestrian walkway. Back and head injuries. Awarded Damages £155,850

Mr M – victim of shooting. Spinal injury. Awarded damages £1,572,877

Mr V – shot. Application rejected because of past convictions and alleged involvement with assailants. Following appeal hearing claim accepted as suitable for damages to be awarded.

Prince Evans represents clients throughout the United Kingdom, and makes home and hospital visits as necessary

England and Wales: Reading and Thames Valley

Field Seymour Parkes
Field Seymour Parkes has many years' experience in dealing with Criminal Injuries Compensation claims, and a long history of handling all types of personal injury claims ranging from the minor to the catastrophic arising from road traffic accidents, accidents at work, industrial diseases, and other causes. Such claims are dealt with by members of the Private Client Litigation Team whose personnel include members of the Law Society's Personal Injury Panel and the Association of Personal Injury Lawyers.

Field Seymour Parkes is included in the Headway (the Brain Injury Association) Personal Injury Solicitors List and we have extensive experience of head injury claims and a close and active association with the local branch of Headway, Headway Thames Valley, with members of the firm holding the offices of President, Vice-President and Secretary of the branch.

In cases where compensation is recovered but the client's affairs need to be managed by a Receiver under the supervision of the Court of Protection we have a wealth of experience and members of the firm are Panel Receivers of the Court of Protection.

Following withdrawal of public funding for personal injury claims we are pleased to advise, and where appropriate, undertake work on a conditional fee basis.

> **Address: Field Seymour Parkes Solicitors**
> **The Old Coronors Court**
> **No. 1 London Street**
> **Reading**
> **Berks**
> **RG1 4QW**
> **Telephone: 0118 951 6200**
> **Fax: 0118 950 2704**
> **E-Mail: mailto:enquiry@fsp-law.com**
> **Website: www.yoursolicitors.com**
>
> **Please contact: Richard Gilby**

We are happy to advise and assist with all levels of claims. Recent Criminal Injury Compensation claims have included:–

Mr A – A fight took place in a public house carpark. The assailant quickly gained the advantage and Mr A made no attempt to defend himself and indicated he had had enough. Notwithstanding this the assailant hit Mr A's head on the ground repeatedly, causing a severe head injury, permanent brain damage and physical disabilities. The application for Criminal Injuries Compensation was refused on the grounds that Mr A was a voluntary participant in a fight and an oral hearing was requested at which we represented Mr A, resulting in the Authority agreeing to make an award of 50% of what Mr A would have been entitled to but for his contributory fault.

Mr B – A hostile atmosphere developed between a group of young people of which Mr B was one and another group, one of whom was the assailant, in a local nightclub. When the nightclub closed a fight broke out in the carpark of the club between members of the two groups, in which Mr B was involved. Subsequently on departing from the scene the assailant deliberately drove his motor car into the group, causing serious injury to Mr B. Despite the Authority alleging Mr B was a voluntary participant in a fight it was persuaded to offer a substantial award of £95,000 representing two-thirds of what Mr B would have been entitled to but for his contributory fault following the submission of expert evidence.

Mrs C – Mrs C was very seriously injured in an assault by her former boyfriend and was left for dead. Fortunately she was found and although in a coma for some weeks, did return to full consciousness. Although her brain injury was 'severe' it was not in the most serious category and some reasonable cognitive functions remain. She will remain in long term nursing care. Her case was settled by CICA in the sum of £72,500, this being approved by the Court of Protection.

England: Essex

Sternberg Reed Taylor and Gill

Victims are frequently let down by the poor quality of advice they receive or by their solicitors' failure to recognise the extent of the injury and advocate this on behalf of their client. At Sternberg Reed Taylor and Gill, one Partner, Angela Nunn, has particular experience of dealing with the majority of CICA cases from inception to the appeals stage, if necessary. Claims vary according to case from minor injuries to a severe head injury and awards ranging from the minimum of £1,000 to the maximum payable of £500,000 under the new tariff scheme.

Directory

Types of cases covered –

- assault
- robbery
- child abuse – where claimants although children will continue to be most physically and emotionally damaged throughout their lives
- child physical abuse and neglect
- indecent assault
- grievous bodily harm
- murder
- post traumatic stress disorder

Address: Sternberg Reed Taylor & Gill
Focal House
12–18 Station Parade
Barking
Essex
Telephone: 020 8591 3366
Fax: 020 8594 4606
E-Mail: angela.nunn@sternberg-reed.co.uk

Please contact Angela Nunn

We believe all CICA work should be dealt with only by specialists. Victims need competent, knowledgeable and strong advocates to act on their behalf to get them through the incredibly adversarial and often distressingly long process under the CICA.

Sample Case Histories

Mr A was an asylum seeker who was the victim of a racially motivated attack. He lost an eye in the unprovoked assault. Due to his status and to his fear of the police he failed to comply with the reporting requirements of the CICA. Nevertheless, by pursuing rigorously the review and appeal process, this appeal was successful and we were able to obtain £12,500 as an expression of sympathy for his injuries.

Ms B was a victim of rape at the age of 17. Her assailant fled the country and could not be prosecuted by the police. Her original application for compensation (made elsewhere) was rejected. We pursued the appeal on her behalf and her compelling and moving statements and evidence led to an award of £13,000 and, more importantly, recognition for her that she was a victim, which recognition had been denied to her by the failure of the criminal process.

Ms C was a canteen assistant in Canary Wharf when a bomb explosion occurred before she had been evacuated from the building. She suffered post traumatic stress disorder and was originally awarded a paltry sum when her CICA application was pursued. A successful appeal by ourselves led to an award of £64,000 being made to reflect the fact that she had been unable to return to work following the injury despite having an excellent previous working history.

Mr D was assaulted in a pub and suffered severe injuries to his arm that rendered that arm in a largely useless state and left him with significant psychological problems. He was refused compensation from the CICB on the basis that he had been equally to blame for the incident. His appeal was successful and he received over £160,000 in compensation that reflected the severity of his injury, his need for care and support and his past and future loss of wages. His comment was that the award changed his life although he still had a long way to go to get over the incident.

Mrs E was a woman in her fifties who had been the victim of persistent sexual abuse from a relative many years previously. Her application for compensation that had been put forward by Victim Support had been rejected, and on review through our efforts she was awarded the maximum award of £17,500.

Master F and Miss G were children who were sexually abused by a family friend. They were awarded £4,000 apiece for their injuries.

England: Kent

T G Baynes
We have 25 years' experience in working successfully with criminal compensation work and long established specialist personal injury and clinical negligence departments

T G Baynes believes many prospective claimants to the CICA get a very poor deal. We have a long established specialist personal injury and clinical negligence departments with over 20 years experience. During that time we have recovered many large awards of damages, some exceeding £1million.

Over the years T G Baynes has pursued the best outcome for every client within the law and exercising a wide degree of legal and practical expertise. Past awards from the CICA/CICB include –

- PTSD £30,500
- shooting of arm and PTSD £185,000
- murder resulting in dependency claim £90,000

FREEPHONE 0800 220 382

Address: **T G Baynes**
Baynes House
102a Station Road
Sidcup
Kent
DA15 7ER
Telephone: **020 8269 8000**
Fax: **020 8302 0157**

Please contact 020 8269 8025 / 8037

Currently, we are working to secure a fair and just award in a case involving severe brain damage with PTSD and physical injuries where the client was involved in an argument outside a pub, threatened with a hammer, turned and ran into the path of a bus. Initially, the Board rejected the claim. The client wished to give up. We encouraged him to appeal and after a hearing the Board accepted 30% liability. We have now obtained a full range of reports describing his psychiatric, neurological and psycho-neurological injuries and valuing the cost of his care and are awaiting a hearing for the claim to be assessed.

Directory

England: Surrey and South London

McMillan Williams

McMillan Williams are specialists in personal injury and clinical and medical negligence cases including Criminal Injuries Compensation cases. Our firm has five offices based in South London and Surrey. We have one member of the Law Society Clinical Negligence Panel, and one member of the Association of Victims of Medical Accidents. McMillan Williams also has two Partners who sit on The Law Society Legal Services Funding Committee.

McMillan Williams undertakes a variety of Personal Injury type Litigation, this includes as stated CICA cases, Clinical Negligence and Personal Injury. In particular, our firm specialises in catastrophic injuries, some involving people with brain damage.

This can include babies suffering from cerebral palsy, individuals who are paralysed, children involved in road traffic accidents who suffer personality problems, difficulties at school and general dysfunction within the family.

McMillan Williams also undertakes Clinical Negligence claims for people who have been damaged because of medical accidents, such as being given the wrong prescriptions causing brain damage and other problems.

McMillan Williams is also a member of Headway – who deal with head injury claims
Royal Society of Medicine
Road Peace – an organisation campaigning about road traffic issues

For emergency help the out of hours care Helpline and police station contact number is 020 8660 3383

> Address: McMillan Williams
> 35 Malcolm Road
> Coulsdon
> Surrey
> CR5 2DB
> Telephone: 020 8668 4131
> Fax: 020 8660 4289
> E-Mail: mcmillanw@btinternet.com
>
> Please contact Colum J Smith

Other areas of legal experience include –
- experience in dealing with sexual abuse
- experience in dealing with child abuse
- experience in dealing with fatalities
- experience in pursuing claims through the full CICA procedure
- successfully attending many hearings where liability is disputed by the CICA
- our firm undertakes general clinical negligence dealing with items such as failure to diagnose cancer, incorrect treatment at Accident and Emergency Departments and other places
- extensive experience of legal aid
- specialism in dealing with people with pre-existing medical problems prior to injury – a factor the CICA always take into account

We operate a 'no win, no fee' undertaking

McMillan Williams is used to coming to see people at home to deal with their problems and takes an overall approach to each case we take on.

We make hospital visits.

Our offices are furnished for disability access and comfort.

We offer an illustration of our commitment to our clients and complexity of CICA work:–

Mr A was assaulted whilst driving a London bus and sustained a serious eye injury resulting in permanent double vision and inability to work again. The CICA offered an award of approximately £20,000; at the final hearing an award was achieved of £120,000. Evidence was collected from not only Mr A and his work colleagues who proved how much he could have earned had he been employed by new bus employers who used new contracts and levels of pay, had Mr A been well enough to work.

McMillan Williams has a support team dealing with matters such as, housing, employment, re-training, admission to brain injury units, contact with MPs, repossession proceedings and all other matters which tend to fall and unduly burden people who are concentrating on dealing with long-term illness or disability.

Address: McMillan Williams
1 Heath Road
Thornton Heath
Surrey
CR7 8NF
Telephone: 020 8653 8844
Fax: 020 8771 7036

Address: McMillan Williams
9 Beddington Gardens
Wallington
Surrey
SM6 0HU
Telephone: 020 8669 4962
Fax: 020 8773 2016

Address: McMillan Williams
19-23 Shrubbery Road
Streatham
London
SW16 2AS
Telephone: 020 8769 1113
Fax: 020 8677 3878

Address: McMillan Williams
56–58 Central Parade
New Addington
Croydon
Surrey
CR0 0JD
Telephone: 01689 848311
Fax: 01689 846946
E-Mail: mcmillanwilliams@ic24.net
Website: www.mcmillan-williams.co.uk

Directory

Attwater and Leill
We have been recovering damages for injured victims for over 20 years. During this time we have developed a specialist department with a team of 12 fee earners. We are dedicated to the pursuit of appropriate levels of compensation for our clients. We take pride in dealing with matters in a sensitive and caring way and our aim is to make the whole process as stress free as possible.

The department is headed by David Kerry, a Partner who is also a member of The Law Society's Personal Injury Panel and Clinical Negligence Panel. David Kerry is also a member of the Headway Panel. We have two further members of The Law Society's Personal Injury Panel and all of the team are members of the Association of Personal Injury Lawyers. We are able to take on all types of claims from minor injuries to those of maximum severity.

Our legal expertise includes the following –

- experience of the full CICA procedure
- experience in dealing with sexual assault
- experience in dealing with child abuse caused by family members and third parties
- experience of difficulties that can arise if the claimant has previous convictions.

We have disabled facilities.

We can offer different types of funding arrangements including 'no win, no fee'.

In appropriate circumstances we can arrange home and hospital visits.

> **Address: Attwater and Leill**
> **Rothwell House**
> **West Square**
> **The High**
> **Harlow**
> **Essex**
> **CM20 1LQ**
> Telephone: 01279 454454
> Website: www.attwaterleill.co.uk

Post–Traumatic Stress Disorder

Scotland: Aberdeen

Centre for Trauma Research at The Royal Cornhill Hospital
The Aberdeen Centre for Trauma Research is not a clinical facility; its primary purpose is to conduct high quality research and to provide training in trauma care. It is however linked to the Traumatic Stress Clinic, also sited on the grounds of the Royal Cornhill Hospital, Aberdeen. The Centre aims to produce research findings which will improve patient care, and the Clinic generates ideas for research.

The staff are:
Professor David A. Alexander (Director), Dr Susan Klein (Research Co-ordinator), Dr Alastair M. Hull (Specialist Registrar in Psychiatry/Lecturer in Mental Health), Dr June Semper (Research Psychologist), and Staff Nurse Linda Bowes.

    Contact: Professor David A. Alexander
    Title: Director
    Address: Centre for Trauma Research
          Bennachie
          Royal Cornhill Hospital
          Aberdeen
          AB25 2ZH
    Telephone: + 44 (0) 1224 681818
    Fax: + 44 (0) 1224 403642
    E-Mail: mental.health.FH@abdn.ac.uk

Brief Biographical Statement
Professor Alexander is Professor of Mental Health at the Medical School, University of Aberdeen, and Honorary Consultant Clinical Psychologist to the Grampian Health Board. He is Director of the Centre and Consultant in Charge of the Clinic.

He has been involved in a number of major disasters in the UK and abroad, including the Piper Alpha oil platform explosion, the Chinook helicopter crash, the Ufa train crash in Russia, the Estonia ferry sinking and the Nairobi terrorist bombing.

He is Consultant to the Scottish Police and has lectured frequently on trauma at the Scottish Police College, the FBI Academy in Virginia, USA, and at other international institutions.

Areas of Specialism –
- Post--traumatic conditions
- The Clinic only accepts adult referrals (ie those over 18 years of age). Most types of trauma have been encountered; referrals include those who have been victims of industrial, domestic and road traffic accidents, helicopter and offshore oil-related incidents, assaults, hostage taking and military combat.

Services Offered and Catchment Area
Our Clinic is exclusively an out-patient service only and we do not have facilities for in-patient needs.

The service is run by Professor Alexander and Dr Hull and with back-up from a Senior Staff Nurse who has extensive orthopaedic and accident and emergency experience. In addition, trainee psychiatrists are attached to the Clinic for supervision and training.
No particular theoretical model is used for treatment; the primary aim is to help patients by whatever means appear to be the most effective and relevant.

Referral Method and Funding Method
Patients must be referred through medical channels only. Such channels include: general practitioners, trauma surgeons and physicians, the military, and occupational physicians from the emergency services. If the patient is referred to the clinic from outside the catchment area, the Hospital Trust does seek reimbursement from the referring agency.

The Clinic is locked into the National Health Service and does not take private patients.

Directory

Assessment Process and Waiting Time
All patients are assessed thoroughly by clinical interview and, where appropriate, by standardised measures. There is no waiting list; rarely do patients have to wait more than three weeks to be seen.

The Clinic also provides an emergency on-call service to Aberdeen Royal Infirmary and to the emergency services.

The treatment approach is deliberately eclectic; psychotherapy (of various forms) and medication are used conjunctively. Also, attention is paid to the patients' diet, exercise, sleep habits and lifestyle.

There is no average treatment time. So much depends on the nature of the trauma, the patients' medical and psychiatric histories, their age, the severity of any physical injuries and other life stressors with which they may have to contend.

Other Areas of Important Work
In addition to the research activity at the Centre, the team regularly present at national and international meetings. They are committed to the development of high quality teaching materials and other materials relevant for patient care. The Centre is attractive to trainee psychiatrists, medical students and other professionals who seek attachments thereto. It also provides a base for a number of candidates for higher degrees.

Medico–legal Reports
Although such reports do have to be provided, and Professor Alexander does on occasions provide Expert Witness testimony, the provision of such reports is much too time-consuming and commonly leads to unrewarding Court appearances. There is little appetite, therefore, among clinical staff to do any more medico–legal work.

Publications
Selected Bibliography 1999–2001:

Human Reactions To Trauma – Their Features and Management in Prehospital Medicine: *Alexander D. A. (1999):* eds I. Greaves and Porter K. published Arnold London

Dynamic Psychotherapy in Clinical Psychotherapy Medical Students and Practitioners: *Alexander D. A. (2000):* 3rd edition ed H. Maxwell published Whurr London

Psychological Reactions To Trauma: *Alexander D. A. (2000):* in **Manual of Advanced Resuscitation** (new national guidelines of evidenced-based practice) eds I. Greaves, K. Porter and J. Ryan, published Arnold London

Bad News Is Bad News – Let's Not Make It Worse: *Alexander D. A. and Klein S. (2000):* (invited article) **Trauma** 2, 11–18

Failure of Emergency Out-patient appointments To Reduce Admission Rates: *Hull A. M. and Morrison A. (2000):* **Health Bulletin** 58(4): 356 (letter)

Personal Safety and The Abuse of Power in a Scottish NHS: *Alexander D. A., Gray N. M., Klein Hall G. and Kettles A. (2001):* **Health Bulletin** 60, 442–449

Is My Stress Greater Than Yours? A Comparison of Policemen and Firemen: *Alexander D. A. and Walker L. G. (2000):* **International Journal of Police Science and Management** 2, 303–312
The Orthopaedic Surgeon and Post-Traumatic Psychopathology: *Sutherland A. G., Alexander D. A. and Hutchison J. D. (2000):* **Journal of Bone and Joint Surgery** 82, 486–488

Triage In Emergency Psychiatry: *Morrison A., Hull A. M. and Shepherd B. (2000):* in **Psychiatric Bulletin** 24, 261–264

A Ten Year Follow-up Study of The Survivors of the Piper Alpha Oil Platform Disaster July 1988: *Hull A. M., Alexander D. A. and Klein S. (2000):* Abstract 3rd World Conference For The International Society For Traumatic Stress Studies, Melbourne Australia

Ambulance Personnel and Critical Incidents – Impact of accident and emergency work on mental health and emotional well-being: *Alexander D. A. and Klein S. (2000):* **British Journal of Psychiatry** 178, 76–81

Suicide by Patients – A Questionnaire Study and Its Effect on Consultant Psychiatrists in Scotland: *Alexander D. A., Klein S., Gray N. M., Dewar I., and Eagles J. M. (2000):* **British Medical Journal** 320, 1571–1574

Caring for others can seriously damage your health: *Alexander D. A. and Klein S. (2001):* Hospital Medicine 62, 264–267

The Aberdeen Trauma Screening Index – An Instrument To Predict Post-Accident Psychopathology: *Alexander D. A., Klein S., Hutchinson J. D., Simpson J. A., Simpson J. M. and Bell J. S. (in press):* **Psychological Medicine**

Debriefing and Body Recovery – Police in a Civilian Disaster in A Critical Appraisal of Practice, Evidence and Clinical Outcomes: *Alexander D. A. (2001):* eds B. Raphael and J. Watson, Cambridge University

Scotland: West Scotland and Glasgow

Royal Hospital for Sick Children
'Thank you for your e-mails to myself and Dr. B. Perhaps we have not given your book the same level of priority that it has for you, but all the information you require is freely available through the University of Glasgow website (www.gla.ac.uk). There is cetainly no wish on our part to obstruct your work and no intention to be secretive about our service, which is widely used both by colleagues in the NHS and lawyers seeking medico–legal assessment.'

E-Mail reply to author's occasional requests for co-operation from March 1999

Address: **Department of Child and Adolescent Psychiatry**
University of Glasgow
Caledonia House
Royal Hospital for Sick Children
Yorkhill
Glasgow
G3 8SJ
Telephone: **0141 201 0223**
Fax: **0141 201 9261**
E-Mail: **ah3e@clinmed.gla.ac.uk**

Directory

Forth Valley Primary Care NHS Trust

The Trauma Clinic is one of the services provided by the Forth Valley Primary Care NHS Trust and is delivered throughout Forth Valley at locations convenient to the patient, usually their local Health Centre or GP practice premises.
Patients from out with the area are seen in Larbert at the address below:

> Contact: Therese McGoldrick
> Title: Head of Service, Behavioural Psychotherapy
> Address: The Forth Valley Primary Care NHS Trust
> Psychotherapy Service
> No. 2 The Bungalows
> Stirling Road
> Larbert
> FK5 4SD
> Telephone: 01324 574321
> Fax: 01324 555080
> E-Mail: therese.mcgoldrick@fvpc.scot.nhs.uk

Areas of Specialism
- Post traumatic stress disorder
- Traumatic grief
- Body dysmorphic disorder

Services offered and catchment area
We also assess and treat other anxiety related disorders such as obsessive compulsive disorder, panic disorder and phobic disorders.

The catchment area is The Forth Valley area in Central Scotland but referrals are accepted from all over Scotland, if funding is agreed with the referring agency.

Assessment Process and Waiting Time.
Assessment and treatment of those suffering from the above disorders. Appointments for first assessment are given within 4–6 weeks of referral. Assessment is usually carried out by a Behavioural Psychotherapist. The assessment is to determine the nature of the sufferer's symptoms and to explain the nature of the treatment. The treatment offered is usually eye movement desensitisation and reprocessing as our research trial (see end) showed this to be the fastest and most effective treatment. It generally takes between 1 and 4 sessions. Explanatory handouts are given about both the condition and treatment at the initial assessment.

Referral Method and Funding Method
Referrals are through the NHS system, generally GPs and Consulting Psychiatrists. We also get referrals from Occupational Health Services, the Fire Brigade and Prison Services. We are funded by our local NHS Trust and also have locality contracts with General Practitioners.

Who is in the team?
Our service consists of a Consultant Psychiatrist and Behavioural Psychotherapists.

Treatment Offered
Treatment is mainly cognitive behavioural psychotherapy and eye movement desensitisation, although drug treatment can be used in combination if indicated as beneficial to a patient.

Medico–legal Reports
We are experienced in providing medico-legal reports.

Other Important Areas of Our Work
- We have carried out a 3 year research trial funded by the Scottish Office, comparing EMDR with Cognitive Behavioural Psychotherapy in the treatment of Post Traumatic Stress Disorder

- One of our staff is a member of EMDR HAP which is an organization providing voluntary training in treating PTSD in disaster stricken countries, including Bangladesh, Turkey and Northern Ireland

Scotland: South East

Royal Edinburgh Hospital

Contact: Dr Christopher P Freeman MB ChB FRCPsych MPhil
Title: Consultant Psychiatrist in Psychotherapy – Lead Clinician
Address: The Cottage
            Royal Edinburgh Hospital
            Morningside
            Edinburgh
            EH10 5HF
Telephone: 0131 537 6708
Fax: 0131 537 6104
Website: www.rivers.il2.com

Areas of Specialism
Specialist service for people affected by post traumatic stress reactions

Services Offered and Catchment Area
Our service is primarily for sufferers in the South-east of Scotland but we will accept referrals from all over Scotland – and from the North of England.

Referral Method and Funding Method
Referrals are through the NHS system, mainly GPs, or from other agencies such as the Scottish Refugee Council. We are funded mainly by our local NHS Trust but do have other contracts with various emergency services.

Who Is In The Team?
Our service consists of Psychiatrists, Psychologists, Nurse Psychotherapists and Counsellors

Treatment Offered
Treatment mainly involves psychotherapy, although drug treatment can be used in combination. Treatment types involve cognitive behavioural psychotherapy, inter-personal psychotherapy, Eye Movement De-sensitisation and Reprocessing (EMDR) and cognitive analytic psychotherapy.

Medico–legal Reports
We have several members of the team who are experienced in providing medico–legal reports.

Other Important Areas of Our Work
Research – we have recently completed a trial of 'psychological debriefing' and are conducting several trials of drug treatment. We are currently planning a treatment outcome trial for Post Traumatic Stress Disorder.

Publications
We have a number of Rivers Centre publications including:–

- A Trauma Manual
- A Self-Help Practical Guide for Trauma Sufferers
- A Manual for Psychological First Aid

For more details please have a look at our website – thank you!

Scotland: Glasgow and West Scotland

Western Infirmary
We are a new and evolving national health resource that provides a liaison psychiatry service within a teaching hospital. We provide services dealing with deliberate self-harm, a generic liaison service and a service to regional and supra regional specialty services – including services for people affected by violent crime.

> **Contact: Dr Tom Brown**
> **Title: Consultant Liaison Psychiatrist**
> **Address: Western Infirmary**
> **Glasgow**
> **G11 6NT**
> **Telephone: 0141 211 2000**
> **E-Mail: Tom.Brown@glacomen.nhs.scot.uk**

Areas of Specialism –
- Medically unexplained symptoms
- Pain

Services Offered
Assessment and Cognitive Behavioural Therapy

Referral Method and Funding Method
GP and 'within hospital' referrals only

Assessment Process and Waiting Time
2 months

Treatment Offered
Pharmacotherapy and Cognitive Behavioural Therapy

Medico-legal Reports
Yes

Wales: Cardiff

University Hospital of Wales

Contact: Dr Jonathan I. Bisson
Title: Consultant Liaison Psychiatrist
Address: Department of Liaison Psychiatry
    Monmouth House
    University Hospital of Wales
    Heath Park
    Cardiff
    CF14 4XW
Telephone: 029 2074 3940
Fax: 029 2074 3928
E-Mail: BissonJI@Cardiff.ac.uk

Areas of Specialism
Assessment and treatment of individuals involved in traumatic events. Research particularly into predictors of and prevention of PTSD following a traumatic event. Teaching.

Services Offered
The service comprises an outpatient clinic and early intervention team developed in partnership with the local Emergency Planning Unit. A variety of evidence-based treatments are provided by one of the psychiatrists, clinical psychologists or specialist nurse therapists attached to the service.

Our Catchment Area
Our catchment area is Cardiff and the Vale of Glamorgan but referrals are seen from throughout Wales and the South West of England.

Referral Method and Funding Method
Referrals are accepted from General Practitioners arid other health care professionals within Cardiff and the Vale of Glamorgan. Out of area referrals are made by mental health professionals when no local service exists. Funding is through the National Health Service.

Assessment Process and Waiting Time
An assessment is performed by a psychiatrist, clinical psychologist or specialist nurse therapist attached to the clinic using standard assessment measures. The current waiting time is approximately eight months although individuals are often seen earlier if they are able to attend an appointment at relatively short notice.

Treatment Offered
The main treatments offered are cognitive-behavioural treatment, eye movement desensitisation and reprocessing and pharmacotherapy.

Directory

Northern Forensic Mental Health Service For Young People

Contact: Nessa Shell – General Manager
Address: Kolvin Clinic
St Nicholas House
St Nicholas Hospital
Jubilee Road
Newcastle upon Tyne
NE3 3XT
Telephone: 0191 223 2226
Fax: 0191 223 2228
E-Mail: kolvinclinic.org
Website: www.kolvinclinic.org

Catchment Area
National

Out patients
The North East of England

In patients
National

Services Offered
The Northern Forensic Mental Health Service for Young People offers specialist mental health services for mentally disordered young offenders and others requiring similar services. The presence of post traumatic stress within this population is known from our own and international research to be high and that is our clinical experience.

Out patient services are offered at the Kolvin Clinic, Newcastle General Hospital and in-patient services at the 18 bedded Roycroft Clinic, St Nicholas Hospital, Newcastle.

Who is Assessed and Treated?
Children and young people between the ages of 10 and 20 years who present with psychological or psychiatric difficulties and whose behaviour places them in conflict with the law. Post traumatic stress is not an infrequent presentation within what are generally complex, multi-factorial presentations. Wherever possible, we involve families in our assessment and treatment.

Who is in the Team?
The team comprises adolescent forensic psychiatrists, psychologists, (including 2 trained cognitive therapists), an analytical psychotherapist, 2 social workers, teachers and nurses.

Waiting Times
Our patient appointments are usually offered within 6 weeks. In patient admission would vary according to bed availability, severity of symptomatology, likelihood of treatability and severity of risk to self and others. The Roycroft Clinic contains a 4 bed ward specifically for girls.

Assessment and Treatment

Families are encouraged to be involved in the assessment and treatment of patients. Out patient assessments are conducted over 1–4 sessions depending on the nature and extent of the difficulties and external factors such as travelling time to the Clinic. The results of the assessment determine the variety of psychological therapies, analytic psychotherapies, pharmaco-therapies and systemic family therapies.

It is recognised that PTSD takes many forms. If the resulting behavioural manifestations of psychological distress is extreme, (severe self harming behaviour or risk to others), then patients can be admitted to our in patient Clinic which provides a secure environment where treatment can be delivered. Assessment for in patient admissions are done jointly by a Consultant Psychiatrist, Consultant Psychologist and a senior member of the nursing team.

Treatment consists of helping the young person and their family to understand and manage their symptoms and assisting them to think about what has happened so they are not overwhelmed by intolerable thoughts and feelings.

Referral Method

- Referrals are welcome from:
- General Practitioners
- Consultant Psychiatrists and Psychologists
- Other NHS professionals and agencies
- Courts, prisons and secure training centres
- Social services
- Probation services
- Youth Offender Teams
- Solicitors – for assessment

The patient's General Practitioner should be aware of the referral and agree that it is appropriate. For all in patients a preliminary assessment is always carried out by appropriate members of our multi disciplinary team. In patient referrals are initiated most effectively through a call to our senior administrator who will post or fax a referral protocol.

Method of Funding

Health Authority agreement will be required prior to admission of in patients to the Roycroft Clinic. It is also required for out patient referrals to the Kolvin Clinic and for all clients who are not within our normal catchment/contractual area, i.e. the North East of England.

England: London

Contact: Dr Gillian Clare Mezey
Title: Consultant Psychiatrist MB BS FRCPsych
     Senior Lecturer in Forensic Psychiatry
Address: Department of Forensic Psychiatry
     St George's Hospital Medical School
     Jenner Wing
     Cranmer Terrace
     London
     SW17 0RE
Telephone: 020 8725 5568

Service Address: Traumatic Stress Clinic
Clare House
St George's Hospital
Blackshaw Road
London
SW17 ORE
Service Address: 020 8725 0355
Telephone: 020 8725 5568
Fax: 020 8725 2475
E-Mail: gmezey@sghms.ac.uk

Areas of Specialism
- Treatment of Post Traumatic Stress Disorder
- Domestic Violence and Sexual Assault
- Academic writing and research
- Teaching in Post Traumatic Stress Disorder – affecting specialist groups

Services Offered and Catchment Area
Referrals accepted from the national catchment area able to provide individual psychological work, assessments and treatments within context of multidisciplinary team.

Referral Method and Funding Method
GP Practices

Assessment Process and Waiting Time
4–6 weeks for weeks for an assessment with a Clinician lasting about two hours, involving clinical interview and questionnaires to complete.

Treatment Offered
- Cognitive Behavioural Therapy
- EMDR
- Individual Treatment for Adults

Medico–legal Reports
Civil medico–legal reports for Plaintiff and Defendant

Publications – abbreviated list

Male Victims of Sexual Assault, *Mezey G. C. + King M. B. (eds)*, Oxford University Press, 2000, 2nd edition

Psychological Trauma: A Developmental Approach, *Black D., Harris-Hendricks J., Mezey G. C., Newman M. (eds)*, Gaskell Press, London, 1996

Violence Against Women, *Bewley S., Friend J., Mezey G. (eds)*, RCOG Press, London, 1997

Chapters in books – abbreviated list

Violence and Women, *Mezey G. C. + Stanko E.,* in **Planning Mental Health Services for Women: A multi-professional Handbook,** Abel K., Buscewicz M., Johnson S. + Staples E. (eds), Routledge, London 1996

An Exploration of Gender Issues in Forensic Psychiatry: Mad, Bad and Dangerous to Know, *Bartlett A. + Mezey G. C.,* in **Special Women,** Hemingway C. (ed), Avebury Press, Aldershot, 1996

Psychological Responses to Inter-personal Violence, *Mezey G. C. + Kaplan T.,* in **Psychological Trauma: A Developmental Approach,** Black D., Harris-Hendricks J., Mezey G. C. + Newman M. (eds), Gaskell Press, London, 1996

Peer-reviewed publications – abbreviated

The Psychological, Behavioural and Emotional Impact of Surviving an Abusive Relationship, *Scott-Gliba E., Minne C. + Mezey G. C.,* J. Forensic Psychiatry, 1995; 6(2): 343–358

Victims and Perpetrators of Child Sexual Abuse, *Hilton M. R. and Mezey G. C.,* **British Journal of Psychiatry,** 1996;169:408-415

Victims of Violence and the General Practitioner, *Mezey G. C., King M., and MacClintock T.,* **British Journal of General Practice,** February 1998, pp 906–908

Recent presentations and lectures – abbreviated

'Developing Women's Services – Research and Training Needs'. Invited speaker at HSPSCB/WISH Joint Seminar, The Future of Women's Secure Psychiatric Services, 8 and 9 May 1997

'Women Who Kill: Characteristics and Legal Outcomes'. XXIII International Congress on Law and Mental Health, 28 June – 3 July, 1998, Paris, France

Other Work Related To Violence Against Women – abbreviated

Report of Mission into the Treatment of Muslim Women in the Former Yugoslavia, *Warburton A., Mezey G. C. contributing author,* Copenhagen, February 1993

Policy Statement on Rape, *Mezey G. C.,* Chair of Working Party for Royal College of Psychiatrists, London, May 1996

Fact Sheet on Domestic Violence, prepared for Royal College of Psychiatrists, in press 2002.

Directory

The Royal Hospital

Contact: Dr C J Churcher-Brown FRCPsych DPM MEWI
Title: Consultant Psychiatrist: Consultant Adviser and Head of Royal Naval
      Psychiatry: Head of Alcohol Education and Treatment: Regional Adviser
      Medical Council on Alcoholism
Address: The Royal Hospital
      Haslar
      Gosport
      Hampshire
      PO12 2AA
Telephone: 023 9258 4255 ext 2421
Fax: 023 9276 2205

Services Offered and Catchment Area

We have a long-standing programme for the management of Post Traumatic Stress Disorder at Haslar, * primarily for the benefit of active servicemen and women.
We are particularly keen to try to assist ex-service personnel suffering as a result of traumatic experiences encountered during the course of their service careers.
* National

Funding For Treatment

Unfortunately, resources are very limited at this time. If ex-service personnel require our services funding must be in place before any assessment or treatment can begin. This financial requirement applies to civilians as well.

Treatment Programme

The Post Traumatic Stress Management Course is run on small group lines with patients attending Haslar on a daily basis and living as a group in nearby self-catering accommodation. The groups are conducted by experienced psychiatric nurses with input from a psychiatrist, clinical psychologist, cognitive and behaviour therapist, hospital chaplain, social worker and others. Spouses, close friends and relatives are encouraged to participate in assessment and open group sessions and may also be able to stay in the accommodation. The residential course lasts for four weeks and attendees are seen for group review over the following twelve months.

Medical and Legal Reports

A number of people are seen at the request of solicitors, insurers, pension funds and other organisations including occasionally CICA claims. Many of these people do not have PTSD but have other post traumatic reactions, which have often gone unrecognised as a result of the emphasis alone upon PTSD. We may be able to arrange treatment for such people on an out-patient basis although this will also require the same funding criteria for fee paying, prior to treatment.

England: Southampton

Chalybeate Hospital

Contact: Dr J Guy Edwards
Title: Consultant Psychiatrist
Address: Chalybeate Hospital
Chalybeate Close
Tremona Road
Southampton
S09 4AX
Telephone: 023 8077 5544

Kindly note I work on my own and see patients from all over the United Kingdom and can only offer a limited service in view of my three to four months' voluntary service as a visiting professor in the Far East.

Services Offered
Assessment and initial treatment programmes.

Types of Referrals
Victims of personal injury and professional negligence.

Referral Method
By formal letter only please.

Waiting Time
An average waiting time for completion of a report is between two to three months.

Medical Reports
Medico–legal assessments and expert witness reports for court.

England: Southampton

Marchwood Priory Hospital

Catchment Area
Anywhere in Southern England

Contact: Dr Austin Tate, MB ChB FRCPsych DPM
Title: Group Medical Director; Consultant Psychiatrist
Address: Marchwood Priory Hospital
Hythe Road
Marchwood
Southampton
SO40 4WU
Telephone: 023 8084 0044
Fax: 023 8020 7554
E-Mail: austintate@marchwood.prioryhealthcare.co.uk
Website: www.prioryhealthcare.co.uk/marchwood

Directory

Areas of Specialism
- Post Traumatic Stress Disorder
- Alcohol and other substance related problems

Medico–legal Reports
Prepare over 100 reports annually

Referral Method
By a General Practitioner
Instruction by Solicitors

Waiting Time For Assessment or Treatment
For treatment 1–3 weeks * this can be faster if admission is required
Court or CICA Report 2–3 months

England: London

The South London and Maudsley NHS Trust

Catchment Area
National

The Child Traumatic Stress Clinic
    Contact: Professor William Yule
    Title: Professor of Applied Child Psychology; Consultant Child Psychologist
    Address: University of London
                Institute of Psychiatry Department of Psychology
                De Crespigny Park
                Denmark Hill
                London
                SE5 8AF
    Telephone: 020 7848 0217 or 7848 0255
    Professor Yule's Fax: 020 7708 3497
    E-Mail: w.yule@iop.kcl.ac.uk
    Website: http://www.iopbpmf.ac.uk

Services Offered and Catchment Area
The Child Traumatic Stress Clinic is located in the Children's Out-Patient Department at The South London and Maudsley NHS Trust Hospital and is a national specialist psychological service offering assessment and treatment of traumatic stress syndromes and anxiety disorders in children and their families.

Who Is In The Team
The Team comprises a consultant psychologist and two clinical psychologists.

Who Is Assessed and Treated
We see children and young people from the ages of 3 to 17 years with post traumatic stress, anxiety and related difficulties, e.g. fears and phobias, sleep problems, separation difficulties, prolonged bereavement reactions or depression. Families are always involved in assessment and this particularly important when the whole family has survived a traumatic event.

Waiting Time
Appointments are usually offered within 6 weeks but sometimes sooner if more urgent and funding is agreed.

Referral Method
Referrals are accepted from general practitioners, the Police, Victim Support and Social Services. Referrals for medico–legal reports are also accepted. Once an appointment has been sent to the family, usually, with permission, we request information from other professionals involved and from the school. Initial assessment usually takes most of the morning or afternoon and if possible involves the whole family. At assessment, we ask parents to give us a full picture of their child, an account of the accident or traumatic event, and a description of the changes or difficulties that have arisen since the event. A full assessment of the child includes talking directly to them about the traumatic event, and is handled sensitively. With younger children, play or drawing might be used; older children might additionally be asked to complete questionnaires.

Depending upon the results of the assessment a variety of treatment options are available –

• group treatment when several children have been involved in the same accident
• individually based cognitive-behaviour therapy aimed at enabling the child to be able to think about what has happened to them without becoming emotionally overwhelmed.

Emphasis is on building effective coping skills. Parents are always involved in treatment, and this is especially so of younger children where emphasis is on supporting parents in helping their children. In many cases 8 sessions is sufficient, but in complex cases should further treatment be necessary this will be negotiated with the referrer.

England: Yorkshire

The Centre For Crisis Psychology

Catchment Area
National and International

Contact: **Barbara Wright**
Title: **Director of Operations**
Address: **The Centre For Crisis Psychology**
Pinetum
Broughton Hall
Skipton
North Yorkshire
BD23 3AE
Telephone: **01756 796383**
Fax: **01756 796384**
E-Mail: **ops@ccpskptn.demon.co.uk**
Website: **www.ccpdirect.co.uk**

Directory

What We Do
- The Centre's Trauma Care work is based within organisations, preparing them to deal with the human aftermath of traumatic events. Client organisations are enabled to develop policy and procedures, and chosen individuals are trained in 'defusing', the process of dealing with reactions in the immediate aftermath of an incident. A series of group and (if necessary) individual meetings that consist of debriefing, education and cognitive-behavioural interventions is carried out.

- The Centre offers training programmes to public service and private sector organisations in the area of trauma.

- CCP Direct offers a general telephone based 'counselling' and advice service.

- CCP Risk offers a tailor-made psychological risk assessment tool that enables organisations to conduct informed identification, surveillance and management of harmful work stressors.

- The Centre does not normally offer individual treatment on a general basis to the patients of GPs or Health Authorities.

Our Background
Michael Stewart (MA Executive Partner) and Peter Hodgkinson (BA MPhil AFBPsS CPsychol Chartered Clinical Psychologist and Honorary Lecturer – London University) the Centre's Partners, forged The Centre For Crisis Psychology from their work in the UK's major disasters of the 1980s. Michael directed aftercare work with the survivors of the Bradford Fire in 1985, and Peter led a team working with the passengers, survivors and bereaved of the Herald of Free Enterprise sinking in 1987. Their joint consultancy established a unique method of working with traumatised individuals. The Centre has deployed these methods with European industry. The Centre's team has a vast depth of experience. Its senior managers have worked with Partners since the early 1990s, diversifying and strengthening the Centre's range.

Our Experience

The Bradford Fire (1985)
The Herald of Free Enterprise Sinking (1987)
The Hungerford Shootings (1987)
The Clapham Train Crash (1987)
The Piper Alpha Explosion (1988)
The Lockerbie Disaster (1988)
The Jupiter Sinking (1988)
The M1 Air Crash (1988)
The Blackburn Town Hall Fire (1989)

The Gulf Hostage Crisis (1990)
The Paris Coach Crash (1992)
The M40 Minibus Crash (1993)
The Bishopsgate Bombing (1995)
The Dunblane Shootings (1996)
The Canary Wharf Bombing (1996)
The Omagh Bombing (1998)
The Hillsborough Disaster (1989)

Publications

Coping With Catastrophe published by Routledge 1998 2nd edition

England and Wales: North West

The Chester Therapy Centre
    Contact: Jeanie McIntee BA (Hons) MSc C Psychol AFBPsS Dip Psychotherapy
    Cert. In Psychodynamic Psychotherapy / Counselling Supervision,
    Chartered Clinical Psychologist
    Title: Consultant Clinical and Forensic Psychologist
    Address: The Chester Therapy Centre
              Weldon House
              20 Walpole Street
              Chester
              Cheshire
              CH1 4HG
    Telephone: 01244 390121
    Fax: 01244 390374
    E-Mail: jmcintee@chestertherapycentre.com

We are open Monday to Friday 9.00am until 5.30pm; at other times there is an answer-phone service with calls being responded to the next working day. Evening appointments can sometimes be arranged.

Background
My name is Jeanie McIntee and I have been dealing with trauma since 1979 and I am the Consultant Clinical and Forensic Psychologist of The Chester Therapy Centre. I trained in assessment and intervention work pertaining to child abuse at Great Ormond Street Hospital in 1984. I have specialised in the trauma field since 1986 and have been providing Expert Witness services since 1989. The Chester Therapy Centre was founded in1988 and is a well-respected referral point with a multi-disciplinary team of professionals providing the following.

Specialist Services Offered
Chester Therapy Centre specialises in trauma and abuse work with –

- Abused Children – physical, sexual, emotional and neglect
- Abused adults – physical, sexual, emotional and neglect
- Risk assessment of children as potential abusers
- Risk assessment of adults as potential abusers
- Risk of families as potential abusers
- Post Traumatic Stress Disorder
- Psychological Assessment for Court
- Therapeutic Services – such as psychotherapy, art, music and play therapies
- Consultancy – and case supervision for professionals and organisations

Forensic work makes up a large part of our specialist work

- Personal Injury work
- Family Court work
- Private Law
- Criminal work

Legal assessment of clients is carried out by our psychologists, who undertake clinical and psychometric assessment, prepare Court Reports and have extensive experience in providing

Expert Witness. Jeanie McIntee is the author of the Reports and has overall responsibility for the information contained within the Reports.

Catchment Area
We are situated in Chester with easy access using public and private transport. We are within travelling distance from Manchester, Liverpool, Wirral, North and Mid-Wales. There are good train routes out of Chester and Crewe; we are within a 15 minute walk of Chester station. Clients travel regularly from a wide geographical area outside the North-west, from London and the Midlands.

Referral Method
Individuals and families may refer themselves to The Chester Therapy Centre. Referrals are also invited from Solicitors, Guardian ad Litem, Court Welfare Officers, General Practitioners, medical insurance companies, probation and Police services and Social Services.

Funding Method
Please telephone The Chester Therapy Centre for our current fees and conditions and at the time of this edition going to print the following fees and conditions apply. The Chester Therapy Centre is an independent service. Private paying clients are charged on a sliding scale from £45 plus VAT per session to £55 plus VAT per session (kindly contact as prices will change from time to time). The cost of sessions is dependent upon their means, who their therapist is and what time their appointment are – evening appointments are more expensive because of overtime rates for CTC employees. The Chester Therapy Centre welcomes clients who have secured funding from statutory agencies in the form of GP referrals, health authority referrals and charitable sponsorship. Information about The Chester Therapy Centre is available for GP and other agencies in order to assist with securing funding. Forensic assessments are currently costed at £65 plus VAT per hour.

Assessment Process and Waiting Time
Resources are available for simultaneous assessment and/or therapy for whole families. The main objective of The Chester Therapy Centre is the successful provision of a high quality specialist service. Assessment and treatment can be provided almost immediately once funding and contracting is completed. Usually, therapy clients are asked to complete an assessment form in advance of the first appointment to assist us in matching client and therapist and to save time and cost on the first two appointments. This allows therapy to commence more quickly and makes the initial sessions more like normal therapy sessions.

Treatment Offered
Chester Therapy Centre offers an eclectic approach to psychotherapy; this is particularly beneficial for clients who have experienced trauma, that is the underlying issue in a large portion of mental health difficulties. The range of brief and long term therapies include:–

- Individual work
- Couples
- Family therapy
- Groups
- Play therapy
- Art therapy
- Music therapy

Medico–legal Reports
We have considerable experience in the preparation of medico–legal reports. Please refer to the specialist services offered at Chester Therapy Centre.

Other Important Areas of Work
The Chester Therapy Centre has many years' experience in the assessment and treatment of trauma and disassociative disorders.

Publications

Trauma: The Psychological Process *1992 McIntee J.* published by The Chester Therapy Centre

Coping With Trauma *1992 McIntee J.* in **Candis** vol 7 book 10, October pp 40–44

Society's Inability To Recognise And Label Sexual Assault *1997 Long N. McIntee J.* in **Clinical Psychology Forum** January 1997

The Psychological Effects Of Trauma On Children in Protecting Children: Challenge and Change *1997 McIntee J. Crompton I. (eds) John Bates Richard Pugh and Neil Thompson* published Arena Publishers Aldershot

The Significance Of Trauma In Problematic Sexual Behaviour *1999 Mulholland S. McIntee J.* in Calder Martin (ed)

Working With Young People Who Sexually Abuse – New Pieces Of The Jigsaw Puzzle published Russell House Publishing Dorset UK

England: Oxfordshire

The Oxford Development Centre Limited

Catchment Area
Regional, National and International

Contact: Dr Claudia Herbert, BSc (Hons), MSc C Psychol, AFBPsS (Centre Director)
Title: Chartered Consultant Clinical Psychologist, Accredited Practitioner in EMDR (Level 2) and UKCP Registered Cognitive-Behavioural Psychotherapist, Trauma Specialist (more details under The Oxford Stress and Trauma Centre)

Address: The Oxford Development Centre Limited
(Registered Company 352 8412) incorporating
The Oxford Stress and Trauma Centre
8a Market Square
Witney
Oxfordshire
OX28 6BB
Telephone: ++ 44 (0)1993 779994, ++44 (0) 1993 779077
or ++ 44 (0) 1865 428426
Fax: ++ 44 (0) 1993 779499 or ++ 44 (0) 1865 428427
E-Mail: claudia.herbert@oxdev.co.uk
Mobile: 07602 831197

Address: The Oxford Stress and Trauma Centre
8a Market Square
Witney
Oxfordshire
OX28 6BB
Telephone: ++44 (0)1993 779077
Fax: ++44 (0)1993 779499
Website: www.oxdev.co.uk

The Clinical Director of The Oxford Stress and Trauma Centre is Dr Claudia Herbert, BSc (Hons), MSc C. Psychol., AFBPsS, a Chartered Clinical Psychologist, a UKCP Registered Cognitive Behavioural Psychotherapist and a Level II trained EMDR Practitioner. She has worked with survivors of many different types of trauma and is the author of self-help literature in the trauma area.

The Oxford Stress and Trauma Centre is the first private facility in Oxfordshire and surrounding counties dedicated to the psychological assessment and therapeutic treatment of trauma and stress-related problems. Although based in Oxfordshire, the Centre accepts private clients nation- and worldwide. Languages spoken at the Centre are English and German. In addition to its therapeutic focus The Oxford Stress and Trauma Centre is a resource for training, supervision, consultancy, education and practice-related research in the areas of Stress and Trauma Work.

The Oxford Stress and Trauma Centre also offers a mail order service for self-help literature, which specializes in a wide range of self-help books, both in the trauma and stress field, as well as in other related areas of psychological health. Book order lists can be obtained from the above website.

Two of her recent self-help publications are:

1. **Understanding Your Reactions to Trauma – A Self-help Guide For Survivors of Trauma and Their Families.** *Dr Claudia Herbert (1996)* – 64 page booklet. Published by The Oxford Stress and Trauma Centre. This booklet has been translated into the Japanese (1999), Spanish (2000) and Turkish (2000) languages and has been distributed to 30,000.00 survivors of the Turkish earthquake. Feedback about the helpfulness of the booklet from survivors of the earthquake has been very positive.

2. **Overcoming Traumatic Stress – A Self-help Guide Using Cognitive Behavioural Techniques.** *Dr Claudia Herbert and Ann Wetmore (1999)* – Published worldwide by Robinson & Constable, London. Special US version of the book published in 2001.

England: Cambridge, East Anglia Region

Medical Research Council

Contact: Dr Tim Dalgleish BA MA MSc PhD
Title: Chartered Clinical Psychologist; Honorary Psychologist at Bethlem and
Maudsley NHS Trust; Research Fellow Clare College Cambridge
Address: Medical Research Council
Cognition and Brain Sciences Unit
15 Chaucer Road
Cambridge
CB2 2EF
Telephone: 01223 355294 ext 630
Fax: 01223 359062
E-Mail: tim.dalgleish@mrc-cbu.cam.ac.uk

Services Offered and Catchment Area
I am a research clinical psychologist specialising in the area of post traumatic stress and my
catchment area is East Anglia. I am very experienced in the preparation of medico–legal
reports and appearing in court.

Referral Method
I am able to accept referrals directly from individuals and happy to work with legally aided
clients.

England: South

Ex-Services Mental Welfare Society

Contact: Dr Morgan R O'Connell MB Bch BAO(NUI) DPM FRCPsych
Title: Chief Consultant Psychiatrist to Combat Stress the Ex-Services Mental
Welfare Society
Address: Wickham House
The Square
Wickham
Hampshire
PO17 5JG

also at –
Address: Marchwood Priory Hospital
Hythe Road
Marchwood
Southampton
Hampshire
SO4 4WU

and –
Address: St Joseph's Centre
Holy Cross Hospital
Haslemere
Surrey
GU27 1NQ

and –
Address: Combat Stress
Tyrwhitt House
Oaklawn Road
Leatherhead
Surrey
KT22 oBX
Telephone: 01329 834512
Fax: 01329 835150
E-Mail: sprint@athene.co.uk

Areas of Specialism
- Post Traumatic Stress Disorder
- Armed Forces Personnel with Service related Pyschological disorder

Services Offered and Catchment Area
- Medical Legal assessment in southern England
- Support for Ex-Service personnel with psychological disorders – national

Referral Method and Funding Method
- via Solicitors
- via War Pensions Directorate – funded by War Pensions

Assessment Process and Waiting Time
Individual appointments with a waiting time in order of 6 weeks.

Treatment Offered
Treatment is mainly offered for Ex-Service Men in one of three homes located throughout the country.

Medico–legal Reports
Significant experience of preparing medico–legal rreports.

Sample of Other Important Areas of Work Experience
Expert witness to the following inquiries –

- Zeebrugge Tribunal
- Hillsborough Disaster
- Kings Cross Fire
- Piper Alpha Disaster

England: North West and London

The Florence Nightingale Hospitals
Florence Nightingale Hospitals specialise in the treatment of psychological and emotional problems, addictions and eating disorders; all within their own specialist areas. With hospitals in London and the North West of England they provide comprehensive services including access to all levels of care allowing patients to 'step down' to less intensive treatment programmes as their condition improves. Emphasis is placed on ensuring patients receive maximum therapy in the shortest possible time.

Florence Nightingale Hospitals are ISO9002 Accredited and are committed to providing the highest quality of service possible to meet each individual client's needs. The hospital group employs Quality Assurance Managers and participates in Clinical Governance. In addition the group have commenced Outcome Monitoring for all treatment programmes.

Areas of Specialism
- Post Traumatic Stress
- Adolescents
- Addictions
- Eating Disorders
- General Psychiatry
- Depression

Contact: Gerry Nurdin
Title: Intake and Admissions Manager

Address: The Florence Nightingale Hospital
11–19 Lisson Grove
London
NW1 6SH
Telephone: 0800 783 0594
Fax: 020 7724 9440
E-Mail: gerry.nurdin@fnhospitals.co.uk
Website: www.florencenightingalehospitals.co.uk

Referral Method
- Florence Nightingale Hospitals do not operate a waiting list and therefore treatment can usually be accessed within the same week
- Patients may self refer or be referred by their GP by contacting the helpline
- Referrals and enquiries can be made 24 hours a day by telephoning the Helpline on 0800 783 0594. The Helpline is staffed by a team of nurse counsellors who can offer an initial free assessment to patients
- Health Authority patients may be referred on a contractual or extra contractual basis. Health Authorities who wish to refer patients should contact the Helpline Team who are usually able to offer immediate access to an in-patient bed
- Referrals are accepted nationally and internationally

Equality in Services
Florence Nightingale Hospitals are committed to achieving equal opportunities in the service it provides. Religious and cultural needs are met. The group employs staff from many different cultural and ethnic groups. Florence Nightingale Hospitals employ clinicians that speak a wide variety of languages. Interpretation services can be arranged when required. Florence Nightingale Hospitals provide independent advocacy services.

Assessment
The initial assessment with a Nurse Counsellor can usually be offered within 24 hours. The assessment lasts for approximately 30 – 40 minutes and enables the Nurse Counsellor to gain a better understanding of the problems the patient is experiencing. Following this the Nurse Counsellor will make a recommendation if needed as to what treatment may be required.

Services Offered and Catchment Area
Florence Nightingale Hospitals provide services on an inpatient, residential, day-patient and out-patient basis. The comprehensive services means patients can step down to less intensive care as their condition improves. All in-patients are offered free aftercare following discharge for one year. Florence Nightingale Hospitals is part of Capio-Healthcare with hospitals in the UK and Europe.

Funding
Referrals and funding enquiries can be made by calling the Helpline on 0800 783 0594. Our client group consists of people who are privately insured, those who self pay for treatment and those referred for specialist treatment by the NHS.

Medico–Legal Reports
Florence Nightingale Hospitals has experienced Consultant Psychiatrists who specialise in medico–legal reports.

For further help and advice in this area please contact the Helpline

England: West Midlands and surrounding regions

Birmingham Nuffield Hospital

> Contact: Dr. David Muss LMSSA
> Title: Director PTSD Unit
> Address: Birmingham Nuffield Hospital
> 22 Somerset Road
> Edgbaston
> Birmingham
> B15 2QQ
> Telephone: 0121 422 1193
> Fax: Same as Telephone
> E-Mail: david@cmuss.freeserve.co.uk
> Website: www.beatptsd.com

Areas of Specialism
- Postraumatic Stress Disorder – adults and children
- Traumatic phobias – adults and children

Medico–legal Reports
- over 250 annually

Referral Method
- By a General Practitioner
- Instruction by Solicitors.

Assessment Process and Waiting Time
- For medical reports – three to four weeks
- Treatment – two to three weeks (outpatient treatment only)

Treatment Offered
- Cognitive behavioural therapy and imagery based techniques including The Rewind Technique, EMDR (Eye Movement Desensitisation and Reprocessing), TIR (Traumatic Incident Reduction) and TFT (Thought Field Therapy).

Publications

1. **A New Technique For Treating Postraumatic Stress Disorder:** British Journal of Clinical Psychology, 1991, 30. 91–92

2. **The Trauma Trap** *by Dr David Muss*, published by Doubleday, 1991. First self-help book for PTSD sufferers published in the UK. ISBN 385-40240-6Csd.

3. **Chapter on CD-ROM: Medico–legal Solutions: Vol 1. Personal Injuries and Criminal Trauma.** ISBN 09533415 OX

United Kingdom

The British Psychological Society
With over 34,000 members, The British Psychological Society is the representative body for psychologists and psychology in the UK. By its Royal Charter, the Society is charged with national responsibility for the development, promotion and application of psychology for the public good. It is funded entirely by member subscriptions or its commercial activities that support its charitable aims.

Its three major aims:
- to encourage the development of psychology as a scientific discipline and an applied profession
- to raise standards of training and practice in the application of psychology
- to raise public awareness of psychology and increase the influence of psychological practice in society.

The Register of Chartered Psychologists is the public list of all registered and conditionally registered Chartered Psychologists. Out of over 9,000 UK based practising Chartered Psychologists around 1,700 have chosen to appear in the *Directory of Chartered Psychologists.* The *Directory* gives them the opportunity to give full details of their specialisms and availability to offer services to the public, including counselling and psychotherapeutic services to groups and individuals. Psychologists can be located on the basis of the services they offer, or the region of the country they work in, via a search on our website (www.bps.org.uk) or by purchasing the *Directory* from the Society.

Our Standards
The Society sets criteria for professional education and training, accredits over 400 university courses and runs its own exams and qualifications. It also maintains a Code of Conduct and investigates complaints about individual psychologists. Details of the complaints procedure and how it works area available on the website or direct from the Society.

The Society is working towards being recognised as the authoritative body to carry out police checks for those practitioners who work solely in the private sector. This will provide assurance to the public that recognised Chartered Psychologists are 'fit' to practise unsupervised and do not have relevant criminal convictions recorded against them.

Directory

Address: The British Psychological Society
St Andrews House
48 Princess Road East
Leicester
LE1 7DR
Telephone: 0116 254 9568
Fax: 0116 247 0787
E-Mail: enquiry@bps.org.uk

Areas of Specialism

Most Chartered Psychologists specialise in certain areas of professional practice including:

- Clinical Psychology
- Counselling Psychology
- Education and Child Psychology
- Forensic Psychology
- Health Psychology
- Occupational Psychology
- Neuropsychology
- Sport psychology
- Teaching and Research

Services Offered

The Society is unable to offer services direct like treatment, or recommend individual psychologists, however it produces the *Register* and *Directory of Chartered Psychologists* to assist in this process. In addition, it produces academic and practitioner guidelines on a wide variety of psychological based topics, which people interested in PTSD may find of interest.

Medico–legal Reports

The Society is currently developing a list of 'expert' psychologists who can offer expert witness services for forensic/legal requirements.

Publications

The Society, as the learned society for psychology in the UK, publishes academic and professional journals, books, leaflets, guidance documents on professional practice and information about psychology training. It also produces guidance on which type of psychologist may be best for the individual. Many of our publications can be obtained direct from our website or from the Society's offices. Books, published through the Society, are available from its partner publisher Blackwell's (www.bookshop.blackwell.co.uk)

The Society's Divisions produce guidance documents on a variety of psychology issues. Many of the Divisions produce journals that may be a useful reference source for academic thinking and research into the treatment of stress and other related illnesses or conditions. Information about subscriptions to journals, or their availability, can be obtained from the website or from the Society's offices. The Society has also issued detailed guidance on a number of topics such as Recovered Memories and Psychological Aspects of Disaster. This is information which is available from the Society's offices.

·